HUGO GROTIUS
AND INTERNATIONAL RELATIONS

Hugo Grotius

(for details of this engraving see p. vi)

Hugo Grotius
and
International Relations

EDITED BY

HEDLEY BULL
BENEDICT KINGSBURY
ADAM ROBERTS

CLARENDON PRESS · OXFORD
1992

Oxford University Press, Walton Street, Oxford OX2 6DP

Oxford New York Toronto
Delhi Bombay Calcutta Madras Karachi
Petaling Jaya Singapore Hong Kong Tokyo
Nairobi Dar es Salaam Cape Town
Melbourne Auckland

and associated companies in
Berlin Ibadan

Oxford is a trade mark of Oxford University Press

Published in the United States
by Oxford University Press, New York

First published 1990
First issued in Clarendon Paperbacks 1992

British Library Cataloguing in Publication Data
Hugo Grotius and international relations.
1. Foreign relations. Theories of Grotius, Hugo, 1583–1645
I. Bull, Hedley, 1932–1985   II. Kingsbury, Benedict
III. Roberts, Adam
327.101
ISBN 0-19-827771-7

Library of Congress Cataloging in Publication Data
Hugo Grotius and international relations / edited by Hedley Bull,
Benedict Kingsbury, Adam Roberts.
Includes bibliographical references (p.
1. Grotius, Hugo, 1583–1645.   2. International law.
3. International relations.   I. Bull, Hedley.
II. Kingsbury, Benedict.   III. Roberts, Adam.
JX2099.H82   1990   327'.092—dc20   89-72116
ISBN 0-19-827771-7

Set by Hope Services (Abingdon) Ltd.
Printed and bound in
Great Britain by Bookcraft (Bath) Ltd.,
Midsomer Norton, Avon

Acknowledgements

THIS book is the brain-child of Hedley Bull, Montague Burton Professor of International Relations at Oxford University and Fellow of Balliol College from 1977 to 1985. It took his fertile and searching mind—at home in the fields of international relations theory, international history, and international law— to conceive and plan a work of this scope. It began with a series of lectures which he organized at Oxford University in Michaelmas Term 1983, to mark the quatercentenary of the birth of Hugo Grotius. He then embarked on the long process of transforming a lecture series into a scholarly book—work which was unfinished when he died on 18 May 1985 at the age of fifty-two after a long illness.

Much has changed in this book since the commemorative lecture series. The original lectures have all been very extensively revised and updated; and some entirely new chapters have been added, by Hidemi Suganami, John Vincent, Rosalyn Higgins, and the undersigned. We are very grateful to all the contributors for their painstaking work, and for their tolerance of editorial whims and delays.

For helpful advice, suggestions and criticisms, we are particularly indebted to Jonathan Barnes, Geoffrey Best, Martin Ceadel, Peter Haggenmacher, Sudhir Hazareesingh, Andrew Hurrell, Maurice Keen, Christopher Kirwan, and Robert S. Summers.

The index was compiled by Mary Bull, to whom we are very grateful for this and much other assistance.

We owe many other debts of gratitude. The board of managers of the Montague Burton Fund at Oxford University facilitated the original lecture series. The typing of successive drafts was undertaken principally by Mary Bügge in Balliol College, and Carole Charlton in the Social Studies Faculty Centre. Carole Charlton, who has worked for three Montague Burton professors, is leaving her job in the same year as this book goes to press. We wish her a retirement as long and happy as it is richly deserved.

Oxford   B.K.
October 1989   A.R.

Jacket and Frontispiece

Hugo Grotius (1583–1645). Engraving by Willem Jacobsz Delff (1632), after a well-known portrait in oils by Michiel Jansz van Mierevelt (1631). The engraving appeared in several different versions over the period 1632–72, although the representation of Grotius and the poem by Heinsius were unchanged throughout. The version reproduced here is from Grotius' *Annales et Historiae de Rebus Belgicis*, Joannis Blaeu, Amsterdam, 1657. Reproduced by courtesy of the Bodleian Library, Oxford. Folio BS 129, opp. p. 1.

Pieter de Groot, Grotius' son, wrote of Delff's engraving: 'The painting of my father can be found in my home in Rotterdam. However, the finest print, than which in my opinion no-one else could ever do better, was made by Willem Delff, son-in-law of Mr Michiel [Mierevelt], from the painting done by Mr Michiel. The plate of this work must now be in the hands of Mr Blaeuw.' See E. A. van Beresteyn, *Iconographie van Hugo Grotius met 65 portretten* (Martinus Nijhoff, The Hague, 1929), pp. 82–3.

Contents

Notes on Contributors

HEDLEY BULL, FBA, who died in 1985, was Montague Burton Professor of International Relations at Oxford University, and Fellow of Balliol College, from 1977 to 1985. His works include *The Control of the Arms Race*, 1961; *The Anarchical Society*, 1977; and (ed. with Adam Watson) *The Expansion of International Society*, 1984.

WILLIAM E. BUTLER, FSA, is Professor of Comparative Law in the University of London, Director, Centre for the Study of Socialist Legal Systems, University College London, and Dean of the University Faculty of Laws (1988–90). His recent works include *International Law in Comparative Perspective*, 1980; and *Soviet Law*, 2nd edn. 1988. His translation of V. E. Grabar, *The History of International Law in Russia, 1647–1917*, was published in 1990.

G. I. A. D. DRAPER, OBE, who died in 1989, became Military Prosecutor before the Military Courts for the trial of war criminals in the British Occupied Zone of Germany in 1945, and thereafter a legal adviser in the War Office (Ministry of Defence). He was Reader in International Law at the University of London before becoming Professor of Law at Sussex University. His works include *The Red Cross Conventions*, 1958.

PETER HAGGENMACHER is Adjunct Professor at the Graduate Institute of International Studies, Geneva. His Ph.D. thesis on *Grotius et la doctrine de la guerre juste* was published in 1983.

ROSALYN HIGGINS, QC, is Professor of International Law in the University of London and teaches at the London School of Economics and Political Science. Her works include *The Development of International Law through the Political Organs of the United Nations*, 1963; and *United Nations Peacekeeping*, 4 vols., 1969–81. She has been the United Kingdom member of the UN Human Rights Committee since 1985.

BENEDICT KINGSBURY is Lecturer in Law at Oxford University
and a Fellow of Exeter College. He specializes in international
law and human rights. A New Zealand citizen, he is doing
research on indigenous peoples and international law. His
works include (ed. with Adam Roberts) *United Nations,
Divided World*, 1988.

ADAM ROBERTS, FBA, is Montague Burton Professor of Inter-
national Relations at Oxford University, and Fellow of Balliol
College. His works include *Nations in Arms: The Theory and Practice
of Territorial Defence*, 2nd edn. 1986; (ed. with Benedict Kingsbury)
United Nations, Divided World, 1988; and (ed. with Richard Guelff)
Documents on the Laws of War, 2nd edn. 1989.

C. G. ROELOFSEN teaches the history of the Law of Nations at
the University of Utrecht. He contributed to *International Law
in the Netherlands*, i, 1978; and (ed. with L. E. van Holk) *Grotius
Reader: A Reader for Students of International Law and Legal History*,
1983.

B. V. A. RÖLING, who died in 1985, was Professor Emeritus of
International Law and former Director of the Polemological
Institute at the Rijksuniversiteit Groningen, and was a judge
at the Tokyo International Military Tribunal. His works
include *International Law in an Expanded World*, 1960; *The Science
of War and Peace*, 1981 (in Dutch); and *International Law and the
Maintenance of Peace*, 1982 (in Dutch).

GEORG SCHWARZENBERGER, who died in 1991, was Emeritus
Professor of International Law in the University of London, and
Vice-President of the London Institute of World Affairs. His
works include *Power Politics: A Study of World Society*, 3rd edn. 1964;
and *International Law as Applied by International Courts and Tribunals*,
4 vols., 1957–86.

HIDEMI SUGANAMI is Senior Lecturer in International Relations
at the University of Keele. His works include *The Domestic Analogy
and World Order Proposals*, 1989.

R. J. VINCENT, who died in 1990, had been Montague Burton Professor of International Relations at the London School of Economics and Political Science since 1989. From 1986 to 1989 he was University Lecturer in International Relations at Oxford University, and Fellow of Nuffield College. His works include *Nonintervention and International Order*, 1974; *Human Rights and International Relations*, 1986; and (ed. with J. D. B. Miller), *Order and Violence: Hedley Bull and International Relations*, 1990.

List of Abbreviations

AJIL   *American Journal of International Law*

ICJ   International Court of Justice

ICLQ   *International and Comparative Law Quarterly*

JB   Alberico Gentili, *De Jure Belli*, first published 1598. (Reference in most cases is to the Rolfe translation, Classics of International Law edition, 1933)

JBP   Hugo Grotius, *De Jure Belli ac Pacis Libri Tres*, first published 1625. (Reference in most cases is to the Kelsey translation, Classics of International Law edition, 1925)

JP   Hugo Grotius, *De Jure Praedae Commentarius*, written c.1604–6, but published only in 1868. (Reference in most cases is to the Williams–Zeydel translation, Classics of International Law edition, 1950)

LNTS   *League of Nations Treaty Series*

Map of the World (1630)
by Henricus Hondius

Overleaf: Map of the world, dated 1630, by Henricus Hondius (1597–1651), a contemporary and compatriot of Grotius. The seventeenth century was a great period of Dutch exploration and also cartography. This map reflects the discoveries of many explorers of Grotius' time, including for example an expedition off the coast of New Guinea in 1623. It is believed to be among the first of such maps to depart (albeit only partially) from the mythical geography of 'terra australis incognita'. It contains some errors typical of the period, including the depiction of California as an island.

The map is believed to have been first published in *Atlas ou représentation du monde universel . . . Édition nouvelle* (Amsterdam, 1633). It is reprinted here from C. H. Coote (ed.), *Remarkable Maps of the XVth, XVIth & XVIIth centuries*, ii–iii, *The Geography of Australia as Delineated by the Dutch Cartographers of the XVIIth century* (Amsterdam, 1895). The size of the original is approximately 55 × 38 cm. Reproduced by courtesy of the Bodleian Library, Oxford. B.1.a.4. (2.3.).

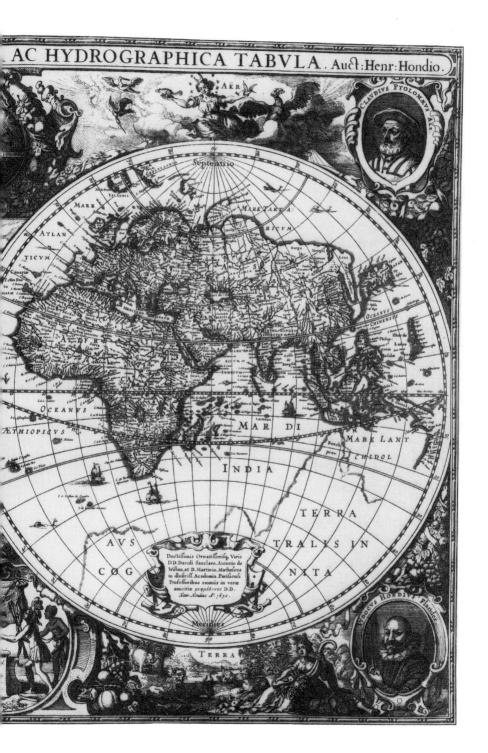

I

Introduction: Grotian Thought in International Relations

BENEDICT KINGSBURY AND ADAM ROBERTS

This work on Hugo Grotius (1583–1645) and international relations is intended to serve three purposes. First, to examine aspects of Hugo Grotius' work touching the fields of international law and international relations, in the historical and biographical context in which he wrote it. Second, to analyse the place of Grotius in a Grotian tradition of thought about international relations. Third, tó contribute to the debate about the issues addressed by that tradition, a debate which is to some extent conducted independently of what Grotius himself actually wrote.

Grotius lived in tempestuous times. His writings reflect the turbulent circumstances of the period, circumstances which also touched his own life: religious controversy with its very high stakes; the brutalities of the Thirty Years War; the struggle of the Dutch for independence from Spanish rule; and the enlargement of Dutch maritime power in the face of Iberian and English obstruction. His writings also engage the changing structures of political power in Europe: the decline of the Universal Church and of the Holy Roman Empire; the gradual emergence of an international system of sovereign states, linked symbolically to the 1648 Peace of Westphalia; and the rising importance of European sea-borne empires.

Subsequent generations have seen Grotius' main contribution to the theory and practice of international relations as lying in his impact on international law. Among scholars of international relations, it is lawyers above all who have been interested in Grotius and claimed him as their own. There are many strong reasons why this should be so, and several of the chapters in this book deal with Grotius' contributions to areas of international law.

While much of Grotius' other work (especially his theo-logical and historical writings) had international political implications at the time,[1] the works which have passed into the literature of international relations are all concerned primarily with the law of nations. They are *De Jure Praedae* (written *c.* 1604–6, but published only in 1868[2]), *Mare Liberum* (first published 1609),[3] and *De Jure Belli ac Pacis* (1625). To modern scholars, Grotius' insights into a number of questions which continue to occupy a central place in contemporary thought about international relations are striking. Several of these questions are explored in the chapters below, although the contributors differ sharply in their evaluations of the coherence and the modern importance of Grotius' views.

The relationships between Grotius' life and works on the one hand, and the political history of the period in which he lived on the other, are examined in several of the chapters below, notably those of Hedley Bull, C. G. Roelofsen, B. V. A. Röling, and Georg Schwarzenberger. That their interpreta-tions differ in certain respects is as much a reflection of the different currents discernible in Grotius' *œuvre* as of differences of perspective among the authors. There may also be a need for revision of some standard views about Grotius: for instance, while Voltaire may have been right that Grotius was 'plus illustre par ses ouvrages que par son ambassade',[4] Roelofsen suggests that Grotius' diplomatic career was not as ineffectual as is often supposed.

(a) THE SIGNIFICANCE OF DE JURE BELLI AC PACIS

While scholars have (for the most part) long-since ceased to debate the *question mal posée* whether or not Grotius was 'the

---

[1] Among the best known of these works are *De Veritate Religionis Christianae* (first published 1627), and *Annales et Historiae de Rebus Belgicis* (first published 1657).

[2] The manuscript was certainly complete by 1609. Part of chap. 12, on the law of the sea, was revised and published separately (and anonymously) as *Mare Liberum* in 1609.

[3] Grotius also wrote a defence of chap. 5 of *Mare Liberum* against Welwod's criticism. It was published only in 1872.

[4] Voltaire, chap. 187 of 'Essai sur les mœurs', in *Œuvres complètes*, xiii (Paris, 1878), p. 119.

father of the law of nations',[5] the significance of his masterpiece *De Jure Belli ac Pacis* in the history of international law remains an important and difficult issue. Peter Haggenmacher has previously argued that it is anachronistic to treat *De Jure Belli ac Pacis* as a systematic study of that collection of issues which was later regarded as constituting the field of international law: it was written as a treatise about the law of war in which other issues were for the most part addressed only as they bore on this central theme.[6] The equation of the scope of Grotius' 'Law of War and Peace' with later textbooks organized under similar headings is a false one. As Haggenmacher points out, the myth of a complete sytem of the law of nations in *De Jure Belli ac Pacis* was sustained by the historicist enthusiasm of subsequent authors, even those who were themselves conscious of the limited ambit of the work. Adam Smith, for instance, in lectures described *De Jure Belli ac Pacis* (not entirely accurately) as 'a sort of casuistical book for sovereigns and states, determining in what cases war may justly be made and how far it may be carried on'. Nevertheless, 'Grotius seems to have been the first who attempted to give the world anything like a regular system of natural jurisprudence, and *De Jure Belli ac Pacis* with all its imperfections, is perhaps at this day the most complete work on this subject.'[7]

This may indeed have been the greatest direct contribution of *De Jure Belli ac Pacis*: the systematic reassembling of practice and authorities on the traditional but fundamental subject of

---

[5] By the 1920s it was widely accepted that the foundational structure of modern international law emerged over a long period, doctrinal responsibility being collegiate and owing a great deal to other historical developments. See e.g. Maurice Bourquin, 'Grotius est-il le père du droit des gens?' in *Grandes figures et grandes œuvres juridiques* (Geneva, 1948); and Coleman Phillipson, 'Introduction' to the Classics of International Law edition of Gentili's *De Jure Belli* (Oxford, 1933), ii, p. 12a, contending that 'no writer can be truly described as the "progenitor" or "forerunner" or "creator" of international law.' The notion that the paternity of international law should be ascribed to Grotius nevertheless still appears occasionally. See also Wilhelm Grewe, 'Grotius—Vater des Völkerrechts?', *Der Staat*, 23 (1984), p. 176, arguing that even if it were possible for there to be a 'father' of classical or post-classical international law, that epithet should not be attached to Grotius.
[6] Haggenmacher, *Grotius et la doctrine de la guerre juste* (Paris, 1983).
[7] Adam Smith, *Lectures on Justice, Police, Revenue and Arms* (c. 1762–3), ed. E. Cannan (Oxford, 1896), p. 1; also id., *Jurisprudence*, ed. R. L. Meek, D. D. Raphael, and P. G. Stein (Oxford, 1978), p. 397. See also id., *Theory of Moral Sentiments* (London, 1759), VII. vi. 37.

4 *Benedict Kingsbury and Adam Roberts*

the *jus belli*, organized for the first time around a body of principles rooted in the law of nature. In his chapter below, Haggenmacher argues that it is this above all which distinguishes *De Jure Belli ac Pacis* from the otherwise comparable treatise of Gentili, *De Jure Belli* (1598).[8] Hedley Bull also emphasizes the unity of the system of *De Jure Belli ac Pacis*, but focuses more generally on Grotius' conception of the nature and workings of international society at an important phase of its evolution.

Several scholars have undertaken studies of the direct influence of Grotius on the theory and practice of international law in particular countries. Poland and China, for instance, have recently been examined;[9] and Professor Butler contributes to this body of literature with his chapter below on the reception of Grotius' works in Russia. Grotius' legal works were cited extensively as authority in judicial decisions, diplomatic practice, and scholarly works in an appreciable number of countries until the late nineteenth century,[10] on such standard issues as the extent of jurisdiction in maritime areas, the immunity of employees of accredited foreign diplomats, and rights and duties in relation to neutral shipping.[11] He is seldom cited as a source of direct modern

[8] For somewhat different interpretations of Gentili, see Diego Panizza, *Alberico Gentili, giurista ideologo nell'Inghilterra elisabettiana* (Padua, 1981); and A. M. Honoré, 'Alberico Gentili nella prospettiva di oggi' (lecture delivered at San Ginesio, 1988, publication forthcoming).

[9] R. Bierzanek, 'The Influence of the Personality and Ideas of Hugo Grotius on Religious and Political Struggles in the Polish–Lithuanian Commonwealth of the 17th and 18th Centuries'; Wang Tieya, 'Grotius' Works in China'; and Hungdah Chiu, 'Hugo Grotius in Chinese International Law Literature'; all in Asser Instituut, *International Law and the Grotian Heritage* (The Hague, 1985). For modern work on Grotius in the USSR and Eastern Europe, see also A. M. Stuyt, 'Grotius et la pensée Marxiste–Léniniste', *Grotiana*, 6 (1985), pp. 25–37.

[10] See e.g. Edwin D. Dickinson, 'Changing Concepts and the Doctrine of Incorporation', *AJIL* 26 (1932), p. 259, n. 132; Hersch Lauterpacht, 'The Grotian Tradition in International Law', *British Year Book of International Law 1946*, p. 15; Robert Feenstra, 'L'Influence de la pensée juridique de Grotius', *XVII͏ͤ Siècle*, 35 (1983), p. 487; Cornelis van Vollenhoven, 'Grotius and Geneva', *Bibliotheca Visseriana*, 6 (1925), pp. 34–41; and Georg Schwarzenberger's chapter below. See also J. G. Starke, 'The Influence of Grotius upon the Development of International Law in the Eighteenth Century', in C. H. Alexandrowicz (ed.), *Grotian Society Papers 1972* (The Hague, 1972), p. 172, asserting that *JBP* 'had little direct effect upon the conduct of States in the eighteenth century.'

[11] E.g. *R.* v. *Keyn* (1876) II Ex. p. 127 per Brett J. A.; *Triquet* v. *Bath* 97 ER 936 (1764), argument of Mr Blackstone, p. 937, and judgment of Lord Mansfield, p. 938;

authority, although his works do retain some special significance in certain esoteric fields of international law which have
been neglected in more recent times, and in areas influenced
by Roman law.[12] His historical examples sometimes find
modern parallels—as, for instance, where he recounts:

Cato wished to have Julius Caesar delivered up to the Germans
because he had made war on them; but I believe that he had in mind
not so much the question of right as a desire to free the city from the
fear of a prospective master. The Germans, in fact, had helped the
Gauls, who were enemies of the Roman people, and consequently
they had no reason to complain that a wrong had been done to them,
provided the Roman people had a just cause for making war on the
Gauls. But Caesar ought to have been satisfied with driving the
Germans out of Gaul, the province which had been assigned to him;
he ought not to have carried war against them into their own territory
without first consulting the Roman people, especially since there
was no imminent danger from that source. The Germans therefore
did not have the right to demand that Caesar be surrendered to
them, but the Roman people had the right to punish him . . .[13]

Much more lasting, though, have been Grotius' ideas on
certain fundamental features of international society. These
ideas have been refined or recast in different ways as later
generations have grappled with old or new problems in their
contemporary contexts. The text has in some measure evolved
away from its author, while retaining an oscillating link to the
system around which he sought to construct it. It is often

The Betsey (Great Britain–United States Mixed Commission, 1796–7), Opinion of
Mr Pinkney, 4 *Moore's International Arbitrations (Mod. Ser.)*, pp. 246–52.

[12] See e.g. Bert Brandenberg, 'The Legality of Assassination as an Aspect of
Foreign Policy', *Virginia Journal of International Law*, 27 (1987), pp. 657–8; and James
A. R. Nafziger, 'The General Admission of Aliens under International Law', *AJIL* 77
(1983), pp. 810–11. Lists of works dealing with Grotius' contribution to Roman law
may be found in several of the bibliographies noted in the Select Bibliography at the
end of this volume, including that prepared by J. C. M. Willems, *Grotiana*, 2 (1981),
p. 128. For a study of the impact of Grotius and other Roman law authorities on
the development of one area of the common law, see Peter Birks and Grant McLeod,
'The Implied Theory of Quasi-Contract: Civilian Opinion Current in the Century
before Blackstone', *Oxford Journal of Legal Studies*, 6 (1986), pp. 55–64.

[13] *JBP*, book I, chap. 3, § 5. On General MacArthur and the Korean conflict, see
e.g. Rosemary Foot, *The Wrong War: American Policy and the Dimensions of the Korean
Conflict, 1950–1953* (Ithaca, NY, 1985); Burton I. Kaufman, *The Korean War: Challenges
in Crisis, Credibility, and Command* (Philadelphia, Penn., 1986); and Peter Lowe, *The
Origins of the Korean War* (London, 1986).

argued that a Grotian tradition of thought about international
relations can be discerned—defined at least by an interest in a
cluster of 'triggers of collective allegiance' deriving originally
from features of Grotius' own thought.[14] The chapters in this
book examine several of these 'Grotian' concerns in the light
both of Grotius' writings and of subsequent debates and
practice in international relations. In the remainder of this
introduction we will allude to some of these more general
Grotian preoccupations, before briefly considering the meaning and value of a 'Grotian tradition' of thought about
international relations.

(b) THE CONCEPT OF INTERNATIONAL SOCIETY IN THE
GROTIAN TRADITION

The contention that there exists an 'international society' has
been fundamental to much of modern scholarship in international relations, especially that falling within the classical
tradition which has remained dominant in Britain.[15] Martin
Wight, for instance, maintained: 'The most fundamental
question you can ask in international theory is, What is

[14] The quoted phrase is Schama's, *The Embarrassment of Riches: An Interpretation of
Dutch Culture in the Golden Age* (London, 1987), p. 82.
[15] See generally the following collections and survey articles: K. Knorr and J. N.
Rosenau (eds.), *Contending Approaches to International Politics* (Princeton, NJ, 1969);
Brian Porter (ed.), *The Aberystwyth Papers* (London, 1972); Alan James (ed.), *The Bases
of International Order* (Oxford, 1973); Michael Donelan (ed.), *The Reason of States*
(London, 1978); James Mayall (ed.), *The Community of States* (London, 1982); M.
Light and A. J. R. Groom (eds.), *International Relations: A Handbook of Current Theory*
(Boulder, Colo., 1985); Roy E. Jones, 'The English School of International Relations:
A Case for Closure', *Review of International Studies*, 7 (1981), pp. 1–13; Hidemi
Suganami, 'The Structure of Institutionalism: An Anatomy of British Mainstream
International Relations', *International Relations*, 7 (1983), pp. 2363–81; Gene M.
Lyons, 'The Study of International Relations in Great Britain: Further Connections',
World Politics, 38 (1986), p. 626; Sheila Grader, 'The English School of International
Relations: Evidence and Evaluation', *Review of International Studies*, 14 (1988), pp. 29–
44; and Peter Wilson, 'The English School of International Relations: A Reply to
Sheila Grader', ibid., 15 (1989), pp. 49–58.
There are also some limited points of contact between the principal modern
conceptions of international society and the theories of 'world society' associated
particularly with John Burton—see e.g. John W. Burton, *World Society*
(Cambridge, 1972); and Michael Banks (ed.), *Conflict in World Society: A New
Perspective on International Relations* (Brighton, 1984).

international society?'[16] While some writers see 'international society' as a society of individuals, of peoples, or of classes, it is most commonly seen as a society composed primarily (though, in many cases, not exclusively) of states. Hedley Bull's definition is broadly representative:

A *society of states* (or international society) exists when a group of states, conscious of certain common interests and common values, form a society in the sense that they conceive themselves to be bound by a common set of rules in their relations with one another, and share in the working of common institutions. If states today form an international society . . . this is because, recognising certain common interests and perhaps some common values, they regard themselves as bound by certain rules in their dealings with one another, such as that they should respect one another's claims to independence, that they should honour agreements into which they enter, and that they should be subject to certain limitations in exercising force against one another. At the same time they co-operate in the working of institutions such as the forms of procedures of international law, the machinery of diplomacy and general international organization, and the customs and conventions of war.[17]

The exact conception of 'international society'—of its nature, membership, and significance—varies amongst different authors who use the term; and in Hedley Bull's own work it is possible to discern differences in his concepts of international society when used as starting-points for different investigations, whether into the place of war, the nature of order, the principles of international justice, or the expansion of international society.[18]

[16] Wight, 'An Anatomy of International Thought', *Review of International Studies*, 13 (1987), p. 222. This is the text of a lecture given in 1960, published posthumously.

[17] Bull, *The Anarchical Society: A Study of Order in World Politics* (London, 1977), p. 13. Bull's systematic exploration of the idea of international society built upon the earlier work of Martin Wight. Concern with the structure of international co-operation in an 'anarchic' international society has generated mounting interest in this analytic concept: see e.g. Oran R. Young, *International Co-operation: Building Regimes for Natural Resources and the Environment* (Ithaca, NY, 1989), pp. 37–44.

[18] See Bull, 'The Grotian Conception of International Society', in H. Butterfield and M. Wight (eds.), *Diplomatic Investigations* (London, 1966), pp. 51–73; id., 'Society and Anarchy in International Relations', ibid., pp. 35–50; id., *The Anarchical Society* (London, 1977); id., *Justice in International Relations* (Hagey Lectures, University of Waterloo, Ont., 1984); id., 'The Revolt Against the West', in Bull and Watson (eds.), *The Expansion of International Society* (Oxford, 1984), pp. 217–28 (these last two were assays into the field of a projected book on *The Revolt against Western Dominance* which

This concept of international society is often described as 'solidarist', meaning that states or other members of the society share a common commitment to the maintenance of the society and its institutions against challenges to them.[19] The concept of solidarity was not articulated by Grotius (or indeed by other writers before the end of the nineteenth century). Solidarist principles are, however, clearly discernible in Grotius' writings, and they may be seen as an implicit concomitant of most early concepts of international society.[20] Explicit discussion of the concept of solidarity in international relations appears to derive from the sociology of Durkheim and others, from which it was incorporated into French political doctrine at the turn of the twentieth century, and thence through natural law doctrines into international theory.[21] General acceptance of such a principle became a necessity if the new institutions of international society, particularly the League of Nations, were to survive and flourish in the conditions of the 1920s and 1930s.[22] That it was a principle of the *via media* is evident from the cautionary remark of the naturalist Le Fur in 1927:

Bull was unable to complete before his death in 1985); id., 'The Emergence of a Universal International Society', ibid., pp. 117–26. See also the Introduction and Conclusion by the editors of that volume.

[19] See e.g. Bull, *The Anarchical Society*, pp. 238–9.

[20] See e.g. Camilo Barcia Trelles, 'Francisco Vitoria et l'école moderne du droit international', *Recueil des Cours*, 17 (1927), pp. 219–31, treating Vitoria as having contributed the seeds of ideas which germinated as the theory of international solidarity prevalent in the 1920s.

[21] Émile Durkheim, *The Division of Labour in Society* (1st pub. Paris, 1893), trans. W. D. Halls (London, 1984), esp. book 1; Célestin Camille Bouglé, *Le Solidarisme* (Paris, 1907); and the discussion in Joseph Charmont, *La Renaissance du droit naturel* (Montpellier, 1910), pp. 138–58. The political doctrine of solidarism was associated particularly with Léon Bourgeois. Related ideas of occupational or class solidarity among workers also gained intellectual and political currency in this period. The solidarist conception is discussed by Maurice Bourquin, 'Grotius et les tendances actuelles du droit international', *Revue de droit international et législation comparée*, 7 (1926), pp. 86–125; and the articulation of Léon Duguit's solidarist premisses is discussed by Marc Réglade in 'Perspectives qu'ouvrent les doctrines objectivistes du Doyen Duguit pour un renouvellement de l'étude du droit international', *Revue générale de droit international public*, 37 (1930), p. 381.

[22] In one of his early works, Riccardo Monaco took the solidarist theory of international law as a necessary starting-point, which he sought to fuse with an institutional theory of law in developing his conception of the international juridical order (dottrina dell'ordinamento giuridico). See Monaco, 'Solidarismo e teoria dell'instituzione: nella dottrina di diritto internazionale', *Archivio Giuridico*, 108 (1932),

à côté de la bonne solidarité, il y en a une mauvaise, celle du maître et de l'esclave par exemple; . . . la solidarité de fait est aussi impuissante que l'individualisme pur à fonder le droit, et c'est en réalité à une notion qui les dépasse, celle du bien commun, qu'il faut pour cela recourir.[23]

An institutional principle of solidarity is very widely accepted by the members of the international society of the UN era. Certain of its precepts have been expounded consensually, especially in Article 2 of the UN Charter and in subsequent interpretive resolutions of the General Assembly.[24] Some of these precepts are discussed below in the chapters by Rosalyn Higgins and Hidemi Suganami. The notion of international 'solidarity' has also been pressed into service for other purposes—including the assertion by proponents of 'new rights' (variously treated as human rights, rights of peoples, or rights of states) to such goods as development, environment, peace, and communication, that these are 'solidarity' rights.[25]

Hersch Lauterpacht, Martin Wight, and Hedley Bull all associated their conceptions of international society with a particular 'Grotian' tradition of thought on this subject.[26] At first sight this may appear somewhat surprising. The most eloquent account of the concept of international society is

[23] Louis Le Fur, 'La Théorie du droit naturel depuis le XVII' siècle et la doctrine moderne', *Recueil des Cours*, 18 (1927), p. 423.
[24] For instance, the Declaration on Principles of International Law Concerning Friendly Relations and Cooperation among States in accordance with the Charter of the United Nations, adopted in GA Res. 2625 (1970); the Definition of Aggression, adopted in GA Res. 3314 (1974); and the Declaration on the Enhancement of the Effectiveness of the Principle of Refraining from the Threat or Use of Force in International Relations, adopted in GA Res. 42/22 (1987).
[25] See Karel Vasak's 'Avant-projet de Troisième Pacte International Relatif aux Droits de Solidarité, in Christophe Swinarski (ed.), *Études et essais sur le droit international humanitaire et sur les principes de la Croix-Rouge en honneur de Jean Pictet* (Geneva, 1984), p. 846; *Conclusions of the International Symposium of Experts on 'Rights of Solidarity and Peoples' Rights'*, Rep. of San Marino, 1982 (Unesco Doc. SS–82/WS/61); Philip Alston, 'A Third Generation of Solidarity Rights: Progressive Development or Obfuscation of International Human Rights Law?', *Netherlands International Law Review*, 29 (1982), p. 307; Farooq Hassan, 'Solidarity Rights: Progressive Evolution of International Human Rights Law?', *New York Law School Human Rights Annual*, 1 (1983), p. 51; James Crawford (ed.), *The Rights of Peoples* (Oxford, 1988).
[26] See Lauterpacht, 'The Grotian Tradition in International Law', pp. 1–53; Wight, 'Western Values in International Relations', in Butterfield and Wight (eds.), *Diplomatic Investigations*, pp. 89–131; and Bull's chapter below.

probably that given, not by Grotius, but by his predecessor Francisco Suarez (1548–1617):

The rational basis, moreover, of this phase of law consists in the fact that the human race, into howsoever many different peoples and kingdoms it may be divided, always preserves a certain unity, not only as a species, but also a moral and political unity (as it were) enjoined by the natural precept of mutual love and mercy; a precept which applies to all, even to strangers of every nation.

Therefore, although a given sovereign state, commonwealth, or kingdom may constitute a perfect community in itself, consisting of its own members, nevertheless, each one of these states is also, in a certain sense, and viewed in relation to the human race, a member of that universal society; for these states when standing alone are never so self-sufficient that they do not require some mutual assistance, association, and intercourse, at times for their own greater welfare and advantage, but at other times because also of some moral necessity or need. This fact is made manifest by actual usage.[27]

This account has been approved by twentieth-century authors whom Wight and Bull might reasonably have located in the Grotian tradition.[28] While it is closer in spirit to what Wight and Bull saw as the Kantian cosmopolitanist tradition than to what might be characterized as the realist wing of the Grotian tradition, Suarez was no Utopian advocate of world government: 'the ordinary course of human nature points to the conclusion that a human legislative power of universal character and world-wide extent does not exist and has never existed, nor is it morally possible that it should have done so.'[29]

Suarez was but one of several writers who expounded theories of international society in the century before Grotius.

---

[27] Suarez, *De Legibus* (1612), book II, chap. 19, § 9. The English translation is in *Selections from Three Works of Francisco Suarez, SJ* (Classics of International Law, Oxford, 1944).

[28] See e.g. J. L. Brierly, 'Suarez's Vision of a World Community' and 'The Realization Today of Suarez's World Community', in *The Basis of Obligation in International Law* (Oxford, 1958). See also Manfred Lachs, 'The Grotian Heritage, the International Community and Changing Dimensions of International Law', in Asser Instituut, *International Law and the Grotian Heritage*, pp. 199–200, arguing that Grotius went much further than Suarez in recognizing the interdependence of states and peoples in the areas of trade and security, and the consequent need for a law between nations to regulate the functioning of international society.

[29] Suarez, *De Legibus*, book III, chap. 4, § 7. The categories used by Wight and Bull are discussed in the final section of this chapter.

Alberico Gentili, in particular, set forth in his *De Jure Belli* a less
visionary and much more structured conception of international
society, very close to that of Grotius.[30] Indeed, Bull noted five
significant features of international society which he associated
not only with Grotius, but more generally with the 'natural-
law thinkers' (referring to Vitoria, Suarez, Gentili, Grotius,
and Pufendorf) of the sixteenth and seventeenth centuries: the
values underlying international society as they conceived it
were Christian; membership of international society was not
governed by any fundamental constitutive principle or criterion;
binding rules of conduct were grounded in natural law much
more than in anything resembling what later came to be
called positive international law; the rules of coexistence were
inchoate, and equivocated between the universalism of a law
common to all nations and true *jus inter gentes*; and finally, no
set of institutions of the international society was specified.[31]
When he identified a return to this conception of international
society as having taken place in the twentieth century, it was
to some of these common factors that Bull referred: the
centrality of Western values in a much wider international
society; vagueness about entities qualifying for membership;
a return to natural law; a revival of universalist or solidarist
assumptions about the rules of coexistence; and the widespread condemnation of secret diplomacy and balance of
power policies.[32]

In seeking to determine what is distinctively *Grotian* about
this modern conception of international society, it is important to observe that while Grotius (unlike Suarez) does not
portray a cosmopolitanist international society consisting

[30] So much so that Coleman Phillipson, discussing Gentili's conception of the
societas gentium, argued that '(though Gentili does not put it this way) the basic axiom
of human solidarity, *"ubi societas ibi ius"* is as applicable to a group of peoples as it is to
a group of individuals. Here Gentili, by his implicit recognition of the principle of
solidarity and interdependence of states as an essential limitation of their
sovereignty, has anticipated a vital conception of our own times, a conception which,
when it comes to be duly realized by the peoples of the world (and more
particularly by their ministers and representatives), will facilitate the working of the
League of Nations organization, and so will pave the way for the consummation of a
rational world polity.' 'Introduction' to Gentili, *De Jure Belli* (Oxford, 1933), ii,
p. 23a. For the definition of international society favoured by Gentili, see *JB*, book 1,
chap. 15.
[31] Bull, *The Anarchical Society*, pp. 28–31.
[32] See esp. ibid., pp. 38–40.

primarily of individual humans,[33] neither does he present an international society comprised only of states or similar entities. For the most part he is concerned with principles applicable to a society of states, and thus with an international society of the sort described by Bull. But he is easily read as allowing some scope for an international society of greater depth—a society which might be described as having matured into an international community—in which states and other international entities are the dominant but not the only participants. This richly textured view of international society has been particularly attractive in the first and last quarters of the twentieth century.[34]

Some commentators have sought to clarify the Grotian conception of international society by positing two different strands in pre-Grotian thought on the subject. One strand is said to treat civil society and international society as being constituted by and under the law of nature, with the achievement of the common good as a primary purpose; while the other strand interprets the basic nature of people as pre-social and pre-rational, the formation of societies being seen as a deliberate decision of those who become members. Grotius is characterized as inclining to the second view.[35] When combined

[33] Van Eysinga has been criticized for treating Grotius as espousing such a 'universal community of mankind'—see e.g. Hendrik van Eikema Hommes, 'Grotius and Natural and International Law', *Netherlands International Law Review*, 30 (1983), pp. 63–4.

[34] See e.g. Hector Gros Espiell, 'En el IV centenario de Hugo Grocio: El nacimiento del Derecho de Gentes y la idea de la comunidad internacional', in *Pensamiento jurídico y sociedad internacional: Estudios en honor del profesor D. Antonio Truyol y Serra*, i (Madrid, 1986), p. 548, arguing that 'aunque todavía no de manera absoluta, la actual Sociedad Internacional—esencialmente universal y embrionariamente organizada, y que es mucho más que una yuxtaposición de Estados—presenta caracteres de Comunidad. La existencia de estos elementos embrionarios hacen que, si bien realísticamente el elemento societario pueda conceptuarse aún como importante, los factores comunitarios se manifiestan ya, con una gran fuerza, en previsible desarrollo.' On the position of the individual in modern conceptions of international society, see also Vincent's chapter below.

[35] See also Mattingly's assessment of Grotius' contribution: 'He was only trying, like most of his contemporaries, to justify what men were doing or thought they ought to be doing, and his standards and value judgements and the rules of international conduct for which he argued were drawn, like most other people's, largely from a medieval past which he never mentioned. But he was the first person to see, or to make clear that he saw, that, to be persuasive, the argument must be couched in the terms not of the interests of a single unitary commonwealth of which the princes and republics of Christendom were subordinate members, but in terms of the interest in

with his conviction that a purpose of law-governed society was to prevent improper interference with the exercise of the natural rights of individuals, Grotius can be read as supporting a limited and essentially rights-based view both of civil society and (by implication) of international society.[36] One such commentator, Michael Donelan, argues:

> The separate states that we form are not an arrangement for the common good of the community of mankind but aim only at the good of those who form them. These states in their international relations will aspire to form one great community of reason, and yet, since each aims at its own good, the basis from which they start will be self-regarding . . . A Grotian state does not seek in its foreign policies to determine international issues for the common good because that is the purpose of its existence, but rather because it sees grounds for doing so in its own interests.[37]

This account expresses one twentieth-century conception of international society. However, the claim that this conception is traceable to the writings of Grotius, or that it is associated with a doubtful distinction between 'Aristotelian' and 'Stoic' positions, is less convincing.

Connections between Grotius' writings and modern views of international society also arise from his accommodation of a wide variety of domestic constitutional structures and political cultures within international society, and from his ready tolerance of religious differences.[38] Setting aside questions as to the

their own self-preservation of the independent, ego-centred, absolutely sovereign states whose aggregate composed the heterogeneous, pluralistic international society of western Europe. That was what the future was going to be like.' 'International Diplomacy and International Law', in R. B. Wernham (ed.), *The New Cambridge Modern History*, iii, *The Counter-Reformation and Price-Revolution 1559–1610* (Cambridge, 1968), pp. 169–70.

[36] See e.g. van Eikema Hommes, 'Grotius and Natural and International Law', pp. 63–4; and Knud Haakonssen, 'Hugo Grotius and the History of Political Thought', *Political Theory*, 13 (1985), pp. 240–4. This conception is evident in many modern views of international society, including perhaps those defended by Terry Nardin, *Law, Morality, and the Relations of States* (Princeton, NJ, 1983), esp. p. 50; and Alan James, *Sovereign Statehood: The Basis of International Society* (London, 1986).

[37] Michael Donelan, 'Grotius and the Image of War', *Millennium*, 12 (1983), p. 241.

[38] On the concept of the state in *JBP* see Richard Tuck, *Natural Rights Theories: Their Origin and Development* (Cambridge, 1979), pp. 77–80. In common with many of his predecessors in the century since the Reformation, Grotius was against religious

extent to which Grotius or modern proponents of international
society have seen tolerance as an intrinsically desirable value
for international society rather than as simply an instrumental
necessity, it is clear that a pragmatic tolerance of diversity
within an overall structure of values embodied in international
society has likewise been an important feature of the theory
and practice of international relations since 1945.

Grotius takes a view of international society which Martin
Wight models, perhaps rather too simply, as two concentric
circles. The inner circle is the society of Christian states,
possessed of special rights and duties originating both in the
commonality of their shared perceptions and in the rectitude
of the Christianity which underlay it.[39] The non-Christian
communities in the outer circle were part of the system not
through positive volitional law, but through natural law.[40]
This is consistent also with Grotius' more general proposition
that 'love is not due to all in the same degree . . . a greater love is
due to a father than to a stranger.'[41] In these respects, Grotius
may be seen as charting an approach in which the objectives of
universality and morality are accommodated in the interstices
of a realistic and pragmatically orientated framework of pre-
scriptions and rules. This too has been a significant attraction
for several twentieth-century theorists of international society.

It is striking that as early as Prolegomena 17 of *De Jure Belli
ac Pacis* Grotius expounds the concept of a law-governed
international society, and returns to this theme in the final

wars: 'Beyond doubt it was rightly said by Philo that to each one his religion seems
the best, since this is most often judged not by reason but by affection.' *JBP*, book II,
chap. 20, § 47.

[39] 'We are bidden to exclude no class of men from our deeds of kindness', says
Grotius, but the Christian law 'ought to be received with due regard to difference in
degree, so that we should be doers of good to all, but particularly to those who share
the same religion'. *JBP*, book II, chap. 15, § 10.

[40] See e.g. ibid., book II, chap. 15, § 12.

[41] Ibid., book I, chap. 2, § 8. Gentili, however, chose to endorse Cicero's view that
'those who say that we should have regard to our fellow citizens, but not to strangers,
destroy the community and the fellowship of the human race'. *JB*, book I, chap. 15.
Note also Grotius' spirited defence of the right of the Dutch to assist the East Indians
against the depredations of the Portuguese, in which he holds: 'the contention that
one must have regard for one's fellow citizens but not for foreigners, is assuredly
equivalent to repudiation of the universal bond of human fellowship, a bond which
one cannot repudiate without being judged impious toward God Himself'. *De Jure
Praedae*, chap. 13 (Classics of International Law, Oxford, 1950, p. 314).

chapter, stressing the role of good faith in sustaining the greater society of states. As to more specific aspects of the Grotian conception, modern assessments have focused especially on Grotius' placing of war within the structure and rules of international society, while recognizing that the treatment of war in *De Jure Belli ac Pacis* was not wholly new. In different ways this theme of the place of war is taken up in most of the chapters below. Similarly, Grotius' extensive treatment of law as an institution of international society was perhaps more systematic and more convincing to subsequent generations than was that of any of his predecessors. Beyond this, what is distinctively Grotian seems—at least in its individual strands—not to be unique to the hero of this eponymous tradition. The Grotian conception of international society, in the form outlined by Hedley Bull in his chapter below, is an earlier conception consolidated by Grotius but transmitted and modulated by very many subsequent authors and practitioners.

(c) GROTIUS AND THE PLACE OF WAR IN INTERNATIONAL SOCIETY

To Hedley Bull, Grotius' most important contribution seems to have lain in his treatment of war as being in some cases contrary to the law of international society, but in other cases sanctioned by it and evidence of its functioning.[42] This interpretation emphasizes Grotius' concern with the solidarity of states in international society: 'The system of rules which Grotius devised was intended to assist the triumph in any war of the party or parties whose cause was just, and who therefore were acting on behalf of the community as a whole.'[43] Edmund Burke may thus be placed squarely within this interpretation of

[42] This view is espoused by Bull in 'The Grotian Conception of International Society', in Butterfield and Wight (eds.), *Diplomatic Investigations*, p. 53. Bull's later work also emphasizes other important features of the Grotian tradition—see e.g. his chapter below.

[43] Bull, *The Anarchical Society*, p. 239. Bull says also: 'The Grotian or solidarist doctrine seeks to achieve a more orderly world by restricting or abolishing resort to war by individual states for political ends, and promoting the idea that force can legitimately be used only to promote the purposes of the international community.' Ibid.

the Grotian tradition when he argues: 'As to war, if it be the means of wrong and violence, it is the sole means of justice amongst nations. Nothing can banish it from the world. They who say otherwise, intending to impose upon us, do not impose upon themselves.'[44] Similarly Michael Donelan discerns three images of war underlying Grotius' thought in *De Jure Belli ac Pacis*: war as a judicial act, war as litigation, and war as a fight for the common good against an enemy who violates the basic norms of international society. Donelan regards the third of these images as enduring. He does recognize that if states must themselves determine the common good (including the good of the opponent), a substantial element of self-interest will inevitably be involved, and there is scope for hypocrisy and for simultaneous self-justification by both sides. But for Donelan the Grotian image of war as a fight for the common good is attractive as a restraining influence primarily because it is premissed upon the maintenance, perhaps even the strengthening, of international society.[45]

Bull and others read Grotius as limiting the just causes of war to defence, the recovery of property and the infliction of punishment. Like Bull, Haggenmacher acknowledges the contribution of Grotius in *De Jure Belli ac Pacis* in circumscribing the just causes of war through listing them exhaustively. Haggenmacher notes, however, that in the Grotian scheme a war may also be started to vindicate an absolute right or to pursue a relative right, although these categories are subject to limitations. In

[44] Edmund Burke, *Letters on the Proposals for Peace with the Regicide Directory of France*, Letter I, in *The Works of the Right Honourable Edmund Burke*, iv (London, 1802), p. 433. Although Burke adduced many arguments in favour of England's war against revolutionary France, the maintenance of international society was certainly one important consideration. 'France, since her revolution, is under the sway of a sect, whose leaders have deliberately, at one stroke, demolished the whole body of that jurisprudence which France had pretty nearly in common with other civilized countries. In that jurisprudence were contained the elements and principles of the law of nations, the great ligament of mankind . . . They have not only annulled all their old treaties; but they have renounced the law of nations from whence treaties have their force. With a fixed design they have outlawed themselves, and to their power outlawed all other nations.' Ibid., p. 423. 'If to preserve political independence and civil freedom to nations, was a just ground of war; a war to preserve national independence, property, liberty, life, and honour, from certain universal havock, is a war just, necessary, manly, pious; and we are bound to persevere in it by every principle, divine and human, as long as the system which menaces them all, and all equally, has an existence in the world.' Ibid., pp. 421–2.
[45] Donelan, 'Grotius and the Image of War', p. 233.

keeping with this scheme, Grotius took a much wider view of what constitutes war than is taken in modern practice, particularly by his inclusion of private war and of measures of extra-judicial enforcement short of full-scale use of force.

Many have expressed much more sceptical views of the content and impact of Grotius' writings on war. Voltaire, for instance, asserted that 'tous les arguments profondément frivoles de Grotius et de Pufendorf' had in practice achieved nothing whatever in the restraint of war.[46] This view is largely shared by Schwarzenberger in his chapter below. From sharply different perspectives, Schwarzenberger and Röling challenge Bull's contention that a doctrine of just war is necessary both to license just wars upholding international norms and to protect the weak through the interdiction of unjust wars.[47]

The sceptical response of Schwarzenberger, and of many others in the realist tradition, is that initial decisions to use force, like the eventual political outcomes of armed conflicts, are determined by considerations of power, not of justice. Higgins contests the assertions of the extreme realists, pointing out that the United Nations has managed, to a limited but significant extent, to raise the cost of certain illegitimate uses of force, and to use peacekeeping forces and diplomacy to moderate the resort to military power in several difficult disputes. Draper develops the further point that restraints on the means of conducting war in the twentieth century, despite their fundamental limitations, have in practice done something to maintain that element of the just war tradition which

[46] *La Tactique* (1773), in Voltaire, *Œuvres complètes*, vol. x (Paris, 1877), p. 193.

[47] In chap. 8 of *The Anarchical Society* Bull examined arguments alleging the decreasing utility of force in the modern era, and concluded that force certainly had not altogether lost its role as an instrument whereby international society enforces its rules. In his article 'New Directions in the Theory of International Relations', *International Studies*, 14 (1975), Bull bemoaned the absence of any study of the changes that have taken place this century in the doctrine of the just war. He subsequently reviewed Michael Walzer's *Just and Unjust Wars* (New York, 1977) with interest, but concluded that studies of a more fundamental kind were required if the just war were indeed to be recaptured for political theory. It is intriguing to note why he felt that Walzer had not succeeded. His criticisms really address Walzer's failure to find a path between a revolutionist and a legalist conception of just war, between an individualist and a collectivist approach to obligation, and between absolutist and relativist conceptions of morality in war. Although he does not say it, he is asking for a Grotian *via media*. 'Recapturing the Just War for Political Theory', *World Politics*, 31 (1979), pp. 588–99.

is concerned with the protection of non-combatants and other 'protected persons'.

The invention of nuclear weapons, and their development and proliferation since 1945, has provided a further ground for scepticism about the contemporary relevance of just war theory. Some, like Professor Röling, contend that these weapons render just war theory contemptible in an age where the essential task for human survival must be the abolition of all war.[48] Others reply that war and threats of war have remained a reality since 1945 and that just war doctrine is relevant to their regulation and limitation.[49]

Three further objections to modern uses of just war doctrine may be mentioned.[50] First, how common in fact are situations where a perspicuous distinction may be drawn between the just and the unjust? There is a risk that such analysis focuses on the aggressor/defender (or defended) dichotomy, leaving the international community more often than not grappling with conflicts subjectively just on both sides, and objectively indeterminable or just on neither side. Second, how far can traditional doctrines of just war accommodate demands legitimated by contemporary principles of justice—for example the principles of decolonization and self-determination? Third, have just war theories encouraged more wars, and more brutality in war, than they have limited? This objection is especially pertinent in view of the number of states—and peoples— which have embraced the notion that the greater the justice of the grounds for wars, the more they should be willing to undertake them and to prosecute them vigorously.

Many reflective theologians and jurists had written eloquent counsels of restraint in war before Grotius embarked on his. Some concentrated on moral arguments—others were more

---

[48] See Röling's chapter below, and his 'Jus ad Bellum and the Grotian Heritage', in Asser Instituut, *International Law and the Grotian Heritage*, p. 111. See also A. J. P. Kenny, *The Logic of Deterrence* (London, 1985); and John Finnis, Joseph M. Boyle, jun., and Germain Grisez, *Nuclear Deterrence, Morality and Realism* (Oxford, 1987).

[49] See James Turner Johnson, *Can Modern War Be Just?* (New Haven, Conn., 1984). See also Paul Ramsey, *The Just War: Force and Political Responsibility* (Cambridge, 1983); David Fisher, *Morality and The Bomb: An Ethical Assessment of Nuclear Deterrence* (London, 1985); and Joseph S. Nye, *Nuclear Ethics* (New York, 1986).

[50] See generally James Turner Johnson, *Just War Tradition and the Restraint of War: A Moral and Historical Inquiry* (Princeton, NJ, 1981).

prudential.[51] Suarez, for instance, discussed cases where it would be just *vis-à-vis* the other side to resort to war, but where waging war would nevertheless be contrary to charity or unjust to the people whose prince had a just cause.[52] Grotius' *temperamenta belli* were certainly a moral and prudential appeal for restraint; the more difficult problem, discussed by G. I. A. D. Draper in his chapter below, is to determine how to place them in the structure of the legal argument (as we now discern it) in *De Jure Belli ac Pacis*.[53]

Grotius' firm location of *jus in bello* in the just war tradition appears on one view as perhaps his most enduring contribution to the law of war. In so doing he drew significantly on Roman sources. Important aspects of just war theory were in fact Roman and pagan in origin, as Grotius recognized. Barnes indeed argues:

the mature theory of the just war—as expounded by Alexander of Hales, Vitoria, Suarez and Grotius—was built upon Roman foundations. The laws of war, or *jura belli*, were born neither in Greek philosophy nor in Christian theology: their paternity must be attributed to the political ideas of the Romans, and more particularly to a pagan and archaic ritual of the Roman Republic.[54]

Whether or not this description undervalues the early contribution of Hebrew law and Christian theology, by the medieval period the just war tradition was overwhelmingly the province of canon lawyers and theologians. The main focus in the later medieval period was upon what came to be called the

---

[51] See generally Christian Lange, *Histoire de l'internationalisme*, i (Kristiania, 1919).

[52] Suarez, *De Triplice Virtute*, 'On Charity', Disputatio XIII, War (hereinafter 'Suarez, *De Bello*'), § 4. 8. An English translation is included in *Selections from Three Works of Francisco Suarez, SJ* (Classics of International Law, Oxford, 1944).

[53] See also Geoffrey Best, 'The Place of Grotius in the Development of International Humanitarian Law', in A. Dufour, P. Haggenmacher, and J. Toman (eds.), *Grotius et l'ordre juridique international* (Lausanne, 1985), p. 101. Best argues that in addressing both the brutal reality of war and the desirability of legal restraints on it, Grotius develops a rich but rather uncomfortable binary doctrine with which Best, at least, is not satisfied. Cf. James Turner Johnson, 'Grotius' Use of History and Charity in the Modern Transformation of the Just War Idea', *Grotiana*, 4 (1983), pp. 21–34.

[54] Jonathan Barnes, 'Cicéron et la guerre juste', *Bulletin de la Société française de Philosophie* (1986), p. 46 (our translation. Footnotes omitted). See also Herbert Hausmaninger, ' "Bellum iustum" und "iusta causa belli" im älteren römischen Recht', *Österreichische Zeitschrift für öffentliches Recht*, 11 (1961), pp. 335–45; and the chapter by Draper below.

jus ad bellum: the authority and state of mind of the person declaring the war, the status (condition) and intentions of those waging the war, the justice of the cause of those on whose behalf the war was waged, and the deserts of those against whom it was waged.[55] A war could not be objectively just on both sides; and little account was taken of the prospect that both sides might genuinely believe that they were justified in resorting to war. Although there were certainly rules about the conduct of war, in the main these were not relevant in medieval thought to the prior question of whether the war was just.

Such a link began to appear more explicitly in writings on the just war in the sixteenth century, fortified by a line of authority dating at least from St Augustine. Vitoria, for instance emphasized:

the obligation to see that greater evils do not arise out of the war than the war would avert. For if little effect upon the ultimate issue of the war is to be expected from the storming of a fortress or fortified town wherein are many innocent folk, it would not be right, for the purpose of assailing a few guilty, to slay the many innocent by use of fire or engines of war or other means likely to overwhelm indifferently both innocent and guilty. In sum, it is never right to slay the guiltless, even as an indirect and unintended result, except when there is no other means of carrying on the operations of a just war.[56]

Suarez held that for a war to be justly waged:

First, the war must be waged by a legitimate power; secondly, the cause itself and the reason must be just; thirdly, the method of its conduct must be proper, and due proportion must be observed at its beginning, during its prosecution and after victory.[57]

Grotius made the observance of *jus in bello* a more central feature of the requirements of just war doctrine. In doing so, however, he has sometimes been construed as having weakened

---

[55] See e.g. Alexander of Hales, *Summa theologica*, iii, § 466. See generally Barnes, 'The Just War', in N. Kretzman, A. Kenny, and J. Pinborg (eds.), *The Cambridge History of Later Medieval Philosophy* (Cambridge, 1982), pp. 773–82.

[56] Vitoria, *De Indis, sive De Jure Belli Hispanorum in Barbaros* (1st pub. 1557), § 37. The English translation is from *De Indis et De Jure Belli Relectiones*, trans. John Pawley Bate (Classics of International Law, Washington, DC, 1917).

[57] Suarez, *De Bello*, § 1. 7.

the restraints on resort to war which were the centre-piece of the medieval just war tradition. This charge of having sold the pass has been levelled with a particular sense of betrayal by those who have seen its recapture as a principal problem of the twentieth century.

An investigation of this charge might begin with Grotius' acceptance that every solemn public war had valid, if limited, legal consequences for *both* sides, regardless of the underlying justifiability of each side's cause.[58] Further, war can be subjectively just on both sides, in the sense not that both sides can be correct about the justice of their causes, but that both sides may be guiltless and thus from a legal viewpoint be entitled to be treated as having engaged in a just war.[59] Here Grotius was in large measure following Vitoria, Suarez, and Gentili[60] in responding to the prevalence of conflicts where each side and its allies asserted their justifications, with no forum in which to resolve the issue other than the justice of the victor. Grotius' view was reinforced by his belief that war is a remedy where law courts are lacking—and that in these circumstances war provides a forum in which 'either party may justly, that is in good faith, plead his case'.[61]

Having elected to acknowledge this reality rather than resist it, Grotius endeavoured to accommodate it within the framework of established just war theory.[62] That he was not wholly successful in doing so was in some respects already evident to his seventeenth-century successors.[63] Following Gentili's approach, Zouche, Textor and others narrowed the definition

[58] A solemn public war is a war between sovereign powers, duly declared.

[59] See esp. *JBP*, book II, chap. 23, § 13.

[60] Vitoria, *De Indis, sive De Jure Belli Hispanorum in Barbaros*, § 32; Suarez, *De Legibus*, book III, chap. 18; Gentili, *JB*, book I, chap. 6.

[61] *JBP*, book II, chap. 23, § 13.

[62] His method of carefully cataloguing the just and unjust causes of war as presented by each party, and the just and unjust means of conducting war in these circumstances, has prompted a few commentators to treat Grotius as formulating doctrines of justifiable and unjustifiable war rather than just and unjust war. Certainly his systematic criteria are vastly different from the doctrines of untrammelled holy war with which the just war tradition was occasionally associated: but Grotius was deeply concerned with the issues addressed and the approaches employed in the literature of the just war tradition, and is properly seen as belonging to it.

[63] As Haggenmacher observes, 'La discordance entre les deux régimes est patente, malgré les efforts de Grotius de l'expliquer par le recours à des sources juridiques distinctes et de l'atténuer grâce à sa célèbre doctrine des *temperamenta belli*: dans cette

of war so that the whole just war theory applied only to Grotius' special category of solemn public wars. Similarly the requirement that the war be declared, already somewhat emasculated in *De Jure Belli ac Pacis*, became further and further attenuated before its final demise in the twentieth century.

The formal separation of *jus in bello* from *jus ad bellum*—and the effective discarding of the latter for practical purposes—is rendered explicit in Vattel's *Droit des Gens* (1758). Among the principles of the voluntary law of nations, to which all states are presumed to have consented, are 'that regular war, as to its effects, is to be accounted just on both sides'; that 'whatever is permitted to the one in virtue of the state of war, is also permitted to the other'; and that the law

does not, to him who takes up arms in an unjust cause, give any real right that is capable of justifying his conduct and acquitting his conscience, but merely entitles him to the benefit of the external effect of the law, and to impunity among mankind.[64]

In addition to *jus in bello*, Grotius also dealt extensively with issues relating to the inception and conclusion of wars, including self-defence as a justification for war and obligations of justice in the conclusion of wars.

For the most part ancient just war theory had placed little emphasis on self-defence as a justification for war: if the attack was justified the defence was not, and vice versa.[65] Grotius, however, seems to imply that self-defence will often be justified, even against a just attacker.[66] The UN Charter completes the

mesure, son essai de synthèse reste imparfait.' 'Mutations du concept de *guerre juste* de Grotius à Kant', in *La guerre* (Cahiers de Philosophie politique et juridique, no. 10, Université de Caen, 1986), p. 110.

[64] Vattel, *Le Droit des gens*, trans. Joseph Chitty (London, 1834), book III, chap. 12, §§ 190–2.

[65] The formalities for a just war were also necessary, even where it was being waged in self-defence. See Barnes, 'The Just War', pp. 753–6.

[66] See esp. *JBP*, book II, chap. 1, § 3, where Grotius says that the right of self-defence for individuals against personal attack arises not from the injustice or crime of the aggressor, but from 'the fact that nature commits to each his own protection'. 'Wherefore, even if the assailant be blameless, as for instance a soldier acting in good faith, or one who mistakes me for someone else, or one who is rendered irresponsible by madness or by sleeplessness . . . the right of self-defence is not thereby taken away.' As to public wars, Grotius does not commit himself unequivocally, but his acceptance that particular acts in war may provide an independent just cause for acts in response, combined with his recognition that a war will often appear just to both sides

inversion: apart from collective action under the auspices of international organizations, self-defence (however broadly construed) is treated as the only legitimate ground for the threat or use of force by states in their international relations.[67] Grotius' quotation from Polybius may be adapted to characterize the appearances many states have thus sought to maintain since 1945: 'The Romans have striven earnestly for this, that they be not the first to lay violent hands upon their neighbours, but that it should always be believed that they proceeded against an enemy in order to ward off injuries.'[68]

Grotius also upheld a significant link between just war theory and the terms of peace at the end of wars.[69] While Grotius held that in law the victor in a just war was entitled to punish the vanquished, he did not wish this right to overshadow all other considerations of justice and prudence. Thus the

interpretation of ambiguous clauses [in peace treaties] ought to be directed to the end that the party who had a just cause of war should obtain that for which he took up arms, and should likewise recover for damages and costs, but that he should not also recover anything by way of penalty, for that would arouse more hatred.[70]

While Grotius recognized that communities and peoples may endure even though all the individuals in them may change, the law should not countenance descendants being punished for their ancestors' sins: 'When, therefore, those individuals are dead through whom the community derived its desert, the desert itself lapses also; and likewise the debt of punishment.'[71]

and that self-defence is a legitimate response to injury received or threatened, suggests that self-defence will often be legally permissible. This issue is discussed by James Turner Johnson, who argues (without citing close textual evidence) that Grotius took a very broad view of the permissibility of self-defence in public wars. Johnson, *Ideology, Reason and the Limitation of War: Religious and Secular Concepts 1200–1740* (Princeton, NJ, 1975), p. 221.

[67] However, not every use of force in self-defence is necessarily just in modern international law: even where an armed attack has occurred, the constraints of necessity and proportionality apply, and certain methods of self-defence are or may be impermissible. Moreover, views differ as to whether 'wars of national liberation', in so far as they are legally permitted, are properly categorized as self-defence.

[68] *JBP*, book II, chap. I, § I.

[69] For one view of the way in which this issue was in general treated in medieval just war theory, see Barnes, 'Cicéron et la guerre juste', pp. 57–8.

[70] *JBP*, book III, chap. 20, § 11.   [71] Ibid., book II, chap. 21, § 8.

Several other aspects of Grotius' writings on the law concerning war continue to have a modern resonance. On the subject of disobedience to unlawful orders, Grotius adopted a well-known maxim: 'if the authorities issue any order that is contrary to the law of nature or to the commandments of God, the order should not be carried out.'[72] Grotius also held that certain barbarous acts are equally forbidden in war as in peace: for instance, acts of rape 'do not contribute to safety or to punishment, and should consequently not go unpunished in war any more than in peace', both as a matter of military discipline and as a matter of that law of nations observed among 'the better' nations.[73] He recognized a useful distinction between territory which is merely occupied in the course of a war, and territory which is conquered and added to the victor's permanent possessions: a distinction sometimes overlooked by later writers.[74] His supplementation of the limited *jus in bello* by *temperamenta belli*, often decried by positivists for their lack of explicitly 'legal' effect,[75] was nevertheless mirrored in the famous Martens Clause included in 1899 Hague Convention II and, with minor variations, in several subsequent instruments on the laws of war:

Until a more complete code of the laws of war is issued, the high contracting Parties think it right to declare that in cases not included in the Regulations adopted by them, populations and belligerents remain under the protection and empire of the principles of international law, as they result from the usages established between civilized nations, from the laws of humanity, and the requirements of the public conscience.[76]

---

[72] *JBP*, book I, chap. 4, § 1. If in such cases the consequence of disobedience is that a capricious sovereign inflicts unjust treatment upon us, 'we ought to endure it rather than resist by force'. Ibid. This Grotius ties to the general illegality of rebellion. See also ibid., book II, chap. 26.   [73] Ibid., book III, chap. 4, § 19.

[74] So territory is not considered as captured at the moment it is occupied, but only when it has been closed to access by permanent fortifications. Ibid., book III, chap. 6, § 4.

[75] Grotius introduces the *temperamenta* with a line Seneca gives to Agamemnon in *Trojan Women*: 'What law permits, this sense of shame forbids to do.' *JBP*, book III, chap. 10, § 1.

[76] The text is in J. B. Scott (ed.), *The Hague Conventions and Declarations of 1899 and 1907*, 2nd edn. (New York, 1915), pp. 101–2. See also 1907 Hague Convention IV (Preamble); 1949 Geneva Conventions I (Article 63), II (Article 62), III (Article 142), and IV (Article 158); 1977 Geneva Protocols I (Article 1), and II (Preamble); and the 1981 UN Convention on Prohibitions or Restrictions on the Use of Certain

In dealing with the *jus in bello*, and even more so in dealing with the *jus ad bellum*, Grotius sought to identify enduring criteria and principles which must be applied in weighing any issue concerning the use of force. While modern international law in these fields contains many more detailed legal instruments, the weighing of these general criteria and principles is still a substantial part of the treatment of use of force issues in such bodies as the UN Security Council.[77]

A number of later writers have attached importance to Grotius' definition of war as status rather than act.[78] While the subsequent development of this approach has been important in international practice and legal analysis,[79] Grotius seems to have chosen this broad definition simply to fit his juridical conception of war as an extension of the lawsuit, encompassing private and public conflicts.[80] His view that all such conflicts were on the same juridical plane did not last; and he himself made little additional use of his definition.

Although there has been considerable scepticism about the impact of Grotius' writings, and indeed of the whole just war tradition, on the prevalence and conduct of war, this scepticism is by no means universal. Meinecke, for instance, in his history of *raison d'état*, expressed a widely held view of Grotius:

Certainly the struggle, waged by his international law and usage of war against barbarism and crude force, was productive of many blessings; and, in spite of the fact that more than one of its requirements has proved excessive, it has also exerted a beneficial influence

Conventional Weapons which May be Deemed to be Excessively Injurious or to have Indiscriminate Effects (Preamble). These texts are in Adam Roberts and Richard Guelff (eds.), *Documents on the Laws of War*, 2nd edn. (Oxford, 1989).

[77] See e.g. D. W. Bowett, 'Reprisals Involving Recourse to Armed Force', *AJIL* 66 (1972), p. 1. The intermeshing of *jus in bello* and *jus ad bellum* issues in practice belies the sharp distinction drawn in some modern theoretical literature. A helpful study is Christopher Greenwood, 'The Relationship between *Ius ad Bellum* and *Ius in Bello*', *Review of International Studies*, 9 (1983), pp. 221–34.

[78] See e.g. Hans Kelsen, *Principles of International Law*, 2nd edn., rev. and ed. Robert Tucker (New York, 1967), p. 23.

[79] See generally Ian Brownlie, *International Law and the Use of Force by States* (Oxford, 1963), chaps. 2 and 23; and Christopher Greenwood, 'The Concept of War in Modern International Law', *ICLQ* 37 (1986), p. 283.

[80] Esp. *JBP*, Prolegomena 25, and *JBP*, book II, chap. 1, § 2. Much of the ground for this view was laid in *JP*, chap. 2: Law XII provides that 'Neither the state nor any citizen thereof shall seek to enforce his own right against another state or its citizen, save by judicial procedure.'

on the practice of nations. Indeed it is seldom that great ethical ideas arise in life which do not carry with them some admixture of illusion.[81]

Meinecke's evaluation, in common with most observations on this theme, is essentially personal. It is not easy to determine how far the incidence and conduct of war have been limited in any particular period by ideas and normative formulations; and it is almost impossible reliably to ascribe such effective limitations as there have been to particular ideas or authors. What is clear is that the issues Grotius addressed, the concepts and language he used, even the propositions he advanced, have become part of the common currency of international debate about war in general, and about particular wars. These concepts and terms are used so widely, and have developed so considerably, that their connection with Grotius is easily, and often, overlooked.

(d) LAW AS AN INSTITUTION OF INTERNATIONAL SOCIETY

Modern proponents of international society have laid particular emphasis on its institutions. According to Hedley Bull's definition: 'By an institution we do not necessarily imply an organisation or administrative machinery, but rather a set of habits and practices shaped towards the realization of common goals.'[82] Bull regarded states as the principal institution of international society, on the ground that they make, promulgate, administer, interpret, legitimize, maintain, enforce, and change the rules of the society. Other institutions listed by Bull include the balance of power, international law, the diplomatic mechanism, the managerial system of the great powers, and war.[83]

    Although Grotius is prayed in aid of these institutional views of international society, his own conception of it was not a

---

[81] Friedrich Meinecke, *Machiavellism*, trans. Douglas Scott (London, 1957), p. 209. The German original, entitled *Der Idee der Staatsräson*, was published in 1924.

[82] Bull, *The Anarchical Society*, p. 74. Robert Keohane provides another useful definition: 'When we ask whether X is an institution, we ask whether we can identify persistent sets of rules that constrain activity, shape expectations, and prescribe roles.' 'International Institutions: Two Approaches', *International Studies Quarterly*, 32 (1988), p. 384; repr. in id., *International Institutions and State Power: Essays in International Relations Theory* (Boulder, Colo., 1989), p. 164.

[83] Bull, *The Anarchical Society*, pp. 71–4.

systematically institutional one.[84] With the central exceptions of war and of international law, he did not have a great deal to say about these institutions of international society. He did associate the historical formation of states with the need to fortify the universal society which links all human beings;[85] and he saw the state or other independent political community as the principal means for the enforcement of the law, whether by judicial means or by war. But the balance of power receives no express mention, and Grotius had no developed concept of great power or superpower management.

He did discuss embassies and the institution of diplomacy, but without adding a great deal to the existing literature in that field[86] or attempting significantly to enhance the role of his final profession.[87] While the structure of diplomacy was only at a relatively early stage of its development by the first quarter of the seventeenth century, there is nothing in *De Jure Belli ac Pacis* comparable to the view of embassies as an essential element in the functioning of international society set forth by, for instance, Emer de Vattel in *Droit des Gens* (1758).[88]

Grotius made no attempt to set out a general scheme for international adjudication (which would necessarily have been Utopian), although he did consider the place of arbitration, both to avoid recourse to war, and to facilitate the ending of wars.[89] The single section in *De Jure Belli ac Pacis* on the use of conferences to settle disputes in doubtful cases has often been

[84] See J. B. Scott's Introduction to Suarez, *Selections From Three Works*, Classics of International Law, ii (Oxford, 1944).

[85] *JP*, chap. 2.

[86] In particular, Gentili's *De Legationibus* (1585).

[87] The overlap between the professions of diplomacy and espionage was perhaps a source of even greater difficulty in the seventeenth century than in the twentieth. Hans Morgenthau cites Grotius as advocating the abolition of permanent diplomatic missions on this ground, although there is no such suggestion in his main discussion of diplomacy in *JBP*, book ii, chap. 18. Morgenthau also cites the remark attributed to Grotius' contemporary Sir Henry Wotton that a diplomat is 'an honest man sent abroad to lie for his country', to illustrate his proposition that 'it is indeed true that the diplomat has been held morally in low esteem throughout modern history'. *Politics Among Nations*, 5th edn. (New York, 1973), pp. 524 and 527. *Satow's Guide to Diplomatic Practice*, 5th edn. (London, 1979), § 10. 16, prefers a version in which Sir Henry is reported as having inscribed in the album of John Christopher Flechammer: 'Legatus est vir bonus peregrè missus ad mentiendum Reipublicae causâ.'

[88] Vattel, *Le Droit des gens*, book iv, chaps. 5–9.

[89] *JBP*, book ii, chap. 23, § 8; book iii, chap. 20, §§ 46–8.

cited,[90] but it cannot credibly be seen in any sense as fore-shadowing such modern institutions as the League of Nations and the United Nations. Certainly Grotius conceived of international society as having no superior body with coercive power: and the international society of the UN period does operate without a supranational body.[91] Much of the impetus for the allocation of significant roles to the United Nations and related organizations may spring broadly from the Grotian tradition. But while *De Jure Belli ac Pacis* may have helped to lay some of the groundwork for international co-operation, it is not a treatise dealing at any length with problems of international organization.[92] In this respect the Grotian tradition has evolved a long way from *De Jure Belli ac Pacis*.

Grotius' contribution to international relations continues to be seen largely as the heritage of international lawyers; a point emphasized by the preponderance of lawyers in the literature on international issues generated by the various commemorations of Grotius in the twentieth century. Lauterpacht expressed a very common view in describing the subjection of the totality of international relations to the rule of law as the central theme of *De Jure Belli ac Pacis*.[93]

The distinction between law applied within all or many nations to matters having an international aspect (*jus gentium*), and law applying and binding between nations (*jus inter gentes*), has been fundamental in the development of modern international law.[94] While the distinction is not always a firm one, and perhaps does not coincide precisely with modern concepts,[95]

---

[90] *JBP*, book II, chap. 23, § 7. A notable reference to this passage is that of the Abbé de St Pierre, who took it as the motto for his *Projet*.

[91] Cf. generally Walter Schiffer, *The Legal Community of Mankind* (New York, 1954), pp. 30–1.

[92] Grotius does refer to the notion of *societas inter populos*, and discusses majority rule, weighted voting, and other principles of decision-making in leagues of cities and other bodies. *JBP*, book II, chap. 5, §§ 17–25.

[93] Lauterpacht, 'The Grotian Tradition in International Law', *British Year Book of International Law 1946*, p. 19.

[94] The terms 'international law' and 'droit international' only came into currency with Bentham, although they draw on the ideas associated with the *jus inter gentes*. See generally Mark W. Janis, *An Introduction to International Law* (Boston, Mass., 1988), pp. 163–9; and Hidemi Suganami, 'A Note on the Meaning of the Word "International"', *British Journal of International Studies*, 4 (1978), p. 226. Modern international law has of course been more centrally concerned with 'states' than with 'nations'.

[95] In the modern period some scholars have advocated collapsing the distinction.

the recognition that a significant body of *jus inter gentes* existed—and might be extended by the express or tacit consent of sovereign actors—was an important refinement of the established Roman concept of *jus gentium*. Although the term '*jus inter gentes*' owes its currency to Richard Zouche and other writers of the second half of the seventeenth century,[96] the distinction had appeared in recognizable form by the early years of the seventeenth century, and is evident particularly in a passage inserted by Grotius in the surviving manuscript version of *De Jure Praedae*.[97] In the Prolegomena to *De Jure Praedae* he develops the idea of what he calls a secondary law of nations, consisting both of precepts agreed to by all states as being for the common international good such as the inviolability of ambassadors, and of widely accepted customary practices such as those concerning servitudes and orders of succession. While states may renounce customary practices, they are bound to adhere to the universally agreed precepts governing their relations *inter se*, as 'whatever all states have indicated to be their will, that is law in regard to all of them.'[98] This notion of the secondary *jus gentium* (similar to *jus inter gentes*) is associated particularly with the express or tacit consent of states in international society, supplementing the

Jessup and others, for instance, contrast international law with 'transnational law', a term used to refer to 'all law which regulates actions or events that transcend national frontiers'. See Jessup, 'The Present Stage of Transnational Law', in Maarten Bos (ed.), *The Present State of International Law and Other Essays Written in Honour of the Centenary Celebration of the International Law Association 1873–1973* (Deventer, 1973), pp. 339–44; and Jessup, *Transnational Law* (New Haven, Conn., 1956). The term 'international law' is used loosely in this Introduction—more specific terms are used where a specific meaning is intended.

[96] Zouche's *Iuris et Iudicii Fecialis sive Iuris Inter Gentes, et Quaestionum de Eodem Explicato* was published in 1650. Earlier incidental references to similar concepts can be found in the works of Vitoria and others.

[97] It was long thought that Grotius was unaware of the distinction when writing the initial version of *JP* in 1604–6, and that he added an exposition of it to the manuscript only after becoming aware of it through the publication of Suarez's *De Legibus* in 1612. See esp. Jan Kosters, 'Les Fondements du droit des gens. Contribution à la théorie générale du droit des gens', *Bibliotheca Visseriana*, 4 (1925), pp. 36–43. More recent study suggests, however, that Grotius may have developed the distinction independently before 1612 through reflection on the logic of the types and sources of law discussed in *JP*. See Haggenmacher, 'Genèse et signification du concept de "jus gentium" chez Grotius', *Grotiana*, 2 (1981), p. 44; and id., *Grotius et la doctrine de la guerre juste*, part I, chaps. 9 and 10.

[98] *JP*, chap. 2—the quotation is Grotius' Eighth Rule.

primary *jus gentium* which has its sources in nature, human
reason, and the divine will. Grotius built upon this structure
in *De Jure Belli ac Pacis*, and in so doing further opened an
avenue for the consent-based accounts of the law between
nations which came eventually to dominate the field.

Beyond and in contrast to this, however, is the widely held
tenet of the Grotian tradition that the binding force of international law may have a source other than the express or tacit
signification by states of their consent to be bound; and that
this law applies universally.[99] The place of natural law, in
particular, as a source of obligation has caused difficulty and
confusion among interpreters of *De Jure Belli ac Pacis*, com-
pounding the problem of determining exactly what natural
law consists of and what its role is in Grotius' thought.[100]
Readers of *De Jure Belli ac Pacis* in a more secular age have also
tended either mentally to excise his passages on divine law, or
simply to conflate divine and natural law.

Grotius saw the sources of the law of nations as natural
(manifest in nature but discerned by human reason), divine
volitional (the law of God), and human volitional.[101] This last
category comprises law made by civil powers and law made
by the will of nations. These human volitional laws supplement
(but do not, in general, override) the divine law and the law of
nature; they exist through human will, but their binding force
comes from the law of nature. They are often difficult to
distinguish in practice from natural law, as the widespread
practice of nations is also used as an important source of
evidence as to the content of the law of nature. Grotius also

---

[99] See e.g. Lauterpacht, 'The Grotian Tradition in International Law', pp. 19–24.
[100] Grotius' treatment of natural law has been considered extensively—see e.g.
Haggenmacher, *Grotius et la doctrine de la guerre juste*; M. C. W. Pinto, 'The New Law of
the Sea and the Grotian Heritage', in Asser Instituut, *International Law and the Grotian
Heritage* (The Hague, 1985), p. 54; and Haakonssen, 'Hugo Grotius and the History of
Political Thought', *Political Theory*, 13 (1985), pp. 239–65. On the sources of Grotius'
thought on natural law, see Robert Feenstra, 'Quelques remarques sur les sources
utilisées par Grotius dans ses travaux de droit naturel', in *The World of Hugo Grotius
(1583–1645)* (Amsterdam, 1984), p. 65; and, more generally, A. Dufour, 'Grotius et
le droit naturel du dix-septième siècle', in *The World of Hugo Grotius (1583–1645)*,
pp. 15–41.
[101] See generally *JBP*, Prolegomena. Although they naturally appear at the
beginning of *JBP*, the Prolegomena seem to embody Grotius' considered reflections
upon completing the work. See generally Haggenmacher, *Grotius et la doctrine de la
guerre juste*, pp. 449–50.

allowed for rules of international obligation based on express consent (most commonly in the form of a promise), but these rank below rules founded upon the other (higher) sources. In this respect the natural law conception commonly associated with Grotius appears antithetical to positivist consent-based accounts of international regulation.[102]

A rather different view of the function of natural law in Grotius' thought is suggested by Olivecrona, Tuck, and others who focus on Grotius' theory of natural or subjective rights.[103] Haakonssen presents his interpretation of the theory succinctly:

> Grotius's most important contribution to modern thought was his theory of rights . . . The central point is that Grotius, in extension of and undoubtedly inspired by various scholastic thinkers, particularly the Spanish neo-Thomists, transformed the concept of *ius* as it is found in Roman law and in Aquinas. Instead of being something that an action or state of affairs or a category of these *is* when it is in accordance with law (*in casu*, natural law), *ius* is seen by Grotius as something a person *has*. The concept becomes 'subjectivized,' centered on the person: It is a power the person has, as such it is also called a moral quality of the person.[104]

These writers argue that Grotius' theory that society and law exist to protect natural rights was sufficient to have enabled him to abandon reliance on natural law altogether. Thus Tuck asserts that in the conception of natural rights developed by Grotius: 'Rights have come to usurp the whole of natural law theory, for the law of nature is simply, respect one another's rights.'[105] Skinner appears to embrace a similar view in associating Grotius with a current of ideas which rejects the

---

[102] Though cf. the contention of Ernest Barker that if each of the three senses which he (Barker) attaches to Aristotle's use of the word 'natural' are taken into account, 'the antithesis between natural and conventional, which is only a *prima facie* antithesis, will disappear; and we shall have a vision of an historically developed law which has both a positive quality and a root in the nature of man.' Translator's Introduction to Otto Gierke, *Natural Law and the Theory of Society 1500 to 1800*, i (Cambridge, 1934), p. xxxv.

[103] See e.g. *JBP*, book I, chap. 1, § 4; and Hugo Grotius, *The Jurisprudence of Holland (Inleidinge tot de Hollandsche Rechts-Geleerdheid)*, vol. i, ed. and trans. R. W. Lee (Oxford, 1926). The theory of natural rights in the latter work is discussed by Richard Tuck, *Natural Rights Theories: Their Origin and Development* (Cambridge, 1979), pp. 66–71. See also Karl Olivecrona, 'Die zwei Schichten im naturrechtlichen Denken', *Archiv für Rechts- und Sozialphilosophie*, 63 (1977), pp. 79–103.

[104] Haakonssen, 'Hugo Grotius and the History of Political Thought', p. 240.

[105] Tuck, *Natural Rights Theories: Their Origin and Development*, p. 67.

proposition that the law of nations is part of the law of nature, and which holds instead that it is a special code of positive human law founded on the principles of natural justice.[106]

Even amongst those who emphasize the natural law aspects of Grotius' thought, Grotius is by no means accorded a pre-eminent place as a representative non-positivist.[107] The evolution from Grotius to Vattel has nevertheless been taken by some writers as a principal phase of the transition to the positivism which remains orthodox in theories about the basis of obligation or the nature of authority in international law. This is what Van Vollenhoven intends when he accuses Vattel of betraying the Grotian conception.[108] There are significant objections to taking either Grotius or Vattel as a paradigm case: the high tide of naturalism is best represented by Pufendorf; and the positivism of, for instance, Bynkershoek was so much sharper than that of Vattel that Vattel has indeed been represented as charting a *via media* between these two.[109] Neither Grotius nor Vattel is fairly characterized by one or other of these rather sweeping labels. For present purposes, it is the depth and subtlety of their accounts of the basis and functioning of international society, and of the place of law within it, which single them out as important exponents of broader

---

[106] Quentin Skinner, *The Foundations of Modern Political Thought*, ii, *The Age of Reformation* (Cambridge, 1978), pp. 152–4. Note also the argument of Massimo Panebianco, *Ugo Grozio e la Tradizione Storica del Diritto Internazionale* (Naples, 1974), that Grotius can be seen as a precursor or even as an initiator of the historical school of international law.

[107] As Kennedy points out, it is possible to read some modern positivists as holding that 'the move from Vitoria to Grotius expresses the foundations of positivism.' 'Primitive Legal Scholarship', *Harvard International Law Journal*, 27 (1986), p. 12.

[108] Cornelis van Vollenhoven, *The Three Stages in the Evolution of the Law of Nations* (The Hague, 1919). Van Vollenhoven's interpretations of several important aspects of Grotius' thought, and the rather misleading contrasts he seeks to draw between the writings of Grotius and those of Vattel, are attacked by Johanna Oudendijk in 'Van Vollenhoven's "The Three Stages in the Evolution of the Law of Nations" ', *Tijdschrift voor Rechtsgeschiedenis*, 48 (1980), pp. 3–27. See also Kooijmans' response to Oudendijk, 'How to Handle the Grotian Heritage: Grotius and Van Vollenhoven', *Netherlands International Law Review*, 30 (1983), p. 81.

[109] See e.g. M. A. Mallarmé, 'Emer de Vattel', in A. Pillet (ed.), *Les Fondateurs du droit international* (Paris, 1904), pp. 481–3, arguing that Vattel is properly placed within the Grotian tradition, and is much closer to Pufendorf than to Bynkershoek and Moser. Cf. generally E. Reibstein, 'Von Grotius zu Bynkershoek', *Archiv des Völkerrechts*, 4 (1953–4), p. 21.

currents of thought on this theme.[110] Vattel described an international society composed of sovereign states whose consent was essential to the formation of norms, and whose discretion as to whether to comply with or to enforce these norms was limited primarily by the self-judged application of principles of morality and proportionality. While there was agreement on certain principles of order, such as a balance of power system to preserve equilibrium and state independence, this agreement did not extend to the enforcement of law or of more elaborate principles of justice or cooperation.[111] In so far as the international society of the modern era has been so limited, the pluralist conception of Vattel is an important paradigm. But the vision among theorists and practitioners concerned with international society has increasingly been one of solidarist international co-operation: in this respect the Grotian conception may be seen as offering either a more accurate description or a more promising prescription for the modern period.

In a general way a concern with natural law has been a feature of the Grotian tradition of thought about international relations;[112] but on more specific issues there has been little convergence of views. Seen as a counterpoint to positivism, natural law largely lost its place as a recognized source of international law in the nineteenth century. This paralleled the demise of natural law among the dominant jurisprudential theories in most of the main Western legal systems. Thus Austin's rejection of Blackstone's views on divine law prevailing over particular human laws has often been taken as embodying a more general positivist position on natural law:

To prove by pertinent reasons that a law is pernicious is highly useful, because such process may lead to the abrogation of the pernicious law. To incite the public to resistance by determinate views of *utility* may be useful, for resistance, grounded on clear and

---

[110] A similar view is defended by Peter Pavel Remec, *The Position of the Individual in International Law according to Grotius and Vattel* (The Hague, 1960), pp. 44–58.

[111] Emer de Vattel, *Le Droit des gens, ou principes de la loi naturelle appliqués à la conduite et aux affaires des nations et des souverains* (Neuchâtel, 1758). See also the discussion of Vattel's conception of the society of states in Andrew Linklater, *Men and Citizens in the Theory of International Relations* (London, 1982), pp. 80–96.

[112] See generally Paul Foriers, 'L'Organisation de la paix chez Grotius et l'école de droit naturel', *Recueils de la Société Jean Bodin pour l'Histoire Comparative des Institutions*, 15 (1961), p. 275.

definite prospects of good, is sometimes beneficial. But to proclaim generally that all laws which are pernicious or contrary to the will of God are void and not to be tolerated, is to preach anarchy, hostile and perilous as much to wise and benign rule as to stupid and galling tyranny.[113]

A standard positivist response to claims that natural law prescribes norms of human behaviour is put by Hans Kelsen:

Nature as a system of facts, connected with one another according to the law of causality, has no will and hence cannot prescribe a definite behavior of man. From facts, that is to say, from that which is, or actually is done, no inference is possible to that which ought to be or ought to be done. So far as the natural-law doctrine tries to deduce from nature norms of human behavior, it is based on a logical fallacy.

The same holds true with respect to human reason. Norms prescribing human behavior can emanate only from human will, not from human reason . . .[114]

The period since 1918 has been marked by at least a limited revival of interest in natural law as a source of international law. One facet of this has been a renewed interest in procedural and interstitial natural law. Hardy Cross Dillard, for example argued in 1935:

a system based on 'natural law' despite many modern deprecations of it is bound to have a constantly recurring appeal. This is so primarily because judges every day everywhere are applying natural law in one form or another. It does not exist as a separate system; it is an inherent part of the judicial process itself. It takes shape in the interstitial applications of law. It does not transcend 'positive law,' as Pufendorf contended; it does not even compete with it. It fills it out.[115]

[113] John Austin, *The Province of Jurisprudence Determined* (London, 1955), p. 186. For a critical evaluation of this position see Deryck Beyleveld and Roger Brownsword, 'The Practical Difference between Natural-Law Theory and Legal Positivism', *Oxford Journal of Legal Studies*, 5 (1985), pp. 9–14. See also their *Law as a Moral Judgment* (London, 1986), chap. 2.

[114] Hans Kelsen, 'What is Justice?' in his *What is Justice? Justice, Law, and Politics in the Mirror of Science* (Berkeley, Calif., 1957), p. 20.

[115] Dillard, 'Review' (of Samuel Pufendorf, *De Jure Naturae et Gentium Libri Octo*), *Virginia Law Review*, 21 (1935), p. 722. This application is mainly at the procedural level, corresponding in some measure to Lon Fuller's 'inner morality of law', which emphasized the procedural requirements of generality, promulgation, prospective application, intelligibility, avoidance of impossible demands, consistency across time,

The standard reading of *De Jure Praedae* and *De Jure Belli ac Pacis* treats Grotius as emphasizing natural law as a source of substantive norms, not merely of procedural requirements; indeed, some passages in *De Jure Belli ac Pacis* suggest that Grotius sees human and divine volitional law as filling out the interstices of the natural law, although he does not adhere systematically to such a position.[116]

Stronger claims have also been made for natural law's contribution to substantive international law. Group of 77 or Non-Aligned Movement states making demands for revision of international law and practice to better correspond with what they describe as universal precepts of justice in some instances assert as international law doctrines whose source is, in effect, closely akin to natural law. Manfred Lachs treats the articulation of claims to designate areas as 'the common heritage of mankind', to the just apportionment of natural resources, and to equity in North–South economic arrangements, as the modern working out of the Grotian conception of international society.[117] In the area of human rights, a continuous tension has existed between the idea that human rights are inherent and inalienable ('natural')[118] and the awkward reality that these rights cannot be authoritatively

and congruence between official actions and the declared rules. An approach similar in substance to that advocated by Dillard, although expressed more sweepingly, is that of Lauterpacht in 'The Grotian Tradition in International Law', pp. 21–4. Note also Sir Gerald Fitzmaurice's contention that 'the principles of natural law . . . form part—and must form part—of the general principles of law as universally recognised.' 'The Future of Public International Law and of the International Legal System in the Circumstances of Today', in Institut de droit international, *Livre du centenaire 1873–1973: Evolution et perspectives du droit international* (Basle, 1973), p. 311.

[116] David Kennedy has no doubt that the role of human volitional law was merely interstitial ('Primitive Legal Scholarship', p. 82); but such passages as *JBP*, book I, chap. 2, § 1, for example, can be interpeted as supporting either position.

[117] Lachs, 'The Grotian Heritage, the International Community and Changing Dimensions of International Law', in Asser Instituut, *International Law and the Grotian Heritage*, pp. 198–206.

[118] The 1948 Universal Declaration of Human Rights, for instance, begins with the natural law recitation 'of the inherent dignity and of the equal and inalienable rights of all members of the human family', but much of international human rights law consists of positive treaty obligations voluntarily undertaken by states, and of procedures for complaints by individuals which depend on express state consent. On theories of natural rights see generally Tuck, *Natural Rights Theories: Their Origin and Development*; and H. L. A. Hart, 'Are There Any Natural Rights?', *Philosophical Review*, 64 (1955), pp. 175–91, repr. in Jeremy Waldron (ed.), *Theories of Rights* (Oxford, 1984), pp. 77–90.

secured in international law except through the consent of states.[119] An element of this tension has been the problem of how much weight to accord to state violations of particular human rights standards in assessing whether these standards command sufficient support to be regarded as customary international law. Grotius was aware of a comparable difficulty: in holding that it was legitimate for persons captured in an unlawful war to escape, taking with them their property and any appropriate compensation, he took the view that

> it does not matter that such flight and abstraction when detected are usually punished with severity. For these things and many others are done by the more powerful, not because they are just, but because it is to the advantage of the more powerful to do them.[120]

But when dealing with the broader issue of the lawfulness of various barbarous acts in war, Grotius found it impossible to overlook the widespread support for several categories of barbarous acts in the practice of states, taking this as evidence that neither the law of nature nor volitional law prohibited such acts.

Grotius' pot-pourri of sources, predominantly classical or biblical but ranging from Polish succession law to Inca social mores, has naturally attracted comment.[121] In some cases this comment also touches on the nature of authority for international legal norms. As early as 1660 Grotius was criticized

---

[119] See also S. Prakash Sinha, 'Freeing Human Rights from Natural Rights', *Archiv für Recht- und Sozialphilosophie*, 70 (1984), p. 342.

[120] *JBP*, book III, chap. 7, § 6. Grotius used a similar method in arguing that the right of retaliation did not extend to killing or mistreating a foreign ambassador; while there were many examples of such vengeance in history, the histories also relate just deeds; and the law of nations safeguards the safety of ambassadors as well as the dignity of those who send them. Ibid., book II, chap. 18, § 7.

[121] Cf. e.g. the opinions of Gibbon and Voltaire. 'Toute l'antiquité se montroit sans voile aux yeux de Grotius: éclairé par sa lumière, il développoit les oracles sacrés, il combattoit l'ignorance et la superstition, il adoucissoit les horreurs de la guerre'. (Edward Gibbon, 'Essai sur l'étude de la littérature' (1761), *Miscellaneous Works*, ed. Lord Sheffield, ii (London, 1796), pp. 452–3.) Voltaire's comment was: 'les compilations de *Grotius* ne méritaient pas le tribut d'estime que l'ignorance leur a payé. Citer la pensée des vieux auteurs qui ont dit le pour et le contre, ce n'est pas penser.' He added that 'la raison et la vertu touchent peu quand elles ennuient'. (Dialogues et entretiens philosophiques, XXIV, 'L'A, B, C', prem. dialogue ('Sur Hobbes, Grotius et Montesquieu'), in *Œuvres complètes*, xxxvi (Paris, 1785), pp. 216 and 213.)

for failing to delineate a hierarchy among his sources.[122] Such criticism became more acute as international lawyers narrowed the range of authoritative sources of international law, and established clear orderings amongst them. This positivist legacy continues to make it difficult for lawyers to feel comfortable with the approach to legal authority manifest in Grotius' texts.[123] Nevertheless, the twentieth-century revival of interest in natural law, and in the classical sixteenth- and seventeenth-century writers whose texts touched upon areas of international law, is in part symptomatic of problems of authority and of method in modern international law. In attempting to address this issue, David Kennedy seeks to draw broad generalizations about differences between three categories of legal scholars: 'primitives' (those writing before 1648), 'traditionalists' (1648–1900), and modernists (1900–80). While this approach is open to considerable criticism, Kennedy identifies a salient theme in contending that

modern scholarship . . . accepts the validity of uniform principles only when methodologically defensible but at the same time is skeptical of all methodological defenses. As a result, modernists think only schemes of internal methodological coherence (such as those of traditional scholarship) can be uniformly principled, but yet have lost faith in each of the traditional schemes.[124]

In his view, 'the primitive text begins with a sense of legal and moral authority from which it derives a social scheme of political and sovereign authority', while the 'traditional text proceeds in precisely the opposite direction'.[125] The problem for modernists is that having 'invalidated the doctrinal distinctions upon which traditional scholars relied to construct their formal legal order', they have 'been unable to

---

[122] Roger Coke, *Justice vindicated from the false focus put upon it, by Thomas White Gent. Mr Thomas Hobbes and Hugo Grotius* (London, 1660).

[123] See Lauterpacht's reproach that Grotius 'will tell us, often with regard to the same question, what is the law of nature, the law of nations, divine law, Mosaic law, the law of the Gospel, Roman law, the law of charity, the obligations of honour, or considerations of utility. But we often look in vain for a statement as to what is *the* law governing the matter.' This Lauterpacht views as 'a defect of method which, apparently, has no redeeming feature.' 'The Grotian Tradition in International Law', pp. 5 and 4. Grotius himself charges several of his predecessors with intermingling and confusing distinct types of law. *JBP*, Prolegomena 37.

[124] Kennedy, 'Primitive Legal Scholarship', p. 7.

[125] Ibid., p. 10.

return to the primitive world of clear distinctions in a single fabric of morality and law'.[126]

A return to the methodology or systems of authority used by the classical writers is not generally seen as a part of the agenda for modern international lawyers, although such an appeal is occasionally evident in the writings of alarmed or despondent idealists. The classical texts have their own frames of reference which are not those of the modern world.[127] They are nevertheless of interest for several reasons, in addition to their intrinsic scholarly and historical significance. They provide insights into recurring issues which, although presenting themselves in different forms to different generations, have the same essence. They provide antidotes to subsequent rigidities and distinctions which we now wish to discard. And they provide 'intersubjective' reference points by which subsequent traditions of thought maintain a certain identity and coherence.

(e) GROTIUS AND THE ENFORCEMENT OF INTERNATIONAL LAW AGAINST THIRD STATES

One important facet of a commitment to an international society is the willingness of its members to uphold its values and institutions against serious challenges. The question of the enforcement of the law of international society beyond mere self-help on the part of victims of violations has remained central. Grotius' acceptance that international law might properly be enforced through punishment inflicted by states which were not themselves direct victims of the delict was seized upon by writers of the 1920s, anxious to legitimate and invigorate the provisions for collective sanctions in the 1919 League of Nations Covenant and the unratified 1924 Geneva Protocol for the Pacific Settlement of International Disputes. Van Vollenhoven, in particular, saw this 'theorem of Grotius' as a central tenet of *De Jure Belli ac Pacis*.[128]

---

[126] Kennedy, 'Primitive Legal Scholarship', p. 9.

[127] As noted by Baron Kaltenborn von Stachau, *Die Vorläufer des Hugo Grotius auf dem Gebiete des Ius naturae et gentium sowie der Politik im Reformationszeitalter* (Leipzig, 1848).

[128] Van Vollenhoven, 'Grotius and Geneva', *Bibliotheca Visseriana*, 6 (1926); id., 'Grotius and the Study of Law', *AJIL* 19 (1925); id., 'Het Theorema van Grotius', *Tijdschrift voor Strafrecht*, 36 (1926).

Grotius' general proposition on the subject was formulated unequivocally:

The fact must also be recognized that kings, and those who possess rights equal to those kings, have the right of demanding punishments not only on account of injuries committed against themselves or their subjects, but also on account of injuries which do not directly affect them but excessively violate the law of nature or of nations in regard to any persons whatsoever. For liberty to serve the interests of human society through punishments, which originally, as we have said, rested with individuals, now after the organization of states and courts of law is in the hands of the highest authorities, not, properly speaking, in so far as they rule over others but in so far as they are themselves subject to no one. For subjection has taken this right away from others.[129]

The principle that enforcement must be the responsibility of those with no superior is not itself a sufficient principle of order where those with no superior are numerous. Grotius seems to have seen it more as a moderating principle: 'Truly it is more honourable to avenge the wrongs of others rather than one's own, in the degree that in the case of one's own wrongs it is more to be feared that through a sense of personal suffering one may exceed the proper limit or at least prejudice his mind.'[130] In this respect the principle is complemented by the chapter of warnings not to undertake war rashly; not least of which is the maxim that 'he who wishes to avenge crimes by armed force ought to be much more powerful than the other party', and ought to be sure that the necessary resources are available.[131]

Nor is this Grotian principle likely to operate as a principle of distributive or commutative justice. Grotius was well aware that those entities with power to punish an offender were in most cases unlikely to do so simply to vindicate an abstract

---

[129] *JBP*, book II, chap. 20, § 40. This passage is discussed in van Vollenhoven, 'Un passage obscur dans le livre de Grotius', *Grotiana*, 5 (1932), pp. 23–5; and Haggenmacher, 'Sur un passage obscur de Grotius: Essai de réponse à Cornelis van Vollenhoven', *Tijdschrift voor Rechtsgeschiedenis* (*The Legal History Review*), 51 (1983), pp. 295–315. See also *JBP*, book II, chap. 25, esp. § 6: 'The final and most wide-reaching cause for undertaking wars on behalf of others is the mutual tie of kinship among men, which of itself affords sufficient grounds for rendering assistance.' This issue is addressed further by John Vincent in his chapter below.

[130] *JBP*, book II, chap. 20, § 40.

[131] Ibid., book II, chap. 24; esp. at §§ 7, 9.

principle of justice. Such gains as they accrued in a war of punishment would by the laws of war be theirs, not those of the victim. In *De Jure Praedae* Grotius had no hesitation in asserting that the Dutch were vindicating the rights of the native East Indies rulers to trade with whomsoever they wished, and exacting retribution for Portuguese outrages against these rulers and their peoples; but Grotius does not suggest that any of these victims should have a share in the booty .of the *Catharina*.[132]

The Grotian principle is qualified by the requirement that injuries punishable by third states are those that 'excessively' (*immaniter*, which could also be rendered as 'monstrously') violate the law of nature or of nations. As examples of such violations he gave impiety toward one's parents, cannibalism, and piracy.[133]

The question of means of enforcement apart, this qualified principle, orientated as it is towards what may broadly be termed humanitarian interventions, finds a modern resonance in the notions of *erga omnes* obligations[134] and of *jus cogens*.[135] Contemporary controversy about these concepts was in some respects foreshadowed by the differences on this issue between Grotius' position, which drew on the ideas of Sinibaldo Fieschi (Pope Innocent IV), Acosta, and especially Gentili,[136] and the position of several of his predecessors, including Vitoria, Vasquez de Menchaca, Azor, Molina, and Suarez. The principal objection was that coercive power to punish did not extend beyond the bounds of civil jurisdiction except to punish an injury sustained by the state or its nationals. Suarez states flatly that

[132] See *JP*, chap. 10, addressing the question 'By Whom May Prize or Booty Be Acquired?'
[133] His later annotations refer also to human sacrifice, castration of male children, and male homosexuality. *JBP*, book II, chap. 20, § 40, footnotes in 1646 edition.
[134] *Barcelona Traction* case, *ICJ Reports*, 1970, para. 33.
[135] The 1969 Vienna Convention on the Law of Treaties, Art. 53. Grotius espoused a similar principle in holding to be impermissible treaties of alliance which provide for a sovereign entity to go to war in support of an ally whose cause was unjust. *JBP*, book II, chap. 25, § 9.
[136] Gentili, *JB*, book I, chap. 16, 'On Defending the Subjects of Another Against their Sovereign', seems to have been a very useful source to Grotius in writing *JBP*, book II, chap. 25. On Grotius' use of Gentili's work generally, see Peter Haggenmacher's chapter below.

Introduction   41

the assertion made by some writers, that sovereign kings have the
power of avenging injuries done in any part of the world, is entirely
false, and throws into confusion all the orderly distinctions of jurisdiction; for such power was not [expressly] granted by God, and its
existence is not to be inferred by any process of reasoning.[137]

There is thus much to support Barnes' conclusion that the
spirit (though not the letter) of medieval just war theory was
against such interventions.[138] Grotius acknowledged the jurisdictional point, noting the objective of preventing people from
provoking wars by usurping the care of things under the
control of others.

If, however, the wrong is obvious, in case some Busiris, Phalaris, or
Thracian Diomede should inflict upon his subjects such treatment
as no one is warranted in inflicting, the exercise of the right vested
in human society is not precluded.

He was aware also of the risk of abuse:

We know, it is true, from both ancient and modern history, that the
desire for what is another's seeks such pretexts as this for its own
ends; but a right does not at once cease to exist in case it is to some
extent abused by evil men. Pirates, also, sail the sea; arms are
carried also by brigands.[139]

In these respects the issues addressed by Grotius remain
central in modern debates about the lawfulness and the desirability of humanitarian intervention.[140]

As to the means of enforcement, Grotius accepted that the
obligations of allies extended as broadly as the terms of the

---

[137] Suarez, *De Bello*, § 4. 3.
[138] Jonathan Barnes, 'The Just War', in N. Kretzman, A. Kenny, and J. Pinborg
(eds.), *The Cambridge History of Later Medieval Philosophy* (Cambridge, 1982),
pp. 778–9.   [139] *JBP*, book II, chap. 25, § 8.
[140] See e.g. Richard Lillich (ed.), *Humanitarian Intervention and the United Nations*
(Charlottesville, Va., 1973); John Norton Moore (ed.), *Law and Civil War in the Modern
World* (London, 1974); Bull (ed.), *Intervention in World Politics* (Oxford, 1984); Natalino
Ronzitti, *Rescuing Nationals Abroad through Military Coercion and Intervention on Grounds of
Humanity* (Dordrecht, 1985); Antonio Cassese (ed.), *The Current Legal Regulation of the
Use of Force* (Dordrecht, 1986); Fernando R. Tesón, *Humanitarian Intervention: An Inquiry
into Law and Morality* (New York, 1987); Cástor M. Díaz Barrado, 'La pretension de
justificar el uso de la fuerza con base en "consideraciones humanitarias". Analisis de
la practica internacional contemporanea', *Revista Española de Derecho Internacional*, 40
(1988), pp. 41–77; and Nigel Rodley, 'Human Rights and Humanitarian Intervention: The Case Law of the World Court', *ICLQ* 38 (1989), pp. 321–33.

alliance were drawn, save only if the cause of the ally was unjust. Beyond this, Grotius had little to say about measures short of war. For him the *juris executio* was war. It is perhaps an indication of progress that the twentieth century has been concerned with such problems as the judicial *actio popularis*[141] and the legality of non-forcible measures against third states,[142] devices which were not then in issue.

(f) GROTIUS AND THE NON-EUROPEAN WORLD

Many twentieth-century idealists have seen Grotius as laying an early foundation for an old order, characterized by state sovereignty and European expansion into the extra-European world, which they regard as discredited and now seek to transcend or supplant. The late Professor Röling saw in European practice a magnification of a form of hypocrisy he perceived in Grotius' own life:

the enormous popularity of Grotius' just war doctrine is rendered comprehensible when we recognize that in theory it could gratify the high-minded and could point to the way which could reasonably lead to a better world, while it did not in any way restrict the endeavour of subjugating the non-European nations to European authority. Grotius' system could afford a pretext for every desired act of violence. Thus the phase was inaugurated in which the aggressive conduct of States could be dressed up in terms of the preservation of law and order and of the costly duty of upholding justice.[143]

[141] The question of the standing of Ethiopia and Liberia to bring a contentious case alleging that South Africa had violated the terms of its Mandate to govern South-West Africa (Namibia) raised this issue, as Ethiopia and Liberia were effectively seeking to act on behalf of the international community of states in general (*actio popularis*) rather than to litigate an issue in which they had particular legal interests greater than those of other states or of the UN. The ICJ was divided on the matter— cf. the *South West Africa* cases (Ethiopia and Liberia v. South Africa), *ICJ Reports*, 1962, and 1966. Note also the total dearth of complaints to the Human Rights Committee under the *actio popularis* procedure for complaints by one State concerning another State's compliance with its human rights obligations set out in Art. 41 of the 1966 International Covenant on Civil and Political Rights.

[142] On counter-measures generally, see e.g. Omer Elagab, *The Legality of Non-Forcible Counter-Measures in International Law* (Oxford, 1988).

[143] B. V. A. Röling, 'Jus ad Bellum and the Grotian Heritage', in Asser Instituut, *International Law and the Grotian Heritage*, p. 122. See also his chapter below.

In assessing this charge that Grotius provided a justificatory text for the forcible subjection of non-European peoples to European colonialism, it must be acknowledged that the theme of relations between Europeans and non-Europeans, or between Christians and non-Christians, was not for Grotius the central concern that it had been for several of his illustrious predecessors, most notably Vitoria. Grotius wrote nothing equivalent to Vitoria's lectures on *De Indis*.[144] *De Jure Praedae* was written in response to events in the extra-European world, but the law concerning the peoples of the East Indies is treated only as an incidental to the main questions between the Dutch and the Iberians. Nevertheless, in *De Jure Praedae* and, more importantly, *De Jure Belli ac Pacis*, Grotius did address several standard questions in legal and theological debate which had a bearing on the legal position of non-European peoples; and he addressed these questions in relatively systematic fashion, albeit within the confines of the structures of these works. Three such questions will be examined briefly here.

On the fundamental question of the rights of Christians to compel unbelievers to the faith, Aquinas had distinguished heathens and Jews, who never having received the faith should not be compelled to faith, from heretics and apostates who should be bodily compelled to fulfil what they had promised and to hold to the faith which at one time they had received. Acceptance of the faith was a matter of voluntary will; keeping it a matter of obligation.[145] The Church had no spiritual jurisdiction over those who had never accepted the faith, but in the exercise of its temporal jurisdiction might tolerate or suppress their rites as circumstances warranted, it

[144] Vitoria, *De Indis Recenter Inventis* (*On the Indians Lately Discovered*), and *De Indis, sive De Jure Belli Hispanorum in Barbaros* (*On the Indians, or on the Law of War made by the Spaniards on the Barbarians*), both first published posthumously in 1557.
[145] Aquinas, *Summa Theologica*, II. ii, Q. 10, Art. 8. Christ's faithful could nevertheless wage war on those who had never accepted the faith to prevent them from hindering the faith. This body of Thomist doctrine might be compared to certain modern secular doctrines concerning heresy and apostasy, including the doctrines enunciated by the Soviet Union at certain times in the post-war period to justify the 'defence of socialism' in eastern European states, most notably in Czechoslovakia in 1968. On the 'Brezhnev doctrine', see Sergei Kovalyov, 'Sovereignty and International Duties', *Pravda*, Moscow, 26 Sept. 1968. An English translation of this article appeared in *Survival* (London), 10 (1968), pp. 375–7.

being necessary to tolerate some evils lest certain goods be lost or greater evils incurred.[146]

Vitoria drew on Thomist principles in arguing that the indigenous inhabitants of the Americas were invincibly ignorant of Christianity.[147] Furthermore:

> The Indians in question are not bound, directly the Christian faith is announced to them, to believe it . . . without miracle or any other proof or persuasion . . . [I]t would be rash and imprudent for any one to believe anything, especially in matters which concern salvation, unless he knows that this is asserted by a man worthy of credence, a thing which the aboriginal Indians do not know, seeing that they do not know who or what manner of men they are who are announcing the new religion to them.[148]

Where no wrong had previously been committed by the Indians, there was no just cause of war. And 'war is no argument for the truth of the Christian faith.'[149] Vitoria explicitly denied that either the Roman Emperor or the Pope had any jurisdiction, spiritual or temporal, over the unbelieving Indians: no Spanish title could derive from these sources.[150] Vitoria's argument on this topic is closely paralleled by several of his successors among the Iberian 'seconda scholastica', including Suarez.[151]

Grotius largely follows this line of argument in *De Jure Belli ac Pacis*.[152] Grotius also accepts the view that war is justly waged against those who actively persecute Christians by reason of their faith.[153] He appears to go further, condoning the punishment of those of whatever persuasion who deny that

---

[146] 'For this reason the Church, at times, has tolerated the rites even of heretics and pagans, when unbelievers were very numerous.' Ibid., II. ii, Q. 10, Art. 11.

[147] In the Thomist tradition, Vitoria treated infidels and apostates separately from the invincibly ignorant Indians.

[148] Vitoria, *De Indis Recenter Inventis*, II, § 10. This was a direct rejection of the *conquistadores'* practice of reading out a *requerimiento* to groups of Indians demanding that they accept the Christian faith—non-acceptance being treated as providing an instant *casus belli*. See generally Pagden, *The Fall of Natural Man* (Cambridge, 1982).

[149] Vitoria, *De Indis Recenter Inventis*, II, §§ 11, 15.

[150] Ibid., II, §§ 1–7.

[151] See Suarez, *De Triplice Virtute*, 'On Charity', Disputatio XIII (De Bello), § 5; and 'On Faith', Disputatio XVIII ('On the Means which May be Used for the Conversion and Coercion of Unbelievers who are not Apostates'), §§ 2–5. The term 'seconda scholastica' is a less accurate description than 'neoscholastics', but the latter term is associated with a later body of Catholic thought.

[152] Esp. in *JBP*, book II, chap. 20, § 48.   [153] Ibid., book II, chap. 20, § 49.

there is a divinity or that he has a care for the affairs of men, arguing that these two fundamental ideas have been preserved throughout the ages and among almost all peoples of whom we have knowledge.[154] Where Vitoria discusses violation of the right to travel as a just cause of war, Grotius (like Gentili) pays more attention to the freedom of navigation and of trade.[155]

On the property rights of native inhabitants, Grotius (like Vitoria) was explicit. Infidels and heathens were able to own property according to their own systems of law,[156] and discovery was no basis to claim what is already held by another, even though the occupants may be wicked, hold wrong views about God, or be dull of wit.[157] The rejection of discovery as a basis for depriving aboriginal inhabitants of their property, with the related holding that their lands are not *terra nullius*, has exerted a continuing influence on municipal and international law and practice.[158] National courts obliged to consider the basis of national title in territories occupied by indigenous peoples have been driven to the recognition of accomplished fact, as exemplified by the statement of Chief Justice Marshall in a judgment of the US Supreme Court in 1823:

However extravagant the pretension of converting the discovery of an inhabited country into conquest may appear, if the principle has been asserted in the first instance, and afterwards sustained; if a

---

[154] Ibid., book II, chap. 20, § 46: 'I think, therefore, that those who first begin to abolish these ideas may be restrained in the name of human society, to which they do violence without a defensible reason.'

[155] Röling, 'Jus ad Bellum and the Grotian Heritage', discusses the question of whether *JBP* introduces exceptions to the principle of freedom of trade enunciated so strongly in *Mare Liberum* and *JP*. See also his chapter below.

[156] *JBP*, book II, chaps. 2–4 and 6–10.

[157] See ibid., book II, chap. 22, § 9, on discovery; citing the view of Vitoria in *De Indis Recenter Inventis*. Grotius also contended that the Portuguese could not have 'discovered' any areas of ocean in the East Indies, for 'surely the Moors, the Ethiopians, the Arabs, the Persians, and the East Indians could not have been unacquainted with the seas near which they themselves dwelt'. *JP*, chap. 12 (Classics of International Law, p. 242).

[158] See e.g. *Worcester* v. *Georgia* 6 Peters 515 (1832), US Supreme Court; and the Advisory Opinion of the ICJ in the *Western Sahara* case, *ICJ Reports*, 1975. See also the Resolutions concerning the Aboriginal and Torres Strait Islander peoples adopted by the Australian Parliament on 23 Aug. 1988, in *Australian Law Journal*, 62 (1988), p. 978.

country has been acquired and held under it; if the property of the great mass of the community originates in it, it becomes the law of the land, and cannot be questioned.[159]

The issue of the property rights of non-Christians and non-Europeans was connected also to the question of the validity of the Aristotelian doctrine of natural slavery. Aristotle had argued: 'Some are by nature slaves, those, to wit, who are better fitted to serve than to rule.'[160] In 1510 the Scottish theologian John Major suggested that this argument applied to the Indians of the Americas, who were assumed to be incapable of reason. Sepulveda built upon this in asserting that the Indians lacked civil society and thus did not have *dominium rerum*. Vitoria rejected this denial of the Indians' *dominium*; the Indians 'make no error in matters which are self-evident to others; this is witness to their use of reason', and

there is a certain method in their affairs, for they have polities which are orderly arranged and they have definite marriage and magistrates, overlords, laws, and workshops, and a system of exchange, all of which call for the use of reason.[161]

They were not to be classed with the slaves of the civil law, even if they were incapable of self-government.[162] The natural God-given right of the Indians to *dominium* was further elaborated by Vitoria's pupils, notably Domingo de Soto and Melchor Cano, over the next half century.

In *De Jure Praedae* Grotius expressly endorsed Aristotle's notion of natural slavery;[163] yet in *De Jure Belli ac Pacis* he denies that anyone is a slave by nature.[164] Grotius does uphold the institution of slavery, and specifically asserts that those individuals or states who from a lawful cause have come into slavery have no general right to liberty and ought to be satisfied with their lot.[165] However, Grotius' acceptance of slavery does not appear to stem from his consideration of issues concerning relations between Europeans and non-Europeans or Christians and non-Christians.

[159] *Johnson* v. *M'Intosh* 21 US (8 Wheat.), p. 591 (1823).
[160] Aristotle, *Politics*, book I; see also book III.
[161] Vitoria, *De Indis Recenter Inventis*, I, § 23.　　[162] Ibid., I, § 24.
[163] *JP*, chap. 6 (Classics of International Law, pp. 61–2).
[164] *JBP*, book II, chap. 22, §§ 11–12; and book III, chap. 7, § 1.
[165] Ibid., book II, chap. 22, § 11; and see generally book II, chap. 5, §§ 27–32.

Röling's spirited criticism of Grotius' works is prompted by developments after these works were written, but it may be that he has treated Grotius and his writings somewhat harshly. Grotius may not have an obvious appeal to those, like Röling, who seek a champion of the oppressed. But it is likewise misleading to read his works as simply an apologetic in support of the powerful. Doubtless opinions will continue to differ as to whether Grotius conceded too much to the realities of power in international relations in seeking to articulate the principles of law which governed them.[166] Nevertheless, a more than cursory theme of *De Jure Belli ac Pacis* is exemplified by Grotius' condemnation of the frequent practice among powerful peoples of equating their own customs with the law of nature, and his accompanying endorsement of Plutarch's remark: 'To wish to impose civilization upon uncivilized peoples is a pretext which may serve to conceal greed for what is another's.'[167]

(g) GROTIUS AND THE UNIVERSALITY OF INTERNATIONAL SOCIETY AND OF INTERNATIONAL LAW

The Grotian tradition is widely associated with a commitment to the universalism of international law—a commitment which is becoming, after a long period of unquestioning acceptance, the subject of more subtle analysis and more rigorous scrutiny. Grotius certainly regarded both the law of nature and the wider *jus gentium* as extending beyond Europe and beyond Christendom. Once the *jus gentium* was established, he did not exempt particular peoples from being bound by it *vis-à-vis* all other peoples. On the other hand, Grotius recognized that additional customary practices or norms of

---

[166] One standard view is exemplified by Roelofsen's observation that the distinctive feature of Grotius' work was 'the combination, on the one hand, of a very considerable expertise in international relations and, on the other hand, a dogmatic conviction of the supremacy of the law in this, as in any sphere of human activity. He found these hard to reconcile.' 'Some Remarks on the "Sources" of the Grotian System of International Law', *Netherlands International Law Review*, 30 (1983), p. 77. Several critics of Grotius, including Röling and Schwarzenberger, reject assessments of this sort as failing to reach the crucial issue, and as unduly flattering.

[167] *JBP*, book II, chap. 20, § 41—quoting Plutarch, *Lives: Pompey*, lxx.

right conduct might grow up among particular groups of peoples. These did not form part of the universal law of nations, but were part of the law binding on these peoples *inter se*. Thus the *jus gentium* provided that all persons captured in public wars became slaves,[168] but in wars amongst Christian peoples Christians as a whole had agreed that captives would not be enslaved. Grotius noted that Muslims followed a similar practice *inter se*, and that under the laws of the Jews and the Franks certain slaves reaching these territories could claim asylum or manumission; but nevertheless he did not find any basis in the law of nature or in volitional law to regard non-enslavement as a rule of the *jus gentium*.[169]

Grotius may thus be understood as embracing a minimum content of universally applicable rules of the *jus gentium* (consisting mainly of the law of nature),[170] with a pluralist overlay of additional norms based on custom or consent or the values of the peoples concerned.

From this it was, for later writers, a short step to the proposition that different groups of peoples may each have their own law of nations,[171] which to a greater or lesser degree included or could be required to include various universal precepts. This was a common view in legal doctrine and in the diplomatic practice of the eighteenth and nineteenth centuries.[172]

During the nineteenth century, however, writers on international law began more often to assume either that international law did not exist outside the territories of the European and American states, or at least that international law was

---

[168] A rule intended to encourage warring parties not to exercise their right under the law of nature to kill all prisoners.

[169] *JBP*, book III, chap. 7.

[170] Ibid., book I, chap. 1, § 14.

[171] 'Not infrequently, in fact, in one part of the world there is a law of nations which is not such elsewhere.' Ibid., book I, chap. 1, § 14.

[172] See e.g. Montesquieu, *The Spirit of Laws* (1st pub. 1748), book I, chap. 3; Ward, *An Enquiry into the Foundation and History of the Law of Nations in Europe, from the Time of the Greeks and Romans to the Age of Grotius* (London, 1795), pp. xiii–xv; Martens, *Précis du droit des gens moderne de l'Europe: fondé sur les traités et l'usage*, 3rd edn. (Göttingen, 1821); Wheaton, *Elements of International Law: With a Sketch of the History of the Science* (London and Philadelphia, Penn., 1836), pp. 44–5; and, on the idea of a public law of Europe, the works discussed by Grewe, *Epochen der Völkerrechtsgeschichte* (Baden Baden, 1984), pp. 47–8.

Introduction 49

generated only by these states.[173] That the development of an increasingly global international society appeared also as the expansion of the European international society was, no doubt, primarily attributable to the power and imperium of European states and of the United States, but the positivism of European international legal theory in the second half of the nineteenth century also played a part. The twin ideas that international obligation depended upon the consent of states to be bound, and that only states meeting certain standards could meaningfully give such consent to the existing rules, fused into the somewhat misleading image of a Eurocentric international society into which non-European states were progressively admitted. The model was of a single (European) international law gradually becoming universal.[174] On one view, the international society of the UN period represents the apogee of this model: in so far as new or revised rules are needed, they can be secured through near-universal custom or multilateral treaties, or more generally through a distillation of the 'common law of mankind'.[175]

This solidarist ideal type represents a view of international law which continues to be widely held. In their chapters below, John Vincent and Hedley Bull justifiably treat the preference for solidarism over pluralism as a feature of the Grotian tradition.[176] But the dominant conception of solidarist universalism fails to capture the whole reality of contemporary international law. Sir Robert Jennings has suggested that

at the present juncture in the development of the international legal system it may be more important to stress the imperative need to develop international law to comprehend within itself the rich diversity of cultures, civilizations and legal traditions, than to concentrate on what might be called the 'common law of mankind approach' which sees importance in those general notions which, so

---

[173] Heffter, for example, doubted that international law existed outside the ambit of the European states: see his *Le Droit international de l'Europe*, trans. Jules Bergson (Berlin, 1857), pp. 1–2.

[174] Cf. Wilhelm Grewe, 'Vom europäischen zum universellen Völkerrecht', *Zeitschrift für ausländisches öffentliches Recht und Völkerrecht*, 42 (1982), pp. 450–79, defending the general accuracy of such a model.

[175] C. Wilfred Jenks, *The Common Law of Mankind* (London, 1958).

[176] See also Bull, 'The Grotian Conception of International Society', in Butterfield and Wight (eds.), *Diplomatic Investigations*.

long as they are stated in sufficiently general terms, are undoubtedly but hardly surprisingly to be found in all systems.[177]

Jennings agrees with Lauterpacht that the Grotian tradition embraces the subjection of the totality of international relations to the rule of law in one common system, but within this system 'universality does not mean uniformity but rather richness of variety and diversity.'[178]

Bozeman argues that in a broad sense *De Jure Belli ac Pacis* 'was designed as an appeal to Western Christendom and . . . does not purport to analyse other cultural orders. However, it is replete with statements and innuendoes which acknowledge the existence of culturally differing frames of reference . . .' From these she draws the Grotian proposition that

The law of nations should not be viewed as either immutably fixed or as universally valid for every people at all times. Rather, its applicability is dependent upon human behavior; and the major tests here seem to be on the one hand self-restraint and the ability to understand and honor obligations, and on the other, willingness to accept political and commercial relations with foreign nations.[179]

The quest for universality has not rested easily with the belief that all cultures and legal systems are entitled to equal respect, and that their moral or juridical values are incommensurable.[180] To the extent that the goal of universality is qualified or reformulated in light of these beliefs, the opposition between solidarism and pluralism which was thought to define a feature of the Grotian tradition may be breaking down.[181]

[177] Sir R. Y. Jennings, 'Universal International Law in a Multicultural World', in Asser Instituut, *International Law and the Grotian Heritage*, p. 195. Adda Bozeman goes much further, arguing that 'the basic principles of the law of nations have no organic place either in Asian or African or in communist societies', and that 'a common understanding of the value and functions of war can no longer be assumed in the world society, and this implies, of course, that there is no common understanding of the law of war.' 'On the Relevance of Hugo Grotius and De Jure Belli ac Pacis for Our Times', *Grotiana*, 1 (1980), pp. 94 and 92.

[178] 'Universal International Law in a Multicultural World', p. 197.

[179] Bozeman, 'On the Relevance of Hugo Grotius and De Jure Belli ac Pacis for Our Times', pp. 100 and 101.

[180] On incommensurability of value see Joseph Raz, *The Morality of Freedom* (Oxford, 1986), and John Finnis, *Fundamentals of Ethics* (Oxford, 1984).

[181] See e.g. The Hague Academy of International Law, *The Future of International Law in a Multicultural World* (The Hague, 1984); and *Is Universality in Jeopardy?* (UN, New York, 1987).

(h) A GROTIAN TRADITION IN INTERNATIONAL RELATIONS?

The claim that there is a 'Grotian tradition' of thought about international relations has often been made rather loosely, with little discussion of what is meant by a 'tradition' or why a particular tradition is held to be 'Grotian'.

Most commonly, the claim that there is a 'Grotian tradition' is intended to embody only a relatively weak sense of 'tradition'; such claims are often based, at core, on the proposition that there can be discerned a pattern of issues, and of approaches to them, with which the tradition has been centrally and distinctively concerned. Claims that there exists a 'Grotian tradition' in this weak sense are readily defended. One such claim asserts that the Grotian tradition is characterized by a commitment to the idea of an international society comprising sovereign entities and other actors who recognize the benefit they derive from maintaining and strengthening the operation of that society. Law is seen as an important regulator of conduct within that society, with particular emphasis on the idea of natural or subjective rights expressed as legal entitlements or claims. The tradition is also seen to have been preoccupied with war: limiting its excesses, placing constraints on its legitimacy, but not denying altogether its role in international society.

A second possible view of the 'Grotian tradition' is preponderantly textual, holding that the tradition is comprised only of Grotius' writings, the commentaries on them, and explorations clearly beginning from and concerned with precepts which either appear in Grotius' texts or can defensibly be constructed from them. While such an approach may command silent support, it has seldom been explicitly espoused; probably because it so narrows the compass of the 'Grotian tradition' as to exclude much of the modern literature with which the tradition is commonly associated. It does, however, raise the wider question of the nexus between the writings of Grotius and the subsequent development of the Grotian tradition: a matter on which there are sharp differences of opinion.

Many modern writers do accept Grotius' works as a useful starting-point. Butler, for instance, takes Grotius' writings as establishing the unadulterated Grotian principle of freedom of the seas, while arguing that the departures from this principle in the 1982 Convention on the Law of the Sea are cautious and are largely consistent with the balancing of interests characteristic of the Grotian tradition as it has subsequently developed.

Other modern authors contend that Grotius' writings were too non-committal to constitute a foundation for any useful and coherent tradition, leading them to deny that any such tradition exists or, at least, to deny its affiliation to Grotius. Shades of this approach are evident in Lauterpacht's view that Grotius too often did not identify a single binding rule of law, and that he therefore could not be considered as a 'Grotian' in the sense of one who has accomplished a workable synthesis of natural law and state practice.[182] In this volume, Schwarzenberger goes further in arguing that Grotius' writings were adaptable to any purpose, and that the most notable use of them was to ornament or mask the unreconstructed *Realpolitik* of the most skilled practitioners of power politics. Röling also treats Grotius' writings as a prop for the most powerful states, but unlike Schwarzenberger does not extend this criticism to the whole of the Grotian tradition. Suganami contends that Grotius had little to say on the important modern subject of the equality of states, and thus that any treatment of this subject within the Grotian tradition owes little directly to Grotius.

Several writers make the more general argument that the world with which Grotius was concerned was simply too remote from our own; and that his writings, while stimulating, are not directly relevant to many of our most pressing concerns. There are certainly grounds for reaching this conclusion. However, on many of the themes canvassed in this introduction and in the chapters in this volume, Grotius' writings are properly associated with important modern approaches and insights. What is clear is that in so far as a Grotian tradition can be said to exist in the twentieth century, its literature must extend beyond Grotius' texts and the small

---

[182] Lauterpacht, 'The Grotian Tradition in International Law', p. 5.

body of works directed specifically at their elucidation. It must include many of the leading analyses of that distinctive body of issues with which the Grotian tradition has long been concerned. These analyses variously involve the application, modification, development, or rejection of approaches and insights previously associated with the Grotian tradition, and often contain no direct reference to Grotius' own works. Opinions will continue to differ as to whether Grotius' contribution to the development of these approaches and insights, and the relevance of his works to them in their modern form, are sufficient to warrant the epithet 'Grotian'.[183]

A much richer but very demanding notion of what is meant by a 'tradition' emerges from the work of Quentin Skinner and other writers sharing his approach to the history of ideas. He seeks to investigate the intellectual context in which a given work was written—to recover the normative vocabulary available to the author from earlier writings, inherited political ideas, and the ambient social, political, and intellectual circumstances in which the author worked.[184] Such investigations may yield valuable insights into particular works, into the relationship between the political theory they embody and political action, and into ideologies with which they were associated. Some such studies of Grotius have been undertaken. But the mammoth task of applying such detailed contextual methods to the long and very broad sweep of a 'Grotian tradition' spanning almost four hundred years has not yet been attempted—if indeed it could ever be attempted.

A fourth approach to the notion of a 'tradition' may be found, lying somewhere between the different approaches already referred to. Such an approach might proceed from a

---

[183] Some uses of the epithet 'Grotian' seem somewhat remote from Grotius or from the core of any possible Grotian tradition. In regime theory, for instance, Stephen Krasner has labelled 'Grotian' an approach which holds that for every political system there is a corresponding regime of implicit or explicit principles, norms, rules, and decision-making procedures around which actors' expectations converge. See Stephen D. Krasner, 'Structural Causes and Regime Consequences: Regimes as Intervening Variables', *International Organisation*, 36 (1982), pp. 185–94; criticized by Jack Donnelly, 'International Human Rights: A Regime Analysis', ibid., 40 (1986), p. 601.

[184] Skinner, *The Foundations of Modern Political Thought*, 2 vols. (Cambridge, 1978), esp. vol. i, pp. x–xv. See also id., 'Meaning and Understanding in the History of Ideas', *History and Theory*, 8 (1969), pp. 3–53.

definition similar to Alasdair MacIntyre's description of a 'tradition of enquiry' as

> more than a coherent movement of thought. It is such a movement in the course of which those engaging in that movement become aware of it and of its direction and in self-aware fashion attempt to engage in its debates and to carry its enquiries forward.[185]

The traditions of enquiry which he discusses merit that description, he argues,

> not just because of the continuities of debate and enquiry which they embodied but also because of the transmutations and translations which they were able to undergo at and through points of conflict and difference. A tradition becomes mature just insofar as its adherents confront and find a rational way through or around those encounters with radically different or incompatible positions which pose the problems of incommensurability and untranslatability.[186]

Here the enterprise would depend upon the identification of distinctively Grotian strands of thought in the history of ideas about international relations; the tracing of these strands from pre-Grotian writings through to modern times; and the investigation of the response of the Grotian tradition to internal conflicts and to encounters with ideas and concepts espoused in other traditions.

Among modern scholars of international relations, an enterprise with some of these characteristics was that undertaken by Martin Wight. As Wight rightly observed, one of the earliest defining features of the Grotian tradition as perceived by pre-Enlightenment writers was its opposition to the *Realpolitik* associated (whether fairly or not) with Machiavelli.[187] In twentieth-century thought about international relations the Machiavellian tradition has been largely subsumed within the very broad ambit of 'Realism'. While there are areas of overlap between such extensive and loosely defined camps as those defined as 'Realist' and 'Grotian', many of the criticisms of Realist positions may be seen to lie

---

[185] MacIntyre, *Whose Justice? Which Rationality?* (London, 1988), p. 326.

[186] Ibid., p. 327.

[187] On Vico's view of Grotius as a preferable alternative to Machiavelli, see Dario Faucci, 'L' "Estimazione del giusto" selon Grotius et selon Vico', *Grotiana*, 1 (1980), p. 135.

within the Grotian tradition, including criticisms pointing to important aspects of reality which Realism is thought to have misunderstood or neglected. Setting aside the question of whether or not the characterization of these criticisms as 'Grotian' is accurate or useful (and there are many alternative ways to characterize each of the positions in this debate), it is clear that this Grotian counterpoint to the Realism dominant in modern international relations theory has often been underestimated.[188] In part this is because in the United States in particular the Grotian–Realist tension has been masked by the terms of political debate between realists and liberals, and by the preoccupation of many scholars with the task of looking over the shoulders of decision-makers. In part also it is because of the difficulty of properly categorizing the various non-Grotian alternatives to Realism, and of assessing their implications for Realist and Grotian positions. Martin Wight addressed this latter issue in his historical investigations by extending the Realist–Grotian interplay to include a third tradition of thought, which he termed cosmopolitanist or revolutionist or Kantian. He used the opposition between these three traditions to generate insights into what he regarded as some of the principal unities or conflicts of ideas in the history of thought about international relations. Although refined somewhat by Hedley Bull, the analytical potential of such an approach has not yet been fully explored.

There are several formidable difficulties with this threefold approach in the form presented by Wight. First, Wight, Bull, and others have treated the Grotian tradition as a residual category, defined in part as the *via media* between the idealized Machiavellian and Kantian positions.[189] Rather than being an

---

[188] Note the emphasis on the Grotian tradition as an alternative to *realpolitik* in e.g. Bourquin, 'Grotius et les tendances actuelles du droit international', *Journal de droit international et de législation comparée*, 7 (1926), pp. 94–5; and Lauterpacht, 'The Grotian Tradition in International Law', pp. 31–5.

[189] This point bears a resemblance to that made by Bruce Kuklick in discussing an aspect of the history of academic philosophy in the United States. He traces what he describes as the 'canonization' of seven philosophers, including Kant, and the perpetuation of this canon in American academic philosophy through what he regards as a victor's history. Giving one example of the constructs which this may entail, he says, 'Kant raised for the Americans the whole issue of the intelligibility of representational realism, and they found in Descartes a realist on whom could be blamed a whole series of errors that Kantian thought could correct.' 'Seven Thinkers

excluded middle, the Grotian tradition has been viewed too broadly. Bull conceded that most professional expositors of international law in the twentieth century belonged to the Grotian tradition.[190] Wight numbered in the ranks of the Grotians figures as diverse as Suarez, Locke, Callières, Burke, Coleridge, Tocqueville, Lincoln, F. D. Roosevelt, and Churchill. It is not easy to identify significant features common to the thought of all the members of this heterogeneous company. This difficulty may be met in part if it is possible to single out points of similarity which, though not each shared by all of them, overlap amongst them, much as members of a family resemble each other.[191] Whether such areas of similarity as can be identified are sufficiently coherent and substantial to constitute the traditions of thought for which Wight and Bull contended is becoming the subject of considerable scholarly investigation.

Second, if the traditions are more than mere insights into the history of past ideas, it must be possible to discern their modern working out in aspects of the contemporary theory and practice of international relations. This raises several problems. Not the least of these is the familiar problem of universality. Thus, for example, one list of the core values of US internationalism includes: international cooperation, consultation and conciliation; international law, institutions, and treaties; international negotiation, norms, and dispute settlement; economic interdependence, growth, and freer trade; international development, aid, and technical assistance; diligence in seeking arms control; and restraint in the use of force, except when responding to clear provocation and then, if possible, employed under multilateral auspices.[192] These are

and How they Grew: Descartes, Spinoza, Leibniz; Locke, Berkeley, Hume; Kant', in R. Rorty, J. B. Schneewind, and Q. Skinner (eds.), *Philosophy in History: Essays on the Historiography of Philosophy* (Cambridge, 1984), p. 130.

[190] Bull, 'Hans Kelsen and International Law', in Richard Tur and William Twining (eds.), *Essays on Kelsen* (Oxford, 1986), p. 323.

[191] The metaphor is borrowed from Wittgenstein's theory of universals, in the *Philosophical Investigations*, para. 67. See generally Renford Bambrough, 'Universals and Family Resemblances', in George Pitcher (ed.), *Wittgenstein: The Philosophical Investigations* (London, 1968), p. 186.

[192] See Thomas L. Hughes, 'The Twilight of Internationalism', *Foreign Policy*, 61 (1985–6), pp. 25–48. On co-operation, see also Robert O. Keohane, *After Hegemony: Cooperation and Discord in the World Political Economy* (Princeton, NJ, 1984).

the values of one contemporary Grotian archetype in the United States, associated with a commitment to international society and to a particular *via media*. But it does not follow that they must be the values of, for instance, an Indian proponent of international society and the *via media*.[193] It may be that the central concerns and approaches which characterize the Grotian, Kantian, and Machiavellian traditions do have meaning beyond a limited range of Western thought: but this has not yet been rigorously established.

This is closely related to a third difficulty, which concerns the extent to which the three traditions discussed by Wight meaningfully define major distinctions in contemporary theories of international relations.[194] To take one of the more recent of many examples germane to the Grotian tradition, the insights contributed by 'interpretive' or 'reflective' theorists of international institutions in the United States represent a challenge to the standard assumption of substantive rationality which the Grotian tradition has tended hitherto to embrace. These theorists point out that institutions themselves shape the preferences and powers of the actors within them, and are in turn shaped both by these actors and by more encompassing institutions. Their assumptions are of intersubjectivity, of continuous shifts in preferences and in institutional dynamics.[195] Whatever view is taken as to the value of 'critical international relations theory' and of its application to international institutions, little or nothing is added by

[193] Among many other challenges to assumptions of 'universality' is that raised by the growing body of work on women in international relations—see e.g the symposium in *Millennium*, 17 (1988).

[194] On such theories, see H. R. Alker and T. J. Biersteker, 'The Dialectics of World Order', *International Studies Quarterly*, 28 (1984), pp. 121–42; K. J. Holsti, *The Dividing Discipline* (Winchester, Mass., 1985); and Biersteker, 'The Emergence and Persistence of Research Traditions in International Relations' (forthcoming).

[195] See the very helpful discussion in Keohane, 'International Institutions: Two Approaches', *International Studies Quarterly*, 32 (1986), pp. 379–96, to which we are indebted. Repr. in Keohane, *International Institutions and State Power* (London, 1989), chap. 7. In addition to the works there discussed, see also R. Roy, R. B. J. Walker, and R. K. Ashley, 'Dialogue: Towards a Critical Theory of International Politics', *Alternatives*, 13 (1988), pp. 77–102; Yosef Lapid, '*Quo Vadis* International Relations? Further Reflections on the Next Step in International Theory', *Millennium*, 18 (1989), p. 77; J. Der Derian and M. Shapiro (eds.), *International/Intertextual Relations: The Boundaries of Knowledge and Practice in World Politics* (Lexington, Mass., 1989); and Y. Lapid, K. J. Holsti, T. J. Biersteker, and J. George, 'Exchange on the "Third Debate" ', *International Studies Quarterly*, 33 (1989), pp. 235–79.

characterizing it in Wightian terms either as neo-Kantian or as the further working out of the Grotian tradition. What is much more likely to be of value, however, is for proponents of such theories, and proponents of attempts to subsume them, to recognize that neither the issues they address nor the approaches they employ are wholly autochthonous, and that reflection on their intellectual antecedents may contribute both to the articulation of the issues and to structuring analysis of them.

The fourth and fifth objections concern Wight's own position on his threefold classification. The fourth objection was expressed well by Hedley Bull:

Much that has been said about International Relations in the past cannot be related significantly to these traditions at all. Wight was, I believe, too ambitious in attributing to the Machiavellians, the Grotians and the Kantians distinctive views not only about war, peace, diplomacy, intervention and other matters of International Relations but about human psychology, about irony and tragedy, about methodology and epistemology. There is a point at which the debate Wight is describing ceases to be one that has actually taken place, and becomes one that he has invented; at this point his work is not an exercise in the history of ideas, so much as an exposition of an imaginary philosophical conversation, in the manner of Plato's dialogues.[196]

Finally, the traditions are perhaps so over-extended as to threaten their usefulness. Acknowledging this problem, Wight described the categories as paradigms rather than as precise lines of argument to which theorists or policy-makers subscribed *in toto*, and experimented with sub-categories and with additional 'traditions'.[197] He accepted that many important writers and historical figures did not fit comfortably into any one tradition, including even the eponyms Machiavelli and Kant. Even with these modifications and concessions, how-

---

[196] Bull, 'Martin Wight and the Theory of International Relations', *British Journal of International Studies*, 2 (1976), p. 111.

[197] In particular, he considered the incorporation of a fourth tradition, that of 'inverted revolutionism'. See generally Bull, 'Martin Wight and the Theory of International Relations', p. 106. Other scholars have proposed further categories— see, for example, Robert Jackson, 'Inverted Rationalism: Martin Wight, International Theory and the Good Life', paper presented at the ISA–BISA meeting, London, Mar. 1989.

ever, it is difficult to devise any set of necessary and sufficient conditions which are both specific enough to identify a definite and useful content for each of Wight's categories, and accurate enough to describe categories of thought which have really existed historically. Wight's categorization may thus appear to equivocate between an attempt to define historical traditions of thought in a manner comparable to that suggested by MacIntyre, and a less ambitious attempt to identify ideal types or paradigms. In so far as Wight's project is of the latter type, it may provide useful insights into many fundamental issues in international relations.[198] While paradigms and ideal types must be used with care,[199] when interpreted as analyses of ideal types the work of Wight and Bull on Grotian thought and its interplay with other patterns of thought is undoubtedly illuminating.

The more difficult issue is whether the idea of a Grotian tradition of enquiry (using the term in MacIntyre's sense) in international relations can be sustained. Clearly Grotius himself offered important insights into the nature and functioning of international society. Many of these were not original to him, but the orientation of his work, the sources he used, the subtlety and depth of his account, and its apparent practicality, convinced contemporaries and his immediate successors of the importance of *De Jure Belli ac Pacis*.[200] In the late twentieth century a recognizably Grotian approach continues to offer an attractive and realistic alternative to stark Realism. But the proposition that the literature and practice spanning almost four centuries is sufficiently unified to constitute a 'Grotian tradition' in this sense remains unproven.

[198] For similar projects, see e.g. Kenneth Waltz, *Man, The State and War: A Theoretical Analysis* (New York, 1959); and Martin Ceadel, *Thinking about Peace and War* (Oxford, 1987). Ceadel agrees with Bull that Grotius is best characterized by his commitment to international society and its institutions and his belief that war will not be abolished. But rather than pursue the idea of a 'Grotian tradition', Ceadel prefers simply to treat Grotius as falling within his category of 'defencists'. See Ceadel, pp. 86–7 and 193–4. Whether Grotius tends towards the 'crusading' or 'pacific-ist' wings of 'defencism' is not discussed.

[199] On some possible hazards in the use of paradigms, see Albert O. Hirschman, 'The Search for Paradigms as a Hindrance to Understanding', *World Politics*, 22 (1970), pp. 329–43.

[200] See Kenneth Simmonds, 'Grotius and the Law of the Sea: A Reassessment', in A. Dufour *et al.* (eds.), *Grotius et l'ordre juridique international* (Lausanne, 1985), p. 46.

Quite apart from specific criticisms of Martin Wight's enterprise, a major obstacle to the accurate description of the lineaments of a Grotian tradition of thought in international relations is the failure of much of that portion of modern international theory which lies outside the realist and Marxist traditions to take adequate account of classical political theory.

The relationship between political theory and international theory has been a source of difficulty for many modern theories of international relations. This has been so especially for those inclined to a 'classical' approach to the theory of international relations;[201] the difficulty is one of the themes in Martin Wight's essay 'Why is there no international theory?'[202] Wight laments:

> it sometimes seems that whereas political theory generally is in unison with political activity, international theory (at least in its chief embodiment as international law) sings a kind of descant over against the movement of diplomacy. Political theory is in a direct relation with political activity—whether justifying recent developments as Hooker did the Anglican settlement and Locke the Glorious Revolution, or providing a programme of action that the next generation carries out, as Bentham did for administrative reform in England or Marx and the other socialist writers for the working-class movement. But international law seems to follow an inverse movement to that of international politics. When diplomacy is violent and unscrupulous, international law soars into the regions of natural law; when diplomacy acquires a certain habit of co-operation, international law crawls in the mud of legal positivism.[203]

In the history of Western political thought, international theory has in large measure been a branch of general political theory. Leaving aside contributions from such disciplines as history, economics, and law, the classics of international

---

[201] See Bull, 'International Theory: The Case for A Classical Approach', *World Politics*, 18 (1966), repr. in (*inter alia*) K. Knorr and J. N. Rosenau (eds.), *Contending Approaches to International Politics* (Princeton, NJ, 1969).

[202] In Butterfield and Wight (eds.), *Diplomatic Investigations*, pp. 17–34. The title suggests a parallel, *mutatis mutandis*, to Isaiah Berlin's 'Does Political Theory Still Exist?', in Peter Laslett and W. G. Runciman (eds.), *Philosophy, Politics and Society*, 2nd ser. (Oxford, 1962).

[203] In Butterfield and Wight (eds.), *Diplomatic Investigations*, p. 29.

theory consist in great part of limited selections from the *œuvres* of the leading political philosophers: Machiavelli, Hobbes, Spinoza, Rousseau, Kant, Marx, even through to Rawls. Recent work on classical theories of international relations has frequently been concerned with tracing the relationship between these often rather scanty excerpts and the wider political philosophy of their authors. Suarez, Grotius, Pufendorf, and other writers on natural law and the law of nations have been treated rather differently, their contributions to international law and international relations being discussed with relatively little regard to studies of their political theory.

Grotius' belief in the immutability of human nature, and his assumption that it may be ascertained with certainty rather than mere probability, were assailed by Vico in a criticism directed also at Selden and Pufendorf.[204] As Berlin neatly puts it, these jurists were attacked by Vico

for their blindness to the idea of development, *nascimento*, coming to birth, from which *natura* is derived, whereby one generation, or culture, grows into another. Blind to this, they cannot see the organic interconnection which unites the various fields of activity which belong to any one particular stage of social growth. Above all, he charges them with ignoring the cardinal truth that all valid explanation is necessarily and essentially genetic, in terms either of human purposes, which change with changing circumstances, or of the alteration of circumstances by these purposes themselves, that is, by human action, or the interplay of purposes and 'blind' circumstances or environment, which often leads to consequences unintended by men.[205]

This dynamic understanding of human history, social organization, and law, represented by Vico as an early exemplar[206] but vastly more influential in the writings of Hegel, Marx, and many others, has penetrated deeply into Western thought; so much so that Grotius' static vision of human activity now seems to miss an entire dimension.

[204] Vico, *Scienza nuova*, §§ 318–29, 338, 350, 394–7, 493, 553, 952–72.

[205] Isaiah Berlin, *Vico and Herder: Two Studies in the History of Ideas* (London, 1976), p. 34. See also A. C. 't Hart, 'Hugo Grotius and Giambattista Vico', *Netherlands International Law Review*, 30 (1983), pp. 5–41.

[206] Vico's writings were acknowledged especially by Croce and Michelet; but their direct influence does not seem to have been great.

Another facet of Grotius' political theory which has provoked later condemnation is his theory of the state and its relationship to its subjects or citizens. Grotius did envisage the possibility of constitutional restraints on the power of the state, provided these limitations were set at the time when sovereignty was acquired: this was a principal basis on which he upheld the lawfulness of the Dutch struggle against Spanish rule.[207] But he also accepted that absolutist rule might be lawfully constituted, and countenanced only a very limited right of resistance for subjects against tyrannical oppression.[208] The Enlightenment reaction against this, exemplified by Rousseau in *The Social Contract*, remains influential:

Grotius denies that all human government is established for the benefit of the governed, and he cites the example of slavery. His characteristic method of reasoning is always to offer fact as a proof of right. It is possible to imagine a more logical method, but not one more favourable to tyrants.[209]

While Grotius' political theory has been extensively explored, not least in relation to human nature, the law of nature, the basis of political community, the nature of the state, the duty of obedience and the right of resistance, and communal and private property, there has been rather less investigation of the relationship between this political theory and Grotius' international theory. Grotius' political theory and his international theory are inextricably linked: in many respects he treated them as a unified body of thought. Investigations of these links are likely to yield further insights both into Grotius' own writings and into the principal concepts embodied in the Grotian tradition of thought about international relations.

Another tendency towards divergence in modern work on

[207] One pamphleteer attempted to use Grotius' writings to justify aspects of the Glorious Revolution in England—see *The Proceedings of the Present Parliament Justified by the Opinion of the most Judicious and Learned Hugo Grotius; with Considerations thereupon, By a Lover of the Peace of his Country* (London, 1689). See also Schama, *The Embarrassment of Riches: An Interpretation of Dutch Culture in the Golden Age* (London, 1987), p. 81.

[208] See the useful discussion of resistance in Skinner, *The Foundations of Modern Political Thought*, ii, *The Age of Reformation* (Cambridge, 1978), pp. 189–348.

[209] Rousseau, *The Social Contract*, book i, chap. 2 (trans. Maurice Cranston, Harmondsworth, 1968).

Grotius results from a degree of separation between international law and international relations as academic disciplines, each exhibiting signs of scepticism about the value of the contributions of the other. In fact there are important connections between these fields, manifest in the work of Grotius and of many subsequent theorists and practitioners, on such subjects as the regulation of resort to war and of the conduct of war, and the allocation of rights in maritime spaces. Recognition of the importance of these connections is an essential element of the Grotian tradition, and an important contribution both to international relations and to international law.

The bearing of past writings and historical practice on current questions remains an important issue in both international relations and international law. To Grotius' contemporaries, many ancient sources were reputable and of considerable persuasive value: 'Let us now peruse our ancient authors, for out of the old fields must come the new corne', wrote Sir Edward Coke apropos of English law.[210] Descartes, however, expressed an opinion which became increasingly influential as scientific inquiry progressed: one 'needs Greek and Latin no more than Swiss or bas-Breton; to know the history of the Roman Empire no more than of the smallest country in Europe.'[211] Rousseau took this line, applying to Grotius the Marquis d'Argenson's remark: 'Learned researches on public law are often only the history of ancient abuses, and one is misled when one gives oneself the trouble of studying them too closely.'[212] Writing in 1970, at the high tide of behaviouralism and problem-specific research, Richard Falk lamented that the classical heritage of international law created by Grotius and others had become 'almost irrelevant to the main lines of current research interest and vocational training in the United States.'[213]

[210] 4 *Institutes of the Laws of England* (London, 1797 edn.), p. 109.
[211] René Descartes, 'La Recherche de la vérité', *Œuvres* (ed. Adam and Tannery), x (Paris, 1908), p. 503. The translation is that of Isaiah Berlin in *Against the Current* (London, 1979), p. 113.
[212] Rousseau adds: 'This is exactly what Grotius does'. Jean-Jacques Rousseau, *The Social Contract* (trans. Cranston, Harmondsworth, 1968), book 1, chap. 2.
[213] Richard Falk, *The Status of Law in International Society* (Princeton, NJ, 1970), p. 38.

The proposition that Grotius' works are no longer worthy of study is ill-conceived. Certainly Grotius must be studied in his context: and this context is substantially different from our own. Yet he presents a thoughtful and pragmatic account of international society and its regulation from which we have much to learn. He grappled with problems which continue to concern us: if some of his solutions seem unsatisfactory or his compromises unwise, they remain sufficiently cogent to provide a starting-point for worthwhile modern debate. This applies, for instance, to his strong (if eventually qualified) formulations of the freedoms of the seas, of trade, and of communication; to his attempts to circumscribe the grounds on which war may be justified; to his emphasis on limitations on the conduct of belligerents; to his significant if limited extension of the ambit of the *jus gentium* beyond the bounds of Christendom; and to the reasons he gives for the binding force of the *jus gentium*. Grotius' works, and the tradition of thought with which they are associated, capture a significant dimension of the past, present, and future of international relations.

2

The Importance of Grotius in the Study of International Relations

HEDLEY BULL

Why, four hundred years after his birth, should Hugo Grotius still be considered an important figure in the study of international relations? His claims to be regarded as the founder of international law have long been disputed. Some say that the mantle should be placed upon the Spanish scholastics of the sixteenth century, Vitoria and Suarez, and that Grotius was simply 'the last of the Spanish school'. Others say that it belongs to Alberico Gentili, the Italian Protestant exile who became Professor of Civil Law at Oxford, where he lectured on the law of war and the law of embassies while Grotius was still an infant. Sir Thomas Erskine Holland proclaimed more than a century ago (in his Inaugural Lecture as Professor of Civil Law at Oxford) that Grotius was no more than Gentili's most distinguished disciple.

The student of international relations today finds the works of Grotius difficult to read, even in English translation, encumbered as they are with the biblical and classical learning with which in Grotius' generation it was thought helpful to buttress theoretical arguments. Martin Wight writes of 'trying to pick a path once again through the baroque thickets of Grotius' work, where profound and potent principles lurk in the shade of forgotten arguments, and obsolete examples lie like violets beneath gigantic overgrown rhododendrons.'[1] Few of us have the stamina to pick this kind of path.

Voltaire said, more bluntly, that Grotius is boring. Rousseau argued, by no means untruthfully, that Grotius, like Hobbes, favoured tyrants; and, indeed, it is a commonplace among

---

[1] Wight, *Systems of States*, ed. Hedley Bull (Leicester, 1977), p. 127.

liberal writers in the Western world, that however much Grotius may be reckoned to have upheld progressive causes in matters of international relations, in his view of domestic society and politics he was the champion of absolutist forms of government, and hostile to notions of popular or national self-determination and to the right of oppressed subjects to rebel against their rulers.

Grotius is also accused by some—for example, by Professor B. V. A. Röling in his chapter below—of propounding doctrines that are permissive to those in authority, and especially of providing justifications for European expansion and imperialism. He has also been charged with varying his interpretations of international law to suit the interests of his clients. It is said, for example, that in 1613 and 1615 when Grotius was a member of Dutch delegations to conferences at which he defended Dutch claims to a monopoly of trade in the East Indies against the challenge of the English, he presented a very different interpretation of the law of the sea from that which he had put forward a few years earlier in *Mare Liberum*, when defending the right of the Dutch to challenge the trade monopoly of the Portuguese.[2]

We are also sometimes told that whatever merits or demerits may have attached to the doctrines of Grotius in earlier times, today these doctrines are, to put the matter crudely, out of date. Grotius' doctrine of just war, for example, is said to be unacceptable in the era of nuclear weapons technology, in which we are as much threatened by just wars as by unjust ones. His doctrine of the freedom of the seas has been in large measure denied in recent years in the process of the enclosure of the oceans by the extension of state claims to territorial waters and exclusive economic zones, now sanctified in the 1982 Law of the Sea Convention.[3]

For all this there is no doubt that the work of Grotius is one of the great landmarks in modern thinking about international

---

[2] For an extensive discussion see G. N. Clark and W. J. M van Eysinga, 'The Colonial Conferences between England and The Netherlands in 1613 and 1615', *Bibliotheca Visseriana*, 15 (1940); ibid., 17 (1951).

[3] See e.g. John Logue, 'The Revenge of John Selden: The Draft Convention on the Law of the Sea in the Light of Hugo Grotius' Mare Liberum', *Grotiana*, 3 (1982), pp. 27–56.

relations, and has lost none of its importance today. In what follows I shall try to show why this is so.

(a) GROTIUS AND HIS CAREER

Grotius was born in Delft in 1583, within a year of the assassination of William the Silent, and died in 1645, while the Peace of Westphalia was being negotiated but three years before it was concluded. His international world was that of the latter phase of the European wars of religion and the formative phase of the secular system of international relations: on the one hand the revolt of the Netherlands against Spain and the Thirty Years War in Germany; on the other hand the dawn of the era of mercantile and colonial rivalries among the European powers.

Quite apart from his contributions to the law of nations and to the study of Dutch domestic law, Grotius was one of the leading intellectual figures, not just of the Netherlands but of Europe, one of the glories of the age of the baroque. He was a child prodigy, who entered the University of Leiden to study under Scaliger when only eleven, published a book at fourteen, and when he visited Paris at the age of fifteen was acclaimed by King Henry IV as 'the miracle of Holland'. His books, which number between fifty and sixty, nearly all written in Latin, embrace theology, biblical criticism, history, philology, and poetry as well as law. His greatest passion, at least in later life, was not the law of nations but the reunion of the Christian churches—at first the reunion of the Protestant churches, later the reunion of Protestant and Catholic Christendom. Loyal to the programme followed in earlier generations by Erasmus and other Christian humanists, Grotius preached the reconciliation of Catholics and Protestants at the height of the Thirty Years War, when this goal had become a chimera and preaching it brought him only vilification from both sides.

As well as being involved in scholarship and intellectual argument, Grotius was involved in practical matters: as a young man in Dutch affairs, and as a mature man in wider European affairs, in neither case at all successfully.

As a young man Grotius held important offices in the Province of Holland as Advocate-Fiscal or attorney-general of the province, and later as pensionary of Rotterdam, a sort of mayor. In this role Grotius from 1608 to 1618 became a prominent political figure and the protégé of Johan van Oldenbarnevelt, the Grand Pensionary of Holland and leader of one of the principal political factions of the country. It was this involvement that led to Grotius' downfall, imprisonment, and exile. The conflict was between parties within the United Provinces of the Netherlands in which several factors were intertwined. One was the struggle between the seven provinces that made up the Netherlands union, and the centre: Oldenbarnevelt and Grotius stood for the independence and sovereignty of the most powerful of the seven provinces, Holland, against the claims of the central power. A second factor was the struggle within the Dutch church between the 'Arminian' or liberal wing of the Calvinists and the orthodox wing, centring upon the doctrine of predestination, which the latter upheld and the former rejected. A third element was the conflict over foreign policy issues, between a conciliatory and militant attitude towards Spain and Catholicism. This was during the period of the Twelve Years Truce in the war with Spain, lasting from 1609 until 1621, when as the truce began to run out the question was being debated whether or not it should be renewed and, if so, on what conditions.

The outcome of the struggle was that a coup brought about the defeat of Grotius' party. Oldenbarnevelt was executed and Grotius was sentenced in 1619 to life imprisonment in the castle of Loewenstein. But two years later, as all Dutch schoolchildren know if they know nothing else about him, Grotius escaped from the castle romantically, and in a manner appropriate to a scholar, in a chest of books. He made his way to France, where Louis XIII's chief minister Richelieu had backed the Oldenbarnevelt faction in the Netherlands. Grotius, now the French King's pensioner, spent the rest of his life as an exile except for a few brief periods, mainly in Paris. It was here that he wrote (among other things) his great work *De Jure Belli ac Pacis*, published in 1625 with a dedication to Louis XIII.

As a mature man in Paris Grotius had his second important

involvement in practical affairs. For his first ten years (1621–31) in the French capital Grotius had devoted himself to bringing about his political rehabilitation in the Netherlands and facilitating a return to the land of his birth. After the final decisive failure of these efforts Grotius accepted an offer that he should become the ambassador of Sweden to the court of Louis XIII, taking up this post in 1635 and retaining it for the last decade of his life. Sweden was a foreign state, but Grotius did not have the opportunity of official work for his own country, and Sweden and the Netherlands were united both as Protestant states and as co-belligerents in the war against Habsburg Spain and the Habsburg Emperor in Germany. Since the death of King Gustavus Adolphus in the battle of Lützen in 1632 Sweden's affairs had been directed by its Regent and Chancellor, Oxenstierna. Grotius' most important business occurred in the first year of his embassy, when he played a part in the negotiation by Oxenstierna and Cardinal Richelieu of the Treaty of Compiègne which brought France fully into the Thirty Years War on the side of Sweden and the Protestant and anti-Imperial German princes, leading to the defeat of the Habsburg cause and the Peace of Westphalia thirteen years later.

Grotius does not seem to have been a success as a diplomatist. Sweden's position in European affairs was deteriorating just as Grotius took up his embassy in Paris, as a result of her defeat by Imperial forces at the battle of Nördlingen in September 1634. In May 1635 the Peace of Prague, a separate peace with the Emperor signed by the anti-Imperial German princes, led to the dissolution of the German Protestant combination to which Sweden was allied. Throughout this period it was not Sweden but France that had the upper hand in the councils of the coalition struggling against Habsburg power.

Richelieu appears to have detested Grotius and sought to have him recalled. The Swedes passed over Grotius in putting together their delegation to the Westphalia conference in 1643, and later failed to renew Grotius' appointment in Paris. As the leading Protestant power on the continent they are not likely to have appreciated his commitment to reconciliation with Catholicism. There is some evidence, moreover, that

Grotius himself was inclined to regard his diplomatic duties as an unwelcome interruption of his studies.

Perhaps the right comment on Grotius' involvement in practical affairs was the one made by King James I on the occasion of the former's visit to London in 1613: 'He was some pedant, full of words and of no great judgement.'[4] Grotius was a typical example of the intellectual in politics, lacking in political tact and common sense and more at home in the world of ideas.

(b) GROTIUS' PRINCIPAL WORKS ON INTERNATIONAL RELATIONS

Grotius' ideas about international relations are expressed chiefly in two works. The first, much the less important, is the Commentary on the Law of Prize, *De Jure Praedae*, which he wrote in his twenties during his early Dutch period but never published in his lifetime—apart from one chapter, *Mare Liberum*, published in 1609. The occasion for Grotius' work on the law of prize was the capture in 1603 of a Portuguese vessel in the Straits of Malacca by a vessel of the Dutch East India Company (which had been founded the previous year), and with it a great deal of booty. This raised international questions as to whether the Dutch East India Company had been within its rights in seizing the Portuguese ship and treating its contents as prize. It also raised domestic questions because some of the shareholders in the Company were Mennonite pacifists who felt both that booty should not be treated as prize, and that in any case all war was wrong. Grotius, it seems likely, acted as advocate for the Dutch East India Company before the prize court, and later set out his argument at length in *De Jure Praedae*. This was that war could be waged justly by Christians, and more particularly that the Company could justly wage a private war in its own defence, before the war was converted into a public one.

In 1609, in the course of the negotiations between Spain and her rebellious Dutch provinces that led to the Twelve

---

[4] W. S. M. Knight, *The Life and Works of Hugo Grotius* (London, 1925), p. 144.

Years Truce, the chapter on the freedom of the seas, *Mare Liberum*, was published, probably to rebut the demands being made by Spain that the Dutch should abandon their commerce in the Far East as part of the price of a peace settlement. One has to remember that at this time the Spanish and Portuguese crowns were united, so that in their conflicts with Spain in Europe and with Portugal outside Europe the Dutch faced in effect a single adversary. The argument of *Mare Liberum* was that neither Portugal nor any other power had exclusive rights to navigation, fisheries, or trade in the East Indies, whether by rights of discovery or by occupation or by Papal donation.

But apart from this chapter the main importance of *De Jure Praedae* was that the material that went into this youthful work of advocacy was absorbed into the writing of the mature and systematic treatise: *De Jure Belli ac Pacis*. John Morley says of this that along with Adam Smith's *The Wealth of Nations* it is 'one of the cardinal books of European history'. It is certainly also one of the cardinal works for the understanding of international relations in modern times, not only in Europe.

(c) GROTIUS AND THE IDEA OF INTERNATIONAL SOCIETY

The work of Grotius is cardinal because it states one of the classic paradigms that have since determined both our understanding of the facts of inter-state relations and our ideas as to what constitutes right conduct therein. This is the idea of international society: the notion that states and rulers of states are bound by rules and form a society or community with one another, of however rudimentary a kind.[5]

In early modern Europe, as states and princes made good their claims to local independence or sovereignty and the super-state pretensions of the papacy and the Holy Roman Empire were brushed aside, two paradigms for relations among these states and princes dominated the field. One was the argument of Machiavelli, Hobbes, Bacon, and their

[5] This idea is further elaborated in Bull, *The Anarchical Society: A Study of Order in World Politics* (London, 1977).

followers that sovereign states and princes in their dealings with one another were in a state of nature, unrestrained by bonds of law or society, and so were free to conduct policies towards one another according to the dictates of the new idea of reason of state. The other was the idea that states and princes could be made subject to a central authority and escape from the state of nature into which they appeared to be drifting: Papal and Imperialist writers urged a restoration of the decaying central institutions of Latin Christendom, while others were beginning to look forward to the construction of new institutions built upon the new forces that were emerging in modern times, to feel their way towards the idea of a perpetual peace made possible by the prospect of human progress, that was later to be given full statement in the writings of Kant.

As against these two doctrines Grotius advanced the third position, that states and the rulers of states in their dealings with one another were bound by rules and together formed a society. On the one hand princes and peoples had indeed become independent of one another and of central authorities and were sovereign. But on the other hand they were not in a state of nature, but part of the great society of all mankind, *magna communitas humani generis*. Even without central institutions, rulers and peoples might constitute a society among themselves, an anarchical society or society without government.

This is the idea that came into its own in Grotius' time and still underlies the relations of states in our own days. It is this idea which, in its many different forms and manifestations over the last four centuries, provides the core of what we may call the Grotian tradition. In its practical embodiment in the modern system of international relations it has undergone great transformations. An international society of princely or patrimonial states has given place to an international society of peoples or nations. An international society of Christian or European states has been replaced by one that is global or all-inclusive in its scope and in which the original European members are a small and dwindling minority. An international society with the bare minimum of agreed rules and with institutions of only the most rudimentary kind, such as was beginning to take shape at the time of Grotius, has become a society whose rules cover the vast range of areas—economic, social, and cultural as well as political and strategic, in which the states and nations of today impinge upon one another. An international society which took for granted the market economy or capitalist system of production, distribution, and exchange, has come to accept the coexistence of these with socialist systems. But the underlying idea, the normative and institutional framework upon which these changes have been constructed, is recognizably the same.

The idea of international society was not, of course, conceived by Grotius alone. In his doctrine that the relations of independent political communities were subject to rules of natural law he followed Vitoria and Suarez among others, and in his exposition of natural law itself he looked back to Aquinas and beyond him to the Christian and pre-Christian Stoics. He was indeed heavily indebted to Gentili in what he said about the laws of war and the law of embassies, and Gentili's views on these subjects are closer to our own ideas than is the doctrine of Grotius.[6] In rejecting the extremes of pacifism and of total licence in resorting to war and in the manner of its conduct, in insisting upon the distinction between just and unjust wars, Grotius was relying on a tradition that stretched back through Aquinas and Augustine to Cicero. In his formulations of so-called human voluntary law or positive law and in applying it to the international circumstances of his time he was not writing in a vacuum, but was able to draw upon the Roman idea of *jus gentium*.

Grotius, indeed, is seldom strikingly original and it is in the vast range of his knowledge, together with his capacity to synthesize this knowledge and focus it upon the issues at hand that he commands our attention. We have to remember also that the ground was prepared for the emergence of the idea of a society of states by earlier systems of ideas that pointed in this direction. The conciliar movement within the Latin Christian church, for example, asserted a collective identity and authority in Christendom, limiting the freedom of action of its parts, apart from the ruling heads of Christendom. Within the Holy Roman Empire of the German nation the

[6] See below, chap. 3.

constitutionalist tradition had long asserted that the many members, ranks, and estates of that complex institution were bound in their dealings with one another by accepted rights and duties, and that neither the Emperor on the one hand nor the princes and cities on the other were free to behave as if they inhabited a legal vacuum.

There are good reasons, however, for regarding the writings of Grotius as those that did most to propagate the idea of international society in early modern times. It was in fact through the numerous editions and translations of *De Jure Belli ac Pacis* in the seventeenth and eighteenth centuries that the idea was chiefly spread. If not the most original treatise written on the law of nations up to that time it was certainly the most *systematic*, dealing with the whole range of relations among independent political communities, with peace as well as with war, and with what today we would call private international law as well as with public, assembling in a single work all the rules which were thought to exist bearing on these matters, and arranging them according to coherent principles. It is Grotius' own claim in the opening paragraph of the Prolegomena that the subject of the law of war and peace has not been dealt with 'in a comprehensive and systematic manner; yet the welfare of mankind demands that this task be accomplished.'[7] This is the task that he made his own.

We have also to remember that Grotius' treatise came at a time when Europe was receptive to many of the ideas which it contained: the rights of princes to independence, the emptiness of the claims of papacy and Empire to authority over them, their right to use force to uphold their rights under agreed law, the equal rights of Protestant with Catholic states, the rights of states to navigate the oceans and to trade, the validity of agreements made with non-Christian powers. In formulating these ideas Grotius was articulating claims that were being put forward by powerful forces in many parts of Europe, and in articulating them, he gave them further strength. Already in Grotius' youth, the argument of *Mare Liberum*, used by the Dutch to press their claims to rights of navigation and trade against the monopolism of the Spanish and the Portuguese,

---

[7] *JBP*, Prolegomena I.

was taken up by the English to buttress their objections to the monopolism of the Dutch. Gustavus Adolphus, as he rode about Germany during the Thirty Years War at the head of the Swedish interventionary force, is supposed to have carried a copy of *De Jure Belli ac Pacis* in his saddle-bag; certainly there is much in it that might have brought comfort to a ruler then asserting a right to intervene within a foreign state in aid of subjects of an oppressive ruler, to wage war justly, and to keep the spoils of conquest. It must also have brought comfort to the cause of the Protestant alliance and the ambitions of German princes to achieve sovereign independence.

(d) THE DOCTRINES OF GROTIUS AND THE PEACE OF
WESTPHALIA

The idea of international society which Grotius propounded was given concrete expression in the Peace of Westphalia, and Grotius may be considered the intellectual father of this first general peace settlement of modern times, just as Richelieu, who like Grotius died before the Peace came about, may be said to have created the political conditions that made it possible.[8] The treaties concluded at Münster and Osnabrück in 1648, bringing to an end the Thirty Years War in Germany and the Eighty Years War between the Netherlands and Spain, did not, as is sometimes said, mark the beginning of the modern international system or states system, which must be dated from the appearance of sovereign states whose behaviour impinged on one another, and began at least as early as the late fifteenth century.[9] Still less does the Peace of Westphalia mark the emergence of a system of *nation*-states, which is a development only of the late eighteenth and nineteenth centuries in Europe, and outside Europe is coming to fruition only in our own times. What the Peace of Westphalia did mark, however, was the emergence of an international society as distinct from a mere international system, the acceptance by states of rules and institutions binding on them in their

[8] The best general account of the Peace of Westphalia is F. Dickmann, *Der Westfälische Frieden* (Münster, 1965).
[9] See esp. Wight's argument in *Systems of States*, chap. 5.

relations with one another, and of a common interest in maintaining them.

By no means all that was affirmed in the Westphalia treaties is consonant with the doctrines of Grotius. Grotius is notoriously silent, for example, on the subject of the balance of power, even though balance of power theory of a rudimentary kind was already extant at this time; indeed, Grotius' doctrine that war may be waged justly only in response to an injury to one's rights sets him at loggerheads with balance of power thinking. The Peace of Westphalia, while it proclaimed no doctrine of the need for a balance of power, did erect such a balance against the Habsburg power by dividing the Spanish from the Austrian Habsburgs, curbing the pretensions of the latter within Germany, and allowing France and Sweden (and in effect Prussia) to advance themselves at the Habsburgs' expense.

There is nothing in Grotius that suggests the role that might be played by a general conference of European powers to give their consent to a settlement of all-European political issues. The Westphalia conference, embracing as it did most of the states of Europe (the Ottoman Empire and England were important absentees), and producing a comprehensive settlement determining the political shape of the European system as a whole, did this, and so came to provide a kind of constitutional foundation of international society such that until the time of the French Revolution European peace treaties referred back to it and reaffirmed it. All this was outside Grotius' experience, and the idea of law-making by multilateral conference, if not inherently hostile to his outlook, has no place in his writings.

It has to be noted also that the solution which was arrived at in Westphalia to the problem of religious conflict in Germany (and by implication, to the wider problem of religious conflict in Europe) was not the one which Grotius preferred. Grotius, as we have seen, sought the end of the schism or schisms within the Christian world; the Peace of Westphalia perpetuated these schisms, by reaffirming and extending the formula *cujus regio, ejus religio*, that had first been laid down in the Religious Peace of Augsburg in 1555. Rulers were left free to determine the confessional allegiance of their states and their subjects, and peace was to be sought by removal of the religious issue from the arena of inter-state relations, and a general commitment to peaceful coexistence. Much of what Grotius had to say served to facilitate this outcome, and it would be wrong to suggest that because the Westphalian solution was not his preferred one he would not have settled for it as a *pis aller*, in circumstances in which reconciliation of Catholics, Lutherans, and Calvinists clearly stood no chance. But one could hardly say that the religious provisions of the treaties were the fulfilment of what Grotius had striven for.

However, in their broad impact on the course of international history the theory of Grotius and the practice of the Peace of Westphalia marched together. The external sovereignty of states was advanced by recognition of the rights of German princes to form alliances outside the Empire, and by recognition of the independence of the Netherlands and of the Swiss Confederation. The internal sovereignty of states was advanced by reaffirmation of the authority of the state over the church, a doctrine as dear to the heart of Grotius as it was to the heart of Hobbes. The ambitions of the Austrian Habsburgs to restore a unified German Reich under their leadership were frustrated, even though the Habsburgs were not deprived of the right to seek to have their candidate elected to the office of Holy Roman Emperor, as some would have liked, and in the event continued to monopolize the office until Napoleon's abolition of the Holy Roman Empire in 1806, except for one brief period. The claims of the papacy to be a super-state institution with a right to pronounce on the validity of treaties concluded among Christian powers were explicitly rejected. (It was the common fate of the works of Grotius and of the Treaties of Westphalia to be denounced by Rome: the papacy for several centuries conducted a rearguard action against the very idea of international law, which it denounced as a Protestant science, and even as late as 1899 the Vatican was refused permission to send a delegation to the Hague Peace Conference because *De Jure Belli ac Pacis* was still on the Index.) At the same time the Westphalia treaties demonstrated in practice, just as Grotius had done in theory, that the independence or sovereignty of states was not

incompatible with their subjection to law or their recognition
of the common bonds of society.

(e) FIVE FEATURES OF GROTIUS' VIEW OF INTERNATIONAL SOCIETY

If we compare the conception of international society set out
in Grotius' writings with the way in which that society came
to be conceived by thinkers and practitioners of international
relations in succeeding centuries, there are perhaps five
features of it that stand out.

1. The Central Place of Natural Law

First, in Grotius' conception of international society natural
law has a central place. Princes are persons, and states or
peoples are collections of persons; a basic reason why relations
among princes and states are subject to law is that they are
subject to the rules of natural law, which bind all persons in
the great society of all mankind. These rules, reflecting the
rational and social nature of man, are known a priori to all
creatures endowed with reason, and also a posteriori because
they are confirmed by the agreement of all, or at least the
agreement of all the best minds. Natural law for Grotius is not
to be equated with the moral law or morality in general; it
comprises only that part of morality that states the rational
principles of conduct in society. The morality of love or
charity, for example, on which Grotius draws in recommending
humanity in warfare (the *temperamenta belli*), lies beyond its
scope. Natural law is for Grotius, however, a body of moral
rules known to all rational beings, against which the mere
will or practice of states can be measured; and this is placed at
the centre of his exposition of international law.

Grotius by no means confines himself to natural law, and
does not adopt the 'pure' naturalist position of his German
successor Pufendorf; along with natural law he draws upon
'human volitional law' or positive law, and especially upon
the emerging positive law of nations, upon Roman law,
Mosaic law, and other systems of law. Grotius does not make

it clear, in cases where the natural law conflicts with the positive law of nations (as it does, for example, in relation to the laws of war), which is to have priority. His method is in fact an eclectic one, and his works seek to assemble all the rules, natural and positive, that can be held to regulate relations among rulers and peoples. It is for this reason that naturalists and positivists both claim that Grotius belongs to their ancestry. It is this also that leads to the complaint that Grotius, while he expounds all the laws that bear upon a particular subject, fails to tell us what is *the* law.[10]

In the eighteenth, nineteenth, and early twentieth centuries the positivist school of international law grew and came to provide the orthodox approach to the subject. Grotius wrote at a time when international law had not yet become a specialist technique, and international lawyers did not yet constitute a distinct profession; when the great compendia or compilations of treaties and customary international law, providing the material on which positivist exponents of the law of nations were able to work, had not yet appeared; and when the positive law of nations that could be derived from ancient and medieval experience contained so many *lacunae* and was of such uncertain applicability to the circumstances of early modern times that it could not provide an adequate guide by itself. As the positive law of nations developed, based upon the accumulating experience of the practice of modern states, the development of archives and records, and the skills of a specialist profession, it came to be held that natural law had served its purpose of easing the transition from medieval to modern times and could now be discarded.

In the period since the First World War there has been a tendency among specialists in international law in Western countries to return to natural law, or at all events to take the view that a purely positivist approach is inadequate. In some cases, natural law criteria are explicitly reintroduced into the exposition of international law; in others, these criteria reappear in the guise of a 'policy-orientated' or 'social needs' approach that will take the place of the objective and value-free rendering of legal rules favoured by the positivists. As in

[10] See e.g. Hersch Lauterpacht, 'The Grotian Tradition in International Law', *British Year Book of International Law 1946*, pp. 1–53.

the case of Grotius, the turn towards natural law in the twentieth century, or search for surrogates for it, reflects a belief that existing positive rules are inadequate to regulate conduct in what are basically new circumstances (the advent of modern military technology, the ideological schism between communist and non-communist states, the emergence of a majority of non-European or non-Western states). It is claimed for an international law hospitable to natural law or to 'policy-orientated jurisprudence' that it provides a flexible instrument for coping with change. We have also to note, however, that the departure from strict standards of evidence of the consent of states, the eclectic method of stating a variety of rules without providing unambiguous criteria for choosing between them, the admission of concepts of 'quasi-law' or 'soft law', leads as in the case of Grotius to a blurring of the distinction between what is international law and what is not.

2. *The Universality of International Society*

Secondly, the international society conceived by Grotius was not composed merely of Christian or European rulers and peoples but was world-wide. This followed from Grotius' emphasis upon natural law as a basis of the rules affecting international relations, for the rules of natural law were rules for all men equally. But he also speaks of the great society of all mankind, and quotes the view of Themistius that wise kings take account not only of the kingdom that has been committed to them, but of the whole of mankind.[11] The independent political communities with which Europeans in Grotius' time were coming into contact in the Americas, on the coast of Africa, and in south and south-east Asia were, in his view, part of the great society of states. Such communities had rights of ownership, and also rights of political independence or sovereignty, of which they could not be deprived merely because they were infidels, or because Christian powers had discovered them, or because of papal donation or on grounds of rights of war.[12]

There was a Christian intellectual tradition which denied that non-Christian peoples could have rights of property or of

[11] *JBP*, Prolegomena 24.   [12] *JP*, chap. 12.

political independence. This was the argument advanced by Henry of Susa, Bishop of Ostia (thus called Ostiensis) in the thirteenth century, that all pagan peoples lost their rights to political independence with the coming of Christ, and that the rights they had previously had were then conferred upon believers. The view of Ostiensis was quoted by the Teutonic Knights at the Council of Constance 1414–18, to justify their wars of expansion against the pagan Lithuanians and against the Poles who were allied to them.[13] This exclusivist view, which divided mankind into Christian peoples who had full rights or who alone had rights, and non-Christian peoples who had only partial rights or were without rights, looked back to the distinction drawn in the ancient world between Greeks and barbarians, and forward to the distinction drawn in later European thought between civilized Europeans and semi-civilized or uncivilized non-Europeans.

In rejecting this view and insisting on the universality of international society Grotius was not stating anything new. The same stand had been taken nearly a century earlier by Vitoria, as Grotius acknowledges, in relation to Spain's conquests in the Indies. It harked back to the doctrine of Paulus Vladimiri, who confronted the views of the Teutonic Knights at the Council of Constance; to the doctrine of Aquinas, which clearly upheld the rights of non-Christian persons to property and non-Christian peoples to political independence; to the doctrine of Augustine, whose view Grotius quotes that Christ's commandment to love one's neighbour is to be understood as a commandment to love all human beings;[14] and ultimately to the Stoic doctrine of world citizenship, to which Grotius appeals in the Prolegomena to *De Jure Belli ac Pacis*.[15]

Grotius, of course, did not think that the rules governing relations among Christian states were *the same* as those affecting relations between Christian and non-Christian states.[16] It was not only by rules of natural law, but also by rules of

---

[13] See E. Christiansen, *The Northern Crusades: The Baltic and the Catholic Frontier 1100–1525* (London, 1980), chap. 9.

[14] *JP*, chap. 13.

[15] *JBP*, Prolegomena 24.

[16] For further discussion of the point see Wight, *Systems of States*, chap. 4, esp. pp. 125–8.

volitional human or positive law that inter-state relationships were constrained, and Christian states had developed among themselves a body of positive law that was of less than world-wide application. Grotius, indeed, has a strong sense of the special ties among Christian rulers and states. In considering just war, for example, he treats the question whether Christian states can justly make war on one another as separate from the wider question whether states in general can justly go to war; he likewise considers separately whether Christian states can seize prize from one another.[17] Grotius, moreover, believed in the propagation of the Christian faith: his *De Veritate Religionis Christianae* (*On the Truth of the Christian Religion*) is thought to have been written to assist seamen to carry out this task when visiting infidel countries.

Grotius accepted the argument of Vitoria that Christian powers were justified in resorting to force to assert their rights to trade; this doctrine, that there is a universal right of peoples to trade with one another, and a right to use force to assert it, formed a vital part of the rationale of European expansion from the time of the Spanish *conquistadores* to that of Commodore Perry. It sets aside the right which some non-European peoples have claimed, to choose to stay outside the international economy and international society, to insulate themselves from contact with other peoples and civilizations, and so to deny foreigners the rights of hospitality and trade to which, according to the mainstream of European or Western thinking, all peoples are entitled.

In the eighteenth century and, to a much greater extent, the nineteenth century, the idea that international society was world-wide and all-inclusive lost ground, both in theory and in practice, to the idea that it was a privileged association of Christian, European, or civilized states, from which other political communities were excluded wholly or in part, at least until such time as they were able to meet the standards laid down for admission by the founder members.[18] 'Europe' came to have a political and cultural (as distinct from a merely geographical) meaning, which it had scarcely yet begun to do

[17] *JP*, chaps. 3 and 4.
[18] See Gerrit W. Gong, *The Standard of 'Civilization' in International Society* (Oxford, 1984).

in Grotius' time.[19] The gap between European states and others in terms of level of economic and technological development, wealth, and military power, perceptible but not yet overwhelming in Grotius' time, was greatly magnified. The exclusivist doctrine of a Europe-centred international society which reached its apogee at the turn of the twentieth century corresponded to new realities of inequality established by the industrial revolution in Europe and America, while also serving to justify their maintenance.

In the twentieth century the European or European-centred society of states has finally given place to one which is global or universal.[20] The universal international society of today is still marked by deep inequalities and is still in many respects describable in terms of centre and periphery: but non-European or non-Western states have multiplied to become a majority of states in the system, and have taken their place as independent actors in the international legal order and in the international diplomatic order as well as in the international economy and the international political system or structure of power. Whereas the universal international society defined by Grotius and other natural law theorists was a merely theoretical or normative one, the universal international society of today is a political and economic reality. Its emergence, however, has stimulated a fresh interest in the writings of the early universalists and made the issues with which they concerned themselves topical once again.

3. *The Place of Individuals and Non-State Groups*

Thirdly, the members of international society in the view of Grotius are not merely states or the rulers of states but include groups other than states and, indeed, individual human beings. International society for Grotius is not just the society of states, it is the great society of all mankind.

Thus in the first paragraph of the first chapter of *De Jure Belli ac Pacis*, devoted to indicating the scope of his work, Grotius speaks not of controversies between rulers or states

---

[19] See Denys Hay, *Europe: The Emergence of an Idea*, 2nd edn. (Edinburgh, 1968).
[20] This theme is explored in H. Bull and A. Watson (eds.), *The Expansion of International Society* (Oxford, 1984).

but of 'controversies among those who are not held together
by a common bond of municipal law', which 'may arise among
those who have not yet united to form a nation, and those who
belong to different nations, both private persons and kings;
also those who have the same body of rights that kings have,
whether members of a ruling aristocracy, or free peoples.'[21]
Grotius, accordingly, deals in his treatise not only with what
today would be called public international law but with
private international law, and also with what might be called
cosmopolitan law or the law of the human community, in a
way suggestive of the emerging 'human rights law' of our own
times.

In dealing with war, for example, Grotius discusses and
upholds the right of private war, or war that is waged without
lawful authority, arguing that individual persons and groups
that are not public authorities do sometimes have the right to
resort to force.[22] He discusses the legality of acts done by
individuals in a public war.[23] He upholds the right of an
individual person to refuse to bear arms in an unjust war.[24] He
discusses good faith among private persons in a public war.[25]
His extensive discussion of the basis of contracts, torts,
promises, and succession, not simply as applied to relationships among states but in general, is beyond the scope of what
is thought of today as international law.

It is true that Grotius does give an especially prominent
place to states as opposed to individual persons and non-state
entities in his exposition of rights and duties, especially when
he is discussing the voluntary or positive law of nations. The
sovereign state, in Grotius' scheme, clearly has a privileged
position in relation to other bearers of rights and duties in the
great society of all mankind. Public war, for example, can be
waged only by those who have the support of the sovereign
power.[26] It is only those who have sovereign power that enjoy
the right of legation or of sending ambassadors.[27] If there is a
right of individuals and non-state groups to resort to private
war, it exists only in abnormal circumstances; under normal

[21] *JBP*, book I, chap. 1, §1.   [22] *JP*, chap. 12.
[23] *JBP*, book III, chap. 18.   [24] Ibid., book II, chap. 26, § 3.
[25] Ibid., book III, chap. 23.   [26] Ibid., book III, chap. 3, § 4.
[27] Ibid., book II, chap. 18.

conditions, the right to resort to force is the privilege of the sovereign state. In Grotius' time neither the sovereign state nor the conventions defining its role in European or world politics were by any means yet fully matured, and the process of homogenization of a variety of kinds of independent political community in Europe into a single political and legal form, carrying with it a single set of rights and duties, was still in an early stage. But the effect of Grotius' discussion of sovereignty, which he defines as not being subject in one's actions to the legal control of another, is to take that process further.

Moreover, it would be quite mistaken to view Grotius as the champion of 'human rights' in the sense in which this phrase is interpreted by Western liberals at the present time. Indeed, there is warrant for the idea often expressed that Grotius, in his view of the relationship between man and the state, was an 'absolutist' or 'Hobbesian'. The subjects of the state, he says, have no right of rebellion by natural law.[28] Sovereignty, he says, does not reside in the people.[29] The desire of a subject people for freedom, he tells us, is not a just cause for war.[30] Sovereign princes, according to Grotius, in some circumstances at least, may enjoy a right of patrimony, that is, of disposing of subject peoples irrespective of their will.[31] Grotius appears very remote from the doctrine of Locke and his disciples among the American and French revolutionaries, that individuals enjoy 'natural rights' against government. Equally, Grotius' ideas are remote from the doctrines with which Rousseau, Vattel, and others in the eighteenth century transformed thinking about international relations: that the true sovereigns are not rulers or governments but peoples or nations; that international relations are therefore relations among these peoples or nations; that peoples have a right to determine who rules them, and cannot be bartered about from one ruler to another without regard for their will.

Nevertheless, Grotius clearly sees the great society of all mankind as the starting-point for his discussion of right conduct in international relations, and regards the society of rulers, governments, or states as no more than part of that

---

[28] Ibid., book I, chap. 4, § 2.
[29] Ibid., book I, chap. 3, § 8.
[30] Ibid., book II, chap. 22, § 11.
[31] Ibid., book I, chap. 3, § 12.

great society. He clearly treats the individual person, endowed with reason and thus with access to rules of natural law against which all merely human volitional or positive law can be judged, as an actor in international relations in his own right, and a bearer of rights and duties that can override those that are imposed by positive law. Moreover, in speaking of Grotius' rejection of the right of people to make war on their rulers, or of nations to liberate themselves, we need to remember that the Dutch struggle for independence from Spain was in one of its several aspects a war of national liberation or self-determination, and that Grotius was a patriotic supporter of this struggle and the author of histories of it.[32] Grotius distinguishes between a state or politically organized community and its prince or ruler, and acknowledges the right of the former to make war upon the latter.[33] While a people as such has no right to resort to force against a ruler, such a right is possessed by an organized community acting under the authority of its magistrates against a prince who has transgressed the law; the Dutch provinces, in resisting the King of Spain, were availing themselves of this right.

From the mid-eighteenth to the early twentieth century a more state-centred conception of international society came to prevail: by the time of the First World War, the orthodox view was that sovereign states were the only subjects of international law, or bearers of rights and duties in it, while individual persons and non-state groups were mere objects of international law, even though they had moral rights and duties as distinct from legal ones. At the same time another change was taking place in the prevailing conception of international society, in some ways antithetical to the state-centred conception, although also antithetical to the doctrine of Grotius. This was the change from the idea of an international society of states or governments to an international society of peoples or nations. The doctrine of national self-determination proclaimed that states should be nation-states, and that nations should be states. Dramatically recognized in the American

---

[32] Most notably, the *Annales et Historiae de Rebus Belgicis*, published posthumously in Amsterdam in 1657.

[33] *JBP*, book 1, chap. 4; *JP*, chap. 13.

and French revolutions, carried forward in the next century and a half in the movements for national unification or independence among European peoples and peoples of European descent outside Europe, the doctrine has more recently extended its impact through the processes of national liberation in Asia, Africa, and Oceania.

In the course of the twentieth century the state-centred view of international law and international morality has gone into retreat. The rights and duties of individual persons have been recognized to have a place in international relations through the 1948 UN Universal Declaration of Human Rights, the 1966 covenants on human rights, and many other documents, just as those of non-state groups have been recognized in response to the growth of international organizations, multinational business corporations, international political movements, and nationalist or national liberation organizations. Some of the confusion and uncertainty as to just who is or is not a full member of international society, evident in the work of Grotius himself, characterizes the present debate among international lawyers and moralists as to who are the bearers of rights and duties in international relations.

4. Solidarism in the Enforcement of Rules

Fourthly, Grotius' particular conception of international society is marked by what we may call solidarism, by the stress it places upon the actual or potential solidarity of international society in defining and enforcing its own rules.[34] His view still carries overtones of the political theory of medieval Latin Christendom, and stands in contrast to the pluralist doctrines of exponents of the idea of international society in the eighteenth and nineteenth centuries.

This comes out most clearly in Grotius' exposition of his doctrine of just war. The distinction between just and unjust causes of war is one which Grotius takes to be apparent to all men, by virtue of their endowment with reason. In accordance with traditional Christian doctrine, Grotius rejects the view

---

[34] The theme of this section is developed at greater length in Bull, 'The Grotian Conception of International Society', in H. Butterfield and M. Wight (eds.), *Diplomatic Investigations* (London, 1966).

that war can be just on both sides, while allowing for the possibility that it may be just on neither side. The grounds for the waging of just war include not only defence, but the recovery of property and the infliction of punishment. Not only does the injured party have a right to wage war to these ends; others have the right to come to the injured party's assistance, indeed there is a general right of participation in a just war conferred by 'the mutual tie of kinship among men'.

Grotius' notion of an objective distinction between just and unjust causes of war that is apparent to all men and confers a general right affects his treatment of the rules governing the conduct of war. In natural law, according to Grotius, just conduct in war derives from the justice of one's cause, and anything is permissible that is necessary for attaining the just end. Grotius goes on to explain that in the voluntary law of nations a lawful war is one waged by a sovereign power and preceded by a declaration of war, and that this holds true irrespective of the justice of the cause. Nevertheless, Grotius does not seek to show whether it is natural law or the voluntary law of nations that should take priority on this issue.[35]

In discussing the role of neutrals or of 'those who are of neither side in war' Grotius argues that their duty is not to be wholly impartial but to discriminate in favour of the party with the just cause, by allowing transit across their territory (the famous doctrine of 'qualified neutrality').[36] The party with a just cause, likewise, has the right to violate neutral territory, whereas the party with an unjust cause does not. In discussing the duty of the individual person to bear arms on behalf of the state, Grotius holds that this is limited by that person's judgement as to whether or not the cause he is being asked to fight for is a just one. Similarly, Grotius holds that the obligations of an alliance are not binding if they are invoked in order to embark upon an unjust war.

International legal theory in the eighteenth and nineteenth centuries came to play down the distinction between just and unjust causes of war, and ultimately to exclude it from positive international law altogether. The doctrine was proclaimed

[35] *JBP*, book III, chaps. 1–9.
[36] Ibid., book III, chap. 17.

that international law sought only to regulate the conduct of war, relegating controversy about the reasons for resorting to war to the sphere of morals or of politics. The view was firmly stated that the law of war applied equally to both sides in any war; that belligerents had the duty to respect the rights of neutrals, and neutrals the duty of absolute impartiality; that international law could have nothing to say about the obligation of the individual citizen to fight for his country, which was a matter of municipal law.

In the period since the First World War there has been a return to the solidarist doctrine of Grotius. In the era of the League of Nations and the United Nations the distinction between just and unjust causes of war was reaffirmed, and written into positive international law. The doctrine of collective security under the League Covenant or the UN Charter brought into question the right of states to remain neutral in an enforcement action approved by the international community as a whole, or to adopt a posture of complete impartiality between the belligerents if they did so. The right, perhaps even the duty, of the individual person to defy his own state if it was engaged in an unjust war, was raised by the Nuremberg and Tokyo war crimes tribunals.

By no means all that Grotius has to say serves to support what we have been calling a solidarist point of view; the pluralist conception may also be found in Grotius who, on this issue as on so many others, may be found wrestling with contending doctrines. Interpreters of Grotius sometimes see him, not unreasonably, as seeking to advance the idea that the laws of war apply equally to both parties, or that belligerents have the duty to respect the rights of neutrals and neutrals the duty to be impartial. Yet if Grotius was moving away from the solidarist viewpoint inherited from the middle ages, he was also deeply marked by it.

5. *The Absence of International Institutions*

Fifthly, Grotius' idea of international society takes little or no account of international institutions. In the eighteenth and nineteenth centuries, and to a much greater extent in the twentieth century, exponents of the concept of an international

society were able to point to institutions which served to
maintain that society and provided concrete evidence of its
existence: international law, the system of diplomatic representation, international organizations, the maintenance of
a balance of power, the special role played by the great
powers. In Grotius' time these institutions existed only in
embryo; the international society he describes is an ideal or
normative one, for which there was as yet little concrete
historical evidence.

Grotius' account of the voluntary law of nations did, it is
true, draw together what was known about the existing
practice of states, and provide a foundation upon which
positive international law was later to build. But in Grotius'
thinking, and indeed in his time, there was not yet any conception of international law as a distinct science, or of international lawyers as members of a distinct profession.

Resident diplomacy was well established throughout Europe
by the time of Grotius, and he himself had experience of it
(although his service as Swedish ambassador in Paris did not
come till a decade after the publication of *De Jure Belli ac
Pacis*). Grotius, moreover, made important contributions to
diplomatic law, especially in elaborating the concept of
extraterritoriality. But the professionalization of diplomacy in
Europe did not come until the eighteenth century, the rise of
functional international organizations until the nineteenth
and the emergence of permanent conference diplomacy, or
general international political organizations, until the twentieth. Grotius does not give much prominence to his discussion
of the law of embassies or seek to treat the diplomatic system
as evidence of the existence of an international society.

From the early eighteenth century until the early twentieth
century it was commonly asserted that the international
system depended upon the preservation of a balance of power;
from the time of Vattel on, this concept found its way into the
writings of international lawyers, some of whom even asserted
that the principle that such a balance should be maintained
was itself part of international law, or at least a condition of its
efficacy. In Grotius' time, however, the concept of the balance
of power had not yet achieved the prominence it was to attain
early in the next century, in the course of the War of the

Spanish Succession, even though it was by no means unknown and in reality a balance between the power of France and that of Habsburg Spain and Austria was already basic to the emerging states system. Grotius makes no mention of the balance of power, and his clear rejection of the concept of preventive war is at loggerheads with balance of power thinking. Nor can we find in the work of Grotius any reference to the concept of a great power, with special rights and duties in relation to the international society as a whole, such as was to emerge in the course of the series of great peace conferences beginning with the Congress of Westphalia and punctuating European history, and is sanctified today in the special rights and duties of a permanent member of the UN Security Council.

(f) GROTIUS AND THE STUDY OF INTERNATIONAL RELATIONS TODAY

Let me return to the question of the bearing of Grotius' ideas on the study of international relations today. It is absurd to read Grotius as if he were speaking to us directly about the problems of our own times. Thus it can make no sense to attempt to harness the name of Grotius to one or another of the political causes of the twentieth century, as many have tried to do. Early in this century, for example, the Dutch jurist Cornelis van Vollenhoven sought to associate Grotius with the cause of collective security and the League of Nations.[37] C. H. Alexandrowicz some years ago, arguing the case for recognition of a universal international society and the need to overcome Eurocentric approaches to international law, seemed to want to make Grotius stand for a more enlightened policy towards the Third World.[38] I have heard it argued that if Grotius were alive today he would have been in favour of the 1982 Law of the Sea Convention.

In the same way it is a mark of shallowness or superficiality in our historical thinking to find fault with views of Grotius

---

[37] C. van Vollenhoven, 'Grotius and Geneva', *Bibliotheca Visseriana*, 6 (1926), pp. 5–44.
[38] C. H. Alexandrowicz, *An Introduction to the History of the Law of Nations in the East Indies* (London, 1967).

formulated against the background and in relation to the problems of the seventeenth century because they offend against some political attitude of our own towards the problems of the present time. The charges, for example, that Grotius was an 'authoritarian' in his approach to domestic politics and government, that like most northern Europeans of his time he was an 'imperialist' inasmuch as he accepted some of the leading justifications for European expansion, or that unlike thinkers of the Enlightenment writing a century or so later he failed to denounce cruel or barbarous practices in warfare in the strong terms we should ourselves use today, involve anachronism and confusion of categories, even if they have some foundation.

It is, moreover, no fair criticism of a view held three centuries ago by Grotius that he did not take account of changes that have taken place in the conditions of international politics that now render it invalid. Thus there would be widespread agreement today with Professor Röling's comment below that in the era of nuclear weapons there can be no basis either in law or in common prudence for the idea that war may be initiated by states not only to defend themselves against military attack but also to defend themselves against a wide range of threats of a non-military nature. Neither the wide interpretation Grotius gave to the right of self-defence, nor the right to resort to force to recover property, nor yet the right forcibly to inflict punishment, command much support today among those who have thought seriously about these matters. But it is not a shortcoming of Grotius' that he formulated his doctrine of *jus ad bellum* in relation to the very different technological conditions of his own times.

We may doubt whether it is a just charge against Grotius that consciously or unconsciously he allowed his views to be influenced by the interests of his client, the Dutch East India Company, or of the Dutch or Swedish state, in whose employ he found himself at different stages in his life. Grotius was in part a visionary, a thinker who in his view of the world was able to stand back from the commonplace assumptions of his time, to conceive alternatives to established ways of doing things in the field of international relations and to urge his contemporaries forward towards new and better goals and means of reaching them. But if he had been only a visionary and not also a man of affairs with views rooted in his own time and place, if his writings had not reflected some of the views of the powerful even while rejecting others, if they had not given some play to the interests that were predominant in seventeenth-century Europe even while condemning others, they could not have had the impact on thought and action that in the event they did have. The seminal works of policy are those whose authors are not mere visionaries but are able to take account of the prevailing forces and reshape or redirect them.

The importance of Grotius lies in the part he played in establishing the idea of international society—an idea that provides one of the several paradigms in terms of which we have thought about international relations in modern times, and that, for better or worse, provides the constitutional principle in terms of which international relations today are in fact conducted. Grotius was not the sole originator of this idea. His own formulations of it, as we have seen, have been subject to frequent modification and remain so. Nor is the idea itself to be regarded as sacrosanct or beyond dispute. But by raising the most fundamental questions about modern international relations, by assembling all the best that has been thought and said in answer to them, and by providing us with a systematic exposition of his own particular conception of international society, Grotius assured for himself a place as one of the master theorists of the subject.

3

Grotius and the International Politics of the Seventeenth Century

C. G. ROELOFSEN

International lawyers generally agree on according Grotius a prominent place among the founding fathers of their branch of jurisprudence, a *communis opinio* to which in 1983 an impressive number of symposia and occasional publications bore witness.[1] Interest in Grotius, however, is not limited to international lawyers, nor is it a transitory curiosity, arising solely from the 1583–1983 quatercentenary. Grotius is generally credited with, and quoted as the proponent of, a 'Grotian' theory of international relations, which is to be found especially in *De Jure Belli ac Pacis*,[2] but which is also detected by some in his other works and is seen as the mainspring of his political and diplomatic activities.[3] The belief in this 'Grotian' model of international relations has undoubtedly added considerably to Grotius' fame. Just as *Mare Liberum* has acquired a new topicality because of the contemporary discussions on the regime of the sea,[4] a view of Grotius as the prophet of an idealistic legal international order has inspired many recent

[1] A. C. G. M. Eyffinger, B. Vermeulen, and J. C. M. Willems, 'Grotius Commemoration 1983', *Grotiana*, 6 (1985), pp. 71–114. A bibliography is regularly published in *Grotiana*, supplementing J. ter Meulen and P. J. J. Diermanse, *Bibliographie des écrits imprimés de Hugo Grotius* (The Hague, 1950); and eid., *Bibliographie des écrits imprimés sur Hugo Grotius* (The Hague, 1961). The most recent biography is H. J. M. Nellen, *Hugo de Groot (1583-1645), De loopbaan van een geleerd staatsman* (Weesp, 1985).
[2] See e.g. Hedley Bull, 'The Grotian Conception of International Society', in H. Butterfield and M. Wright (eds.), *Diplomatic Investigations* (London, 1966), pp. 51–73.
[3] P. H. Kooijmans, 'How to Handle the Grotian Heritage: Grotius and Van Vollenhoven', *Netherlands International Law Review*, 30 (1983), pp. 81–92, is a good example.
[4] See Asser Instituut, *International Law and the Grotian Heritage* (The Hague, 1985), pp. 54–110.

publications.[5] Around Grotius, it is fair to say, a legend has grown. His name is one to conjure with, particularly of course in the Netherlands, where C. van Vollenhoven initiated something like a cult of Grotius.[6] This has stimulated research, leading to the publication of important source material, like Grotius' correspondence,[7] and the records of Anglo-Dutch negotiations in 1613 and 1615.[8]

The rich documentation on most stages of Grotius' career which we have thus acquired, mostly under the inspiration of the 'Grotian legend',[9] enables us critically to examine that legend. But at the same time it enormously adds to our task of reassessment, particularly since there is as yet no fully documented modern biography of Grotius.[10] Yet it is of

---

[5] C. S. Edwards, *Hugo Grotius, The Miracle of Holland: A Study in Political and Legal Thought* (Chicago, Ill., 1981) and its introduction by R. A. Falk may be quoted as instances of this interpretation.

[6] C. van Vollenhoven, *The Three Stages in the Evolution of the Law of Nations* (The Hague, 1919); and id., 'Grotius and Geneva', *Bibliotheca Visseriana*, 6 (1926), pp. 1–81. For van Vollenhoven's interpretation of Grotius see also id., 'The Land of Grotius', *Lectures on Holland for American Students, Leyden University July 1924* (Leiden, 1924), p. 113: 'But, if my notion be right and my interpretation true, Grotius's book, though old-fashioned in its Latin form and its quotations, is a quite modern book; for it is only since the first Peace Conference (1899) or rather since the outbreak of the war (1914) that the problem of punishing a culprit occupies the public mind.'

[7] By 1988 twelve volumes had appeared under the title *Briefwisseling van Hugo Grotius* (The Hague, 1928–), bringing the publication of Grotius' correspondence (both his own and the letters addressed to him) up to 1641. Publication of the Grotius correspondence is undertaken by the Grotius Institute (established in The Hague) of the Royal Netherlands Academy. A modern edition of Grotius' letters to the Swedish Chancellor Axel Oxenstierna is *Rikskanseleren Axel Oxenstierna Skrifter och Brefvexling, utgifna af. Kongl. Vitterhets-Historie och Antigvitets-Akademien: Hugonis Grotii Epistolae ad Axelium Oxenstierna* (2 vols., Stockholm, 1889, 1891).

[8] G. N. Clark and W. J. M. van Eysinga, 'The Colonial Conferences between England and The Netherlands in 1613 and 1615', *Bibliotheca Visseriana*, 15 (1940); ibid., 17 (1951).

[9] The publication of the correspondence was undertaken at the instance of van Vollenhoven and continued after his death (1933), to a large extent because of the influence exercised by W. J. M. van Eysinga.

[10] Nellen's short biography (n. 1 above) is, as the author correctly describes it, an elaborated version of his essay 'Hugo Grotius (1583–1645): Geschichte seines lebens basierend auf seiner Korrespondenz', *Nachbarn* (Publications of the Dutch embassy in the German Federal Republic), 28 (1983). It is much to be regretted that the late Prof. Poelhekke could not finish his essay on Grotius' political aspirations. J. J. Poelhekke, 'Hugo Grotius as a frustrated Dutch Statesman', *Hugo Grotius, A Great European 1583–1645: Complete Translations of the Dutch Articles Abridged for the Exhibition Catalogue Het delfts Orakel, Hugo de Groot*, pp. 67–78; and id., 'Grotius a Frustrated Dutch Statesman?' in *The World of Hugo Grotius (1583–1645)* (Amsterdam, 1984), pp. 13–14. The use of Grotius' letters as the foremost, and now readily available,

considerable importance, if we want to avoid the rather indiscriminate use of the epithet 'Grotian' in combination with terms like 'heritage', 'tradition', or 'concept',[11] to examine the circumstances surrounding the composition of Grotius' major works on international law, and Grotius' own attitude to the 'Grotian' concept held to be enshrined in them. Of course, an author, particularly after his death, is not responsible for the interpretation given to his works. It may be argued that, since *De Jure Belli ac Pacis* exercised an undoubted influence towards the general adoption of the 'Law of Nations', the *jus gentium*,[12] as the expression of a legal relationship between the members of the community of states, Grotius' own views matter much less than his intellectual parenthood of the ideas that go by his name. Why, indeed, drag in the author if only his books really matter? This attitude, sensible in many cases where one has to deal with authors who are intellectuals first and foremost, and where textual criticism is indeed the appropriate method of analysis, is in our opinion not satisfactory as regards Grotius. This is especially so as he never considered himself as an 'author', but continually aspired to public office.

Grotius' own attitude therefore warrants our attempt to arrive at an analysis of his works, at least those of a legal and political character,[13] by starting from his career. The major works with which we are here concerned, *Mare Liberum* and *De Jure Belli ac Pacis*, owe much to their author's political ambitions and to his experience of public affairs. Their publication is more or less closely connected with Grotius' career. Indeed, while it would be an exaggeration to describe Grotius' interest

source of information has its hazards. Since other sources of the same intimate nature are often lacking, we may tend to describe events too much from Grotius' point of view.

[11] See above, nn. 2–4.

[12] On Grotius' own use of the term, see P. Haggenmacher, 'Genèse et signification du concept de "ius gentium" chez Grotius', *Grotiana*, 2 (1981), pp. 44–102. The standard account is A. Nussbaum, *A Concise History of the Law of Nations* (New York, 1962), p. 109.

[13] This is not to suggest that Grotius' literary and theological works did not have political implications. Indeed, distinctions are often hard to draw in this respect, but a discussion of Grotius as a man of letters is not intended here. See Eyffinger, *Grotius Poeta, aspecten van Hugo Grotius' dichterschap* (The Hague, 1981), English summary, pp. 301–19; and C. Gellinek, *Hugo Grotius* (Boston, Mass.; 1983).

in international law as *merely* incidental to his role in Dutch and international politics, there would be rather more truth in that than in the converse position, namely, of considering the 'sage of Delft' as the impartial jurisconsult of mankind in accordance with his declaration in the Prolegomena.[14] It is fair to warn the reader that the elaboration of our subject as defined in this introduction will suffer from lack of space and, more seriously, from lack of information on some crucial questions.[15] Yet it seems preferable to offer suggestions which may be questioned, rather than present the reader with an exposition of Grotius' career that does not try to establish the connections between the politician/diplomat and the author of *De Jure Belli ac Pacis*.

(a) GROTIUS AT THE PERIPHERY OF DUTCH POLITICS, 1599–1613

Any description of Grotius' career has to start with the milieu in which he was born, since this exercised an important and lasting influence on his position in Dutch society as well as on his political and religious views. As the son of an influential burgomaster of Delft, traditionally one of the leading cities in the County of Holland, Grotius belonged to the town's small circle of ruling families: in other words, he was a member of the patriciate of so-called 'regents' which dominated public life in Holland and Zeeland. The family connections of the De

---

[14] *JBP*, Prolegomena 58. The edition by the Carnegie Institution, ed. James Brown Scott (Classics of International Law, Washington, DC, 1913), a reproduction of the text of 1646, omits the division of the Prolegomena into paragraphs which was introduced only after Grotius' death. The English translation by F. W. Kelsey (Classics of International Law, Washington, DC, 1925; repr. New York and London, 1964) retains the numbering. As Feenstra has demonstrated, the usual division of the Prolegomena is not always correct: 'Hugo de Groots oordeel over de 16e eeuwse beoefenaars van het Romeinse recht, Een herinterpretatie van par. 55 der Prolegomena', *Na oorlog en vrede* (Arnhem, 1984), pp. 23–9. See also the critical remarks on the editions of *JBP* by Feenstra in 'Quelques remarques sur les sources utilisées par Grotius dans ses travaux de droit naturel', in *The World of Hugo Grotius*, pp. 67–71.

[15] As the edition of Oxenstierna's letters has not yet been continued, it is for instance hardly possible to assess Grotius' diplomatic activities from the viewpoint of his employer.

Groot family[16] were not unimportant, since members of the family had already been sitting on the town corporation well before 1572. Oldenbarnevelt, the Advocate of Holland, was a friend of Jan de Groot, Grotius' father. So was the leading scientist of the Dutch Republic, Simon Stevin.[17] In this intellectually stimulating climate the precocious Grotius developed to a remarkable degree the characteristic attitudes of the Holland regents. His cultivation of humanistic studies, though exceptional in its level, fitted in with traditions cherished since at least the time of Erasmus.[18] Religious toleration, mixed with a good share of anti-clericalism, together with the veneration of *bonae literae*, is generally described as a major characteristic of the 'regents', and is loosely called 'Erasmian', or, alternatively, 'Erastian'.[19] Grotius, himself the son of a mixed marriage,[20] had the broad Protestant religious opinions that were usual among the leading circles of the Dutch Republic at about 1600.[21] In his

[16] Or more correctly 'Cornets de Groot', since the family descended from the Burgundian nobleman Corneille Cornets who married the daughter of the Delft burgomaster De Groot at the beginning of the 16th century.

[17] Did Stevin exercise an intellectual influence on Grotius, and is Grotius to be reckoned among the adepts of a 'mathematical method', or 'mos geometricus'? See H. van Eikema Hommes, 'Grotius on Natural and International Law', *Netherlands International Law Review*, 30 (1983), pp. 61–72. We rather agree with A. Dufour, 'Grotius et le droit naturel du dix-septième siècle', in *The World of Hugo Grotius*, pp. 15–42. The *Briefwisseling* only mentions Stevin as a go-between of Prince Maurice's after Grotius' arrest on 29 Aug. 1618.

[18] Was there a difference between the intellectual climate of Holland (at least before the Revolt) and that of the other provinces, the Holland patricians being less inclined to academic studies, as is suggested by J. den Tex in his classical biography of Holland's leading politician? *Oldenbarnevelt* (5 vols., Haarlem, 1960–72), i. 29–30. We quote from the Dutch original edition; an English translation exists under the same title (2 vols., London, 1973). On Grotius' own appreciation of Erasmus, see R. Pintard, *La Mothe le Vayer, Gassendi, Guy Patin. Etudes de bibliographie et de critique, suivies de textes inédits de Guy Patin* (Paris, 1943), pp. 69–86.

[19] After Thomas Erastus, theologian at Heidelberg, whose views on the relation between Church and State, or rather on the subordination of the former to the latter, were very influential. Den Tex, *Oldenbarnevelt*, i. 62 ff.; iii. 14 ff.; and v. 95.

[20] There is a well-known anecdote of Grotius, aged twelve, converting his Roman Catholic mother to Protestantism. Van Eysinga, *Huigh de Groot* (Haarlem, 1945), p. 7, after Caspar Brandt's biography. There is nothing unusual in such a mixed marriage. Among the prominent groups in the Dutch Republic, for instance among the nobility of Holland, Roman Catholics were not exceptional; H. F. K. van Nierop, *Van Ridders tot Regenten* (Dieren, 1984), p. 208.

[21] This is to be stressed in view of the often depicted 'evolution' of the 'Calvinist' Grotius towards broader religious views. It seems more correct to describe Grotius' religious position as essentially unchanging in its confrontation with the assertion of

choice of a career, too, he conformed to the regular practice by establishing himself as an advocate in the Hague, at the bar of the two supreme courts of Holland and Zeeland in 1599,[22] after a brief study of law.[23] The legal profession, very much the usual preparation for public office at the time,[24] was probably taken up by Grotius for social reasons, in preference to a university career as a philologian, which was no doubt open to him.[25]

Ambition, particularly *political* ambition, seems the main-spring of young Grotius' activities, both as a lawyer and as a publicist. His successes at the bar, attested by his remarkable rise to high legal office already in 1607,[26] led to consultations on legal-political questions by the Stadtholder, Prince Maurice,[27] and by the powerful Dutch East India Company. Grotius' political reliability was reflected in his appointment (1601) as Latin historiographer of Holland. The position was one of trust, in view of the delicate questions bound up with the description of the recent past. The interpretation of the Dutch Revolt against Spanish rule had important implications both for constitutional practice in the Republic of the United Netherlands and for its international position. Most observers outside the Dutch Republic (and a considerable section of its inhabitants too) entertained serious doubts about the legitim-acy of the States regime and considered it unworkable in the long term. This attitude, that was to persist up to about

Calvinistic orthodoxy. A. H. Haentjens, *Hugo de Groot als godsdienstig denker* (Amsterdam, 1946). The recently discovered manuscript of Grotius' first theological work is briefly discussed by G. H. M. Posthumus Meyjes, 'Het vroegste theologische geschrift van Hugo de Groot herontdekt, zijn *Meletius* (1611)', in S. Groenveld *et al.* (eds.), *Bestuurders en Geleerden: opstellen aangeboden aan J. J. Woltjer* (Amsterdam, 1985), pp. 75–84. See also below, n. 87.

[22] The traditional 'Hof' (dating from 1428) and the recent 'Hooge Raad' (1582).
[23] Did Grotius study law at Leiden? His uncle Cornelius was one of the professors of the law faculty. Apart from the date of Grotius' doctorate at Orléans (5 May 1598), we know nothing about his studies in France. He appears to have been a self-taught lawyer.
[24] For instance Oldenbarnevelt and John de Witt both started their careers at the bar. See H. H. Rowen, *John de Witt* (Princeton, NJ, 1975), p. 21.
[25] See *Briefwisseling*, vol. i, p. xvi.
[26] His appointment as 'Advocaat Fiscaal' of the States of Holland. This office combined the duties of public prosecutor in criminal cases and of legal adviser to the States.
[27] E.g. regarding Maurice's succession to the County of Mörs (Meurs) in the Rhineland, D. P. de Bruyn (ed.), *The Opinions of Grotius* (London, 1894), pp. 311 ff.

1630,[28] was all too understandable at the beginning of the seventeenth century, because the Dutch, losing their French and English allies in 1598 and 1604 respectively,[29] found themselves confronting the Spanish monarchy alone. It seemed unlikely that a ramshackle republic would be able to maintain itself against the great military power of the age. Of course, there were elements of strength in the Dutch position too, such as their formidable defensive situation and their economic prosperity.[30] Yet in the last resort the Dutch Republic had to rely on foreign assistance, called forth by fears of Habsburg dominance in Europe, especially once the financial drain of the 'guerra de Flandes' had been removed from Spain.

In the circumstances, to present the Dutch case in terms that made sense to the European learned public was a task of some importance. Grotius performed it by creating, or at least divulging, an historical apology for the States regime, comparable with other national histories produced by the humanist historiographers of the sixteenth and seventeenth centuries.[31] The thesis of continuity between the Batavian Republic of antiquity and the Holland of his own day, outlined in Grotius' *De Antiquitate*, first published in 1610,[32] may strike the modern reader as extremely implausible from the start, and was indeed perhaps doubted by Grotius himself at a later stage in his life.[33] It has, however, to be compared

[28] J. J. Poelhekke, *'t Uytgaen van den Treves* (Groningen, 1960), pp. 120 ff. See also J. I. Israel, *The Dutch Republic and the Hispanic World 1606–1661* (Oxford, 1982), pp. 18, 78 ff.

[29] By the treaties of Vervins and of London, the one concluded under duress by the French King Henry IV, the other inaugurating James I's pacific reign.

[30] G. Parker, *Spain and the Netherlands, 1559–1659* (Glasgow, 1979), pp. 199 ff., provides a convenient summing-up. See also Israel, *Dutch Republic*.

[31] A. E. M. Janssen, 'Grotius als Geschichtsschreiber', *The World of Hugo Grotius*, pp. 161–78; J. Bell, *Hugo Grotius Historian* (Ann Arbor, Mich., 1973; fac. copy of Ph.D. thesis Columbia University), pp. 303 ff.

[32] Ter Meulen and Diermanse, *Bibliographie*, 1950, nos. 691–710A. See also Eyffinger *et al.* (eds.), 'De Republica emendanda', *Grotiana*, 5 (1984), pp. 34–40.

[33] At least if the well-known admissions in his correspondence that he had written in his youth much that was to be ascribed to, and excused by, his youthful patriotic ardour are considered as referring *inter alia* to the constitutional aspects of *De Antiquitate*. Of course, Grotius never publicly disavowed the 'Batavian' thesis. *De Antiquitate* was still reprinted to provide an argument in the current discussion on the Republic's constitution as late as 1757. Ter Meulen and Diermanse, *Bibliographie*, 1950, no. 708.

C. G. Roelofsen

with the Trojan and Greek genealogies, still current at the time, if we want to appreciate its impact. It provided a much-needed 'classical' justification for the constitutional theory with which the Dutch Revolt was associated from its beginning: the doctrine of the States' rights. According to this, the provincial States as constitutional legislative institutions held an important position in government independent of the monarch's wish to consult them.[34] Grotius, setting the pattern followed by the great majority of Dutch constitutional theorists up to 1795, pretended that sovereignty rested with the provincial States, not only since the Revolt, but also in the 'monarchical' period of the 'Hollandic, formerly Batavian Republic'. The Counts of Holland, according to Grotius, had never been 'monarchs' in the real sense, but only the hereditary executive officers of the Republic, appointed by the States. This theory, still upheld in *De Jure Belli ac Pacis*,[35] absolved the Dutch from the accusation of being rebels against their lawful ruler—a very serious accusation in the eyes of monarchical Europe, and in those of the legally minded regents themselves.[36] Still, though Grotius was to

[34] E. H. Kossmann and A. F. Mellink, *Texts Concerning the Revolt of the Netherlands* (Cambridge, 1975) contains most key documents of the constitutional conflict.

[35] It is explicitly stated in *JP*, chap. 11, part 1, art. 1: 'Hollandiae, quae justa jam a septem saeculis respublica est, Ordinum auctoritas' ('Shortly thereafter, the States Assembly of Holland (which has been a true commonwealth for all of seven centuries) added its authority to the movement. For it is, of course, a well-known fact that this body was set up in addition to the princes and governing officials, as a guardian of the rights of the people' (Classics of International Law, p. 169)).

The discussion of the relations between rulers and subjects in *JBP*, book 1, chaps. 3 and 4 is of course much more general. Grotius explicitly rejects a *general* right of subjects to resistance (chap. 4, §§ 2–6). In particular he attacks the French Calvinist school of so-called 'monarchomachs' who upheld a right of resistance against monarchical authority, to be exercised if not by private individuals at least by subordinate officials (chap. 4, § 6. 1). However, Grotius modifies his defence of 'sovereign authority' by the admission of the historic rights of States Assemblies, especially in chap. 4, § 14. Grotius' reference to the historic rights of Brabant and Flanders (chap. 4, § 14, n. 3) in particular fits in with the by then traditional 'constitutional' motivation of the Dutch Revolt.

See also Q. Skinner, *The Foundations of Modern Political Thought* (2 vols., Cambridge, 1978), ii. 309 ff. on the Calvinist doctrine. Kossmann, *Politieke Theorie in het 17e-eeuwse Nederland* (Amsterdam, 1960), pp. 19, 78 considers *JBP* as 'absolutist' in tendency. In view of Grotius' qualifications, indicated above, we think this conclusion too precise.

[36] However, doubts as to the legitimate character of the Republic still lingered on. The French King Henry IV is recorded as having called the Dutch provinces 'libres, mais non pas souverains', in a conversation with the English ambassador Carew in Jan. 1609; S. Barendrecht, *François van Aerssen* (Leiden, 1965), p. 220.

present himself throughout as a defender of the 'aristocratic' constitution of Holland—and consequently of the Dutch Republic—he seems at the beginning of his career to have had his doubts about some of its characteristics. The criticism in his manuscript *De Republica emendanda* directed against the preponderant position of the provincial States, and favouring a stronger central government, makes rather odd reading if one considers Grotius' later impassioned defence of provincial sovereignty.[37] Projects of reforms like those sketched by Grotius were, however, not unusual at the time. Indeed, even Oldenbarnevelt seems to have toyed with similar ideas.[38] Besides, it is hardly to be doubted that *De Republica emendanda* remained strictly *in petto*. It represents a mental exercise, interesting as indicating one of the first stages, indeed probably the first stage, of Grotius' political development, but nothing more.[39]

Being a lawyer with a growing reputation, a Latin author of

[37] 'De Republica emendanda', p. 53: 'In provinciali imperio nimis ampla conventus ordinum potestas videtur'; likewise Grotius favours a restriction of the power of the States General (ibid., p. 54), and a strengthening of the Council of State, to be presided over by a 'summus praefectus', also commander-in-chief. The States General were to be a consultative assembly (ibid., p. 59). Grotius in fact reverts to a great extent to the situation before the Revolt. The Council of State, formerly advising the Prince or his Governor General, now is to exercise sovereign powers ('cui leges de re quavis ferendi, iubendique omnibus potestas sit, qui de bello, pace, federibus statuat'). The new president of the Council of State makes the impression of a surrogate monarch, whose position as Governor of the Republic as a whole would have been considerably stronger than that of the stadtholders, mere *provincial* governors.

[38] Den Tex, ii. 413 ff. describes two secret deliberations in 1602 and 1603.

[39] French projects for a monarchic form of government in the Netherlands, discreetly introduced in 1607–9, aimed at French sovereignty with Maurice as viceroy (den Tex, ii. 555). Grotius was probably aware of such suggestions through his relations with both Oldenbarnevelt and the French ambassador Jeannin, whose letters are our main source. See *Négotiations de Jeannin* (4 vols., Amsterdam, 1959), i. 332, on King Henry IV's policy. See also van Eysinga, *De wording van het Twaalfjarig Bestand* (Amsterdam, 1959), p. 107. Even though the French proposals, e.g. for strengthening the authority of the Council of State, showed great resemblance to those in 'De Republica emendanda', Grotius never remarked upon this. The fragments of Grotius' manuscripts in various public libraries, which have been inventoried by Eyffinger (report not yet published) appear not to contain any reference either. During his trial in 1618 Grotius mentioned his unpublished (and recently discovered (see above, n. 21)) *Meletius*, but he only referred to *De Antiquitate* for his opinions on the constitution of Holland. R. Fruin (ed.), *Verhooren en andere bescheiden betreffende het rechtsgeding van Hugo de Groot* (Werken uitgegeven door het historisch Genootschap gevestigd te Utrecht, 14, Utrecht, 1871), p. 6.

recognized standing, and, last but not least, well acquainted
with Dutch and European political affairs, Grotius was in
1604 a likely choice as publicist in defence of the Dutch East
India Company, the VOC as it is usually called.[40] The
occasion for the call on Grotius' services, the capture of the
Portuguese carrack *St Catharine* in February 1603, has often
been described. Indeed the whole episode, leading to the
composition (1604–6) of a manuscript *De Jure Praedae*, of
which the twelfth chapter appeared in the beginning of 1609
with some minor emendations as *Mare Liberum*, has been
studied by such a host of scholars that it is surprising to find it
still surrounded with questions.[41] Thanks to the late Professor
Coolhaas, we know that Grotius' documentation on Asian
affairs consisted of some testimonies by Dutch sea-captains on
their encounters with the Portuguese. No extensive study
involving an examination of the VOC archives was undertaken
by Grotius himself. Also, it is quite unlikely that Grotius had
any real knowledge of Asian legal systems, and/or of Asian
(Indian, Malay, and Chinese) rules regarding the free use of
the sea and the regulation of trade.[42] He relied on the
information supplied by the VOC and on classical descriptions
like Pliny's.[43] While the character of Grotius' sources for his
description of Dutch and Portuguese activities in the East is
fairly clear, it remains something of a puzzle how certain
passages of chapters I and VIII of *Mare Liberum*, defending an
absolute freedom of trade,[44] can have been published by an

[40] The abbreviation standing for 'United East India Company'.

[41] Thus den Tex, iv. 171, supposes Grotius to have drawn up the *intendit* (act of
accusation) in the prize procedure against the *St Catharine*. However, van Eysinga,
'Mare Liberum et De Iure Praedae', *Sparsa Collecta* (Leiden, 1958), pp. 324–35,
rightly as I think, concludes with Molhuysen from Grotius' letters that he cannot
have been acting on behalf of the VOC. Nellen, p. 16 nn. 38–9, states that the exact
nature of Grotius' relations with the VOC still remains uncertain.

[42] W. P. Coolhaas, 'Een bron voor het historische gedeelte van Hugo de Groots De
jure praedae', *Bijdragen en Mededelingen van het Historisch Genootschap*, 79 (1965),
pp. 415–540. C. G. Roelofsen, 'Review Article', *Netherlands International Law Review*, 31
(1984), pp. 117–20.

[43] *Mare Liberum*, chap. 2. The edition in general use, J. B. Scott (ed.), 1916 (ter
Meulen and Diermanse, *Bibliographie*, 1950, no. 551) has an English translation
beside the Latin text. The translation is to be used with caution. See L. E. van Holk
and C. G. Roelofsen (eds.), *Grotius Reader* (The Hague, 1983), pp. 95–6.

[44] Chap. 1: 'Sequitur ex sententia Lusitanos, etiamsi domini essent earum
regionum ad quas Batavi proficiscuntur, iniuriam tamen facturos si additum Batavis

author well versed in Dutch politics and familiar with the VOC's policies in Asia.

Indeed, if one considers that company's position at the time Grotius wrote *De Jure Praedae*, boldness stands out as a main characteristic of Grotius' apology for the VOC. The VOC had been established as a monopolistic chartered company by the amalgamation of various merchant associations interested in direct trade with the East Indies. A good deal of pressure had been necessary to overcome opposition by various groups.[45] With some reason it had been declared that the exclusive rights conferred on the VOC constituted a notable breach of the general principles of Dutch policy which favoured freedom of trade and free enterprise. Besides, the directors of the newly founded company showed few scruples about turning their position to good account at the expense of the shareholders. The VOC's dividends were meagre, its capital being swallowed up by military expenditure on the construction of fortifications and the fitting out of its fleet.[46] Such investments made sense only if one considered the VOC not as a simple commercial venture, like its English counterpart, but as an instrument of warfare against the Spanish/Portuguese empire. Oldenbarnevelt, the VOC's creator, was in reality led by strategic and political considerations rather than by the expectation of immediate profits. The attack on the Portuguese communications in the Indian Ocean, as well as on their none-too-well-established sphere of influence in the Indonesian archipelago, forced Philip III to divert considerable resources to the defence of Portugal's 'Estado da India'.[47] The Dutch presence in Asia, a well-advertised challenge to Spain's imperial position, focused attention once again on the Dutch Republic in its favourite role of champion of Protestant Europe against Spanish arrogance. Even if the VOC's nuisance value at that time rather exceeded its immediate importance to the Dutch

---

et mercatum praecluderent.' Chap. 8: 'Commercandi igitur libertas ex iure est primario gentium, quod . . . tolli non potest . . .'.

[45] Den Tex, ii. 392 ff.

[46] H. den Haan, *Moedernegotie en Grote Vaart* (Amsterdam, 1977), pp. 111–22. The first dividend was only paid in 1610.

[47] Israel, *Dutch Republic*, pp. 8–9, on the strategic importance of the Dutch advance in Asia.

economy,[48] Oldenbarnevelt had acquired an important asset for his foreign policy. Against this, he had to accept some domestic and foreign liabilities. The foundation of the VOC had created a vested interest that could seriously influence Dutch politics. In some cities directors of the VOC's chamber were leading political figures, the outstanding example being Reynier Pauw in Amsterdam.[49] Concessions to Spain in the East Indies, urged upon Oldenbarnevelt by the French and English mediators during the negotiations of 1607–9, thus risked alienating important elements of the patriciate on whose confidence Oldenbarnevelt's position rested. On the other hand, jealousy of the Dutch successes in Asia, and justified fears of their supplanting the Portuguese as monopolists, complicated the relations between the Dutch Republic and those European powers whose good will in the struggle with Spain was indispensable, namely France and England.

This rather delicate situation has to be borne in mind to understand both the contents of *Mare Liberum* and the book's delayed publication in 1609. For all the apparent straightforwardness of Grotius' defence of the natural freedoms of trade and of navigation[50] against the 'usurping Portuguese', the author must, at least soon after completing *De Jure Praedae*, have understood the serious risks connected with a semi-official exposition of Dutch policy in Asia in terms of a 'crusade for free trade'. Unlike Dutch pamphlets destined for home consumption,[51] a Latin publication would arouse interest abroad and would indeed be intended for a European public. While a good case was to be made against Portuguese pretensions in so far as they rested on the occupation by discovery of the sea-routes to Asia and on Papal grants,

[48] See above, n. 46. The importance of colonial trade for the Dutch 17th-century economy tends to be overrated.

[49] Amsterdam's staunch opposition to the Twelve Years Truce was 'motivated by its concern for the East India trade', Israel, *Dutch Republic*, p. 40. Grotius' home town, Delft, was also much influenced by the East India interest, ibid., pp. 36, 41; den Tex, ii. 663.

[50] See F. de Pauw, 'Grotius and the Law of the Sea', *Studies en Voordrachten Vrije Universiteit Brussel*, 1964-II (Brussels, 1964), pp. 31 ff.

[51] Israel, *Dutch Republic*, p. 36 suggests that the VOC abstained from participation in the 'pamphlet war'. This seems unlikely. R. Kaper, *Pamfletten over Oorlog en Vrede 1607–1609* (Amsterdam, 1980), p. 57 n. 24 lists five pamphlets as probably inspired by the VOC. The freedom of the seas is prominent in their argumentation.

religious issues had to be shunned because of French Roman Catholic public opinion.[52] Above all, the VOC's actions had to be represented as originating in legitimate defence only. Of course this was misleading in view of the monopolistic tendencies already manifested by the Dutch soon after their arrival in Indonesian waters.[53] Grotius had to tread warily in order to present a convincing indictment of Portugal without at the same time compromising the Dutch position, built upon monopoly treaties—the so-called 'contracts', concluded with Indonesian chiefs and rulers.[54] On the whole, *Mare Liberum* suited both purposes. Its resounding refutation of the Spanish/ Portuguese claims is justly famous as a brilliant example of scholastic, deductive argumentation. In accordance with the time-honoured logical method, Grotius established general principles from authoritative texts, namely Holy Writ and the classics,[55] here followed up by extensive quotations from recent Spanish authors, mainly Vitoria and Vasquez.[56] From the general rules thus set out, the inevitable conclusions are drawn in favour of the Dutch competition with Portugal in the East Indies. The remarkable persuasive powers of Grotius' short pamphlet are not to be accounted for by the original character of the argumentation—originality was not sought by Grotius[57]—but by its well-ordered composition and, not least, by its masterly rhetorical style.[58]

[52] Grotius carefully hides behind Roman Catholic authors, especially Vitoria, in refuting the Spanish–Portuguese 'missionary title'. See *Mare Liberum*, chaps. 2 and 4. Also J. Fisch, *Die europäische Expansion und das Völkerrecht* (Wiesbaden, 1984), p. 251.

[53] Even before the founding of the VOC, already in 1600, a monopoly contract was concluded at Amboina. For a description of the Dutch system, see M. A. P. Meilink-Roelofsz, *Asian Trade and European Influence in the Indonesian Archipelago (1500–1630)* (The Hague, 1962, repr. 1969), pp. 172 ff.

[54] J. E. Heeres and F. W. Stapel, *Corpus Diplomaticum Neerlando-Indicum*, i (The Hague, 1907).

[55] Biblical precedents, however, are rare in *Mare Liberum*. See chap. 1 on the right of passage denied by the Amorites, and chap. 4, an indirect quotation from Matt.

[56] On F. Vazquez de Menchaca see Fisch, *Die europäische Expansion*, pp. 243–4; also A. Truyol y Serra, 'Grotius dans ses rapports avec les classiques espagnols du Droit des Gens', *Recueil des Cours*, 182 (1984), pp. 431–51.

[57] Or, rather, his originality resides not in the introduction of new arguments, but in his new arrangement of traditional elements. See Haggenmacher, *Grotius et la doctrine de la guerre juste* (Paris, 1983), p. 176 and n. 679.

[58] Of Grotius' style the accomplished use of classical quotations with their then generally recognized symbolic function constituted one of the main attractions. See Roelofsen, 'Some Remarks on the "Sources" of the Grotian System of International Law', *Netherlands International Law Review*, 30 (1983), pp. 74–5.

Why was *De Jure Praedae* never published by Grotius, and why did its twelfth chapter, *Mare Liberum*, appear only in March/April 1609, and anonymously at that? As we already suggested, it seems a plausible explanation that the VOC and/or Oldenbarnevelt considered publication inadvisable for political reasons. One may surmise that before 1607 these were of a domestic nature:[59] Dutch opponents of the VOC's monopoly could find plenty of ammunition in this defence of free trade! Afterwards, at the beginning of 1607, negotiations between Spain and the Dutch Republic started, in which the continuation of Dutch trade with Asia was one of the crucial issues. Spain was only willing to recognize Dutch independence if there was official toleration of Roman Catholicism in the Republic, and if the Dutch abstained from infringing the Spanish/Portuguese monopolies of trade outside Europe.[60] Both the mediating powers, France and England, were not fundamentally opposed to the Spanish demands. Grotius, from 1607 as Advocate-Fiscal, the official legal adviser to the States of Holland,[61] would not, indeed presumably *could* not, publish a pamphlet on such an important affair without the fiat of his official superior and patron, Oldenbarnevelt. We know that, during the negotiations, Grotius collaborated with Oldenbarnevelt;[62] and that Grotius made acquaintance with the foreign special ambassadors at the Hague, particularly with the French plenipotentiary Jeannin.[63] After August 1608, when it had become clear that peace was not to be attained, negotiations were continued for the purpose of reaching a long-term truce. This necessitated on the part of Spain only a

[59] The new edition of the first volume of *Briefwisseling* which is under preparation will apparently not add anything to our knowledge on this point (friendly communication by the director of the Grotius Institute, J. H. M. Nellen).

[60] Van Eysinga, *De wording van het Twaalfjarig Bestand*, pp. 116–7; Israel, *Dutch Republic*, pp. 8–9. The Spanish demands as regards extra-European trade were set forth on 13 Feb. 1608.

[61] See above, n. 26.

[62] For example, he drafted a note (May 1607?) summing up the arguments *against* peace with Spain at the Advocate's request; van Eysinga, 'Eene onuitgegeven nota van de Groot', *Sparsa Collecta*, p. 495. It is, however, to be remarked that Grotius during these negotiations served Oldenbarnevelt without really appreciating his policy. As he was later to remark: 'He found the Advocate to have acted much better and more prudently then he had ever believed' (my translation); *Briefwisseling*, ii. 441, confidential letter of 4 Apr. 1625 to N. van Reigersberch.

[63] *Briefwisseling*, i. 97.

provisional recognition of Dutch independence, deliberately couched in ambivalent terms. French pressure on the Dutch to abandon their trade in Asia abated.[64] In these circumstances, while the question of whether the conclusion of a truce would not fatally weaken the international position of the Republic as well as impair its cohesion led to a passionate debate, the decision to print *Mare Liberum* was taken, at the demand of the VOC's directors.[65]

An explanation for Grotius' sudden pulling out of a drawer the manuscript finished some three to four years before[66] may be found—rather than in Grotius' own later, general explanation[67]—in the political situation of November–December 1608. A considerable opposition to a long-term truce had arisen among the regents, led by the Stadtholder, Prince Maurice. This was particularly strong in Amsterdam and in Grotius' own Delft. Whereas Maurice was probably motivated by distrust of Spain, the interests of the VOC exercised considerable influence on the regents adhering to his views.[68] Oldenbarnevelt, insisting on full powers to conclude the truce, was opposed by a powerful coalition, but once more proved himself the dominant figure in Dutch politics. An important factor contributing to his victory was French assistance: Maurice expected in vain that the French king, Henry IV, would repudiate Jeannin's policy.

At this time, in mid-November 1608, publication of *Mare Liberum* by Oldenbarnevelt's protégé served the purpose of somewhat reassuring the 'East India interest' that the Republic would continue to reject the Spanish/Portuguese monopoly. Also, in view of the rather dubious attitude of the mediating

---

[64] Jeannin's speech in the assembly of the States General (27 Aug. 1608) conceded the point; *Négotiations de Jeannin*, ii. 413.

[65] *Briefwisseling*, i. 128, letter of 4 Nov. 1608 from the Zeeland Chamber of the VOC. What relations did Grotius entertain with the VOC Chamber in Delft? The question, like that of Grotius' relations with the patriciate of his home town, would bear investigating.

[66] On the date of Grotius' finishing the manuscript of *JP*, see Haggenmacher, 'Genèse et signification du concept de "ius gentium" chez Grotius', *Grotiana*, 2 (1981), pp. 88–9.

[67] In his *Defensio capitis quinti Maris Liberi* (1613); ter Meulen and Diermanse, *Bibliographie*, 1950, nos. 688–9.

[68] Den Tex, ii. 645–6.

powers in an earlier stage of the negotiations,[69] *Mare Liberum* discreetly (hence its anónymity)[70] deployed against the Iberian pretensions a juridical argumentation from which England and France would find it hard to dissociate themselves.[71] Thus day-to-day circumstances may explain the guise in which a part of Grotius' manuscript was finally published. This hypothesis agrees with what we know about the relation between Grotius and Oldenbarnevelt. Grotius was fast becoming the Advocate's juridical expert and was soon also to become his adviser on church policy. Grotius' subservient attitude towards Oldenbarnevelt, by general consent a domineering character, is fairly clear, making it rather plausible that *Mare Liberum*'s publication took place only after the Advocate had given the (unofficial) *imprimatur*.

Clearly, in 1608–9 *Mare Liberum* fitted in very well with the purposes of Oldenbarnevelt's foreign policy: obtaining a formal recognition of Dutch independence from the enemy while at the same time increasing the Republic's practical freedom of action, particularly in its relations with France and England. Both were served by the conclusion at Antwerp of the Twelve Years Truce (9 April 1609), even though this was but an uneasy compromise, guaranteed by the French and English mediators. Spanish prestige suffered, but the Spanish monarchy remained the dominant power in European politics. For various reasons, discontent with the terms of the Truce was to become widespread in Spanish political circles.[72] Thus the Habsburg danger remained. In consequence, Oldenbarnevelt could not really emancipate Dutch foreign policy from French and English 'advice'. Yet English influence

---

[69] The French tried· to found a French East India Company with Dutch participation; van Eysinga, *De wording van het Twaalfjarig Bestand*, p. 116.

[70] The first (Dutch) edition which mentioned Grotius as the author appeared in 1614; ter Meulen and Diermanse, *Bibliographie*, 1950, p. 211. Already in 1613 Grotius' authorship was known in England; Clark and van Eysinga, 'The Colonial Conferences', *Bibliotheca Visseriana*, 17 (1951), p. 71. One wonders whether, informally, Grotius was not from the start fairly generally recognized as the writer of *Mare Liberum*.

[71] See *Négotiations de Jeannin*, ii. 145 (letter to Henry IV of 7 Mar. 1608) concerning the Spanish/Portuguese pretensions: 'Puis il semble chose injuste et *contre le droit des gens*, de leur [sc. the Dutch] défendre ce trafic ès lieux ou ils [sc. Spain and Portugal] ne tiennent rien, attendu que les Roys et peuples qui y ont l'interest, le consentent' (emphasis added).

[72] Israel, *Dutch Republic*, pp. 55, 64.

weakened.[73] Relations with France took on a new complexion as a result of the murder of Henry IV in 1610. During the anarchical regency of Maria de Medici the Huguenot party once again reared its head, protesting against the supposedly pro-Habsburg orientation of the regent's advisers. In consequence, Dutch foreign policy was presented with the opportunity of interfering in French domestic politics by assistance to anti-Spanish factions among the nobility. This 'interventionist' line of action was favoured by the Dutch ambassador in Paris, François Aerssen. However, Oldenbarnevelt withstood temptation and persevered in cultivating his relations with the French government.[74] Once again Oldenbarnevelt proved himself a 'politique', refusing to admit the prior claims of religious solidarity (that is, with the Huguenots) over considerations of *raison d'état*.[75] As a result, Oldenbarnevelt earned himself the assistance of the French government as well as the hatred of Aerssen, who was deprived of his embassy by a rather shady intrigue.

Grotius' role in the elaboration of Dutch foreign policy during the first years of the Truce, while restricted to some aspects of Anglo-Dutch relations, was not unimportant. Economic rivalry over issues like Arctic whaling, herring fishing in the 'English seas', and trade in the Moluccas led to serious incidents, embarrassing James I as well as Oldenbarnevelt, both of whom for their own reasons wished to maintain the alliance which had nominally existed since 1585.[76] Grotius' juridical argumentation in favour of the freedom of fishing in his *Mare Liberum*, even though the question is only casually treated here, provided the stock-in-trade of Dutch negotiators for some sixty years as far as the British claims to a *dominium maris* in the North Sea and in the waters surrounding Spitzbergen were concerned.[77] In the East

---

[73] Traditionally symbolized by the withdrawal of English troops from Flushing and The Brill (1616) in consequence of the termination of the Treaty of Nonesuch (1585) and the end of the last vestiges of the English 'protection'; den Tex, iii. 525 ff.; see also A. T. van Deursen, *Honni soit qui mal y pense?* (Amsterdam, 1965), an analysis of Dutch foreign policy in 1610–12.

[74] Den Tex, iii. 241.   [75] Ibid., pp. 349 ff.

[76] And renewed by the English (and French) guarantee of the Truce.

[77] *Mare Liberum*, chap. 5; J. K. Oudendijk, *Status and Extent of Adjacent Waters* (Leiden, 1970), p. 64.

Indies, the VOC's increasingly effective monopoly of the spice trade[78] was hardly to be defended by *Mare Liberum*. Indeed, the Dutch position in Asia rested on sea-power, systematically used to control particular branches of Asian trade. As Meilink-Roelofsz showed, the Dutch took a leaf out of the Portuguese book.[79] Of course, this laid them open to the same reproaches which they had themselves heaped upon Portuguese 'insane ambition'. Grotius, apparently still the VOC's legal adviser, was entrusted with formulating the Dutch case in Asia against the English and other European would-be competitors. Therefore he was an obvious choice as a member of the Dutch delegation to the Anglo-Dutch conferences on Asian affairs of 1613 and 1615, which were to provide him with his first major diplomatic experience.[80]

However, rather than in his close connections with the VOC, it is in his relation with Oldenbarnevelt that we have to seek the reasons for Grotius' career in Dutch politics. Of paramount importance was his participation with the Advocate in the conflict which disrupted the Reformed State Church from 1610 onwards. The theological controversy between the parties, Remonstrants and Contra-Remonstrants, was serious. The Contra-Remonstrants held to the Calvinist doctrine of predestination, while the Arminians or Remonstrants tried to find a compromise between predestination on the one hand and human free will in rejecting or accepting divine grace on the other. In consequence, the Remonstrants were with some reason accused of 'papist' or even Arian/Socinian inclinations.[81] Such accusations point to the political implications of the debate. In European political theory, conformity in religion was generally considered essential for the cohesion of

---

[78] For instance in 1609 the monopoly of nutmeg and mace was established by treaty; P. J. Drooglever, 'The Netherlands Colonial Empire: Historical Outline and Some Legal Aspects', in H. F. van Panhuys *et al.* (eds.), *International Law in the Netherlands* (Alphen aan den Rijn, 1978), p. 109.

[79] Meilink-Roelofsz, *Asian Trade and European Influence*, p. 120.

[80] If we leave aside his being (probably as juridical adviser) among the Dutch delegation sent in 1611 to East Frisia.

[81] It was especially the nomination of C. Vorstius as theology professor at Leiden (1611) which lent credibility to accusations of Socinianism, i.e., 'unitarianism'. James I, a theologian in his own right, had his ambassador protest in Sept. 1611; den Tex, iii. 191 ff.

the State.[82] It was also usual to trust to religious solidarity as the best guarantee of common alliances.[83] Thus, the threatened schism in the Dutch established church gravely weakened the international position of the Republic, quite apart from the serious menace to public order in many towns resulting from schisms within the local congregations of the Reformed Church.[84] Town corporations tried to assert their authority, but found the Contra-Remonstrants hard to handle. They, being clearly the stronger and the more popular party, refused to tolerate government interference with church *doctrine*, while at the same time insisting that it was the government's 'proper role' to assist the Reformed Church, *inter alia*, in the enforcement of church discipline and the maintenance of outward religious conformity.[85] At one time or another, most seventeenth-century governments had to deal with problems of this kind.[86] However, Calvinist established churches, as demonstrated by the experience of Scotland, were particularly hard to handle because of their democratic organization and theocratic leanings. It was therefore no mean task which Grotius set himself of formulating a compromise, to be accepted by both Arminians and Contra-Remonstrants and to be imposed on them by the States of Holland, in accordance with their duty as an ordained Christian government. Grotius' treatise on toleration—the recently rediscovered (and previously unpublished) *Meletius*[87] —was to be only the first of his many theological works.[88] Against the charge of heterodoxy,

---

[82] U. Scheuner, 'Staatsräson und religiöse Einheit des Staates', in R. Schnur (ed.), *Staatsräson, Studien zur Geschichte eines politische Begriffs* (Berlin, 1975), pp. 365–6 and *passim*.

[83] See Gentili, *JB*, book i, chap. 15, pp. 116–17. The English interpretation of the Vorstius affair as an indication of the pro-French inclinations among the nobility and patricians in the province of Holland is a striking example of the direct connection between religion and politics; van Deursen, *Honni soit*, pp. 81–2.

[84] Notably in Rotterdam; den Tex, iii. 175 ff.

[85] A new decree against Roman Catholic priests entering the Republic (1612) was drafted by Grotius; van Deursen, *Honni soit*, p. 92.

[86] Scheuner, 'Staatsräson und religiöse'.

[87] Posthumus Meyjes (ed.), *Meletius sive de iis quae inter Christianos conveniunt epistola: Critical edition with translation, commentary and introduction* (Leiden, 1988). See also above, n. 21.

[88] A summary is given by Haentjens in *Hugo de Groot als godsdienstig denker*; see also Posthumus Meyjes, 'Hugo Grotius as an Irenicist', and H. J. de Jonge, 'Hugo Grotius: exégète du Nouveau Testament', in *The World of Hugo Grotius. Posthumus*

made against Oldenbarnevelt's party by the Contra-Remonstrants, Grotius was the one publicist able to defend the Erastian policies of the States before the forum of the European Protestant commonwealth.[89] His family background, as well as his marriage in 1608 into a not unimportant Zeeland 'regent' family, the Reigersberchs,[90] also pointed to a political career. His juridical and theological qualifications were of particular value at that moment and, of course, he was well known to Oldenbarnevelt after some years of often close collaboration. So the Advocate decided to choose Grotius as his lieutenant in the States of Holland by offering him the position of pensionary of Rotterdam. This had become vacant on the death of Elias, the Advocate's brother. Grotius, after some hesitation, accepted (4 March 1613), exchanging his office of Advocate-Fiscal with its prospect of a legal career for a position that was much more important than its humble description of town secretary and legal adviser seems at first sight to warrant.[91]

(b) GROTIUS AS OLDENBARNEVELT'S RIGHT-HAND MAN AND HIS DOWNFALL, 1613–1621

The years 1613–18 provided Grotius with his sole experience of real political power. Of course, in a formal sense, he was merely the servant of the town corporation. However, the members of the 'vroedschap' were only part-time politicians. They expected to take important decisions themselves, by a majority vote, but they left daily affairs very much to the

Meyjes, ibid., p. 46 n. 15, accepts Grotius' description of himself as a 'lawyer satisfied with a little theology'; *Briefwisseling*, i. 159, 24 Dec. 1609. It seems more likely that Grotius did already have a much more intimate knowledge of the questions at issue than he admitted.

[89] For instance by his correspondence with I. Casaubon. See Nellen, 'Le Rôle de la correspondance de Grotius pendant son exil', *The World of Hugo Grotius*, p. 136.

[90] Nicolaas van Reigersberch, Grotius' brother-in-law, was after 1621 to become one of Grotius' most regular correspondents. Van Reigersberch, a lawyer, was appointed a member of the 'Hooge Raad' (above, n. 22) in 1625. As a favourite of Frederick Henry he was the natural intermediary between the Stadtholder and his brother-in-law, Grotius' correspondence with him being intended to inform the Stadtholder of political events in Paris as well as to prepare Grotius' return from exile; Nellen, ibid., p. 139.

[91] Nellen, 'Hugo de Groots geschil met de stad Rotterdam over de uitbetaling van zijn pensionaristractement', *Rotterdams Jaarboekje*, 9th ser. 2 (1984), pp. 212–13.

pensionary, a trusted member of their own 'regent' class who often turned out to be the real director of policy. As a rule, therefore, until the end of the *ancien régime*, the pensionaries of the major towns were key figures in the States of Holland.[92] Grotius' power base seems to have been particularly secure because of the docility of the Rotterdam 'regents' at the time. They appear to have been rather unimaginative supporters of Oldenbarnevelt, quite content to follow their brilliant pensionary's lead.[93] Legally speaking, responsibility for Grotius' actions rested with the town corporation of Rotterdam, a point that Grotius was later to emphasize in his defence.[94] As a matter of fact, he enjoyed considerable freedom of action and was expected to play a leading role in Dutch politics.

This political career was inaugurated by a diplomatic mission to England in March–May 1613. The avowed purpose of Grotius' appointment, together with three members of the VOC's board of directors, was to provide the Dutch delegation in the negotiations on Indian affairs with a legal expert.[95] In fact, Grotius acted as spokesman of the Dutch delegation throughout the conferences with the English delegates, as well as on ceremonial occasions. His Latin speech at the first audience of the Dutch at court was much admired. King James seemed favourably impressed, at least according to as shrewd an observer as the Dutch Ambassador Caron, and to Grotius himself.[96] Here much more was at stake than Grotius' fame as a humanistic orator. James I was a theologian in his own right and considered himself somewhat like a Protestant Pope, keeping watch over the orthodoxy of foreign churches as well as over the English and Scottish ecclesiastical establishments. As was to be expected, the king was keenly interested in the struggle between Arminians and

[92] The one exception being the pensionary of Amsterdam, who traditionally was relegated to a secondary role by the city's four burgomasters. The career of Pieter de Groot, Hugo's son, pensionary of Amsterdam from 1660 to 1667, offers a good illustration; M. van Leeuwen, *Het leven van Pieter de Groot* (Utrecht, 1917), pp. 105 ff.
[93] The Contra-Remonstrants were exceptionally weak in Rotterdam.
[94] Nellen, 'Hugo de Groots', p. 215; Fruin, *Verhooren en andere bescheiden betreffende het rechtsgeding van Hugo de Groot*, p. 98. See also H. Gerlach, *Het Proces tegen Oldenbarnevelt en de 'Maximen in den Staet'* (Haarlem, 1965).
[95] Clark and van Eysinga, 'Colonial Conferences', *Bibliotheca Visseriana*, 17 (1951), p. 52.
[96] Ibid., p. 61.

Contra-Remonstrants. At Oldenbarnevelt's prompting, James declared himself satisfied with the States' decisions in the controversy and wrote, just before Grotius' arrival in England, some letters to that effect.[97] If Grotius could ingratiate himself with James and the leading Anglican theologians he might strike a decisive blow for his party. Without hopes of international approbation of their 'extremist' opinions, the Contra-Remonstrants would probably accept the 'reasonable' compromise imposed by the government. The controversy would abate. Once more the States of Holland, guided by their Advocate, would have vindicated their authority.

Such flattering prospects, together with a well-established confidence in his own abilities, animated Grotius in his intense lobbying. Most notably, he obtained a private audience with the king to confirm James in his apparently favourable opinion of Oldenbarnevelt's policy. We may assume that intellectual curiosity on the king's part played a role in granting the interview, and also that after the conversation, this will have been assuaged. Grotius held forth on the compatibility of the Arminian position with Christian doctrine as established by the Early Church, particularly by St Augustine and the other Fathers, and in consequence defended the toleration granted to the Arminians within the Dutch Reformed Church.[98] With the wisdom of hindsight, we may wonder whether it never occurred to Grotius to question Oldenbarnevelt's instructions in this respect. The English, invited by both Dutch parties to decide the conflict,[99] were seriously divided over the theological issues involved. James himself, in spite of his Erastian sympathies with the States, was very much an uncertain quantity, as he had shown by his hesitant policy on many occasions. However, such considerations were quite alien to Grotius. Almost till the end he acted on the assumption that his theological arguments in favour of toleration, supported by the sovereign authority of the States

[97] Den Tex, iii. 284.

[98] Clark and van Eysinga, 'Colonial Conferences', *Bibliotheca Visseriana*, 17 (1951), p. 80; Fruin, *Verhooren en andere bescheiden betreffende het rechtsgeding van Hugo de Groot*, pp. 223–4, 311; *Briefwisseling*, i. 234–6.

[99] Reynier Pauw, the Contra-Remonstrant Amsterdam regent, one of the members of the delegation of 1613, tried in vain to obtain a private audience with James; *Briefwisseling*, i. 238.

of Holland, would sooner or later convince the moderates among the Contra-Remonstrants, just as they had (or so he at least temporarily believed) convinced his English interlocutors in 1613. This over-confident assessment of the English political situation was considered by Molhuysen to be Grotius' first capital mistake.[100] It was aggravated by the publication in October 1613 of his famous *Ordinum Pietas*, a defence of the conduct of the States of Holland in such vehement terms that the dispute between the parties took on a new edge, Grotius himself becoming the foremost controversialist of his party.[101]

Since this is not a complete political biography of Grotius, but only a sketch of his role in international affairs, we can leave aside much of his political activity of these years. Still, we have to keep in mind the importance of foreign policy considerations in this Dutch domestic crisis. As the antagonism between Oldenbarnevelt's party and the Contra-Remonstrants developed, and the Advocate's position was threatened by an important Contra-Remonstrant minority in the States of Holland as well as by the Contra-Remonstrant majority in the States-General, the Dutch Republic lost the energetic leadership so long provided by Oldenbarnevelt's control of foreign policy. This was the more serious because of the tense situation in central Europe. The Bohemian states, seeking allies among the Protestant powers against their Habsburg ruler, had hopes of Dutch as well as English assistance.[102] While both parties in the Netherlands agreed on the general anti-Habsburg tenor of the Republic's foreign policy, there were significant differences of emphasis. Oldenbarnevelt's party had excellent relations with the French government, while their opponents relied on the English ambassador, Sir Dudley Carleton. The Contra-Remonstrants, who from July 1617 were openly led by Prince Maurice, had crystallized into the 'Orangeist' party, traditionally connected in Dutch history with Great Britain by religious and dynastic ties.[103] Accusations of treason against the 'Arminians' were bandied

---

[100] Ibid., vol. i, p. xxiii.
[101] Ter Meulen and Diermanse, *Bibliographie*, 1950, nos. 817–54.
[102] Den Tex, iii. 587.
[103] Was Maurice's choice already clear in 1609? van Deursen, *Honni soit*, pp. 52 ff.

about, because of their alleged Catholic leanings and their alliance with the Roman Catholic French government. Oldenbarnevelt's hesitant attitude towards intervention in German affairs was ascribed to Spanish bribes:[104] the real reasons for this reluctance, the desire to preserve the nominal 'neutrality' of the Empire in the Spanish–Dutch conflict,[105] and to prevent a rupture of the Truce, were not appreciated by Oldenbarnevelt's opponents.

Did even Grotius do full justice to the Advocate's foreign policy? One may doubt it. In January 1619, as a prisoner, Grotius was willing to interpret some of Oldenbarnevelt's actions as 'suspicious', and as perhaps confirming the treasonable intentions of the Advocate.[106] The episode is very discreditable to Grotius,[107] but some justification for his behaviour may, at least from a psychological point of view, be found in his strictly subordinate role as far as foreign affairs were concerned. The pensionary of Rotterdam was used in the management of Anglo-Dutch relations,[108] and entertained close relations with foreign envoys like the French ambassador du Maurier,[109] yet he seems not to have acquired a broad grasp of matters such as would have enabled him to take the measure of Oldenbarnevelt's foreign policy. France, to the Advocate, was the necessary pivot of a European coalition against the Habsburgs. If she could or would not play this role, the Republic had to maintain its freedom of action, and to avoid entanglements with weak and exposed allies like the Elector Palatine.[110]

Engrossed in legal and theological controversy, elaborating time and again compromise proposals for toleration within a

---

[104] Poelhekke, *Het verraad van de pistoletten* (Amsterdam, 1975), published Spanish reports that seem to prove that many leading Dutch politicians, Grotius among them, indeed accepted Spanish bribes. It is hard to accept this as regards Grotius.

[105] 'Neutrality' at the time of course having quite other legal implications than nowadays. See *JBP*, book II, chap. 2, § 10.

[106] Fruin, *Verhooren en andere bescheiden betreffende het rechtsgeding van Hugo de Groot*, pp. 42, 47.

[107] Ibid., pp. 225 ff.; den Tex, iii. 690–1; *Lettres, mémoires et négociations du chevalier Carleton . . . 1616–1620* (3 vols., The Hague and Leiden, 1759), ii. 332, and iii. 79.

[108] Esp. in East Indian affairs. On his role in the Anglo-Dutch conference at the Hague, see Clark and van Eysinga, 'Colonial Conferences', *Bibliotheca Visseriana*, 17 (1951), p. 113.

[109] According to whom Grotius in July 1618 had grown distracted with concern. *Briefwisseling*, i. 619 n. 6.   [110] Den Tex, iii. 587; Carleton, *Lettres*, iii. 15, 17.

'broad' Dutch Reformed Church, Grotius seems only at a very late stage of the conflict to have realized what formidable forces were arranged against his party. Maurice's immense popularity as a 'Protestant hero', his constitutional position as Stadtholder as well as his command of the army enabled him to decide the outcome of the conflict, particularly since the authority of the 'Oldenbarneveldist' town corporations was often undermined by popular demonstrations under the leadership of Contra-Remonstrant ministers. In addition, important groups among the 'regents', like the dominant faction in Amsterdam, were opposed to their long-time leader for various reasons—religious convictions as well as jockeying for position playing a role.[111] It says much for the confident mood of the regent oligarchy, generated by some thirty years of unopposed domination, that the majority of the States of Holland did not capitulate until Maurice actually arrested Oldenbarnevelt, Grotius, and the pensionary of Leiden, Hogerbeets, on 29 August 1618.

Grotius, on whom the strains of the long struggle had been telling, broke down. He wrote rather abjectly to Maurice, asking for his protection and blaming both Oldenbarnevelt and the Rotterdam town corporation.[112] His excuses sound none too good, particularly coming from the high-minded defender of Holland's sovereign rights.[113] They were also of no avail, since Grotius had rendered himself particularly odious to Maurice.[114] Indeed, the pensionary of Rotterdam fell between two stools. In the final stage of the conflict his credit among his own party had been diminished by his proposing fundamental concessions to the Contra-Remonstrants. Yet the victors held him, together with the Advocate, responsible for the persistent opposition of the majority of the States of Holland to resolutions on ecclesiastical affairs passed by the

---

[111] Israel, 'Frederick Henry and the Dutch Political Factions, 1625–1642', *English Historical Review*, 98 (1983), p. 3.

[112] Fruin, *Verhooren en andere bescheiden betreffende het rechtsgeding van Hugo de Groot*, pp. 87 ff.

[113] Grotius even alleges his youth! (ibid., p. 97).

[114] Esp. because of his leading role in the crisis of July 1618 at Utrecht, where Maurice considered himself to have been in danger; den Tex, iii. 608. This, after Grotius' earlier attempts at accommodation (ibid., iii. 584) irrecoverably discredited him with Maurice.

majority of the States-General. The stubborn refusal to accept these decisions had been backed by the raising of armed forces in the towns of Holland, including Rotterdam, and by a threatened refusal to pay Holland's share in the national budget. Such extremist measures had put the 'Union'—that is, the existence of the Dutch Republic as a state—in jeopardy. Grotius had on many occasions formulated his party's views and had acted as the main spokesman of the 'Arminians'.[115] Among the strict Calvinists Grotius was hated with an intense *odium theologicum*. In these circumstances his condemnation, together with that of Oldenbarnevelt and some other leading figures of the defeated party, by the special tribunal instituted for the occasion, was a foregone conclusion. The judges found both the Advocate and Grotius guilty of high treason. Grotius' sentence—imprisonment for life, instead of exile as requested—seems to have been partly suggested by fears of his talents as a controversialist.[116] Oldenbarnevelt's execution on 13 May 1619 grimly marked the beginning of a new regime and the end of Grotius' political career. Thereafter, it is often assumed, Grotius was a spent force in Dutch politics. The former pensionary of Rotterdam naturally returned to his literary, legal, and theological pursuits, which were henceforth to constitute his main occupation. Seen in this perspective, the two years of Grotius' stay at Loevestein Castle up to his escape on 22 March 1621 are sometimes considered as a particularly useful period of preparation, marked by the composition of some of his best-known works such as *Introduction to the Jurisprudence of Holland* and *De Veritate Religionis Christianae*.[117] However, did Grotius himself really accept the verdict of 1618–19 as irreversible, and was he prepared to abandon his 'rightful position' in Dutch politics? The answer to this question is important for our interpretation of some of his later works, above all *De Jure Belli ac Pacis*.

---

[115] Even to the point that a very successful pamphlet was generally, though wrongly, ascribed to him.

[116] Carleton, *Lettres*, iii. 85.

[117] Gellinek, *Hugo Grotius*, pp. 40, 108 ff., for short summaries.

(c) GROTIUS IN EXILE, 1621–1645

After Grotius' escape and his settling in Paris, where he was to stay until November 1631, his correspondence begins to assume impressive dimensions, even by seventeenth-century standards. Indeed, the completeness and accessibility of this source can constitute a serious pitfall for a biographer, who is inevitably tempted to adopt Grotius' point of view as expressed in his letters. However, did even the confidential correspondence between Grotius and his brother-in-law Nicolaas van Reigersberch present a sincere picture of Grotius' current mood and real intentions?[118] Also, Grotius' relations with the leaders of the various factions at the French Court would have to be analysed if we were to arrive at an adequate description of his situation in Paris during this crucial period in French politics, when Richelieu was rising to power.

During his short stay at Antwerp in 1621 Grotius received a letter of invitation from Jeannin,[119] which he was to quote in 1624 as the principal inducement for his coming to France.[120] Grotius could be reasonably certain of a good reception from the French government, which considered him one of the leading members of a Francophile party. He was awarded a not insignificant pension, presumably for services to be rendered to the French Crown. However, Grotius in his letters to Dutch correspondents studiously gives the impression that he hardly did anything to deserve his money and had retained his freedom of action.[121] His continuous complaints about delays of payment are, then, not very surprising; nor, for that matter, are they exceptional for the time.

If it seems wise not to accept Grotius' assertions at face value as far as his relations with the French government are

---

[118] As Nellen points out, the—varying—risks of interception have also to be taken into account; 'Le Rôle de la correspondance de Grotius', p. 139.

[119] *Briefwisseling*, vol. ii, no. 629; also an invitation from du Maurier, ibid., no. 624.

[120] Ibid., no. 896.

[121] Ibid., no. 883, 15 Feb. 1624 to N. van Reigersberch; Grotius wrote that in the receipt of his pension he had been mentioned as 'historiographer', evidently—according to Grotius—because the French government wished to improve relations with Prince Maurice. This sounds rather far-fetched.

concerned, what are we to think of his affirmations to Reigersberch regarding his eventual return to Holland?

It is fairly certain that at least at times Grotius cherished hopes of a future in Dutch politics. Illusory as these were to prove, they were certainly not unfounded. The events of 1618–19 were of such an unprecedented nature that they soon appeared of dubious legality to most members of the Dutch political class. The city of Rotterdam did not dare to appoint another pensionary instead of Grotius, who had been engaged in 1613 for life! The new regime proved weak and was not much respected by the populace in some towns. The 'old regents', those deposed in 1618 by Maurice, continued to enjoy great social prestige.[122] In 1621 the Twelve Years Truce expired and the war with Spain was duly resumed. But Oldenbarnevelt's foreign policy was vindicated, since England proved but a broken reed. French assistance had once more to be requested and 'godly' close relations with the Huguenots were once more sacrificed to Reason of State.[123] Besides, Maurice's successor-designate, his younger half-brother Frederick Henry, showed leanings to the 'Arminian' party and was clearly as much of a 'politique' as Oldenbarnevelt himself. Maurice was in bad health. At his death, would not the tables be turned on the victors of 1618? Grotius' high expectations no doubt found confirmation in his confidential correspondence with Frederick Henry, for which Nicolaas van Reigersberch served as intermediary.[124]

It is this rather ambiguous situation of the author of *De Jure Belli ac Pacis* that is too often overlooked in assessments of that famous book. Grotius, in spite of his experiences of 1618–19, did not look upon himself as a spent force in Dutch politics. Though he protests his disinterestedness,[125] the author remains at heart the former legal adviser to Oldenbarnevelt, cherishing

---

[122] Poelhekke, *Frederik Hendrik* (Zutphen, 1978), pp. 177 ff.; Israel, 'Frederick Henry and the Dutch Political Factions', p. 5.

[123] *Briefwisseling*, vol. ii, no. 963, 4 Apr. 1625 to N. van Reigersberch. Grotius comments on the Dutch naval assistance to the French army against the Huguenots: 'It is much that in our country they begin to distinguish rebellion from religion.' It is a surprise that the Huguenots tried to engage Grotius. Was his loyalist attitude not as generally known as one would suppose? *Briefwisseling*, ii. 471, 22 Aug. 1625 to van Reigersberch.

[124] Poelhekke, *Frederik Hendrik*, pp. 168 ff.   [125] *JBP*, Prolegomena 58.

hopes of a return to office. It is no doubt too crude to describe *De Jure Belli ac Pacis* as simply a bid for employment. Still, *pace* C. van Vollenhoven[126] it was at least partly that. Indeed, Grotius' European reputation, enhanced by his immediately famous book,[127] clearly pointed to his taking up a new political or legal career. There is little, if anything, in *De Jure Belli ac Pacis* that can be considered as conflicting with such aspirations. To put it more bluntly: Grotius' exposition of the Law of Nations was not at all that revolutionary condemnation of existing state practice for which it is often taken.[128] The reservation made in the Prolegomena[129] regarding the *political* as opposed to the *juridical* approach to international affairs, though it somewhat confirms our point of view, is not as important as the analysis of the text itself. The modern reader, swept along by Grotius' grand style, is apt to overlook the qualifications added to statements such as those concerning the place of law in international affairs,[130] or the 'duty' to take sides in a *bellum justum*.[131]

Of course, this is not to deny that Grotius' view of the 'society of mankind', ruled by law like any other society, is an impressive one; nor that in its systematic exposition it is rather more attractive than, for instance, Gentili's.[132] But, to Grotius' contemporaries, the idea in itself of the rule of law in international relations can hardly have come as a surprise.

---

[126] Van Vollenhoven, 'The Land of Grotius', p. 113, protesting against W. S. M. Knight's suggestion that *JBP* 'was written largely with a regard for its possibilities as an introduction to diplomatic service'.

[127] See Ter Meulen and Diermanse, *Bibliographie*, 1950, pp. 222 ff., for the impressive list of editions in Grotius' lifetime.

[128] For example, Edwards, *Hugo Grotius*, p. 181, says that Grotius 'postulated a system of universal law to bring about world order, but people since have been resistant to his vision.' Arguing from a philosophic viewpoint Tuck arrives at the opposite conclusion: he suggests a fundamental conformity between Grotius and Hobbes, even though the latter 'would make an unlikely tutelary god for a Peace Palace'; Richard Tuck, 'Grotius, Carneades and Hobbes', *Grotiana*, 4 (1983), p. 61.

[129] *JBP*, Prolegomena 57.

[130] See ibid., Prolegomena 22 and 23, where the 'utilitarian' argument for international law is put forward; also *JBP*, book II, chap. 23, § 13, and chap. 24, esp. § 9.

[131] See *JBP*, book II, chap. 25, § 7, and book III, chap. 17, § 3. Van Vollenhoven's thesis about punitive war being at the centre of *JBP* was already refuted by D. Beaufort, *La Guerre comme instrument de secours ou de punition* (The Hague, 1933), pp. 165 ff.

[132] See Grotius' remark on Gentili's lack of method, *JBP*, Prolegomena 38. Also, anti-papist outbursts impair *JB*: see book III, chap. 19, pp. 661–2.

Indeed, in spite of Grotius' famous criticism of the current
'lack of restraint in relation to war',[133] it is the general respect
paid to legal considerations that strikes the modern observer
of early seventeenth-century state practice. At least among
Christian rulers, war was seldom if ever proclaimed without
invoking juridical arguments, such as feudal or dynastic titles
to territory. Medieval legal traditions were still very much
alive in the Empire—where the Thirty Years War was, after
all, fought over the juridical definition of the position of the
States and the Emperor—as well as in Western Europe.[134]
There were some instances in which legal title was dis-
regarded, but it appears that only towards the end of the
seventeenth century, with the famous 'partition treaties'
between William III and Louis XIV, were dynastic considerations seriously weakened in favour of the more power-
political *droit de convenance*.[135]

If, then, the connection between *De Jure Belli ac Pacis* and
contemporary international politics was not essentially different from that between modern expositions of international law
and current international affairs, why is this connection ob-
scured by the almost complete absence of references to recent
practice? This forms one of the major stumbling-blocks for
modern readers of *De Jure Belli ac Pacis*, and has led to many
reproaches against Grotius' 'antiquarian' tendencies.[136] How-

[133] *JBP*, Prolegomena 28: 'levibus aut nullis de causis ad arma procurri'.
[134] For instance the Spanish intervention in Mantua in 1627, clearly motivated by
strategic considerations, was justified as safeguarding imperial rights in the duchy;
J. H. Elliott, *Richelieu and Olivares* (Cambridge, 1984), p. 95. See F. Dickmann, *Der
westfälische Frieden* (Münster, 1972), p. 223, on the necessity of a juridical title
according to Richelieu. Also, Poelhekke, *De vrede van Munster* (The Hague, 1948),
p. 339.
[135] The use of several ecclesiastical principalities to provide territorial 'compensa-
tions' to Brandenburg and Sweden may be considered one of the first instances of
such 'utilitarianism' on a large scale. For a typical remark of John Oxenstierna, the
Chancellor's son, about the relative character of ancient rights, see Dickmann, *Der
westfälische Frieden*, p. 320. On the importance of dynastic right, see M. A. Thomson,
'Louis XIV and the Origins of the War of the Spanish Succession', in R. Hatton and
J. S. Bromley (eds.), *William III and Louis XIV: Essays 1680–1720 by and for Mark A.
Thomson* (Liverpool, 1968), pp. 142 ff. The phrase *droit de convenance* was, according to
Meinecke, first used by the French refugee publicist Jean Rousset in 1735;
F. Meinecke, *Die Idee der Staatsräson in der neueren Geschichte* (Munich and Berlin, 1929),
p. 322.
[136] G. Mattingly, *Renaissance Diplomacy* (London, 1965), p. 273; also id., 'Inter-
national Diplomacy and International Law', in R. B. Wernham (ed.), *The New*

ever, such criticisms fail to take into account the scholarly methods of the early seventeenth century. Classical antiquity and Holy Writ still enjoyed prime authority as 'sources' of law.

Even though Grotius ostensibly bases his legal system on natural law, in practice he subordinates his naturalist argumentation to the interpretation of recognized classical and biblical precedents. As a rule, he reasons as it were 'by quotation'.[137] This did not, as one might expect, reduce the value of *De Jure Belli ac Pacis* as a textbook for practical statesmen. Rather, in an age which set store by rhetorical ornaments, the reverse was probably true. Grotius' massive erudition, thus offered ready for use, was much appreciated, even if direct quotations from *De Jure Belli ac Pacis* in official documents seem to have been few, at least in the seventeenth century.[138] Finally, we cannot resist suggesting that the book's lasting popularity as a classic owes much to the ambiguity which is not the least important of its characteristics. It has been interpreted as a defence of absolutism; it has also been called by conservatives a dangerous work because of Grotius' contractual constitutional theories.[139] Grotius has been called a 'realist' for his description of the laws of war, as well as a visionary reformer.[140] Such contradictions are not merely the result of different views among Grotius' interpreters: they are inherent in the text itself. Time and again, the author of *De Jure Belli ac Pacis* is struggling with contrasting propositions and tries to strike a mean, generally by qualifying his conclusions. It is not surprising, then, that 'Grotian' ideas have been made to serve widely different purposes.[141]

Cambridge Modern History, iii, *The Counter-Reformation and Price Revolution 1559–1610* (Cambridge, 1968), pp. 169 ff.

[137] The relation in *JBP* between the principles of natural law and the 'illustrations' (Prolegomena 39 and 40) is of course much more complicated than we may seem to suggest. What we are concerned with here, however, is the practical use made of *JBP* in its own time. For a criticism of some methodological interpretations of *JBP*, see Vermeulen, 'Discussing Grotian Law and Legal Philosophy', *Grotiana*, 6 (1985), pp. 84 ff.

[138] L. V. Ledeboer, *Beroep op volkenrecht voor 1667* (Amsterdam, 1932), p. 13.

[139] Above, n. 35.

[140] M. Roberts, 'The Military Revolution, 1560–1660', *Essays in Swedish History* (London, 1967), p. 216: 'The limits he [Grotius] did set were appallingly wide.' On the other hand see Nussbaum, *A Concise History of the Law of Nations*, p. 110: 'Grotius opened a new path.'

[141] See Willems, 'How to Handle Grotian Ambivalence', *Grotiana*, 6 (1985), pp. 106 ff.

As Grotius saw his book through the press, Maurice lay dying. He died on 23 April 1625. Frederick Henry succeeded as Stadtholder and was soon found to favour at least some members of the 'Arminian' faction.[142] In Amsterdam something like a 'restoration' took place. However, Frederick Henry attempted to effect a reconciliation between the factions rather than disowning the events of 1618–19. Indeed, imposing himself as umpire between the parties, he tried to rule above the fray of factional strife.[143] Was there ever any place for Grotius in this system? It is hard to answer the question wholly in the negative. Of Frederick Henry's personal regard for his fellow-townsman (both were born in Delft) there can be no doubt. Still, a sensational return from exile for one who was, after all, still a condemned prisoner would hardly have fitted in with political prudence. The strict Calvinist ministers remained among the most vociferous elements of Dutch society, staunch Orangeists, but hardly ready to welcome the author of *Ordinum Pietas* back to an eminent position in Holland, even at Frederick Henry's bidding. On the other hand, Grotius firmly refused a return to Holland that would not be an annulment of the verdict passed in 1619 and a vindication of his conduct as pensionary of Rotterdam. A deadlock ensued. With the mirage of a glorious home-coming before his eyes, Grotius found something of a substitute for action in historiography, continuing his increasingly weary stay in Paris. At last, in October 1631, he took the plunge and returned to the Dutch Republic, notifying the Stadtholder, and also the magistrate of Rotterdam, of his arrival.[144] Evidently Grotius expected to take up his career, if not as he had left it in 1618, at least in a way compatible with what he thought was due to him.[145] He was sadly disappointed.

---

[142] 'Arminian' in the sense of the 'political Arminianism' of those patricians who adhered to the Reformed State Church, but opposed the persecution of the Remonstrant Church and wished to grant it the same—unofficial—toleration accorded to other Protestant communities, such as the Lutherans and Anabaptists. Israel, 'Frederick Henry and the Dutch Political Factions', p. 8.

[143] Ibid., p. 10.

[144] *Briefwisseling*, vol. iv, no. 1688, 2 Nov. 1631 to Frederick Henry; and no. 1703, 1 Dec. 1631 to the magistrate of Rotterdam. In his letter to the Stadtholder Grotius mentioned the 'well-known nullity of the legal proceedings' of 1618–19.

[145] Ibid., Grotius' letters of Nov. and Dec. to his brother Willem and to van Reigersberch. Grotius' refusal to *request* a pardon, nos. 1710, 1711, and 1721.

In April 1632 the States of Holland decided to have Grotius apprehended again if he did not leave the Republic. He fled in time, to Hamburg. There, at the end of 1633, negotiations began between Grotius and the Swedish Chancellor Axel Oxenstierna. After an interview at Frankfurt-on-the-Main in May 1634, Grotius accepted his appointment as Swedish ambassador at the French Court.[146] Sixteen years had passed, but in the end Grotius found himself back in European politics.

There can be no doubt that Grotius' choice of a diplomatic position was deliberate. It cannot be ascribed to any reasons other than his own conviction that a high-ranking political or legal office was the only employment he could honourably accept. However, this does not explain why Oxenstierna chose Grotius for the top post in the Swedish diplomatic service, nor why Grotius was only recalled from Paris in 1644, after serving for some ten years. It is hard to reconcile this long stay in post with the common charge that Grotius was inept as a diplomat.[147] Unfortunately we still lack an informed analysis of Grotius' role in Oxenstierna's system of diplomacy.[148] Making some guesses, one can build up a picture. To begin with, it is hardly conceivable that in 1634 Oxenstierna would not have been well briefed on Grotius. If he sent to Paris a European celebrity and a man grown punctilious after long years of disappointment, it was because he had a use for him there. Sweden's foreign policy—which after Gustavus Adolphus' death was Oxenstierna's policy—was a desperate

---

[146] *Briefwisseling*, vol. v, no. 1928; Oxenstierna's invitation to Grotius, 15 Feb. 1633, ibid., no. 1815; see also van Vollenhoven, *De Groots Sophompaneas* (Amsterdam, 1923), pp. 24 ff. It is not clear whether serious Swedish attempts to engage Grotius had been made before Oxenstierna's letter of 1633. A letter from Gustavus Adolphus, probably of Mar. 1626, was never received by Grotius. P. C. Molhuysen, 'Twee brieven uit de correspondentie van Grotius', *Mededeelingen der Koninklijke Akademie van Wetenschappen, afdeeling Letterkunde*, 74 Ser. B (1932), p. 31.

[147] Nellen, *Hugo de Groot*, p. 64, puts the question whether Oxenstierna's decision to send Grotius to Paris was not a mistake in view of his strained relations with Richelieu. On the traditional opinion of Grotius as a somewhat clumsy diplomatist, see R. Zuber, 'La Triple Jeunesse de Grotius', *17e Siècle: Revue publiée par la Société d'études du 17e siècle*, 35 (1983), p. 449.

[148] Roberts, 'Oxenstierna in Germany, 1633–1636', *Scandia*, 50 (1982), p. 86 does not even mention Grotius. S. Tunberg *et al.*, *Histoire de l'administration des affaires étrangères de Suède* (Uppsala, 1940), pp. 110 ff., is a useful but superficial account of Grotius' career as Swedish ambassador from the Swedish official sources.

gamble. Maintaining the Swedish military position in Germany meant maintaining a coalition of Protestant German princes, even if few among them were anything more than very reluctant allies against the Emperor. Only by posing as the 'head' of the German Protestants, as the defender of the *Corpus Evangelicorum* against Catholic aggression, could Sweden justify its continuing intervention.[149] All in all, with minimal resources of its own, Sweden was engaging in a daring, even reckless, imperialist policy. It clashed with Richelieu's conception of a new order in Germany. Though the French might be ready to use and even to subsidize the Swedes against the Habsburgs, for religious as well as political reasons they did not accept that Sweden was an ally on equal terms. There was a keen rivalry between France and the upstart Great Power, taking on somewhat the character of a duel between Richelieu and Oxenstierna. Experience had taught Oxenstierna that it was imperative to have in Paris a representative who would not deal with the French on his own, but who would present a bold front against French pretensions.[150]

All these requirements were admirably fulfilled by Grotius. As a foreigner he had no 'base' in Swedish policy-making bodies, but being Oxenstierna's 'creature' he would remain completely dependent on the Chancellor. During his first stay in Paris Grotius had acquired an insight into French politics that could not but be useful to the Swedish ambassador. It may not have escaped Oxenstierna that Grotius' acquaintances were often to be found among groups adverse to Richelieu's virtual dictatorship. That also might serve Sweden's interest. Last but not least, Sweden no doubt gained in 'reputation' by drawing Grotius to its cause. The man was, after all, an acknowledged genius and a great figure in the European 'république des lettres'.

---

[149] Dickmann, *Der westfälische Frieden*, pp. 152 ff. On the Swedish image of the Swedish people as the champion of Protestantism see B. Ankarloo, 'Europe and the Glory of Sweden: The Emergence of a Swedish Self-Image in the Early Seventeenth Century', in G. Rystad (ed.), *Europe and Scandinavia: Aspects of the Process of Integration in the Seventeenth Century* (Lund, 1983), p. 238.

[150] Roberts, 'Oxenstierna in Germany', p. 85. A treaty concluded with Richelieu on 1 Nov. 1634 by deputies from Sweden and its German allies had proved unacceptable to Oxenstierna.

Assuming Oxenstierna to have reasoned along these lines, he found his expectations realized. Grotius did not play an important role in Swedish–French negotiations, but that was probably expected. Adler Salvius at Hamburg and Oxenstierna himself between them controlled Sweden's German policy and managed the strained relations with the French representatives in Germany. The routine duties of the Swedish ambassador in Paris were not in themselves of great political weight. Grotius may have fallen short of expectations as a political cor-respondent,[151] and have shown a lack of diplomatic finesse,[152] but he proved a not unworthy ambassador, a respected representative of his adoptive country. However, if his appointment turned out on the whole to Oxenstierna's satisfaction, it is fairly clear that Grotius was gradually coming to feel frustrated. Indeed, it was a natural sentiment in one who for all his outward trappings of dignity had no real influence on Swedish policy. His zealous identification with the cause of Sweden was attested by his edition of the classical sources of Swedish history,[153] as well as by the choice of a military career for two of his sons,[154] but all this met with little appreciation. It seems likely that his final recall in December 1644 was inspired by Queen Christina's disagreement with Oxenstierna's policy towards France.[155] Grotius was still the Chancellor's protégé and was apparently offered no further employment. It was a dismissal, to which Grotius' death in Rostock on 28 August 1645 was the dramatic sequel.

From our point of view Grotius' Swedish career is interesting mainly for one reason, namely his taking political office under

[151] Grotius' letters to Oxenstierna rarely contain anything of great political interest. Still, he no doubt had his merits as an independent observer. *Briefwisseling*, vol. x, no. 4252, 13 Aug. 1639.

[152] Corroboration of this is generally found in the ending of direct relations with Richelieu because of the Cardinal's pretensions of precedence. Though it seems hardly likely that an 'expedient' could not have been found saving both parties' formal positions, one must keep in mind the supreme importance of matters of 'precedence' in 17th-century diplomacy.

[153] Ter Meulen and Diermanse, *Bibliographie*, 1950, no. 735. On the 'Gothic Myth' see Roberts, *The Swedish Imperial Experience 1560–1718* (Cambridge, 1979), p. 71. Also, Ankarloo, 'Europe and the Glory of Sweden', p. 241.

[154] Both Diederik and Cornelis were expressly ordered by Grotius not to leave Swedish military service, a career most unlikely for scions from a Dutch patrician family.

[155] Dickmann, *Der westfälische Frieden*, p. 304.

Oxenstierna at all. This in itself goes far to disprove the view of the 'sage of Delft' as a dispassionate prophet of the rule of law. Those who try to give Grotius some credit for promoting the 1648 peace settlement in Westphalia[156] are, in our opinion, taking his own pious utterings in his letters to Dutch friends far too seriously. However reluctantly, it seems that we have to reconcile ourselves to a Grotius acting the part of an ornament to Oxenstierna's war machine. It may have been a somewhat incongruous role, but Grotius stuck to it—albeit with some hesitations and misgivings.[157]

At the same time his main intellectual activity of this period, his critical study of the dogmatic disputes between the Protestant and the Roman Catholic churches, clearly pointed in a direction which diverged from Sweden's religio-political stance in European politics. Grotius refuted the Protestant tenets regarding the Pope as the Antichrist, and in general he seriously undermined the Protestant position against Roman Catholicism. Understandably, the rumour of his conversion ('Grotius papizans') spread. In an age in which religious controversies inevitably had political impact, Grotius took great risks in provoking the retorts of a host of dogmatic Lutheran and Calvinist theologians.[158] His political credit cannot but have suffered. It is a tantalizing question, here for several reasons to be left unanswered, how Grotius reconciled his loyalty to Sweden's cause with his 'ecumenical' views.[159]

This chapter has suggested that there is a case for a more holistic view of Grotius and his works, particularly of the famous *Mare Liberum* and *De Jure Belli ac Pacis*, than is generally adopted. With someone as versatile as Grotius, the inevitable division of 'Grotian studies' among members of several different

---

[156] Gellinek, 'Hugo Grotius und Gerard ter Borch; Neues zum Kampf um den Westfälische Frieden', *Simpliciana: Schriften der Grimmelshausen-Gessellschaft*, 3 (1982).

[157] It would be easy to gather an impressive list of complaints, mostly about the delays in payment of Grotius' salary (e.g. *Briefwisseling*, x. 703). Such complaints are, however, so much part and parcel of 17th-century diplomatic correspondence that it is hard to take them very seriously.

[158] H. Bots and P. Leroy, 'Hugo Grotius et la réunion des Chrétiens: Entre le savoir et l'inquiétude', *17e Siècle*, 35 (1983), p. 459.

[159] Nellen, *Hugo de Groot*, p. 85, mentions that according to van Reigersberch (Aug. 1644) Grotius had by his theological works lost his credit with Oxenstierna.

faculties may cause serious distortions that can only be cor-
rected by an attempt at restoring Grotius' own perspective. It
seems incontrovertible that among the motives determining
Grotius' activities, his political aspirations played a constant
and considerable, even a dominant role. His major theological
and historical works are not to be understood if one does not
take into account the author's purpose. The same applies to
Grotius' works on international law. That these were written
with a political purpose is of course clear as regards *Mare
Liberum*, but applies also, though much more subtly, to *De Jure
Belli ac Pacis*.

4

Grotius and Gentili: A Reassessment of Thomas E. Holland's Inaugural Lecture[1]

PETER HAGGENMACHER

Le père du droit des gens, c'est une société en nom
collectif, si j'ose ainsi m'exprimer; c'est une série de
penseurs et de juristes, dont les uns ont précédé Grotius,
dont les autres ont élargi et développé son œuvre, au
cours du XVIIe et du XVIIIe siècles.

Maurice Bourquin[2]

No direct link seems to exist between Grotius and the City of
Oxford: he never studied at its University, nor was he even
able to pay it a visit during the two months he spent in
England on his diplomatic mission in 1613.[3] Yet some link
was at least indirectly established when, over a century ago,
an Oxford professor, Thomas Erskine Holland, put forth the
first real challenge to Grotius' undisputed reputation as the
founder of international law by drawing attention to an earlier
Oxonian, Alberico Gentili (1552–1608), who had in his eyes
'some claim to dispute with Grotius himself the title of "father
of International Law"'. Holland's inaugural lecture, delivered

[1] Cordial thanks are due to José Mico who helped to render this paper somewhat
more reminiscent of English than its author alone could have done.
[2] Bourquin, 'Grotius est-il le père du droit des gens? (1583–1645)', in *Grandes figures
et grandes œuvres juridiques* (Mémoires publiés par la Faculté de Droit de Genève, no. 6,
Geneva, 1948), p. 94.
[3] Such a visit seems in fact to have been contemplated in the company of Isaac
Casaubon and Sir Henry Savile who had together left London for Oxford to do some
research in the Bodleian Library. In his letter to Grotius of 19 May 1613, Casaubon
complains of his absence which deprives him of their 'confabulations': 'Valde autem
dolemus et nobilissimus Savilius et ego, non licuisse tibi per tua negotia hoc iter una
nobiscum conficere.' *Briefwisseling van Hugo Grotius* (The Hague, 1928–), vol. i,
no. 264, p. 238. The Dutch mission to England lasted from 22 Mar. to 27 May 1613.
Most of Grotius' time was certainly spent in London; yet he visited several royal
castles, as witnessed by some of his epigrams in: *Poemata Omnia*, 4th edn. (Leiden,
1645), pp. 269–70. For the negotiations, see below, n. 41.

at All Souls College on 7 November 1874, was entirely
devoted to this Italian who had fled his native country on
account of his Protestant faith, come to England in 1580, and
taught law in Oxford for almost two decades.[4] It seems
therefore opportune to consider Grotius' relation to Gentili,
and by the same token to review Holland's vindication of him.

(a) PROFESSOR HOLLAND'S CLAIM

There may be some exaggeration in Holland's assertion that
Gentili's memory had 'wellnigh perished',[5] suggesting as it
does that it had to be restored altogether. In fact Gentili was
never entirely forgotten, even during the eighteenth and
nineteenth centuries when Grotius had come to be generally
regarded as the sole founding father of the *jus naturae et gentium*,
bringing forth at a single Promethean stroke, as it were, a
twofold science that was to shed light on a vast field
supposedly immersed in deep obscurity ever since the end of
antiquity.[6] No doubt Gentili's reputation in the seventeenth
century, culminating in the inclusion of an article on him in
Pierre Bayle's *Dictionnaire*,[7] suffered a severe set-back during
the period following the Peace of Utrecht. But it did not
vanish altogether. Thus Glafey's *Geschichte des Rechts der
Vernunft* praises his work in a separate paragraph.[8] In 1770 an

---

[4] The text of the lecture is reproduced with several appendices in: Thomas E.
Holland, *Studies in International Law* (Oxford, 1898), pp. 1–39 (hereinafter cited as
Holland, 'Alberico Gentili').

[5] Ibid., p. 2.

[6] Such was still e.g. Dietrich H. L. von Ompteda's view: 'Die Zeiten des
Mittelalters, worunter ich hier den Zeitraum seit der Publication der im vorigen
Abschnitte berührten römischen Gesetzbücher bis zu Erscheinung des vortrefflichen
Werks des Grotii vom Rechte des Krieges und Friedens, welches ein helleres und ganz
neues Licht in Ansehung des Völkerrechts anzündete, mithin vom ersten Viertel des
6ten bis zum ersten Viertel des 17ten Jahrhunderts, oder vom Jahre 533 bis zum
Jahre 1625 verstehe, sind für die Wissenschaft des Völkerrechts äusserst unfruchtbar,
und kaum kommt in diesem ganzen den Wissenschaften überhaupt so ungünstigen
Zeitverlaufe irgend etwas in Ansehung dieses Theils der Gelehrsamkeit vor, was nur
eine Erwähnung verdiente.' *Litteratur des gesammten sowohl natürlichen als positiven
Völkerrechts* (Regensburg, 1785), § 45, p. 162 (hereinafter cited as *Litteratur*).

[7] Pierre Bayle, *Dictionnaire historique et critique*, 5th edn. (Amsterdam, 1734), iii. 33–4
(1st edn., 1695–7).

[8] Adam Friedrich Glafey, *Geschichte des Rechts der Vernunft* (Leipzig, 1739), book III,
§ 4, p. 85 (1st edn., Frankfürt, 1723).

edition of his *Opera Juridica Selectiora* was started, although publication was interrupted after two volumes owing to the editor's death.[9] Fifteen years later Martens, in one of his early works, considers Gentili the only predecessor of Grotius worth mentioning,[10] whilst Ompteda declares him 'the first scholar to have earned himself some merit in the promotion of the science of the Law of Nations'.[11] In 1795 he appears in Ward's famous *Enquiry* as the one 'who bore the palm from all the jurists before Grotius'.[12] During the first half of the nineteenth century he is discussed in Hallam's *Introduction to the Literature of Europe*[13] as well as in Wheaton's *History of the Law of Nations*.[14] These and other examples show that there is a continuous 'thread of reference to his work'[15] up to the time of Holland's lecture.

For all these favourable comments, Gentili was still regarded as a mere 'predecessor' of Grotius, and his work as a rather imperfect prefiguration of the great book of 1625. Thus Kaltenborn's monograph of 1848, the first to be especially devoted to Grotius' 'forerunners', keeps looking upon Grotius

---

[9] Coleman Phillipson, Introduction to Gentili, *De Jure Belli Libri Tres* (Classics of International Law, Oxford, 1933), ii. 15a–16a n. 1 (hereinafter cited as Phillipson, 'Introduction'). See also Giorgio del Vecchio, *Ricordando Alberico Gentili. Con un saggio di bibliografia gentiliana*, 2nd edn. (Rome, 1936), p. 10.

[10] 'Post exigua nonnullorum sec. 16 et initio sec. 17 circa studium iuris naturae et gentium molimina e quibus solus Albericus Gentilis nominandus videtur, longe feliciori successu Hugo Grotius in immortali suo de belli et pacis opere cum universalis, tum iuris gentium practici principia exposuit . . .' Georg Friedrich von Martens, *Primae Lineae Juris Gentium Europaearum Practici in Usum Auditorum Adumbratae* (Göttingen, 1785), Prolegomena, § 7, p. 6.

[11] Ompteda, *Litteratur*, § 49, pp. 168–9. 'Er . . . hat besonders die Materie vom Rechte des Krieges und vom Gesandtschaftsrechte zu allererst auf eine der Sache ziemlich angemessene Art ausgeführet.' Ibid., p. 168. Concerning more especially Gentili's *De Jure Belli*, Ompteda observes: 'Dieses Werk des Albericus Gentilis . . . ist ziemlich ausführlich und gründlich, doch freilich nach dem Geschmacke damaliger Zeiten, und heutiges Tages wenig brauchbar.' Ibid., § 290, p. 615.

[12] Robert Ward, *An Enquiry into the Foundation and History of the Law of Nations, from the Time of the Greeks and Romans, to the Age of Grotius* (London, 1795), vol. ii, chap. 18, p. 608; but see also p. 612.

[13] Henry Hallam, *Introduction to the Literature of Europe in the Fifteenth, Sixteenth, and Seventeenth Centuries* (Paris, 1839), vol. ii, chap. 4, §§ 90–2, pp. 153–5.

[14] Henry Wheaton, *Histoire des progrès du droit des gens en Europe et en Amérique depuis la Paix de Westphalie jusqu'à nos jours*, 3rd edn. (Leipzig, 1853), i. 49–53.

[15] Kenneth R. Simmonds, 'Hugo Grotius and Alberico Gentili', *Jahrbuch für Internationales Recht*, 8 (1959), p. 85 (hereinafter cited as Simmonds, 'Hugo Grotius and Alberico Gentili').

as the *Epochemann*,[16] Gentili being no more than an important precursor. Not before Holland, then, was Gentili perceived in his own right for the part he played in the genesis of international law. This probably accounts for the emphatic terms of the inaugural lecture. Holland saw in him the first writer to have reached a clear conception of international law as a separate legal discipline, Grotius merely completing the picture sketched by him some decades earlier.[17] The lecture did succeed in drawing attention to Gentili in an unprecedented way. Grotius was never thereafter to regain the lonely and absolute position he had traditionally enjoyed. Indeed, for some time the two authors would almost appear like two runners in a stadium, each encouraged by his own supporters, Grotius mostly a little ahead of his 'forerunner',[18] both of them soon to be joined by several eminent Spaniards—especially Francisco de Vitoria, Fernando Vasquez de Menchaca, and Francisco Suarez—all of whom had shared Gentili's long sojourn in the purgatory of fame.[19]

[16] Carl Baron Kaltenborn von Stachau, *Die Vorläufer des Hugo Grotius auf dem Gebiete des Jus naturae et gentium sowie der Politik im Reformationszeitalter* (Leipzig, 1848), part I, p. 229 (hereinafter cited as *Die Vorläufer*). This judgement, however, is derived from Grotius being crucial both for the law of nations and for the law of nature. Considering the former in itself, Kaltenborn thinks very highly of Gentili and may to that extent have inspired Holland's appreciation: 'Er [i.e. Gentili] ist der erste wichtigere Autor des modernen Völkerrechts und in dieser Beziehung als der eigentliche und unmittelbare Vorläufer des Grotius zu betrachten. Ja ich halte ihn für die unmittelbare Grundlage des Grotius, dem ich desswegen im gewissen Sinne seine Originalität und seine gerühmte Vaterschaft der modernen Völkerrechtswissenschaft in etwas abzusprechen nicht unterlassen kann.' *Die Vorläufer*, part I, p. 228. See also, id. *Kritik des Völkerrechts* (Leipzig, 1847), pp. 34–7.

[17] Holland, 'Alberico Gentili', p. 2.

[18] For this posthumous competition, enhanced by blooming nationalisms, see esp. ibid., Appendix no. 9, pp. 37–8; and Gesina van der Molen, *Alberico Gentili and the Development of International Law*, 2nd rev. edn. (Leiden, 1968), pp. 60–3 (hereinafter cited as van der Molen, *Alberico Gentili*).

[19] Although these authors were not entirely forgotten, their importance tended to be minimized in the literature on the Law of Nations, widely dominated as it was by Protestant authors, as appears e.g. in Kaltenborn's revealing appreciation, *Die Vorläufer*, part I, pp. 124–90. All the more noteworthy are Robert Fruin's and Gerard Hamaker's judgements declaring Vitoria, Soto, Covarrubias, and Vasquez de Menchaca to be by far more important with respect to Grotius than was Gentili, whose accomplishments had been stressed the year before by W. A. Reiger, *Commentatio de Alberico Gentili, Grotio ad condendam juris gentium disciplinam viam praeeunte* (Groningen, 1867); see Fruin, 'Een onuitgegeven werk van Hugo de Groot', *De Gids*, 1868, translated as: 'An Unpublished Work of Hugo Grotius's', *Bibliotheca Visseriana*, 5 (1925), pp. 60–1 (hereinafter cited as Fruin, 'An Unpublished Work'); Gerard

Whereas the influence of the theologians and jurists of Spain's Golden Century on Grotius has since been widely studied—with the unexpected result that he sometimes appears to be merely their late follower—there has been a tendency to neglect his relation to Gentili. There are, it is true, numerous incidental observations by many authors, including some relevant comments in Gesina van der Molen's monograph on Gentili: but only a few—notably Kenneth R. Simmonds, Fujo Ito, and Hugo Fortuin—have examined this relationship in itself.[20] The purpose here is to reconsider it more especially with regard to the debt owed by Grotius to his Italian predecessor, a debt he is suspected to have insufficiently acknowledged. This at least is what Holland seemed to imply when he stated:

> Grotius confesses his debt to Gentilis, though in words which hardly suggest its full extent. 'Albericus Gentilis', he says, 'cuius diligentia sicut alios adiuvari posse scio, et me adiutum profiteor'. In point of fact, the general scheme of the immortal work of Grotius is taken from that of his predecessor, and both works rest upon the same conception of natural law. The finished picture has, however, consigned the sketch to oblivion, and the merits of the earlier jurist by no means receive the recognition which they deserve.[21]

To be sure, other parts of the lecture tend to show that Holland was 'by no means concerned to place Gentilis on a level with his undeniably greater follower'.[22] He recognized the difference between their works and thought it comparable to the distance separating Marlowe from Shakespeare. Yet whatever their actual achievements, he still regarded their merits in bringing about the discipline of international law as at least equivalent. It was Gentili whom he credited with

---

Hamaker, 'Praefatio' to *Hugonis Grotii De Jure Praedae Commentarius* (The Hague, 1868), p. xi.

[20] Van der Molen, *Alberico Gentili*, esp. pp. 113, 124–37, 149, 162–7, 176–82, 240–5; K. R. Simmonds, 'Hugo Grotius and Alberico Gentili'; id., 'Some English Precursors of Hugo Grotius', *Transactions of the Grotius Society*, 43 (1957), pp. 143–57; F. Ito, 'Alberico Gentili e Ugo Grozio', *Rivista internazionale di filosofia del diritto*, 41 (1964), pp. 621–7 (hereinafter cited as Ito, 'Alberico Gentili'); Hugo Fortuin, 'Alberico Gentili en Hugo de Groot', *Netherlands International Law Review*, 16 (1969), pp. 364–90 (this article is actually a review of van der Molen's above-mentioned monograph).

[21] Holland, 'Alberico Gentili', p. 2.　　　　　[22] Ibid., p. 23.

having accomplished the real pioneering work by combining the practical but rather sterile endeavours of 'Catholic casuists'[23] with the supposedly more enlightened Protestant speculations on natural law into a genuine science of international law: Grotius, he thought, had but to follow in 'the path thus opened up' by his predecessor.[24]

In Holland's opinion, then, Gentili's sketch was at least as meritorious as Grotius' ensuing picture, entitling its author to an equal share in the 'paternity' of international law. More than a century has elapsed since his inaugural lecture. This chapter attempts a re-examination of his judgement on the respective positions of the two authors in the emergence of international law as a legal discipline, particularly with reference to Gentili's influence on Grotius. First, however, a brief account of their writings, as far as relevant to the present subject, would appear useful.

(b) GENTILI'S WRITINGS ON THE LAW OF NATIONS

Born in 1552, Alberico Gentili began his legal career in his native country, the March of Ancona, around 1573;[25] yet it was only after he came to England in 1580 that he seems to have touched upon that particular sphere of law he calls *jus gentium*, as opposed to *jus civile*, municipal law, in the terminology of the Roman jurisconsults. His first publication in that field was a treatise on embassies, *De Legationibus Libri Tres*.[26] Written in 1585, this work dates from the period of his first stay in Oxford from December 1580 to the summer of 1586. It had grown out of a legal opinion he had given in 1584—the year of the assassination of William the Silent—in

[23] Holland, 'Alberico Gentili', pp. 20–3. See also Holland's subsequent lecture of 1879 (quoted below, n. 93), pp. 57–8.

[24] Holland, 'Alberico Gentili', p. 21. In the introduction to his edition of Gentili's *De Jure Belli* (Oxford, 1877), Holland calls it the *archetypus* of Grotius' treatise and hence the 'real cradle of the modern Law of Nations', Grotius being therefore but the 'most famous of Albericus' imitators' (p. xxi).

[25] The biographical facts concerning Gentili are mainly based on van der Molen, *Alberico Gentili, passim*, esp. chap. 2, pp. 35–63.

[26] *De Legationibus* was reproduced in the edition of Hanau, 1594, with a preface by Ernest Nys (Classics of International Law, New York, 1924). See also van der Molen, *Alberico Gentili*, chap. 4, pp. 87–112.

the case of the Spanish ambassador, Don Bernardino de Mendoza, involved in the Throckmorton conspiracy against Queen Elizabeth. Dissenting from the opinion of the Privy Council which recommended punishing the ambassador, Gentili held, together with Jean Hotman who had been consulted on the same question, that in the circumstances his actions were still covered by criminal immunity. This opinion was accepted and led to Mendoza's expulsion from England. Soon after, Gentili delivered a lecture on the rights and duties of ambassadors, and the following year he wrote in comparatively short time the three books of his treatise *On Embassies*. It was published in July 1585 and dedicated to Sir Philip Sidney, Gentili's protector. Whatever predecessors he may have had in this particular field, his work is undoubtedly the first successful attempt to encompass diplomatic law as a coherent whole.[27]

Gentili's next study on the Law of Nations took him much longer, its genesis extending over the major part of what may be called his second Oxford period. He had in fact decided in 1586 to leave England, and settled in Wittenberg. But the following year he was called back to Oxford and appointed Regius Professor of Civil Law, a position he held until 1600. During that period he wrote his main contribution to international law, his work on the law of war.

Like the previous one, this treatise arose from a concrete incident, again involving Spain, although on a vastly greater scale—the attempted invasion of England by the Invincible Armada. On 30 June 1588, about three weeks before the rival fleets were to meet for a ten days' struggle culminating in the Battle of Gravelines, Gentili informed his friend John Bennett that he was to deliver during the forthcoming *Comitia* an oration on the law of war, especially 'on the causes that justify its beginning and on the manner of conducting it, on the rights of the victors and the vanquished'. Moreover he was to take part in a disputation on

---

[27] Diplomatic law as such appears especially in book II, whilst book I mainly deals with definitions and historical aspects, and book III with the qualities required in an ambassador. Questions of diplomatic immunities as raised by the Mendoza incident are discussed in chaps. 17–21 of book II.

Whether a war may be just on both sides; whether the right of
embassies subsists in a civil war; whether the subject of a prince
whose religion is different from his may take up arms against a
prince of his own creed, in other words whether a papist may
legitimately fight against the Pope in the service of his sovereign the
Queen.[28]

The last point was of course specially relevant in view of
current political developments. The whole letter throws
valuable light on the circumstances giving birth to a work
which, from a mere academic discourse, was to grow into an
elaborate treatise—probably the largest written on the subject
until then.

   The substance of Gentili's oration was published towards
the end of 1588 under the title *De Jure Belli Commentatio Prima*.
It was to be followed by a *Commentatio Secunda* at the beginning
of 1589, both being printed together shortly afterwards at
Leiden. A *Commentatio Tertia* appeared that same year. But
Gentili did not rest there: he continued his investigations into
the law of war for almost a decade, which enabled him in 1598
to put into print a totally revised version of the three
commentationes, about five times as long:[29] this was to be the *De
Jure Belli* as we know it—and as Grotius himself was to know
it very soon after its publication.[30]

   Meanwhile, Gentili had set out on an additional enquiry
into the lawfulness of war on the basis of some cases taken
from Roman history. He thus examined the main wars of the
Romans in two parallel studies. The first, entitled *De Injustitia
Bellica Romanorum, Actio*, shows that all those wars were
unlawful; the second was a *Defensio* of the same Roman wars.
Both appeared together in 1599 under the title *De Armis
Romanis et Injustitia Bellica Romanorum Libri Duo*.[31] The essay is
significant mainly on account of the historical material it
contains. It proves Gentili's sustained interest in the legal
problems of war and no doubt greatly helped him in recasting

---

[28] This author's translation; for the Latin original, see Holland, 'Alberico Gentili',
Appendix no. IV, pp. 29–30; see also van der Molen, *Alberico Gentili*, p. 53.

[29] See van der Molen, *Alberico Gentili*, p. 54.

[30] *JB* was reproduced in the edition of Hanau: Apud Haeredes Guilielmi Antonii,
1612 (Classics of International Law, Oxford, 1933). See also above, n. 9.

[31] Repr. under the title *De Armis Romanis* in Gentili's *Opera juridica selectiora*,
i (Naples, 1770). See also above, n. 9.

his *Three Books on the Law of War*. These were in turn to assist Grotius, mainly on account of the emphasis placed on the actual practice of belligerents, the most authoritative among them being precisely the practice of the Romans.

Up to that time Gentili had considered the Law of Nations partly as a legal adviser, partly—and above all—as a scholar. Shortly before his death came his last opportunity to dwell upon it, this time as a lawyer. He had become a member of Gray's Inn in 1600, ceasing thereby to teach the law in order to serve it as a practitioner. As such he reverted to international questions five years later. The occasion was again brought about by Spain, though in a reversed setting, for he was now to defend Spanish interests before the Admiralty Bar against Dutch claims arising out of the war between Spain and the United Provinces, England being a neutral power. Gentili had been appointed Advocate to the Spanish Embassy in 1605 and thus, paradoxically, the Protestant refugee had come to side with the main Catholic power against the country which was steadily becoming a bastion of Calvinism. He was to hold this position until his death three years later. His pleas, notes, and opinions were subsequently collected by his brother Scipio Gentili, who published them in 1613 under the title *Hispanicae Advocationis Libri Duo*.[32] This 'first case-book of the Law of Nations',[33] as it has been somewhat exaggeratedly called, is obviously quite different from Gentili's earlier, scholarly works. It is interesting mainly for the shrewd, if not unbiased, light it sheds on contemporary maritime practice.

(c) GROTIUS' WRITINGS ON THE LAW OF NATIONS

Grotius, born in 1583, was Gentili's junior by thirty-one years. Of legendary precocity, it took him less than three decades to

---

[32] The *Hispanica Advocatio* was reproduced in the edition of Amsterdam: Johannes van Ravesteyn, 1661, with an Introduction by Frank F. Abbott (Classics of International Law, New York, 1921). See also van der Molen, *Alberico Gentili*, chap. 6, pp. 159–96; and Simmonds, 'Alberico Gentili at the Admiralty Bar, 1605–1608', *Archiv des Völkerrechts*, 7 (1958–9), pp. 3–23.

[33] Travers Twiss, *Two Introductory Lectures on the Science of International Law* (1856), p. 12, quoted Simmonds, 'Alberico Gentili', p. 22.

become Gentili's equal, even though his initial interests did not concern law. At first he devoted himself mainly to philology and history,[34] and it is doubtful whether he even studied law at the University of Leiden,[35] where he remained from the age of eleven to fifteen. Only later, during his visit to France in 1598, did he touch upon the field of jurisprudence which more than anything else was to secure his fame in the eyes of posterity. Shortly before the turn of the century he was admitted to the Bar of The Hague. He was by then barely 17 years old, but seems to have become very soon as able a lawyer as Gentili, who started to practise law about a year later in London at the age of 48.

Unlike Gentili, it was in this capacity, in 1604, that Grotius first came upon international legal relations. Although the case he had to deal with also involved Spain, his immediate adversaries were actually Dutch—a group of shareholders of the United Netherlands East India Company. An admiral of the Company had captured a Portuguese ship—a carrack— in the Straits of Malacca. This action seemed gravely objectionable to the Mennonite shareholders, who regarded any kind of violence as contrary to Christ's teachings, and threatened to withdraw from the recently founded Company in order to set up a rival institution on French territory. The directors of the Company therefore turned to Grotius for a legal opinion justifying the incident as well as the warlike attitude underlying it.[36] Grotius was doubtless delighted by this assignment, which caused him to write between 1604 and 1606 his first[37] study on the Law of Nations, commonly known as *De Jure Praedae Commentarius.*[38]

[34] Willem J. M. van Eysinga, *Hugo Grotius: Eine biographische Skizze*, trans. Plemp van Duiveland (Basle, 1952), pp. 20–30. On the relevant cultural influences, see more generally Fiorella de Michelis, *Le origini storiche e culturali del pensiero di Ugo Grozio* (Florence, 1967).

[35] Van Eysinga, 'Quelques observations sur Grotius et le droit romain', *Grotiana*, 10 (1942–7), p. 18.

[36] Fruin, 'An Unpublished Work', pp. 13–36.

[37] This distinction was claimed by van Eysinga for Grotius' *Parallelon Rerumpublicarum*, a study comparing Athens, Rome, and Holland, apparently written shortly after 1600; see van Eysinga, 'Het oudste bekende geschrift van de Groot over volkenrecht', *Mededeelingen der Nederlandsche Akademie van Wetenschappen*, afd. letterkunde, nieuwe reeks, deel 4, no. 11 (1941), pp. 463–74. Yet, although book 3, chap. 6 (*De fide et perfidia*), has some bearing on international law and morality, Grotius' perspective in this work is not a specifically legal one at all, since he more generally compares the

To prove that the prize was not a mere act of piracy but a legitimate act of war, Grotius first endeavoured to show that it had occurred in the course of a just war. This induced him to discuss the general conditions of just war, and in turn the very foundations of the law of war and of law in general. Though limited in scope by the concrete case under examination, *De Jure Praedae* therefore contained a whole theory on the law of war, which had been precisely the subject of Gentili's great treatise.

It is not entirely clear why *De Jure Praedae* was not published upon completion in 1606. As a matter of fact, the work remained unknown until it came to light in 1864 at a sale of Grotian manuscripts in The Hague.[39] Grotius nevertheless managed to publish at least a fragment of it in 1609 when the major part of chapter 12 was printed and anonymously

customs and national characters of the three communities. It is therefore doubtful whether this chapter can be regarded as the origin of *JP*, as seemingly held by W. Fikentscher in a stimulating though rather debatable essay: *De fide et perfidia—Der Treuegedanke in den 'Staatsparallelen' des Hugo Grotius aus heutiger Sicht* (Munich, Bayerische Akademie der Wissenschaften, Philosophisch-historische Klasse, Sitzungsberichte, 1979, 1). The few years separating the composition of the two works actually brought about a decisive shift in Grotius' general conceptions and outlook.

[38] Richard Tuck's recent suggestion to replace the present title by *De Indis* is rather unfortunate ('Grotius, Carneades and Hobbes', *Grotiana*, 4 (1983), pp. 44 and 49). Whatever its precise origin, the title *De Jure Praedae* is in fact quite appropriate (and in this writer's opinion basically Grotian too). To be sure, in one of his rare allusions to the manuscript Grotius calls it *de rebus Indicis opusculum* (letter to Lingelsheim of 1 Nov. 1606, *Briefwisseling*, vol. i, no. 86, p. 72); but this was merely an easy way of referring to the work which indeed had to do with a dispute concerning Holland's 'Indian affairs' (not 'the Indians' as in Dr Tuck's suggested title) through the action taken by the East India Company. The gist of the manuscript (considered as a whole, not merely with regard to its twelfth chapter) was precisely the lawfulness of this 'action', i.e. the prize case examined at length in it. The initial controversy raised by the Mennonites was an internal one and did not concern the trade with the East Indies as such—which no Dutchman had of course ever objected to—but the warlike means whereby the Company had resolved to carry it on. Only later, in 1608–9, under the influence of the negotiations with Spain, did the emphasis shift to the *Indicana commercia* mentioned in the subtitle of *Mare Liberum* (see below, n. 40); this evolution is reflected in the introductory sentences of the *Defensio Capitis quinti Maris liberi oppugnati a Guilielmo Welwodo* (see below, n. 42), where Grotius mentions the 'rather ample commentary which I hitherto refrained from publishing' (whence apparently the term *commentarius* was derived by the editors). Yet these were obviously second thoughts; they should not be confused with Grotius' initial intentions in 1604–6.

[39] The manuscript was bought by the University of Leiden and first edited in 1868 by G. Hamaker (see above, n. 19). A collotype reproduction of the manuscript was edited by Gwladys L. Williams with an English translation (Classics of International Law, Oxford, 1950).

published as an independent work under the celebrated title of *Mare Liberum*, to support the Dutch position in the negotiations with Spain—negotiations which were shortly to bring about the Twelve Years Truce. Though anonymous, this was his first actual publication in the field of the Law of Nations: it came out less than a year after Gentili's death.[40]

While the Truce provisionally halted the young Republic's external struggle for independence, it opened up a period of inner turmoil during which Grotius played an ever-increasing part on the side of Oldenbarnevelt and the ruling oligarchy of Holland against the claims of the orthodox Calvinist party. The crisis was abruptly ended by Prince Maurice's *coup de force* in August 1618, which entailed *inter alia* the fall and execution of Oldenbarnevelt as well as Grotius' trial and sentence to life imprisonment. This period was therefore hardly conducive to his activity in the sphere of international relations, with the possible exception of his participation in the Anglo-Dutch negotiations of 1613 in London and of 1615 in The Hague,[41] as well as an unfinished draft defending his *Mare Liberum* against a Scottish professor of civil law, William Welwod.[42]

Only after his celebrated escape from the fortress of Loevestein in 1621 was he able seriously to revert to what he deemed 'the noblest part of law', the *jus naturae et gentium*. It was in Paris between 1623 and 1625 that he wrote the treatise which was to become his masterpiece, *De Jure Belli ac Pacis*

---

[40] *Mare liberum, sive de jure quod Batavis competit ad Indicana commercia, dissertatio* (Leiden, 1609). The work underwent several editions and was reprinted as an appendix in many editions of *JBP*; see J. ter Meulen and P. J. J. Diermanse, *Bibliographie des écrits imprimés de Hugo Grotius* (The Hague, 1950), nos. 541–51, pp. 210–16.

[41] For these negotiations, see G. N. Clark, 'Grotius' East India Mission to England', *Transactions of the Grotius Society*, 20 (1935), pp. 45–84; van Eysinga, 'Huig de Groot als Nederlandsch gezant', *Mededeelingen der Nederlandsche Akademie van Wetenschappen*, afd. letterkunde, nieuwe reeks, deel 3, (1940), pp. 359–77; Clark and van Eysinga, 'The Colonial Conferences between England and The Netherlands in 1613 and 1615', *Bibliotheca Visseriana*, 15 (1940); ibid. 17 (1951).

[42] Having shared the fate of *JP*, this manuscript was likewise bought by the University of Leiden in 1864 and subsequently edited by Samuel Muller as an appendix to his *Mare clausum: Bijdrage tot de geschiedenis der rivaliteit van Engeland en Nederland in de zeventiende eeuw* (Amsterdam, 1872), pp. 331–61. For an English translation, see Herbert F. Wright, 'Some Less Known Works of Hugo Grotius', *Bibliotheca Visseriana*, 7 (1928), pp. 154–205. A collotype reproduction was published by the Carnegie Endowment for International Peace *c*.1951.

Libri Tres.[43] This work, basically a revised and greatly elaborated version of the theoretical part of *De Jure Praedae*, again dealt with the law of war: once again therefore Grotius was treading the same ground as Gentili, whose fate as an exile he had by now come to share.

De Jure Belli ac Pacis was to be his major, but also his last, contribution to the Law of Nations. His later interests focused mainly on theological questions, his foremost preoccupation being the reunification of Christianity.[44] He was, however, involved in international affairs after 1635 as Swedish ambassador to the court of Louis XIII, and left an impressive amount of correspondence reflecting contemporary international practice.[45] But he wrote no further legal work in this particular field, limiting himself to several thorough revisions of *De Jure Belli ac Pacis*,[46] which he obviously—and understandably—considered as his last word on the question.

(d) GENTILI'S PLACE IN GROTIUS' WORKS

Such, then, are in rough outline the respective achievements of the two authors with regard to the Law of Nations. We now revert to the question raised earlier: to what degree is Gentili

[43] For the genesis of *JBP*, see Jesse S. Reeves, 'The First Edition of Grotius' De Jure Belli Ac Pacis, 1625', *AJIL* 19 (1925), pp. 12–23; and P. C. Molhuysen, 'Over de editio princeps van Grotius' De Iure Belli ac Pacis', *Mededeelingen der Koninklijke Akademie van Wetenschappen te Amsterdam*, afd. letterkunde, deel 60, serie B, no. 1 (1925), pp. 1–8. Editions and translations of *JBP* were very numerous: see ter Meulen and Diermanse, *Bibliographie*, 1950, nos. 565–676, pp. 222–300. The best edition is the *Editio major* prepared by B. J. A. de Kanter-van Hettinga Tromp (Leiden, 1939).

[44] On this point, which is of course not entirely devoid of international implications, see in particular Antonio Droetto, 'La formula giuridica dell'ecumenismo groziano', *Rivista internazionale di filosofia del diritto*, 41 (1964), pp. 515–38, repr. in A. Droetto, *Studi Groziani* (Turin, 1968), pp. 163–88; and Dieter Wolf, *Die Irenik des Hugo Grotius nach ihren Prinzipien und biographisch-geistesgeschichtlichen Perspektiven* (Marburg, 1969).

[45] The last two years of Grotius' correspondence are not yet published in the *Briefwisseling*; see, however, *Hugonis Grotii . . . Epistolae Quotquot reperiri potuerunt* (Amsterdam, 1687). For Grotius' diplomatic activities in Paris, see W. S. M. Knight, *The Life and Works of Hugo Grotius* (London, 1925), pp. 224–44 (hereinafter cited as Knight, *Life and Works*).

[46] On Grotius' revisions, see Cornelis van Vollenhoven, 'L'Édition de 1631 du De Jure Belli ac Pacis de Grotius (1625)', *Mededeelingen der Koninklijke Akademie van Wetenschappen*, afd. letterkunde, deel 66, serie B, no. 2 (1928), pp. 31–60.

present in Grotius' writings and how far did he influence his thinking?

Gentili's name appears first in *De Jure Praedae*, with ten references[47] to his *De Jure Belli*—an appreciable number, even though other sixteenth-century or medieval jurists are mentioned more often. Thus Balthazar Ayala, a Belgo-Spanish military judge who had died the year after Grotius' birth, the author of an important work on the law of war, appears 16 times.[48] Pope Innocent IV and Panormitanus, the two great canonists of the thirteenth and the fifteenth centuries, are both mentioned 25 times. Diego de Covarrubias, the famous Spanish bishop and canonist of the sixteenth century, 34 times. Baldus de Ubaldis and his master Bartolus de Saxoferrato, the two foremost civilist commentators of the fourteenth century, 51 and 57 times respectively. Fernando Vasquez de Menchaca, a Spanish jurist greatly revered by the young Grotius who found in his work one of the key texts in defence of the freedom of the sea,[49] appears 74 times. Finally, the *Summa Summarum* of the canonist Sylvester Prierias is cited no less than 90 times.[50]

Against these figures the ten references to Gentili's work may seem negligible. They are not, however, when compared to the use made of other equally important jurists of the three preceding centuries. This is particularly the case for a group of sixteenth-century humanist jurists, whose influence on Grotius' legal thinking is undoubtedly crucial, but who are mentioned less frequently than Gentili.[51] The same is true for several medieval legists of the Bartolist school, some of whom Grotius held in great esteem.[52] Thus, although by this purely

[47] This and the following figures are based on the indexes in the Classics of International Law editions.

[48] Balthazar Ayala, *De Iure et Officiis Bellicis et Disciplina Militari Libri III* (Douai, 1582; repr. Classics of International Law, Washington, DC, 1912).

[49] *Mare Liberum*, chap. 7; the quotation is from Fernandus Vasquez de Menchaca, *Controversiarum illustrium aliarumque usu frequentium . . . pars prima* (Venice, 1564), book I, chap. 89, §§ 30–44.

[50] Sylvester Mozolini (also: Mozzolino, Mazzolini, or Mazolini) Prierias, *Summa summarum que Sylvestrina dicitur* (Strasburg, 1518; 1st edn., 1515).

[51] The most important among them, with the number of references by Grotius, are the following: Hugo Donellus (9), Jacobus Cuiacius (6), Franciscus Duarenus (5), Franciscus Connanus (3), Andreas Alciatus (1), Guilielmus Budaeus (1).

[52] Apart from his natural 'humanist' prejudice against the 'inelegance' of these lawyers, Grotius' general appreciation of them was in fact quite positive, as appears

numerical evidence Gentili does not seem to rank among his main legal authorities, the *De Jure Belli*—then one of the latest publications on the subject—can safely be supposed to have played at least some part in his study on the law of prize.

De Jure Belli ac Pacis contains a dozen references to three of Gentili's works, *De Jure Belli*, *De Legationibus*, and the *Hispanica Advocatio*. On the whole this points to an increased interest in his writings, the more so since the references to the other jurists cited in the earlier work tend to decline.

Firm conclusions could only be drawn from such quantitative evidence after a thorough qualitative analysis. What can safely be said in the case of jurists is that Grotius hardly ever mentions them for purely ornamental purposes, as happens sometimes with other categories of authors such as poets and orators.[53] Therefore a large number of references to a jurist tends to indicate a real use of his work and hence a corresponding influence. But a low number does not necessarily imply that an author did not exert at least a comparable influence. In fact Grotius seems to have relied a great deal

in *JBP*, Prolegomena 54. Many of the Bartolists are cited in his works, although it is not always certain to what extent it is merely through references by other authors (for this question, see hereafter). The same favourable opinion prevails for the Schoolmen in general, despite what is usually held to the contrary (see Prolegomena 52). Through the 16th-century Spaniards, Grotius is in many respects indebted to what has aptly (if not unparadoxically) been called 'humanist scholasticism'; see Ernst Lewalter, *Spanisch-Jesuitische und Deutsch-Lutherische Metaphysik des 17 Jahrhunderts: Ein Beitrag zur Geschichte der Iberisch-Deutschen Kulturbeziehungen und zur Vorgeschichte des deutschen Idealismus* (repr. Darmstadt, 1967), p. 22 n. 3. Equally unjustified is the frequent assertion that Grotius was a fervent anti-Aristotelian. The Stagirite in fact appears in the Prolegomena as holding 'deservedly the foremost place among the philosophers', although Grotius admittedly claims for himself a degree of liberty towards him (Prolegomena 42). He does indeed interpret Aristotle rather freely and sometimes even flatly contradicts him (e.g. Prolegomena 43–4). But those instances do not amount to an utter rejection. Grotius' intellectual temperament was anything but Manichean: in the very passage referred to above he proclaims himself an eclectic, following the example set by the early Christians, out of a deep conviction that 'no philosophic sect had ever encompassed all truth nor any of them failed to perceive at least some aspect of truth' (Prolegomena 42). One of his most typical tendencies was to discover truth beyond divergent opinions, whilst showing by the same token to what degree it was reflected in each of them; which, incidentally, may also account for his often criticized propensity to luxuriant quotations. In all these respects he stands in sharp contrast to writers like Descartes or Hobbes, his two younger contemporaries, both of whom show an evident distaste for tradition and especially scholasticism, however much they may owe to it. See also below, n. 105.

[53] This is openly acknowledged by Grotius in *JBP*, Prolegomena 47.

more on Gentili's writings than mere statistical evidence
might suggest.

Thus concerning *De Jure Praedae*—and more specifically
chapter 12 which became *Mare Liberum*—William Knight
observed that a section of it, including about two dozen
references, appears to be entirely drawn from one chapter of
Gentili's *De Jure Belli*, 'the only acknowledgement that jurist
receives being a single reference as one of the general
company.'[54] In spite of his otherwise rather superficial
analysis, Knight's opinion seems quite plausible, and it might
well prove to be correct with regard to other parts of Grotius'
first work—Gentili being probably not the only victim.

Such practices, which today seem surprising and rather
questionable, were not then exceptional. Humanist vanity and
'elegance' induced scholars to hide their real, direct sources,
in order to show only the pure wisdom of antiquity, which was
of course supposed to have been drunk at its very spring, not
from some intermediary vessel. Moreover, a generally accepted
tendency prevailed among lawyers to muster as many
references as possible in order to bring home a point; it was
therefore understood, and widely practised, that in addition to
the real source of a quotation one mentioned all the authors
referred to therein, without checking them and without
specifying which one was the key to the others. Grotius was
both a humanist and a lawyer, so there was nothing unusual
about his method, even though his work was obviously far
removed from standard legal practice. No doubt Gentili had
resorted to similar expedients. It should also be pointed out
that the relevant books were sometimes difficult to obtain.

Such difficulties were especially numerous and pressing in
the rather uneasy circumstances in which Grotius wrote his
De Jure Belli ac Pacis. His personal library had been confiscated
in 1619 after his conviction[55] and, though he had access to
some of the best libraries in Paris[56] he seems to have relied on

---

[54] Knight, *Life and Works*, p. 94. The chapter concerned is *JB*, book 1, chap. 19,
pp. 138–49.
[55] On the library of Grotius, see P. C. Molhuysen, 'De bibliotheek van Hugo de
Groot in 1618', *Mededeelingen der Nederlandsche Akademie van Wetenschappen*, afd.
letterkunde, nieuwe reeks, deel 6, no. 3 (1943), pp. 45–63.
[56] Esp. the libraries of President Jacques-Auguste de Thou (who had died in 1617,

his memory or on fellow authors for many of his quotations. Hence one is not surprised to find in *De Jure Belli ac Pacis* quite a few errors of quotation and citation—several of them being, however, of great help in detecting Grotius' real sources.

Barbeyrac, though not a very faithful translator of Grotius since he deliberately valued elegance above accuracy, was most scrupulous as an editor,[57] and pointed out several quotations and references which merely repeated errors by Gentili.[58] Some additional examples, having escaped Barbeyrac, may be mentioned here by way of illustration.

Thus, when discussing the question whether a war might be just on both sides, Grotius calls in aid several standard authorities on this widely debated sixteenth-century commonplace.[59] Most of them are already mentioned in Gentili's chapter on this subject.[60] Both Gentili and Grotius refer, among others, to an Italian professor of philosophy, Francesco Piccolomini, their common citation being *De Civili Philosophia*, book 6, chapter 21. In fact no such title seems to exist at all. The reference actually rather concerns Piccolomini's *Universa Philosophia de Moribus*.[61] It is true that chapter 21 of book 6 deals with suicide instead of war; but chapter 22 bears on the

but with whose still youthful son, François Auguste, Grotius was on friendly terms) and President Henri de Mesmes.

[57] His edition of the *JBP* was first published in 1720 and remains quite useful even today; his famous French translation appeared in 1724 in Amsterdam. See ter Meulen and Diermanse, *Bibliographie*, 1950, nos. 601, 602, and 654, pp. 250–1 and 283–4.

[58] These places are pointed out by Jules Basdevant, 'Hugo Grotius', in A. Pillet (ed.), *Les Fondateurs du droit international* (Paris, 1904), p. 221 n. 1 (hereinafter cited as Basdevant, 'Hugo Grotius'). See also van der Molen, *Alberico Gentili*, pp. 318–19 n. 241, and C. G. Roelofsen, 'Some Remarks on the "Sources" of the Grotian System of International Law', *Netherlands International Law Review*, 30 (1983), p. 75 n. 14, and p. 77 n. 30.

[59] *JBP*, book II, chap. 23, § 13. The doctrinal ancestors of this topic seem to be: among the jurists, Raphael Fulgosius (1367–1427), see *In Primam Partem Pandectarum Commentarium* (Lyons, 1554), ad Dig., 1, 1, 5 nn. 1–5; among the theologians, Alfonsus Tostatus de Madrigal (c.1400–55), see *Commentaria in Josue* (Venice, 1615), chap. 11, qu. 9, p. 12.

[60] *JB*, book I, chap. 6, pp. 47–52.

[61] Franciscus Piccolomineus, *Universa Philosophia de Moribus* (Frankfurt, 1601). The preface is dated July 1583, and the 1st edition seems in fact to have appeared that year in Venice. It is not clear why Gentili refers to it as *De Philosophia Civili*, though Piccolomini does describe its proper object as *civilis scientia*. No evidence of an earlier version of the book possibly bearing the title indicated by Gentili could be found by this author. At any rate Gentili mentions it several times and seems to have greatly valued it.

duel and incidentally on bilateral justice in war. The error common to both authors is obviously more than a coincidence. Grotius probably just took his reference from Gentili—as he had already done in *De Jure Praedae* where the same reference occurs.[62] He may never even have seen Piccolomini's treatise.

Another instance is to be found in the third book of *De Jure Belli ac Pacis*, where Grotius quotes a passage from Cicero's *Fourth Philippic*, seemingly giving a general definition of lawful enemies (*hostes*); it reads as follows in Grotius' formulation: '*Ille hostis est*, ait Cicero, *qui habet rempublicam, curiam, aerarium, consensum et concordiam civium et rationem aliquam si res ita tulerit pacis et federis*.'[63] Checking this definition, which appears as a quotation, against Cicero's text, one finds that, in spite of a general correspondence of the features supposed to define lawful enemies, the meaning of the original sentence was different. Cicero may certainly have had in mind the Roman conception of lawful enemies, but he did not intend in that passage to give it a general expression. He merely pointed out to the senators that their ancestors had always confronted enemies of this type, whereas now the enemy, Mark Antony, had none of those characteristics and was therefore little more than a brigand, worse even than Spartacus or Catiline.[64] Still, the idea of extracting from this text a general definition of lawful enemies was by no means absurd, provided the operation remained clearly recognizable: which was precisely what Gentili had done in a chapter defining brigands as opposed to lawful enemies, where his reference to, and approximate rendering of, Cicero's text was indeed meant to

[62] *JP*, chap. 7, fo. 35ᵛ. In all probability Grotius had the manuscript of *JP* with him when writing *JBP* in Paris. This assumption is strongly affirmed by Fruin ('An Unpublished Work', p. 57), and may be considered as fairly sound despite the lack of any direct evidence. *JP* was possibly included in *illis puerilibus quibus valde opus habebamus* which he thanks his brother Willem de Groot for sending over to him in Paris: letter of 20 June 1622, *Briefwisseling*, vol. ii, no. 767, p. 225.

[63] *JBP*, book 3, chap. 3, § 1.2.

[64] 'Ac maioribus quidem vestris, Quirites, cum eo hoste res erat, qui haberet rempublicam, curiam, aerarium, consensum et concordiam civium, rationem aliquam, si res ita tulisset, pacis et foederis: hic vester hostis vestram rempublicam oppugnat ipse habet nullam.... Est igitur, Quirites, populo Romano victori omnium gentium, omne certamen cum excursore, cum latrone, cum Spartaco. Nam quod se similem Catilinae esse gloriari solet: scelere par est, belli industria inferior.' Cicero, *In M. Antonium ad Quirites*, *Philippica Quarta*, 14–15, in *M. Tullii Ciceronis Opera omnia quae extant, a Dionysio Lambino ex codicibus manuscriptis emendata* (Geneva, 1624), p. 657.

have a general validity, but was not put forward as a quotation.[65] As to Grotius' purported quotation, it turns out, upon comparison, to be absolutely identical to Gentili's paraphrase. In fact there is hardly any doubt that he just reproduced Gentili's text without checking it against Cicero's original and mistakenly took it for a genuine definition. Gentili is mentioned twice towards the end of that chapter, but on other points and only to be refuted.[66]

Of course such examples are of limited significance and do not amount to anything remotely like plagiarism. A close scrutiny would doubtless reveal additional cases, but this in no way detracts from the value of Grotius' work. Again, such practice was common at a time when today's sense of intellectual property and propriety did not prevail. Nor can it be denied that Grotius' knowledge of ancient letters was enormous: he certainly did not need such intermediary sources as Gentili; if he used them it was for practical reasons, because time was lacking or because the primary source was not at hand. A striking illustration of this is given by the second example set out above, the sentence from the *Fourth Philippic* on lawful enemies: it appears in *De Jure Praedae* in a similar context, but not as a quotation, and in an almost exact rendering probably based on the text itself.[67] In fact Grotius had been steeped in Cicero ever since his early years.

Yet these two examples do at least show that he used Gentili's works more extensively than would appear at first glance. He might even have kept the *De Jure Belli* on his desk as a permanent companion while writing his own Three Books on the subject. Such an assumption becomes all the more plausible in the light of several passages of his correspondence.

(e) REFERENCES TO GENTILI IN GROTIUS' LETTERS

Grotius' high valuation of Gentili appears in a famous letter, dated 13 May 1615, to Benjamin Aubéry du Maurier, the French ambassador to The Hague, who had requested his advice on the education of his son. This remarkable document,

[65] *JB*, book i, chap. 4, p. 38.
[66] *JBP*, book iii, chap. 3, §§ 11 and 12.   [67] *JP*, chap. 13, fo. 136^{r-v}.

which was reprinted along with similar writings by other humanists like Erasmus, gives us a vivid summary of his intellectual outlook and ideals, in many respects reminiscent of the great humanist of Rotterdam.[68] Concerning jurisprudence, Grotius recommends the study of several parts of Emperor Justinian's *Digest* and *Code* relating to public law. As to more recent jurists, he observes that only a few of them dealt with the *jus gentium ac publicum*—which he already identifies with the *jus belli ac pacis*, following yet another cherished Ciceronian phrase[69]—and he thinks it all the more worth while to mention three of them: Fernando Vasquez de Menchaca, François Hotman, and Alberico Gentili.[70] In such a context this was certainly no little compliment, coming as it did, not from a youthful lawyer, but from a man at the height of his intellectual powers.

The next important testimony is a series of letters addressed to his brother Willem de Groot from Paris, after the escape from Loevestein, between November 1622 and March 1623. In the first letter, dated 12 November 1622, Grotius draws attention to a list of books he needs 'for some legal comment', and he asks Willem to send them post-haste: '*Mitto indiculum librorum quibus opus habeo ad aliquid de iure commentandum. Eos rogo quam fieri ocissime potest mihi mittas.*'[71] This is actually the earliest hint of his intention to write the *De Jure Belli ac Pacis*. The enclosed *indiculus* is not extant, but Gentili, as well as Ayala, was most probably among those listed, as the two subsequent letters show. One of them, dated 12 January 1623, deals desultorily with a number of practical points, in particular the books Grotius had asked for: 'I remember having had in my prison Alberico's *De Jure Belli* as well as his *Hispan-*

---

[68] *H. Grotii et aliorum Dissertationes De Studiis instituendis* (Amsterdam, 1645), pp. 1–6. Grotius' veneration for Erasmus is significantly reflected in one of the first things he did during his short-lived attempt to return to Holland in 1631: he visited Erasmus' statue in Rotterdam. Grotius is a direct spiritual descendant of Erasmus; both are outstanding representatives of Christian humanism.

[69] See Cicero, *Pro L. Cornelio Balbo*, 15. The original meaning of the phrase was slightly different: Cicero had not in mind a separate legal 'science' as Grotius implies but Pompey's 'knowledge' of the problems of war and peace. Grotius was obviously under the spell of the formula which is already quoted in the introductory chapter of *JP* (fo. 4ᵛ).

[70] *Briefwisseling*, vol. i, no. 402, p. 386.

[71] Ibid., vol. ii, no. 796, p. 254.

icas Advocationes. I am urgently expecting the books.'[72] The sudden appearance of these two sentences suggests that the subject was perfectly familiar to the addressee and that Gentili's works must therefore have been included in the list, which is implicitly referred to in the second sentence. This is clearly confirmed by the letter of 23 March 1623, which contains another two sentences on the subject: 'I found Ayala and Albericus elsewhere. Therefore do not worry with that mission.'[73] However brief these statements, they leave little doubt that Grotius found Gentili's writings immensely important to the treatise he was to publish almost exactly two years after the last-mentioned letter.[74]

(f) GROTIUS' AMBIGUITIES: PROLEGOMENA, PARAGRAPH 38

Yet this impression seems but partially borne out by what is probably Grotius' most important utterance on Gentili, the very passage containing the sentence quoted in Holland's inaugural lecture.[75] It is taken from the Prolegomena, the famous preface introducing the Three Books to their reader. Since that statement is crucial for Grotius' understanding of, and general attitude towards, Gentili, it deserves to be quoted in full. First, however, a brief description of its context is appropriate.

The passage is included in paragraph 38 of the Prolegomena, itself part of a development starting at paragraph 36.[76] Having drawn the general plan and pointed out the

---

[72] 'Albericum de Iure Belli, item Advocationes Hispanicas in carcere habuisse memini, hic neutrum habeo. Libros avide expecto.' Ibid., vol. ii, no. 815, p. 274.

[73] 'Ayalam et Albericum nactus sum aliunde. Itaque noli de hoc mandato esse sollicitus.' Ibid., vol. ii, no. 822, p. 283.

[74] *JBP* appeared at the Frankfurt book fair during the second half of Mar. 1625; the *summa privilegii* figuring in the 1st edition is dated 17 Mar. 1625.

[75] See above, text accompanying n. 21.

[76] The division of the Prolegomena into paragraphs is not due to Grotius himself, but to his son Pieter de Groot who introduced it first in the edition of 1667; see van Vollenhoven, 'Notice sur le texte du *De iure belli ac pacis*', Grotiana, 2 (1929), pp. 36–7. At the same time the paragraphs in the text were divided into subparagraphs. This fragmentation is often rather incongruous, esp. in the Prolegomena; its only use is to facilitate reference.

contents of the three books in paragraphs 33 to 35, Grotius sets out to recall in paragraph 36 the endeavours of his predecessors in the field he is dealing with, which he pronounces *partem iurisprudentiae longe nobilissimam*. None of them, he thinks, has ever treated the subject in its entirety, and those who examined parts of it left a great deal to be done by others. In antiquity he sees nothing worth mentioning. As to the Middle Ages, he acknowledges the value of the *summae casuum*, the penitential books he used extensively as evidenced by his frequent citation of the *Summa Summarum* of Sylvester Prierias.[77] He goes on to list, in paragraph 37, some medieval and sixteenth-century theologians and jurists who left works bearing specifically on the law of war, all regarded as rather incomplete and confused. In paragraph 38 he starts by favourably commenting on Pierre du Faur, whose legal and philological research he greatly appreciated, especially for its historical insights, so painfully absent in the traditional scholastic works.[78] Then he names the two authors whose achievements he considers the most significant in this field, Balthazar Ayala and Alberico Gentili, that is, the very two writers he had mentioned in his letter of 23 March 1623 to his brother Willem. Both, he says, made extensive use of historical evidence, like du Faur, and both, moreover, tried to order this congeries of facts into some general categories, which is especially the case with Gentili. Thereupon follows the passage opening with the words quoted by Holland:

Knowing that others can derive profit from Gentili's painstaking, as I acknowledge that I have, I leave it to his readers to pass judgement on the shortcomings of his work as regards method of exposition, arrangement of matter, delimitation of inquiries, and distinctions between the various kinds of law. This only I shall say, that in treating controversial questions it is his frequent practice to base his conclusions on a few examples, which are not in all cases worthy of approval, or even to follow the opinions of modern jurists, formulated in arguments of which not a few were accommodated to the special interests of clients, not to the nature of that which is equitable and upright. The causes which determine the character-

---

[77] Above, n. 50.

[78] See esp. Petrus Faber Saniorensis (i.e. Pierre du Faur de Saint-Jorry), *Semestrium liber unus* (Lyons, 1590), and *Semestrium liber secundus* (Lyons, 1592).

ization of a war as lawful or unlawful Ayala did not touch upon.
Gentili outlined certain general classes, in the manner which seemed
to him best; but he did not so much as refer to many topics which
have come up in notable and frequent controversies.[79]

Grotius then goes on in the rest of the Prolegomena to present
his own method purporting to remedy the deficiencies of his
predecessors.

Obviously the above-quoted passage is crucial in assessing
his position towards Gentili. Yet what is its precise import?
How far is it in line with Grotius' earlier references to his
Oxonian predecessor?

At first sight it is difficult to escape a feeling of ambiguity.
True, Grotius considers Gentili as the one who came nearest
to his own intentions in dealing with the *jus belli*; in this
respect he does compare him favourably with all his other
predecessors and acknowledges the assistance received from
his work: *cuius diligentia . . . me adiutum profiteor.* To that extent
the impression gained from his correspondence would seem to
be confirmed. But on the other hand he emphasizes the
shortcomings of Gentili's work and, on the whole, shows
considerable reservations: his judgement he finds verging on
the superficial, his classifications somewhat arbitrary and
incomplete, his method unsound, hardly apt to disclose the
true nature of the problems; for the rest the reader is invited to
judge by himself which of the two works he regards as superior
with respect to systematic order and legal acumen. On the
whole, a rather critical, if not negative appraisal, leaving an
uneasy impression of insufficient acknowledgement—as

---

[79] *JBP*, Prolegomena 38 (Kelsey's trans.). The Latin text of Prolegomena 38 reads
as follows: 'Quod his omnibus maxime defuit, historiarum lucem, supplere aggressi
sunt eruditissimus Faber in Semestrium capitibus nonnullis, sed pro instituti sui
modo, et testimoniis tantum allatis; diffusius, et ut ad definitiones aliquas
exemplorum congeriem referrent, Balthazar Ayala, et plus ·eo Albericus Gentilis,
cuius diligentia, sicut alios adiuvari posse scio et me adiutum profiteor, ita quid in
docendi genere, quid in ordine, quid in distinguendis quaestionibus, iurisque diversi
generibus desiderari in eo possit, lectoribus iudicium relinquo. Illud tantum dicam,
solere eum saepe in controversiis definiendis sequi, aut exempla pauca non semper
probanda, aut etiam auctoritatem novorum Iurisconsultorum in responsis, quorum
non pauca ad gratiam consulentium, non ad aequi bonique naturam sunt composita.
Causas unde bellum iustum aut iniustum dicitur, Ayala non attigit: Gentilis summa
quaedam genera, quo ipsi visum est, modo delineavit, multos vero et nobilium et
frequentium controversiarum locos ne attigit quidem.'

Holland and others apparently felt.[80] To what extent is that feeling justified? Is it conceivable that Grotius tried to cut his predecessor and avowed source of inspiration down to size in order to make himself appear—successfully as it turned out— as the sole creator of a new legal discipline, nay, as the reformer of jurisprudence itself?

Any sound assessment would of course depend upon a careful comparison of the two works to which the subsequent observations will be confined, namely, Gentili's *De Jure Belli* and Grotius' *De Jure Belli ac Pacis*. Nothing more can be attempted here than to suggest some possible guidelines for an answer.

(g) THE TWO MAJOR TREATISES COMPARED

The reader is confronted with two seemingly opposite findings. On the one hand there are few things in *De Jure Belli* that do not somehow reappear in *De Jure Belli ac Pacis*: the similarities between the two works are in fact substantial, and whatever other sources Grotius may have used—some of them no less important—little doubt is left as to Gentili's central place. On the other hand, however, Grotius hardly ever fails to transform what he borrows from him so as to infuse it with a new significance. Perhaps these two statements may account for his ambivalent attitude towards Gentili.

As to the first aspect, the likeness between the two works is fairly obvious. They both essentially consist of three books on the law of war. At first sight, to be sure, the scope of the Grotian treatise appears to be wider since the title mentions a *jus pacis* in addition to the *jus belli*, suggesting that it covers the whole field of international law, whereas Gentili limits himself to the law of war. Grotius' supposed law of peace is generally

[80] Phillipson even calls Grotius' judgement 'excessively deprecatory, not to say arrogant', and 'unjustifiably contemptuous'. 'Introduction', pp. 10a–11a n. 13, and p. 20a n. 2. Such an impression may possibly find some confirmation in Gentili's absence from the *Loci scriptorum in hoc opere specialiter explicati, aut examinati, aut emendati*, a list of passages the discussion of which Grotius regarded as especially noteworthy. Among the *jurisconsulti* he included there Bartolus, Zasius, Covarrubias, Vasquez de Menchaca, Menochius, Bodin, Barclay and Connan.

perceived to materialize in the second book.[81] In fact, however, *De Jure Belli ac Pacis* contains no international law of peace in the accepted sense of the term: like Gentili's work it deals essentially with the law of war.

As pointed out by Holland, both writers follow roughly similar schemes.[82] They start with introductory observations on their legal premisses, on the definition of war,[83] and on its general lawfulness.[84] Both go on to state who is entitled to wage war, that is, the lawful belligerents;[85] on what grounds, that is, the lawful causes of war (which constitute the real subject of Grotius' second book);[86] in what manner, that is, the lawful conduct of war as well as its lawful effects;[87] both ending with considerations on the termination of war (which is actually the part meant by Grotius' *jus pacis*: there is in fact quite an important counterpart to it in the twelve last chapters of Gentili's third book).[88] The two works, then, are built along similar lines and encompass approximately the same subject-matter: the law of war and the conclusion of peace. Neither of them intends to deal with international law in the modern sense: this must be stressed before entering upon the second point set out above, regarding the differences between the two authors.

It is indeed essential to a proper understanding to consider them with reference, not to modern international law, but to

---

[81] See e.g. Fruin, 'An Unpublished Work', p. 56. This interpretation also seems to underlie Holland's perception: see 'Alberico Gentili', p. 23.

[82] Above, n. 21; see also van der Molen, *Alberico Gentili*, p. 113, and Ito, 'Alberico Gentili', pp. 622–3.

[83] *JB*, book I, chaps. 1–2; *JBP*, book I, chap. 1. The two points are discussed in reverse order.

[84] *JB*, book I, chap. 5; *JBP*, book I, chap. 2. The order with the following point is reversed in Gentili.

[85] *JB*, book I, chaps. 3–4; *JBP*, book I, chaps. 3–5.

[86] *JB*, book I, chaps. 7–25; *JBP*, book II, chaps. 1–26.

[87] *JB*, book II, chaps. 2–24, and book III, chaps. 1–12; *JBP*, book III, chaps. 1–18.

[88] *JB*, book III, chaps. 13–24; *JBP*, book III, chaps. 19–25. Gesina van der Molen sees Gentili's law of peace as covering the whole of book III, which is in a way correct, since that book deals with the rights *post bellum*, as opposed to the rights *in bello* discussed in book II; it must be noted, however, that Gentili clearly divides the rights *post bellum* into those concerning the liquidation of the past (*ultio*: chaps. 2–12) and those concerning the establishment of the future peace (*pax*: chaps. 13–24); the first part is actually covered by what Grotius calls the lawful 'measure' or effects of war (see *JBP*, book III, chaps. 1–18, which, however, also comprise the matters discussed in Gentili's book II).

the medieval discipline of the law of war as brought to its final shape during the sixteenth century.[89] The two things are quite distinct. It would be inadequate to look upon that *jus belli* as part of an incipient international law. Whatever international relations may have existed in fact, whatever their legal regulation, they were not yet thought of in terms of international law during the Middle Ages.[90] Conversely, the medieval *jus belli* did form a self-contained doctrinal corpus and to some extent an individualized legal discipline, however little it would fit into any of today's juridical categories.[91] After about two centuries of scattered reflections, glosses, and comments on the subject, starting with the *Decretum Gratiani* around the middle of the twelfth century and leading up to Bartolus in the fourteenth century, it had assumed a distinct shape by around 1360 in Giovanni da Legnano's *Treatise on War, Reprisals and Duel*—another work to be brought to wider attention by T. E. Holland.[92] In fact Holland was among the first to perceive the cohesion of the steadily growing current of legal and theological literature on war during the later Middle Ages.[93] The unity of

---

[89] The author takes the liberty to refer on that point to his doctoral thesis, *Grotius et la doctrine de la guerre juste* (Paris, 1983), *passim*, esp. pp. 11–49 and 615–29.

[90] For international relations in the Middle Ages see e.g. R. Ago, 'Il pluralismo della comunità internazionale alle sue origini', *Studi in onore di Giorgio Balladore Pallieri* (Milan, 1977); and, by the same, 'Les Premières Collectivités interétatiques méditerranéennes', in *Mélanges offerts à Paul Reuter* (Paris, 1981). Such relations were not unknown even within the Catholic part of Christianity, which very soon witnessed the emergence of *de facto* independent powers; see e.g. F. A. von der Heydte, *Die Geburtsstunde des souveränen Staates* (Regensburg, 1952). Yet no corresponding conception of international law was worked out. Possibly the persistent effects of the 'imperial' ideology—especially through the texts of the *Corpus Juris Civilis*, the authority of which was comparable to the Holy Writ itself—may have prevented it from being crystallized (although expressions like *jus gentium* and *jus naturae* were current and frequently discussed, precisely on the basis of the Roman sources and the *Etymologies* of Isidore of Seville). To that extent the catalytic effect of the confessional split of the 16th century as well as of humanism cannot be denied, inasmuch as they removed or at least diminished an obstacle to such a new conceptualization; see, however, below, text accompanying n. 137.

[91] In addition to international law, it would partly stretch over several fields presently covered by municipal law, such as the law of torts, the law of contracts, criminal law, and constitutional law.

[92] Giovanni da Legnano, *De Bello, de Represaliis et de Duello*, ed. Thomas E. Holland (Classics of International Law, Oxford, 1917). The work had been printed in vol. xvi of the *Tractatus Universi Juris*, published by Ziletti in Venice in 1584. Gentili and Grotius probably knew it in this version.

[93] See his lecture 'The Early Literature of the Law of War', delivered in 1879, repr. in *Studies in International Law* (Oxford, 1898), pp. 40–58.

this law of war was secured by the fact that it governed the activity of a fairly distinct, though quite heterogeneous, class of men, that is, those following the profession of arms.[94] The medieval *jus belli* underwent an important evolution during the sixteenth century, especially under the influence of Spanish and Italian theologians and jurists, who adapted it to the changed political setting. Through that process it came nearer to what is now seen as the classical framework of international law, but it did not cease to constitute an autonomous body of legal thought and practice, at the centre of which stood, in all its complexity, the social fact of war. It is against this background that both Gentili's and Grotius' works have to be appreciated. Both in their way represent a restatement of the traditional law of war, which accounts for their striking analogies. But it is also against this common background that their important differences appear in their proper light.

This leads immediately to our second statement: in spite of the similarity of the two works, in spite of their material analogies, there are few elements that are not significantly altered in Grotius' treatise, almost as if transposed into a different key. The contrast stems no doubt from a variety of factors, some of them general, some personal; they may, however, be conveniently summed up in the proposition that the two scholars, though roughly contemporaries, belong to fairly distinct legal worlds.

Gentili, who had studied in Perugia around 1570, is a spiritual descendant of the Bartolists. His legal training and method are typical of the school of the medieval commentators, the so-called *mos Italicus*.[95] He consciously adhered to this tradition and defended it with great determination against the onset of legal humanism, as shown by his first important

---

[94] For an admirable account, see Maurice H. Keen, *The Laws of War in the Late Middle Ages* (London, 1965). See also Philippe Contamine, *Guerre, État et société à la fin du Moyen Âge: Études sur les armées des rois de France 1337–1494* (Paris and The Hague, 1972).

[95] On the *mos Italicus*, see Roderich Stintzing, *Geschichte der deutschen Rechtswissenschaft*, i (Munich and Leipzig, 1880), pp. 102–39 (hereinafter cited as Stintzing, *Geschichte der deutschen Rechtswissenschaft*), and Paul Koschaker, *Europa und das römische Recht*, 4th edn. (Munich and Berlin, 1966), chap. 7, pp. 87–105 (hereinafter cited as Koschaker, *Europa und das römische Recht*). For Gentili's relation to the *mos Italicus*, see Gesina van der Molen, *Alberico Gentili*, chap. 7, § 2, pp. 206–10.

Peter Haggenmacher

publication in England, the six dialogues *De Interpretibus Juris*, where the Bartolist method is upheld as the only true one against the intrusions of history and philology in the field of law.[96] He remained faithful to this position even in works basically unconnected with civil law.[97] This is also the case with *De Jure Belli*,[98] even though its general composition and style clearly belong to the sixteenth century, and though the many references to historical examples and quotations from antiquity admittedly contrast with the rather dry comments of Bartolus, Baldus, or Paulus Castrensis on Roman law. Nor is Gentili a genuine systematizer. Whatever systematic elements there are, they remain a simple veneer. His method is essentially casuistic and topical;[99] in the best Bartolist tradition it has its roots in the medieval *disputatio*.[100] What may at times look like a system is hardly more than a skilful, often

[96] *De Juris Interpretibus Dialogi Sex* (London, 1582); reissued by G. Astuti, Turin, 1937 (Istituto giuridico della R. Università di Torino, Testi inediti o vari, no. 4). On the significance of this work, see Koschaker, *Europa und das römische Recht*, pp. 110 and 111.

[97] Though Gentili does not follow the Bartolists uncritically he often mentions them in almost affectionate terms. Thus Alexander Imolensis once appears as *doctissimus*, and Paulus Castrensis as *optimus*; see *JB*, book III, chap. 18, p. 635.

[98] Phillipson's judgement would not seem quite accurate on this point: 'Whilst Gentili belonged to the Bartolists, so far as municipal jurisprudence was concerned, he adopted an independent, and what was then a revolutionary attitude with regard to the law of nations.' 'Introduction', p. 20a. No doubt Gentili very consciously tends to separate *jus gentium* from *jus civile*; yet his legal argumentation, and often the arguments themselves, are to a great extent 'civilian' and Bartolistic: 'Gentili was irrevocably a civilian, steeped in the "written reason" of the *Corpus juris civilis*', Percy E. Corbett, *Law in Diplomacy* (Princeton, NJ, 1959), p. 19. Occasionally he would even purely and simply identify civil law with the Law of Nations: 'Ius etiam, illis perscriptum libris Iustiniani, non civitatis est tantum, sed & gentium, & naturae, & aptatum sic est ad naturam universam, ut imperio extincto, & ipsum ius diu sepultum surrexerit tamen, & in omnes se effuderit gentes humanas. Ergo & Principibus stat: etsi est privatis conditum a Iustiniano.' *JB*, book I, chap. 3, p. 26; see also the following pages, to p. 29.

[99] See on this question esp. Theodor Viehweg, *Topik und Jurisprudenz*, 2nd edn. (Munich, 1963).

[100] Quite significantly Gentili once refers to a previous chapter in his book as a 'disputation': 'sed reverentia quadam iurisiurandi (ut dixi in disputatione De mendaciis) clementer servatum est.' *JB*, book III, chap. 19, p. 651. Although he could mean his *De Actoribus et de Abusu Mendacii Disputationes duae* (written in 1597 but published only in 1599), he more probably has in mind *JB*, book II, chap. 5, where the question of oaths is incidentally discussed at pp. 243–6 (on this last page, however, Gentili seems to refer to *De Abusu Mendacii*). At any rate the structure of Gentili's chapters is reminiscent of academic disputations, to one of which the whole work after all owes its origin; see also Phillipson, 'Introduction', p. 16a.

quite elegant, discussion of the topical questions as raised and formulated by successive generations of lawyers and theologians in the particular field of the law of war.

Grotius, on the other hand, despite an excellent knowledge of the Italian masters, is a genuine offshoot of legal humanism as it had developed during the sixteenth century along two main lines, the one philological and historical (with scholars like Budé, Cujas, and du Faur), the other dogmatic and systematic (for example, Connan, Le Douaren, and Doneau). Together, these currents were to form the so-called *mos Gallicus*, in conscious opposition to the older *mos Italicus*.[101] Grotius, who significantly had obtained his legal doctorate at the French university of Orléans, was under the influence of both tendencies of the *mos Gallicus*, but its systematic strand became especially important to his legal thought. What the French systematizers had done for Roman civil law—an orderly reconstruction of the materials afforded by the *Corpus Juris Civilis* according to logical principles—he was to accomplish for the whole field lying beyond the ken of civil law, that is, the *jus belli ac pacis*, the part of social relations where no civil magistrate was competent to settle the disputes and where consequently war had to be considered as a lawful institution: *ubi judicia deficiunt, incipit bellum*.[102]

Hence his criticism of the earlier writers on the *jus belli* and even of Gentili's monumental work: above all it is their lack of method, of order, and of system that leaves him dissatisfied. Accordingly, his own treatise was to be dominated by an all-embracing systematic intent, which reveals at the same time one of his deepest and most constant tendencies, equally

---

[101] On the *mos Gallicus*, see Stintzing, *Geschichte der deutschen Rechtswissenschaft*, esp. vol. i, chap. 10, pp. 366 ff.; Otto von Gierke, *Das deutsche Genossenschaftsrecht*, iv (1913, repr. Graz, 1954), §§ 10–11, pp. 153–204; Koschaker, *Europa und das römische Recht*, chap. 9, pp. 105–24. But, as pointed out esp. by the last-mentioned author, the opposition between *mos Gallicus* and *mos Italicus* should not be exaggerated. More often than not both tendencies are perceptible to some degree in the same jurist. Moreover the older 'Italian' manner, far from being simply discarded by its 'French' rival, in fact retained considerable vitality among practitioners who continued to work and think *more Italico*, whilst the 'elegances' *moris Gallici* remained in many respects a purely academic matter. This may explain why Grotius, though clearly on the 'French' side owing to his humanist education and outlook, by no means spurns the 'Italians'.

[102] *JBP*, book ii, chap. 1, § 2.1.

perceptible in other parts of his work such as his theological writings.[103] No subject within the ambit of the traditional *jus belli* is left untouched: not just to be reviewed with arguments for and against as in Gentili, but to be dissected and broken down to its basic elements, and then rebuilt in the light of a true legal system, entirely founded on a few clearly articulated principles allegedly consonant with the rational and social nature of man. Especially apparent in his first work on the subject, *De Jure Praedae*,[104] this twofold process of 'resolution' and 'composition', of analysis and synthesis, may remind one of the contemporary reflections by Galileo (d. 1642) and Descartes (d. 1650) on scientific method. The parallel should not, however, be taken too far: apart from natural reason, the principle of authority plays no small part in Grotius' construction, his method remaining in that respect essentially eclectic.[105] No wonder therefore that the practical results of the whole operation do not generally lie far from those reached by earlier writers; this indeed may account for the analogies pointed out earlier with Gentili's views. Yet the whole field is renewed, from within as it were, all its traditional parts reappearing after their analytic isolation and synthetic reconstruction as elements of an overall legal mechanism.

---

[103] See e.g. Grotius' 'bestseller', *De Veritate Religionis Christianae*, which appeared in its Latin version in Leiden, 1627. Grotius' frequent use of dichotomies may be the result of Ramist influence (quite conceivable at Leiden University), though there is no direct evidence for it (unlike e.g. in the case of Johannes Althusius).

[104] *JP* is ostensibly built in the manner of a treatise of geometry. On the possible origin of this 'Euclidean' structure, see Ben Vermeulen, 'Simon Stevin and the Geometrical Method in De Jure Praedae', *Grotiana*, 4 (1983), pp. 63–6, who fails, however, to give any stringent demonstration. A possible link between Grotius and Stevin was already hinted at in 1925 (Knight, *Life and Works*, pp. 20–2).

[105] The constant interaction of reason and authority is among the basic features of all Grotian argumentations, be they legal or theological. It is already clearly perceptible throughout the *JP* (see esp. chap. 1, fo. 4ᵛ–5). For its theological aspect, see Rene Voeltzel, 'La Méthode théologique de Hugo Grotius', *Revue d'histoire et de philosophie religieuses*, 32 (1952), pp. 126–33. On some more general implications of this method, see Franco Todescan, *Le radici teologiche del giusnaturalismo laico*, i, *Il problema della secolarizzazione nel pensiero giuridico di Ugo Grozio* (Per la storia del pensiero giuridico moderno, no. 14, Milan, 1983), pp. 21–41.

(h) AN ILLUSTRATION: THE LAWFUL CAUSES OF WAR

Such, then, are the basic similarities and the basic differences between the two works when they are examined, as they should be, against the tradition of the law of war. Both aspects could be illustrated by many examples: one is of particular interest, since it bears on the very point mentioned in paragraph 38 of Grotius' Prolegomena in relation to Ayala and Gentili, namely, the question of the lawful causes of war.[106]

Both Gentili and Grotius indulge in extensive disquisitions on that problem. Gentili's exposition is undoubtedly the largest ever presented up to his time, covering three-quarters of book I of his *De Jure Belli*.[107] His predecessors had usually been content with either some general formula characterizing a war as just, or an enumeration of different kinds of just wars, without even isolating the concept of just cause. In this light Gentili's attempt to go through the whole range of possible lawful grounds for war by mustering an impressive array of historical materials, as well as to classify these grounds according to some general categories, is indeed quite new and noteworthy. Yet upon closer examination the system turns out to be rather loosely knit and partly incoherent, based as it is on a somewhat haphazard set of classifications. At first the main criterion seems to be drawn from the type of legal rule involved, whence the distinction between 'divine', 'natural', and 'human' causes of war. In the course of the discussion, however, two other criteria appear—one proceeding from the offensive or defensive nature of the war, the other from its 'necessary', 'useful', or 'honourable' character—and in the end these apparently subordinate divisions partly take precedence. Such lack of consistency does not in fact diminish the value of Gentili's investigation. It simply reveals how inessential his pseudo-system really is. In truth he merely restates the main topoi and reviews them in a convenient order. The alleged system has no impact on the real substance of the discussion.

[106] See above, pp. 154–5.
[107] *JB*, book I, chaps. 7–25, pp. 53–208.

Grotius' examination of the just causes of war is of an altogether different nature. It does form a genuine system, and this may even be its dominant characteristic. This system is developed in the first twenty-one chapters of book 2 of *De Jure Belli ac Pacis*, the remaining five chapters providing some further considerations, especially on doubtful and unjust causes. Altogether, book 2 represents about half the whole treatise. The fact that it is entirely devoted to the question of just causes of war (whereas Gentili had treated that point as part of his first book) is quite revealing. For Grotius this was undoubtedly the central and most important part of the whole work.

He begins by asserting the need for a just cause and clarifies the concept by distinguishing the *causa justifica* from the *causa suasoria*.[108] The contrast between just causes and mere pretexts is sharply drawn and immediately differentiates Grotius from Gentili who has a constant tendency to blur the separation. On this basis Grotius then goes on to enunciate what appears as an axiom: *Causa iusta belli suscipiendi nulla esse alia potest, nisi injuria*.[109] In itself this formulation was not new: Vitoria had used a similar phrase in his *Relectio de Jure Belli* of 1539,[110] and this was probably Grotius' direct source, though the idea is much older and can be traced at least as far back as St Augustine.[111] It is actually the gist of the whole Christian, and especially scholastic, doctrine of just war. At the same time, however, it is one of its most critical aspects because of the great difficulty of assessing what an *injuria* really is and on which side it lies (whence the above-mentioned problem of a war being lawful on both sides). At precisely this point Grotius attempts to present a new solution: his ambitious aim is to provide an exhaustive set of criteria enabling anybody to

[108] *JBP*, book II, chap. I, § 1.1. Both categories are in turn contrasted, as grounds for war, against the *belli principia*, the historical causes of a given conflict.

[109] *JBP*, book II, chap. I, § 1.4.

[110] 'Unica est et sola causa iusta inferendi bellum, iniuria accepta.' Franciscus de Victoria, *Relectio de Jure Belli*, § 13, in *Obras de Francisco de Vitoria. Relecciones teologicas* (Madrid, 1960), p. 825.

[111] The *locus classicus* was St Augustine, *Quaestiones in Heptateuchum*, book VI, question 10 (on Josh. 8: 2, in J.-P. Migne, *Patrologia latina*, XXXIV, cols. 780–1), widely quoted on account of its inclusion into the *Decretum Gratiani*, part 2, causa 23, quaestio 2, canon 2. See also *De Civitate Dei*, book XIX, chap. 7, which is quoted by Grotius at *JBP*, book II, chap. I, § 1.4.

make out infallibly what is a just ground for war and what is not.

What he does is essentially to focus on *injuria* with greater precision. He defines it simply as the violation of a *jus*. Hence this further question: What is a *jus*? A right in its subjective meaning, Grotius answers, which in turn leads him to a complete assessment of all the rights 'naturally' enjoyed by human beings.[112] Such rights fall under four headings, and their violation gives rise, accordingly, to four types of legitimate actions: self-defence, including the defence of one's property; the vindication of a right *in rem*; the pursuit of a right *in personam*; and the infliction of a punishment. These legitimate types of actions—which represent as many types of reactions to injury—are then identified with the four categories of causes of war Grotius is ready to recognize as lawful.[113] The possible realization of such a cause is thus supposed to be objectively ascertainable by reference to the general system of law set out in book 2. The validity of the system, based as it is on human nature itself, is claimed to be universal, permanent, and in some respects absolute (although superficial modifications brought about by agreements of *jus civile* or *jus gentium* remain possible and play an important part for Grotius); its basic 'natural' features are binding upon any human being of whatever status, and are therefore relevant to any kind of war,

---

[112] Grotius sharply distinguishes the subjective from the objective meaning of *jus*, respectively defined at *JBP*, book i, chap. i, §§ 4–8 and 9–15. He was credited with the first real definition of subjective rights by Michel Villey, 'Les Origines de la notion de droit subjectif', in *Leçons d'histoire de la philosophie du droit* (Paris, 1962), pp. 221–50. In fact similar formulations occur in several slightly earlier scholastics like Francisco Suarez, *Tractatus de Legibus ac Deo Legislatore* (Coimbra, 1612), book i, chap. 2 nn. 4–6, pp. 11–12; or Leonard Lessius, *De Justitia et Jure ceterisque Virtutibus cardinalibus libri quatuor* (Milan, 1618; 1st edn. 1605), book ii, chap. 2 nn. 1–7, pp. 15–16.

[113] Grotius is usually said to have recognized three categories of just causes, but this is the result of a superficial reading of *JBP*, book ii, chap. i, § 2.2: 'Plerique bellorum tres statuunt causas iustas, defensionem, recuperationem rerum, et punitionem . . .' In fact, all Grotius does here is to report a general opinion he regards as lacking in precision. Therefore he specifies at the end of that sentence: 'in qua enumeratione nisi vox recuperandi sumatur laxius, omissa est persecutio eius, et quod nobis debetur.' Already in *JP*, chap. 7 (the remote ancestor of *JBP*, book ii) he had insisted on including into his classification the pursuit of rights *in personam*, the *debitum* as opposed to the *suum*. This distinction, probably borrowed from Doneau, is not without important consequences for the general structure of *JBP*, book ii, which discusses rights *in rem* in chaps. 1–10, and rights *in personam* in chaps. 11–19.

whether 'public', among nations, or 'private', among individuals.

The distance between the Grotian construction and Gentili's discussion is readily apparent. It arises from the very fact that Grotius provides a system, as opposed to a mere catalogue—a system deemed to answer the question of just causes of war absolutely and completely by reference to the basic rights of human beings. This system in itself was an outgrowth, not of the traditional theory of just war, but of some civil law constructions of humanist inspiration (especially by Doneau), one of Grotius' major contributions being the combination of these two currents. Intended to be at the same time a system of just causes of war and of rights in general,[114] it was in turn to supply the basis for the natural law theories of Pufendorf and his successors.[115]

Limited though it is to a single, if important, aspect, the above comparison highlights the difference in outlook and method of the two authors, as well as their more general attitude towards the doctrinal tradition concerning just war. Gentili restates that tradition, discusses its various parts and considerably amplifies it by an important accretion of historical evidence. Grotius reworks it from within, and recasts it into a general theory on the legitimate use of force among human beings considered beyond the scope of municipal law. Gentili, while he does contribute to a redefinition of the *jus belli*[116] by

---

[114] Grotius' conception of a limited number of types of subjective rights, of legal powers 'naturally' belonging to any human person, is historically important. He was criticized by many (starting with Jean-Jacques Rousseau) for his conservative outlook on resistance against established authority. Yet, structurally speaking, his natural rights conception is rather 'modern' (whatever its medieval antecedents) and, though not directly put to such use by Grotius, quite relevant to the history of human rights theories. Grotius' ambivalence in that respect is well shown in Richard Tuck, *Natural Rights Theories: Their Origin and Development* (Cambridge, 1979), chap. 3, pp. 58–81.

[115] Samuel Pufendorf was to hold the chair specially created in 1661 at the University of Heidelberg with the purpose of teaching the *jus naturae et gentium* along the lines of the Grotian treatise.

[116] He is credited by Holland with having performed this task alone: 'The Early Literature', pp. 57–8. In fact, such a move was already effected earlier by Vitoria's *Relectio de Jure Belli*, and basically corresponds with the Thomistic tradition as explained by Cardinal Cajetan. Holland's otherwise excellent perception of this point remains partly anachronistic: viewed in their proper historical context, matters such as 'the principles of army organization, and the disciplinary rules which are

discarding a number of components traditionally included in it from Giovanni da Legnano down to Pierino Belli and Balthazar Ayala, still remains basically in line with these predecessors. Grotius, no less anxious than Gentili to stay within the confines of law,[117] is nevertheless more than a jurist. His view of the subject is also that of a philosopher, as the three methodological rules at the end of his *Prolegomena* admirably show:

In my work as a whole I have, above all else, aimed at three things: to make the reasons of my conclusions as evident as possible; to set forth in a definite order the matters which needed to be treated; and to distinguish clearly between things which seemed to be the same and were not.[118]

In this perspective, then, the 'finished picture' of 1625 is not only superior to the 'sketch' of 1598: it is of another kind. The difference is not merely one of degree; the two writers move on qualitatively distinct levels. This goes a long way to explain Grotius' critical and seemingly ambivalent judgement on his predecessor. To that extent Holland's appreciation of their relationship would not seem to be wholly accurate: in construction and system as well as in general intention and plane of thought they lie much further apart than his inaugural lecture would imply, provided, again, that they are seen against the background, not of present international law, but of the traditional law of war, their common and natural frame of reference.

(i) THE COMPARATIVE MODERNITY OF GENTILI

Such a conclusion, however, has no direct bearing on the respective significance of Gentili and Grotius with regard to

administered by courts-martial' were not just 'incongruous topics' (ibid., pp. 56 and 57), but very naturally belonged to the *jus belli* in its wider sense as described above, pp. 158–9.

[117] Both authors share this concern, though Grotius' understanding of it is slightly different from Gentili's; cf. e.g. *JB*, book III, chap. 1, p. 588, and *JBP*, Prolegomena 57.

[118] *JBP*, Prolegomena 56 (Kelsey's translation). The original text reads as follows: 'In toto opere tria maxime mihi proposui, ut definiendi rationes redderem quam maxime evidentes, et ut quae erant tractanda, ordine certo disponerem, et ut quae eadem inter se videri poterant nec erant, perspicue distinguerem.'

our modern discipline of international law. If it is accepted that international law as we know it was not yet familiar to them, it still remains legitimate to ask which of the two conceptions is more in conformity with it.

Paradoxically, from that point of view Gentili appears in many respects at least as modern as his Dutch follower.[119] *De Jure Belli* often seems closer, if not to the 1899/1907 Hague Rules of Land Warfare, at least to the spirit of eighteenth-century warfare as reflected by authors like Moser or Vattel,[120] than is the Grotian system, however elaborate, coherent, and profound it may be. Possibly the very fact that Grotius had in view such an all-embracing system is what caused him to leave what appears in retrospect as the main path eventually leading up to the emergence of modern

---

[119] 'A study of the production of Gentili—and to appreciate it duly it must be constantly borne in mind that he was Grotius' predecessor—will show what a high place he really occupies in the history of modern international law, and particularly in regard to its development on the positive side; and it will be seen that because of the greater affinity between his point of view and that of modern States and jurists he is, in that respect, as much as, if not more than, Grotius, the progenitor of the existing law of nations.' Phillipson, 'Introduction', pp. 11a–12a. The contrast on this point strikingly appears in the 'practice' both writers adduce in support of their arguments: while Grotius almost exclusively relies on examples from antiquity as supplied by classical literature, Gentili draws at least as much on contemporary, sometimes most recent, history.

[120] Thus Gentili's consistent opposition to 'internecine' war (e.g. *JB*, book II, chap. 2, p. 227, and chap. 23, p. 442; book III, chap. 2, p. 474) seems to foreshadow Montesquieu's famous description of the Law of Nations as being 'naturellement fondé sur ce principe que les diverses nations doivent se faire, dans la paix, le plus de bien, et, dans la guerre, le moins de mal qu'il est possible, sans nuire à leurs véritables intérêts' (*De l'Esprit des Lois*, book I, chap. 3); and his frequent appeal to *humanitas* (e.g. *JB*, book I, chap. 3, p. 25; book II, chap. 17, pp. 351 and 369; book II, chap. 24, pp. 457, 463, 469), although of Ciceronian descent, also points to the 'laws of humanity' set out in the 1868 Declaration of St Petersburg ('the only legitimate object which States should endeavour to accomplish during war is to weaken the military forces of the enemy').
It is therefore not quite accurate to say that, whilst 'both writers adopt the medieval concept of war as a punitive weapon . . . Grotius is not, however, so dogmatic an advocate of this concept as is Gentili', or 'that nowhere in the *De Jure Belli ac Pacis* does he seem so shackled by the medieval concept of the "just war" as is Gentili' (Simmonds, 'Hugo Grotius and Alberico Gentili', pp. 89 and 94). In fact (with the exception of some passages, especially in the first half of book III, e.g. *JB*, book III, chap. 8) the medieval conception of just war is on the whole implicitly neutralized in Gentili's thinking, whilst it is explicitly, and emphatically, upheld by Grotius, in spite of the important exceptions he allows for. See on this point one of Gentili's most determined present-day 'supporters', Carl Schmitt, *Der Nomos der Erde im Völkerrecht des Jus Publicum Europaeum* (Cologne, 1950), pp. 123–31.

international law: a path which Gentili, again in retrospect, seemed content to tread as others had done before while remaining as attentive and sensitive as possible to surrounding political and legal conditions.[121] This is aptly illustrated by their respective definitions of war, by their views on the Law of Nations, and by their conceptions of the international community.

Their definitions of war are equally famous: whilst Gentili describes it as *publicorum armorum iusta contentio*, Grotius defines it as *status per vim certantium*.[122] Gentili's formula is usually held to be superior precisely because it is more in keeping with the spirit of classical international law. Not only does he limit war to a contest between sovereign powers—whereas Grotius expressly includes private warfare in his definition[123]—he also stresses the idea of legality and regularity which is conspicuously absent from the Dutchman's formula. The criticisms voiced against the Grotian definition are of course hardly justified. They fail to perceive it as embodying a deliberate methodological choice directly reflecting a specific approach to the *jus belli*: the idea of justice, Grotius explains, remains outside his definition because it is the very thing his treatise is supposed to reveal; private war, on the other hand, is included because he endeavours to pronounce upon the legality of the whole field of war, the complete range of possible manifestations of physical contest among men. The Grotian definition is comparable to a scientific hypothesis; war stands in it for a wide, philosophical notion of human conflict akin to the *pugna exterior* of Suarez.[124] Yet this is precisely why it appears so

[121] Such seems to be Phillipson's appraisal: 'But parts of his [i.e. Grotius'] work were in some respects retrograde, at all events unprogressive, and in other respects were alien to the circumstances and requirements of the age. Hence not infrequently his method, exposition, and reasoning are very much like those of an abstract *a priori* treatise. Gentili, on the contrary, always considered actual conditions and potentialities, and he never forgot that a body of rules governing the relationships between men or between states is necessarily of an organic nature; so that he avoids all arbitrary dogmatic methods.' 'Introduction', p. 51a.

[122] *JB*, book I, chap. 2, p. 17; *JBP*, book I, chap. 1, § 2.1; see on that point also Ito, 'Alberico Gentili', pp. 623–6.

[123] *JBP*, book I, chap. 1, § 2.1–2. Grotius nevertheless recognized that public war was war *par excellence*; *JBP*, book I, chap. 1, § 2.3.

[124] Franciscus Suarez, *Opus de Triplici Virtute theologica, Fide, Spe et Charitate* (Coimbra, 1621), *De Charitate*, disp. 13: *De bello*, i. pr., p. 797 (Classics of

different from the technical concept of war as understood by international lawyers today; a concept which, in turn, seems better embodied in Gentili's more restrictive, essentially legal, formula.

The same kind of paradox is noticeable if one compares their views on the Law of Nations. Holland seemed to consider these as substantially similar, essentially hinging on enlightened and secularized natural law theories of Protestant jurists, in opposition to the scholastic and obscurantist 'casuistry' of Catholic theologians.[125] Yet, looking beyond the all too simple nineteenth-century cliché that underlies this appreciation,[126] it will appear that the Catholic conceptions of natural law, especially as developed on a Thomistic basis by sixteenth-century Hispanic Dominicans and Jesuits, are clearly better articulated, and for that matter more 'secular', than is most of contemporary Protestant thought on the subject. Moreover, the positions of Grotius and Gentili differ widely from each other on this point. If indeed Gentili is in line with the bulk of Protestant legal theory, Grotius is moving—at least in his mature treatise[127]—closer to the latest Spanish theologians of his time. Gentili's position is Protestant especially through its lack of precision: it deliberately identifies *jus gentium* with *jus naturale*, both being in turn an expression of divine will—which, incidentally, makes it a rather unfortunate choice as a 'secular' conception, despite Gentili's often quoted sentence reminding theologians to stay within their bounds.[128] Grotius, on the other hand, clearly

International Law). Unlike Grotius, but in agreement with the Thomistic tradition, Suarez avoids the word *bellum* when speaking in generic terms of a 'struggle opposed to external peace'.

[125] Holland, 'Alberico Gentili', p. 2 (see also above, pp. 137–8) and pp. 20–3. Holland seems to be in that respect under the influence of Kaltenborn's somewhat idiosyncratic view on the respective merits of Protestant and Catholic writers. The confessional factor is less essential than is usually held. While they were both genuine Protestants, Gentili and Grotius appear, as jurists, remarkably free from confessional prejudice with regard to their substantive solutions. See, however, the following footnotes.

[126] For similar views, see e.g. Phillipson, 'Introduction', pp. 22a–26a; and van der Molen, *Alberico Gentili*, pp. 1–34.

[127] Unlike his conception in *JP* which is at first sight rather 'Protestant' owing to its extreme voluntarism. Grotius' evolution on this point is difficult to account for. Probably it is more a matter of show than of substance. See also below, n. 129.

[128] 'Silete theologi in munere alieno'; *JB*, book I, chap. 12, p. 92. The significance

distinguishes *jus naturae* and *jus gentium*: his law of nature derives directly from immutable human nature as an independent basis, and is therefore declared, in no less famous a sentence, to be valid even if God did not exist;[129] whilst the law of nations proceeds from human will and is therefore merely 'positive' and mutable; one of Grotius' foremost aims being to hold *jus naturae* and *jus gentium* apart—in accordance with his third methodological maxim[130]—and to show their constant

of this sentence (the meaning of which in the context remains partly unclear) has perhaps been exaggerated. 'Secularization' in the modern sense of the expression, be it of law in general or of international law in particular, was hardly a concern of Gentili. In *JB* he could of course not do away with biblical evidence and as a faithful Christian had obviously no intention of doing so (see e.g. *JB*, book II, chap. 21, p. 417; and book III, chap. 7, p. 525). On the other hand he did time and again insist on the distinction between the respective jurisdictions of the *jurisconsulti* (who often appear as '*nostri*') and the *theologi* (see also van der Molen, *Alberico Gentili*, pp. 210–14). This leads him at times to abandon a question in whole or in part to the theologians, especially when it relates to the first three commands of the Decalogue. Thus he declares in *JB*, book III, chap. 15, p. 611, with regard to the lawfulness of duels between princes when their state is thereby jeopardized: 'Forte tamen hic quaestio est prioris tabulae [i.e. of the Decalogue]: quae supra iurisconsultum est'; or again in book III, chap. 19, p. 649, concerning treaties concluded with men of another religion: 'Atque est quaestio partim theologalis, tractataque theologis; partim & nostris tractata civilis'. It is such a division of competences, rather than a general secularization of law, which seems to be at the bottom of Gentili's celebrated exclamation. The sentence is probably also an echo of the bitter quarrel that had opposed him to the puritan faction in the University of Oxford. See on this problem Diego Panizza, *Alberico Gentili, giurista ideologo nell'Inghilterra elisabettiana* (Padua, 1981), pp. 55–87 and 92–3; an excellent account which unfortunately came to the writer's notice only during a late revision of this paper.

[129] 'Et haec quidem quae iam diximus [i.e. the basic rules of natural law], locum aliquem haberent, etiamsi daremus, quod sine summo scelere dari nequit, non esse Deum, aut non curari ab eo negotia humana.' *JBP*, Prolegomena 11. This sentence was put to similar use as Gentili's phrase discussed in the previous footnote, with similar exaggerations. The sentence itself makes it clear beyond doubt that Grotius took it as a mere hypothesis he was by no means ready to accept. Moreover the *locum aliquem haberent* indicates an important restriction: in fact the Grotian natural law derives at least indirectly from divine will; though not free to order anything *different* from what natural law prescribed, God still had to *order* it if it was to become a binding norm of conduct the violation of which was not only evil but sinful; see also *JBP*, book I, chap. 1, § 10.1 and 5. This actually represents a subtle compromise between intellectualism and voluntarism, as had already been reached by several Spanish scholastics, especially Suarez. Yet Grotius' obvious implication was to play the volitional element down (as much as he had played it up twenty years earlier), and he was usually understood in that way by his successors, although he had no intention, any more than Gentili before him, of 'secularizing' natural law. The whole debate on Grotius' supposed secularization is to a great degree anachronistic, confusing as it does his real intentions with the subsequent effect of his writings viewed in a nineteenth- or twentieth-century perspective.

[130] See above, n. 118.

interactions. This acute analysis goes well beyond his predecessor's thought on the matter, and yet, by a curious reversal, it is again Gentili's blurred conception of *jus gentium* which seems less at variance with classical international law viewed as a homogeneous set of legal rules governing inter-state relations, the more so since custom is its favoured expression. Grotius' *jus naturae et gentium*, by contrast, does not constitute such a uniform corpus of law: its two components are independent of, sometimes even in conflict with, each other, reaching a semblance of unity only through their common opposition to the *jus civile*.[131] Thus once again the very precision and penetration of the Grotian construction make it seem further removed from classical international law than Gentili's position, however vague and inarticulate.

Finally, a similar impression prevails as to their respective conceptions of the international community. Most of the time Gentili implicitly thinks in terms of inter-state relations such as Italy had known since the later Middle Ages, and which had clearly come to dominate Europe in the time of Jean Bodin; in that respect, again, the climate of his treatise is not essentially different from what we find in Moser or Vattel. Grotius, too, is of course fully aware of the importance of independent nations and their sovereigns in international life, and they do play a central part in his theory of war; any other position would have been hopelessly out of touch with the political reality of his day. However, his ultimate frame of reference remains the Ciceronian *humani generis societas* inherited from Stoicism,[132] a society of mankind rather than of states.[133]

---

[131] It must be stressed that the Grotian *jus naturae* is *real* law, not just a lofty moral ideal. It is no less 'positive' (that word being taken in its modern, not its Grotian, sense) than the *jus gentium*, and cannot therefore be discarded as binding 'only' in conscience, as some eminent authors have done in the light of present conceptions of law; see J. Basdevant, 'Hugo Grotius', pp. 236–8; and Maurice Bourquin, 'Grotius et les tendances actuelles du droit international', *Revue de Droit international et de Législation comparée*, 53 (1926), pp. 112–16.

[132] See e.g. Cicero, *De officiis*, 1, (14)42–(18)59; 3, (5)21–(8)37; *De finibus bonorum et malorum*, 3, (19)62–(22)76.

[133] 'Il y a chez lui une tendance marquée à considérer l'individu plutôt que l'État et sa conception de la communauté internationale vise plutôt une communauté humaine que la société des États.' Basdevant, 'Hugo Grotius', p. 254.

(j) THEIR RESPECTIVE ROLES IN THE DEVELOPMENT OF INTERNATIONAL LAW

Considering, then, both authors with regard to current international law, Gentili would appear to be at least as modern as Grotius.[134] This, it is submitted, was actually Holland's vantage-point, and to that extent his appreciation remains quite plausible. But it is important to remember its inherent anachronism, based as it is on the categories of a legal discipline with which neither of the two writers was yet familiar, and which neither of them had any intention of propounding to the world, since all they had in mind was a reformulation of the traditional *jus belli*.

Yet, however anachronistic Holland's perception, if it does correctly assess Gentili's position with regard to modern law, we may still ask why it was Grotius who none the less was seen as the fountain-head in the subsequent crystallization of international law, to the point of having allegedly begotten it all by himself. It may be doubted whether this was really due to any 'crusading and reforming spirit'[135] such as was thought to prevail in *De Jure Belli ac Pacis*. In fact Gentili's solutions are no less 'progressive and forward-looking', and throughout his *De Jure Belli* the same 'urgency and conviction' prevails as in Grotius.[136] Besides, Grotius had no intention of proclaiming any 'new' law. In his own view the law he expounded was 'old', as old in its basic part as humanity itself. It was therefore supposed to be as valid in his time as it had been in

---

[134] Equally significant is Gentili's advocacy of pacific settlement of disputes (*JB*, book I, chap. 3, pp. 23–32); although less articulate than Grotius' (exaggeratedly praised) proposals (*JBP*, book II, chap. 23, §§ 7–9), his insistence on this point is at least as forceful and convincing. Grotius may have realized this when, in 1642, he attached to the paragraph dealing with arbitration (ibid., § 8) a lengthy footnote setting out the more recent practice on the subject (it was possibly inspired by Gentili, Grotius referring to Connestagio's work on the union of the kingdoms of Castile and Portugal, which is discussed in the other work, loc. cit.; the initial paragraph was already indebted to Gentili, as shown by Barbeyrac; see also above, n. 58). For a divergent opinion on these passages, see Simmonds, 'Hugo Grotius and Alberico Gentili', p. 90.
[135] Simmonds, 'Hugo Grotius and Alberico Gentili', p. 99.
[136] Ibid., pp. 97 and 99.

Roman times.[137] All he intended was to *remind* his contemporaries of it.[138] If anything, Grotius was 'backward-looking'. Never would he—any more than Gentili—have thought of himself as the prophet of a new legal order or as the 'father' of international law.

Thus it is not to any subjective intent that the success and influence of Grotius' work has to be ascribed. Rather it is to the reactions of posterity to some of its objective features. Clearly the philosophical substance and 'geometrical' construction of *De Jure Belli ac Pacis* appealed more to the age of system-builders like Pufendorf, Spinoza, Leibniz, and Wolff than did the 'plain empirical approach of Gentili'.[139] Beyond the properly 'international' aspects of the treatise, it was above all the general system of rights set out in the second book of *De Jure Belli ac Pacis* which was to become in some way the stage and scenery where future actors were to perform the plot of which modern international law was to be one of the main outcomes.[140] The parts played by these generations

[137] Quite significant is Grotius' clearly uttered intention not to allow for current disputes and particular facts, 'just as geometricians treat their figures as abstracted from bodies' (*JBP*, Prolegomena 58; the *mathematici* mentioned by Grotius seem to be 'geometricians', rather than 'mathematicians' as translated by Kelsey). This again forms a marked contrast to Gentili's constant attention to current events. Grotius was of course quite familiar with, and greatly interested in, the political situation and events of his time, as his correspondence amply shows. But it is misleading to perceive his treatise essentially as a response to that situation and an attempt 'for the first time to demonstrate that an international legal system can be constructed in accord with the new conditions following upon the collapse of the Universal Empire and the Universal Church' (Simmonds, 'Hugo Grotius and Alberico Gentili', p. 99). His achievement basically remains within the realm of ideas and concepts; for the most part, the relation of his thinking to the contemporary political context is only indirect, however considerable its subsequent influence may have been.

[138] See *JBP*, Prolegomena 26 and 28: 'Sileant ergo leges inter arma, sed civiles illae et iudiciariae et pacis propriae: non aliae perpetuae et omnibus temporibus accommodatae . . . Ego cum ob eas quas iam dixi rationes compertissimum haberem, esse aliquod inter populos ius commune quod et ad bella et in bellis valeret, cur de eo instituerem scriptionem causas habui multas ac graves.' The last sentence is immediately followed by the famous complaint on the barbarous conduct of belligerents in Grotius' time—one of the most often quoted sentences of the whole work—and which does of course show that he did not lose sight of the present: the foregoing observations are not intended to deny his very real practical purposes—except that he was not concerned with setting up international law in our sense but with limiting warfare by recalling the law governing it since times immemorial.

[139] Simmonds, 'Hugo Grotius and Alberici Gentili', p. 99.

[140] It was of course only one of the possible outcomes of this complex plot. No less important, and certainly more central, was Grotius' impact on general legal theory,

of thinkers were at least as influential in the subsequent
evolution as Grotius' original intents, with which their
interpretations did not always coincide. Once a work has left
the mind of its author it takes on a life of its own, the course of
which is determined by all its successive readers. Thus it is
that international law could grow out of a treatise which its
author had basically intended to bear only on the law of war. If,
therefore, Grotius prevailed over Gentili in point of historical
influence, it was not because he had a clearer vision of international law as such: it was the indirect result of some catalytic
features of his work, which soon were to confer on it the status
of a standard textbook such as Gentili's treatise could hardly
have become.

Still, whatever its influence, the *De Jure Belli ac Pacis* is but
one of many forces, intellectual or other, to have shaped
international law. Some similar legal discipline would certainly
have come into existence even without the Grotian treatise,
although its aspect might not have been quite the same. An
important benefit of Holland's inaugural lecture was no doubt
to destroy for good the myth of a single creative genius
producing at once a fully fledged system of international law.
Nowadays it is generally acknowledged to have been a
collective creation stretching over more than a century. In the
complex interactions surrounding that process, Grotius'
Three Books obviously had a crucial place. But they could not
have become what they were, nor could their historical role
fully have been what it became, without their author's
predecessors. Grotius' very awareness of the advance he had
effected may have induced him to minimize his debt to their
works.[141] This accounts for his marked reservations towards

giving rise to the rationalist school of natural law and more especially to an important
current of 'natural private law', leading up to the Prussian, French, and Austrian
codifications of civil law; see in particular F. Wieacker, *Privatrechtsgeschichte der Neuzeit*
(Göttingen, 1952), pp. 133–216; Hans Thieme, 'Natürliches Privatrecht und
Spätscholastik', *Zeitschrift der Savigny-Stiftung für Rechtsgeschichte: Germanistische Abteilung*,
70 (1953), pp. 230–66; Robert Feenstra, 'Grocio y el Derecho privado europeo',
Anuario de Historia del Derecho Español (Madrid, 1975), pp. 605–21 (as well as other
studies by this author on private law aspects in Grotius).

[141] 'Les écrivains catholiques et protestants de la Renaissance avaient ouvert la
voie. Plus qu'il ne le dit—et je crois aussi plus qu'il ne le pense—Grotius s'est enrichi
du fruit de leur labeur. Il n'en reste pas moins qu'il les dépasse incontestablement, car

them, no exception being made even for the writer he mentions last in the Prolegomena and values most, Alberico Gentili. Yet, keeping in mind the above considerations, his judgement cannot be looked upon as entirely unfair, although it probably fails to spell out the constant and decisive inspiration afforded to him by the eminent Italian of Oxford.

avec lui, pour la première fois, cet effort collectif s'épanouit en une vaste et majestueuse synthèse.' M. Bourquin, 'Grotius et les tendances actuelles', p. 95.

5

Grotius' Place in the Development of Legal Ideas about War

G. I. A. D. DRAPER

(a) GRAECO-ROMAN DEVELOPMENT OF THE DOCTRINE OF THE JUST WAR

The history of the doctrine of the 'just war' is long and complex. In its earliest traces the doctrine was primarily religious. In general, a religio-juridical doctrine of the 'just war' is not ascertainable among the Greek philosophers. Aristotle, in his *Politics*, reflected ideas from an earlier period when he classified non-Greek peoples as natural enemies destined by nature to serve the Greeks as slaves. Warfare with these barbarians was, in his estimation, more truly considered as a hunt. Such wars Aristotle described as 'just by nature'.[1] By way of contrast, wars between Greeks were not properly 'wars', but 'disease and discord', according to the view Plato attributed to Socrates. Further, Socrates thought that if such wars could not be avoided they should nevertheless be fought with moderation.[2]

The doctrine of the 'just war', as it came to be known in the civilization of Western Europe, was an inheritance from early Roman religio-legal ideas dating from the era of the Roman kings (735–508 BC). This idea was unique and precocious as to its legal content. Rome shared with other and older civilizations the association of war with religious beliefs and sacrificial rituals. Rome from its earliest history had invoked and implicated the gods in such important public transactions as making war and entering into treaties of alliance and peace. The committal of the gods of both peoples to a treaty of peace

[1] A. Nussbaum, *A Concise History of the Law of Nations*, rev. edn. (New York, 1954), p. 5.
[2] Ibid., p. 9.

was the most powerful sanction then known to ensure its observance. Although priests were frequently used as diplomatic envoys and dispatched on embassies for a specific transaction, their more important role in ancient Rome was the sacrificial rites accompanying the making of war and peace. In early Rome, in the period of the kings, the law governing the making of war, of peace, and of treaties of alliance with other nations formed part of the *jus sacrum*, a body of rules, practices, and rituals performed by the college of priests (*fetiales*). It was the religious task of the *fetiales* to decide whether or not the foreign nation or city had committed an 'injury' or 'wrong' against Rome. If the *fetiales* were so satisfied, they took an oath to that effect to the gods of Rome and demanded satisfaction from the foreign nation for the 'wrong' done. In the ceremonies that accompanied these proceedings the *fetiales* concluded their solemn oath with the invocation of the execration of the gods upon the Roman people if their claim should prove to be 'unjust'. If time were demanded by the opposing city or nation to consider Rome's claim, a period of thirty to thirty-three days was normally granted for that purpose. In default of satisfaction being offered to Rome, the *fetiales* would so certify, in Republican times to the Roman senate, the existence of a 'just cause' for resort to war. The final decision whether war or peace should result rested with the 'senate and Roman people'. A war so declared was considered as *bellum justum et pium*.[3]

In the course of time the *jus fetiale* faded. The 'pium' element became vestigial, and the 'justum' element became the essence of the idea. Implicit in this modified Roman *bellum justum et pium* is a juridical idea of considerable importance, although details of its origins may be lost in the pagan religious beliefs of antiquity. It marks the advent of the idea of some, limited, moral and legal restraint upon the resort to war. The idea of a legal wrong done to Rome being requisite before a war waged by Rome on that account could be considered 'justum', i.e. right and lawful, was a progressive one. The Roman sense of law and of order derived from the idea of 'causes of action' (*legis actiones*), known to the *jus civile*

---

[3] A. Nussbaum, *Concise History*, p. 10.

and required before a remedy could be sought under the Roman legal system. The *bellum justum et pium* was an institution of Roman public law, of which the *jus sacrum* originally formed an important part. The significance of such legal ideas when Rome was considering the resort to war is apparent. The Roman *bellum justum et pium* unmistakably emanates from an age when *fas, jus*, and *mos* have not yet been at all sharply distinguished.

Cicero (106–43 BC) made an important contribution to Roman ideas on just war, drawing particularly on the Stoic conception of universally applicable rules of natural law. The law of nature was a 'law' of order visible in nature, and was perceived by man through the use of his reason.

In the mature stage of the Roman conception of the 'just war' four 'just causes' were recognized:

(i) violations of the frontiers of Rome;
(ii) violations of the persons of, or insults to, Roman ambassadors;
(iii) violation of treaties made with Rome; and
(iv) support given to an enemy of Rome by a nation which hitherto had been friendly to Rome.[1]

(b) EARLY CHRISTIAN IDEAS ON JUST WAR

The passage of this Roman idea of the 'just war' into Christian theology and apologetics is one of the more remarkable facets of the history of Western thought. Early Christian history, both in the era up to the persecutions under Diocletian (AD 284–305) and thereafter, shows a considerable hesitancy and ambivalence in the Christian attitude to war and the participation of Christians in war. The Church took an unfavourable view of soldiers already in the Roman army who became Christians after the Edict of Milan (AD 313). In the Eastern Church some of the Church fathers, such as St Basil (AD 326–79), expressed disapproval of Christian participation in all warfare.

[1] L. Oppenheim, *International Law*, i, 8th edn., ed. H. Lauterpacht (London, 1955), pp. 76–7.

In the Western Church, hesitancy and conflicting views continued long after Christianity had become the official religion of the Roman Empire. Eventually the writings of St Augustine (AD 354–430), the most influential of the Western fathers, virtually settled the controversy in the Christian Church with a formula which has validity to this day.[5] In a famous polemic against the Manichaean heresy, *contra Faustum*, written towards the close of the fourth century, St Augustine replied to a question asked by his opponents whether it was necessarily sinful for a Christian to take part in a war. This had proved a major issue of the time, because orthodoxy and heresy were not infrequently determined by resort to arms. In his youth St Augustine, as a student of the Latin classics, had been powerfully impressed by the writings of Cicero, both for their exquisite Latinity and for the philosophical ideas which he found in them. In fact, such ideas were not original and reflected much Greek and particularly Stoic philosophy.[6]

St Augustine adopted the view of Cicero that in the last resort war is waged in order that genuine peace may be restored.[7] Wars waged, he urged, for lust of destruction or revenge or power, were, by definition, 'unjust'. On the specific question posed to him by Faustus, St Augustine gave the answer that a war is not necessarily sinful (for Christians) if, but only if:

(i)   it was waged for a 'just cause';
(ii) it was waged with a 'right intention', i.e. to do good or to avoid evil; and
(iii) it was waged on the authority of a prince.

In this formula, St Augustine had thus chosen a *via media*, adopting neither the view that for a Christian wars were generally permissible, nor that all war was forbidden to Christians. The 'just war', as envisaged by St Augustine, must be one waged (1) for 'avenging' an injury suffered (not 'taking revenge upon'), or (2) when a nation or city fails to punish a bad act, or (3) when a nation or city fails to return what has been unjustly taken. To St Augustine, the *outcome* of the war is not the determinant of its 'justness' or otherwise. That is a

---

[5] Nussbaum, *Concise History*, pp. 35–6.   [6] Ibid., p. 15.
[7] M. H. Keen, *The Laws of War in the Late Middle Ages* (London, 1965), pp. 65–6.

matter for God and the Day of Judgement, a fate for the individual soul and not for the nation. This was a marked departure from the ideas of the old Roman religion.

The immense authority of St Augustine in the Western Church, in theology, philosophy, and apologetics, was such that it bestrode the medieval world 'like a Colossus'. In particular, the teaching of St Augustine dominated medieval thinking about the doctrine of the 'just war'. Theologians, the schoolmen, canon and civilian lawyers accepted his views. Such men refined and elaborated the doctrine of the 'just war' with the subtleties and distinctions that were the hallmark of the schoolmen.

(c) CHRISTIAN DOCTRINES OF JUST WAR IN THE MIDDLE AGES

St Thomas Aquinas (1226–74) was the most outstanding thinker of the schoolmen. He adopted and elaborated St Augustine's classical formulation of the three conditions of the just war. The idea of 'just war' was thus elevated into a Christian doctrine and was impregnated with Christian theology and moral teaching.[8] It formed the main strand of thought about war throughout the Middle Ages and into the late sixteenth century when the new secular national states were established upon the dissolved system of the *imperium* and *sacerdotium* of the Middle Ages.

For St Thomas Aquinas a 'just cause' for all kinds of war, public or private, is essential. He treats the 'just war' as a moral question and therefore of direct concern to the church. To the men of his time, theology, morality, and law were not distinct. In the Thomist scheme the formulation of the 'just war' idea embraced all three, as interrelated in a form of hierarchy. The 'just causes' encompassed such topics as sovereignty, territorial claims, treaties, the right of legation, and related matters.

To the schoolmen who followed in the Thomist tradition, the 'just causes' of war, although ultimately subject to

---

[8] Nussbaum, *Concise History*, pp. 36–7.

theology, were moral questions first and foremost, with certain juridical qualities as secondary features. The school-men, canonists, and civilians saw war in a wide perspective which included private wars, particularly the feudal forays endemic in medieval society. The church did its best to limit these private wars through the 'truce of God', and by anathematizing mercenaries and *routiers*, although often to little effect. The essential requirement for a 'just war' both to St Augustine and St Thomas Aquinas—that the war should have the authority of a prince—thus had a sound practical purpose as well as a moral basis.

St Raymond of Pennaforte (*c.*1185–1275), one of the most distinguished of the thirteenth-century canonists, expressed a mature form of doctrine of the 'just war' which can be summarized thus:

(i) It must be 'just' in regard to those who wage it: thus a war waged by clerks could not be 'just'.

(ii) It must be 'just' in regard to its 'object': that is, it must be to redress an injury to property or person, or for violation of some right.

(iii) It must be 'just' in regard to its 'cause': that is, it must be a necessary 'cause' in the sense that there was no alternative way of securing that object other than recourse to arms.

(iv) It must be 'just' in intention: that is, it must be waged out of a desire to do justice and not out of greed or hate.

(v) It must be waged on a valid authority: that is, that of the Roman Emperor or of the Universal Church or of a sovereign prince.[9]

If a war were 'just' in this sense (which is largely what is now called *jus ad bellum*), then it could not only legitimize acts that would otherwise have been criminal—e.g. killing as an act of war, as opposed to brigandage—but also confer on such acts legal consequences, including, for example, legal title to a ransom for a prisoner lawfully taken or to spoils so taken in a war. An 'unjust' war lacked legal standing of any kind and therefore did not have comparable legal consequences. As one

---

[9] Keen, *Laws of War*, pp. 66–7.

writer put it (with the taking of spoils in mind): 'Knights who take part in a war without just cause should rather be called robbers than knights.'[10]

Gradually it came to be accepted that princes and lawyers were unwilling to view any war other than one levied on the authority of the prince as a 'just' war. By the late Middle Ages a war waged on the authority of the prince (although there might be much legal debate about which princes had that right), was presumed to be a 'just war'—that is, one that had met the stringent criteria which determined whether a particular war was 'just' or not. The prince being sovereign, it followed that in practice there was no other authority to pass judgement upon the 'wrong' alleged by the prince who declared the war. The only practical standard of justice to be applied was that the war had been levied on the authority of a prince. There evolved a practical presumption that if both sides believed in the justice of their cause they were entitled to the benefit of the doubt. Traces of these arguments can be seen in the work of Grotius, who had made a deep study of the medieval writers. This development brings us nearer to the modern idea of a public war in which the parties are equally bound by the laws of war independently of the 'just' or 'unjust' cause for which the war is being fought. Only in such public wars was the full 'right of war' (*jus in bello*) available to both sides, with the further restriction that in wars between Christians the enslaving of prisoners was not permitted. Therefore ransom had to be permitted for Christian captives. Important questions, including the legitimacy of claims to huge sums of money, turned on the existence of a public war declared by a king or a ruling prince. A difficult legal question was determining whether such a prince had indeed authorized an act of war, a matter which could lead to close argument before a military or other tribunal on, for instance, a claim of debt arising out of a promise to pay ransom. The other principle clearly established by the fifteenth century was the converse: 'private wars' conferred no title to ransom or spoils, particularly if they were fought between subjects of the same superior.[11] This is a phase in the gradual transition from warfare seen as

[10] Ibid., p. 65, quoting Nicholas of Tudeschi.
[11] Ibid., pp. 78–81.

a form of private *commercium* by military personnel to the idea of war as a public military service in a sovereign's army. Nevertheless, the idea of war as a form of private enterprise died slowly.

(d) EFFECTS OF JUST WAR DOCTRINES ON THE CONDUCT OF WAR IN THE MIDDLE AGES

It was a marked weakness of the medieval approach to war that the theorists generally had little to say about the manner in which war was to be waged. Clerics could not wage war; and war should not be waged against women and children. Apart from permitting stratagems and ruses and forbidding bad faith in adherence to promises given to an adversary, the canonists and the schoolmen said little about the humane treatment of enemies in warfare. Although the use of the crossbow and longbow was restricted by the Second Lateran Council of 1139 as 'deadly and odious to God',[12] the later canonists considered that such restrictions applied only to those waging an 'unjust war'. The paramount issue was the right to wage war.

In the early Middle Ages the theological doctrine of the indivisibility of the Will of God had precluded acceptance of the contentions of both sides that they were fighting a 'just war'. Further, the Will of God was made manifest in Christian thinking by the outcome of the war, a form of *arbitrium Dei* seen in victory or defeat. An elaboration of this doctrine enabled the victorious prince to be seen as enforcing the Judgement of God against the wicked defeated 'on this earth as the devils in hell will do in the next'.

These ideas did little to abate the fury and brutality of medieval warfare, and may indeed have aggravated it. In general the doctrinal aspects of the 'just war' theory had little or no effect on the conduct of war. In the secular 'law of arms' the right of war enured for both sides provided it was 'public and open' war. If the authority of the prince was lacking, then the war was not 'public and open': therefore such rights were

---

[12] Nussbaum, *Concise History*, p. 18.

not permissible, and the normal belligerent acts of killing, wounding, taking prisoners, ransoms, spoils, etc. became brigandage and banditry inconsistent with the honour of the military calling. Such matters as the existence of a 'regular and open' war would make the difference for the professional military classes between a fortune and a hanging. Whereas the rights under the 'law of arms' (*jus in bello*) were minutely governed, and argued with considerable subtlety by civilians and canon lawyers before the military tribunals, in which experienced knights and heralds often acted as judges, the doctrine of the 'just war' rarely restrained resort to war either by private foray or by princes who could authorize public wars. These were questions of conscience and were for the internal forum of penance.

The 'law of arms' was applied in the military jurisdiction and was seen as part of the *jus gentium*. The secular content was derived from chivalry and the customs of the knights.[13] Thus an act of perfidy would be considered as an act *contra fidem et jus gentium*, the 'faith' in this context being the faith and honour of a knight, a matter which could be enforced by the degrading process of 'dishonour'.

In the later Middle Ages, no prince, in practice, was prepared to admit that a war he had 'avowed' was other than 'just'.[14] It was not easy for third parties not engaged in the war to determine which side was waging a 'just war'. Such matters, it came to be accepted, were best left to the determination of the belligerents. This had important legal consequences as it affected the lawful rights of both belligerents under the law of arms to kill or to take prisoners, ransom, and spoils. These were matters of the utmost importance to those engaged in professional military business and were adjudicated in the feudal and military courts of Christendom, the law of arms being universal.[15] Such developments rendered nugatory in practice the theological aspect of the 'just war' doctrine which regarded the adversaries of the belligerent waging a 'just war' as no more than brigands waging an 'unjust war'.

---

[13] Keen, *Laws of War*, pp. 15–18.
[14] Ibid., pp. 68–70.
[15] Ibid., p. 70.

(e) THE PRELUDE TO GROTIUS

The Spanish theologian-jurists of the late fifteenth and sixteenth centuries inherited the scholastic doctrine of the 'just war' with all its elaborations and imperfections. This included a conception of Christian moral theology, which left the final determination of the 'just' nature of the war primarily to theologians and theologian-jurists. Such thinking was not in harmony with the rise of secular states in Europe and their accompanying political and legal claims to unrestricted sovereignty. The strictly scholastic approach to the 'just war' could not easily be reconciled with the idea that a war might be 'just' for both belligerents. The natural law had to be in harmony with the divine law: it could not stand independently of, or in conflict with, the Will of God. The Will of God was not, in theological terms, divisible.

The idea that both belligerents could not be waging a 'just war' had the consequence that the adversary opposed to the belligerent waging the 'just war' might be precluded from the benefits of such limited restraints upon the conduct of warfare as existed, particularly in relation to the taking of prisoners. The Spanish theologian-jurists were fully aware of the brutalities of medieval warfare which were in part attributable to this position, the ascendancy of which precluded the possibility that all parties to a war could be equally bound by, and entitled to, the benefit of the rules for its conduct. Such a posture would have demanded a secular and legal approach, which the Spanish theologians were not in a position to adopt. This led them to resort to artificial reasoning to impose limitations upon the idea of the 'just war' as they had inherited it from the schoolmen. To that extent the Spanish jurists were theologically inhibited from adopting a modern doctrine of international law in relation to war.[16]

Prominent in the development of the doctrine of the 'just war' in the Spanish school were the Dominican theologian Francisco de Vitoria (1480–1546), and the Jesuit theologian Francisco Suarez (1548–1617).

---

[16] Nussbaum, *Concise History*, pp. 72–3.

Vitoria held the Professorship of Theology at Salamanca, where he delivered lectures on 'The Indians Recently Discovered' and 'The Law of War Made by the Spaniards on the Barbarians'. These lectures, the notes of which were taken by his pupils and published posthumously, were probably delivered in about 1539. Thoroughly imbued with the scholastic ideas of St Thomas Aquinas, Vitoria examined the question whether the Spanish war against the American Indians was a 'just war'. His work is characterized by humane ideas and considerable courage in opposing the claims of his king, Charles V, to imperial mastery of the world. He castigated the inhumane practices of the *conquistadores* against the Indians. He pointed out that the Indians were in fear of the Spanish soldiers armed with novel weapons. He was prepared to allow to the Indians the exception of 'excusable ignorance' as to the legitimacy of the Spanish claims to the New World. He was further prepared to allow that the Indian resistance to the Spaniards might accordingly be viewed as 'just' but only on a subjective basis.

The novelty of Vitoria's thinking lay in his development of the idea that heathens might be subject to legitimate princes of their own, and in his contention that a war against them must be for a 'just cause'. Such a 'just cause' might exist, Vitoria thought, if the Indians resisted the work of the Spanish missionaries or directed their actions against Indians already converted to Christianity. This was not a claim for the 'equality' of Christians and heathens. Neither could there be any question of non-Christian missionaries being allowed to work among the Indians.[17] Vitoria's ideas were based upon the divine law (the Scriptures), natural law, and the *jus gentium*, deduced in the scholastic tradition.

To a limited extent Vitoria was willing to accept that a war might be 'just' on both sides, although he was prepared to concede the role of 'judge' to the victorious prince if his 'cause' were objectively just.[18] He enumerates the grounds upon which the war of the Spaniards against the Indians and the occupation of their territory might be 'just'. At the same time, he considered the hypothesis that his reasons for that

[17] Ibid., p. 82.
[18] Ibid., p. 83.

conclusion might not be valid. However, the fact that large
numbers of Indians had been converted to Christianity by the
Spaniards meant that it would not be right for the King of
Spain to withdraw entirely his administration of the 'provinces' taken from them. This being the age of 'discovery' and
of Spanish ascendancy, Vitoria's views are understandable,
but as a Christian theologian he was bound to warn the
conquistadores against the abuse of that ascendancy over the
Indians: he did not hesitate to condemn the Spaniards'
misdeeds. Behind his thinking, whether about the 'just war' or
other matters of international interest, lies his firm support of
papal claims over the secular authorities, and of the need for
the layman to follow the advice of the priest. Vitoria thus
stands as an enlightened traditionalist.

The Jesuit theologian Francisco Suarez was, like his
distinguished predecessor, a Spaniard and Professor of Theology. In 1596, in the period after the conquest of Portugal by
Philip II of Spain, Suarez was appointed by the king to the
Chair of Theology at Coimbra. He was a prolific writer and a
powerful thinker. Steeped in the scholastic tradition, he was
known by some as the 'last of the schoolmen'. His main
discussion of the law of war is found in his *De Triplici Virtute
Theologica*, published posthumously in 1621, in which there is
a substantial section on charity. This treatment again reflects
the Thomist tradition, war being here considered as contrary
to charity. His approach is analytical, detached, and primarily
juridical. Suarez' thinking on the doctrine of the 'just war' is
concerned with the relationship between 'justness' and charity
which he analyses in conceptual terms. He asks whether a war
can have a 'good cause' and yet violate charity, and if so, what
reparation must be made. Again, he asks whether a war could
be undertaken in which neither belligerent had a good 'cause'.
Would such a war be contrary to justice and to charity? Can
'just' causes derive from those based upon natural reason?
Although Suarez is not entirely consistent on this issue, he
largely rejected the thesis of Vitoria that a war might be 'just'
subjectively on both sides.

In the tradition of scholastic moral theology Suarez held
that a war may justly be waged even though it is not certain
that the prince's claim is valid: it is sufficient if the claim is

supported by the 'more probable' opinion. Thus a mercenary in doubt about the 'justness' of the 'cause' of the war is protected by the law if the doubt be 'negative', that is, if he is unaware of 'probable reasons' favourable to the opponent. If he is aware of such 'probable reasons' he must follow them: otherwise he would be at the mercy of his captors.

Unlike Vitoria, Suarez develops a 'judicial' theory of the just war and makes it a primary part of his legal ideas on the subject. The prince waging the 'just war' has a real jurisdiction in respect of his belligerent act, as if it were a decree of a court of law. This jurisdiction is part of 'vindicative justice'. This dual role of the prince waging the 'just war', as both prosecutor and judge, is unobjectionable in Suarez' view— because war is, in his definition, an act of vindicative justice necessary for mankind and for which no better substitute has been found. Such views did not escape criticism from his contemporaries in the Society of Jesus, such as Molina and Vasquez.[19]

Among the military law writers who served as military auditors in the armies of King Philip II, Pierino Belli (1502–75) and Balthazar Ayala (1548–84) both expressed views on the 'just war'. Belli, an Italian, published his work *De Re Militari et Bello Tractatus* in 1563. He urged that if one party is willing to submit a controversy to arbiters, then the other should cease waging the war lest it become 'unjust': this is novel, but is expressed in an unconvincing manner.

Ayala was Auditor-General in King Philip's armies in the Netherlands and published his book *De Jure et Officiis Bellicis et Disciplina Militari* in 1582. He based his theory of the 'just war' doctrine on 'equity and the duty of a religious man' rather than on legal considerations. In his view, it was not appropriate to discuss the 'equity of the cause of a war between sovereign princes'. If such a war were lawfully conducted it might be 'just' on both sides. Such an idea had no place, however, in the war between the Spaniards and the Netherlanders. Such a struggle was rebellion, analogous to heresy and parricide, the King of Spain being a kind of parent even to his rebellious subjects. Ayala proceeded to assert that the laws

---

[19] Nussbaum, *Concise History*, pp. 90–1.

of war did not apply to rebels any more than to pirates and robbers.

Alberico Gentili (1552–1608) was a North Italian Protestant who became Regius Professor of Civil Law at Oxford. His work, *De Jure Belli*, gave the doctrine of the 'just war' a central place. The third part of that work dealt with treaties and alliances. According to Gentili, third states ought to assist allies beyond the terms of the alliance whenever those allies were unjustly attacked, as well as assisting all other nations close in blood, race, or religion to the third state. This was in effect a claim for Protestant solidarity dressed in the guise of the 'just war' idea. His list of 'just' causes of war does not extend to wars for the propagation of the Christian faith or in opposition to the acceptance of it. The scholastics' views were not acceptable to Gentili. In particular, he advocates that a war may be 'just' on both sides, and not merely by reason of excusable ignorance, but also in the objective sense. What is more important is that Gentili was prepared to hold that the rights of a belligerent in war, for example, to take prisoners, ransoms, and booty, are independent of the 'justness' of the cause for which that belligerent resorted to war.[20] Gentili does not enquire further as to whether there remains any legal significance for the doctrine of the 'just war'. In the main, Gentili was not a theoretical writer, but approached his subject in a pragmatic and polemical manner. He wrote essentially as an advocate. He desired the sparing of women, children, and priests from acts of war, not by reason that they had no hand in the starting of war, but on the ground of 'humaneness'. This quality he derived from classical sources rather than the Gospels and Christian apologists, although he paid considerable deference to St Augustine.

Gentili did much to free international law from its theological background and to focus attention on legal rather than moral considerations. His writings received little recognition in his day and for a long period thereafter. His important influence for secularization is epitomized by his memorable remark: 'Let theologians hold their peace in work that belongs to

---

[20] Nussbaum, *Concise History*, p. 97. This is an advance in thought for which Gentili probably did not receive the credit to which he was entitled. See the chapter by Peter Haggenmacher in this volume.

others than they.'[21] It is doubtful whether full justice has yet
been done to Gentili.

(f) GROTIUS' WRITINGS ON JUST WAR

The two great works which have made Grotius famous are *De
Jure Praedae*, which (with the exception of one chapter, *Mare
Liberum*, published in 1609) was not discovered or published
until the 1860s; and *De Jure Belli ac Pacis*, published in Paris in
1625 after his escape from Holland. Some scholars have seen
the earlier work as a form of first edition of the latter, although
others have detected a development of his ideas in the twenty-
year period that elapsed between the two works.[22]

De Jure Belli ac Pacis, dedicated to King Louis XIII of
France in 1625, while the Thirty Years War (1618–48) was in
progress, secured for its author a European reputation rarely
enjoyed upon publication. So great was this reputation that it
is doubtful whether the predecessors of Grotius have received
their due acclaim for their part in the development of the Law
of Nations. Although several further editions of the work were
published during his lifetime the rest of his life was not
devoted solely to the law. His later years were increasingly
given up to literature and theology, and particularly to the
idea of the unification of the Christian church with the
accompanying benefit of achieving peace after the prolonged
horrors of the Thirty Years War.[23]

Grotius, like his most important predecessors, was con-
versant with and much influenced by the writings of the
scholastics, both in his adoption of subtle distinctions and in
his extensive reliance upon biblical and classical sources. The
display of erudition was brilliant, but the methods of
presenting his views had numerous defects.

The success of *De Jure Belli ac Pacis* was due not only to

---

[21] *De Jure Belli*, book I, chap. 12; and J. L. Brierly, *The Law of Nations*, 6th edn., ed.
H. Waldock (Oxford, 1963), p. 27.

[22] Hersch Lauterpacht, *International Law: Collected Papers*, vol. ii, part 1, ed.
E. Lauterpacht (Cambridge, 1975), p. 311. For a detailed account see J. B. Scott's
Introduction to the translation of *De Jure Belli ac Pacis* (Classics of International Law,
Washington, DC, 1925), vol. ii, pp. ix *et seq.*

[23] Lauterpacht, *International Law*, p. 309.

Grotius' reputation but also to the time and circumstances in which it was compiled. It was the time of Holland's greatness. The country had been recently liberated by popular struggle from the rule of Spain and was already an independent state. Political liberty, religious toleration, commercial success, and a high degree of culture all united to make the Netherlands probably the most enlightened and advanced political society in the Europe of the day.[24]

1. Grotius' Approach and Methods

There has been much criticism of the work *De Jure Belli ac Pacis*, not least in its method of presentation and also on account of a confusion and contradiction surrounding some of his fundamental conceptions such as natural law, the Divine Law, and the *jus gentium*, and the nexus and interplay between them. Grotius makes more reference to biblical events and classical precedents than to wars in his own day. However, the appeals for moderation in the conduct of war contained in his discussion of *temperamenta belli* in book III, show that he was only too well aware of the harshness of current war practices and of the need to mitigate their severity.

A major criticism of *De Jure Belli ac Pacis* is that about half of it is not concerned with international law in the modern sense. It embraces the law of property, contract, delict, reparation, jurisprudence, and much else. It extends to a general theory of constitutional law, drawing in ideas of sovereignty and of the social contract. The explanation for this may not be difficult to establish. It is part of the originality of Grotius that he saw the 'just war' idea primarily in juridical and moral terms, that is, as the lawful response to threatened or actual violation of a right known to the law, or to a refusal of reparation for such violation. It was necessary to give a detailed exposition of the substantive internal law, as any part of this could be engaged by a breach of a legal duty. A further explanation may be that Grotius had already prepared a great deal of the material used in *De Jure Belli ac Pacis* when writing *De Jure Praedae* twenty years earlier.[25]

---

[24] Brierly, *The Law of Nations*, 6th edn., pp. 28–9.
[25] Nussbaum, *Concise History*, pp. 107–9.

A further defect of presentation is readily discernible on nearly all topics. Grotius informs his reader of the position under Divine law, natural law, and the *jus gentium*, but it is often impossible to ascertain his views on what the law actually is or was on any given case. This is particularly true of the law of war, the central concern of the work. This is highlighted in book III where, after reciting the harsh nature of the law of war in actual practice, that is, under the Law of Nations, he has this to say under the rubric 'With what meaning a sense of honour may be said to forbid what the law permits':

> I must retrace my steps, and must deprive those who wage war of nearly all the privileges which I seemed to grant, yet did not grant to them . . . I bore witness that many things are said to be 'lawful' or 'permissible' for the reason that they are done with impunity . . .[26]

To explain this passage Grotius cites the answer given by Agamemnon to Pyrrhus who had claimed that the full power over prisoners lay with the victor—namely, that such conduct, although permitted by law, may be contrary to our sense of justice and thus forbidden. Such an appeal from law to justice is made, according to Grotius, only in relation to things done in an unjust war, though undertaken in a lawful way. In such a war, he says, 'all acts which arise therefrom are unjust from the point of view of moral injustice.'[27] This is confusing. While Grotius does make this broad distinction between 'just' and 'unjust' wars, in general he moved some way towards the position where *jus in bello* came to be viewed as applicable irrespective of the justness or unjustness of a war.[28]

In much of the treatise it is uncertain whether Grotius is concerned with law or morals. His part in reducing the dependence of the doctrine of the 'just war' on theology had not yet enabled him to make law and morality distinct. His belief in natural law as the source of all law in his scheme of thought meant that he could not draw an explicit distinction between law and morality. He defined the law of nature as:

---

[26] *De Jure Belli ac Pacis*, book III, chap. 10, § 1. 1.
[27] Ibid., book III, chap. 10, § 3.
[28] Ibid., book III, chap. 4, § 4.

a dictate of right reason, which points out that an act, according as it is or is not in conformity with rational nature, has in it a quality of moral baseness or moral necessity; and that, in consequence, such an act is either forbidden or enjoined by the author of nature, God.[29]

Grotius asserts that the law of nature is the law that is most in conformity with the social nature of man and the preservation of human society. This law of nature in its 'primary sense' prohibits the taking of what belongs to others, demands restoration to others of what is their property, imposes the duty to fulfil promises and to make reparation for injury, and confers the right to inflict punishment.[30] In other words it yields the requirements for 'just war'.

2. *The Just Causes of War*

Grotius made a major advance upon the work done by his predecessors in his detailed and systematic elaboration of the 'just causes' of war. In order that a war may be 'just' there must be, in Grotius' view, a 'just' and lawful 'cause', on the analogy of a 'cause of action' which would be recognized as affording a remedy before a municipal court of law. He states:

It is evident that the sources from which wars arise are as numerous as those from which lawsuits spring; for where judicial settlement fails, war begins. Actions, furthermore, lie either for wrongs not yet committed, or for wrongs already done.

He was convinced of the reality of a society of states, just as there was a society of men comprising a state.[31]

Some have seen the analogy of a 'cause of action' as far-fetched and artificial, but it provided a basis for his distinction between 'just' and 'unjust' wars. In an age when the new sovereign territorial states were novelties the analogy had relevance. At the same time, it enabled Grotius to introduce in book II a vast amount of jurisprudential and legal material which would not find a place in modern treatises on international law.

---

[29] *JBP*, book I, chap I, § 10. 1.
[30] Ibid., Prolegomena 8.
[31] Ibid., book II, chap. I, § 2. 1.

In default of judicial proceedings, war was the method adopted by states to settle their claims. No other method existed which offered an effective disposal of state disputes. If war had to be recognized by the law, it was then necessary that war should have a 'just cause', as would a lawsuit before a court between citizens within a state. From these premisses Grotius advanced to the key proposition that a war initiated without a basis in strict justice is an 'unjust war'. These 'just causes' are based on natural law and the law of nations. They extend to:

(i) defence against an injury, actual or threatening, but not anticipatory;
(ii) a recovery of what is legally due to the aggrieved state; and
(iii) the infliction of punishment upon the wrongdoing state.[32]

By this scheme of thought Grotius accepted the reality of war as a phenomenon recognized by the law, but at the same time sought to eliminate unlicensed and unrestrained resort to war by demanding 'just' and legal grounds for wars.

As to anticipatory self-defence, Grotius is clear that the 'just causes' of self-defence do not extend to a potential, as distinct from actual, threat to the security of a state: 'That the possibility of being attacked confers the right to attack is abhorrent to every principle of equity. Human life exists under such conditions that complete security is never guaranteed to us.'[33] Elsewhere in his treatise he says:

Fear with respect to a neighbouring power is not a sufficient cause. For in order that a self-defence may be lawful it must be necessary; and it is not necessary unless we are certain, not only regarding the power of our neighbour, but also regarding his intention; the degree of certainty required is that which is accepted in morals.[34]

3. The Consequences of the Distinction between 'Just' and 'Unjust' Causes

The categorization of 'just' and 'unjust' causes of war in the treatise is not novel, and much of it echoes the thinking of the

---

[32] Ibid., book II, chap. 1, § 2. 2.　　　[33] Ibid., book II, chap. 1, § 17.
[34] Ibid., book II, chap. 22, § 5. 1.

schoolmen. However, the detailed practical consequences which Grotius draws from the distinction mark a considerable departure from the earlier writers on these subjects. Grotius traces these consequences in several innovative directions. Thus, wars waged without any 'cause' are 'unjust'; a treaty of alliance is not binding in relation to a state waging an 'unjust war'; a state waging a war against an adversary engaged in a 'very unjust war' has a right to inflict capital punishment on those carrying contraband; the claim of a subject people to attain their freedom is 'unjust', as is the claim to universal empire.[35]

His treatment of these practical consequences extends to the question of the duty of the subject to serve in a war which is 'unjust' or doubtful. Grotius is firm that a subject ordered to take up arms in an 'unjust war' has the duty to refuse. With some hesitation he is prepared to counsel this duty to refuse where the 'justice' of the cause is doubtful, although he admits that there is in such a case a risk of disobedience ensuing. If a war be 'unjust' then there is no disobedience in refusal to take up arms. If either course of action be uncertain, then the lesser evil should be followed. However, the ruler is entitled to impose an extraordinary tax upon those who refuse to take up arms in a doubtful war.[36]

One of the practical legal consequences of the moral element inherent in the 'just' and 'unjust' war dichotomy was that the concept of absolute impartiality or neutrality could not be accommodated. International law could, in theory, establish that some wars were 'unjust' and criminal and yet demand that neutral states act with absolute impartiality as between the aggressor and the victim state. Such a posture would, in legal terms, be open to doubt and in moral terms would be manifestly wrong. The spirit of Grotius' treatise rendered absolute 'impartiality' impossible. In book III, Grotius broke new ground in propounding the doctrine of qualified neutrality. Under the heading, 'What the Duty of those at Peace is towards Belligerents', he writes:

It is the duty of those who keep out of a war to do nothing whereby he who supports a wicked cause may be rendered more powerful, or

---

[35] *JBP*, book II, chap. 22.   [36] Ibid., book II, chap. 26, §§ 3–5.

whereby the movements of him who wages a just war may be hampered . . .[37]

This does not imply a duty to assist actively those waging the 'just war', but it does not debar the right to do so. The duty not to hamper may not be easily distinguishable from the right to render assistance to the party waging the 'just war'. Grotius asserts that the right of passage ought to be denied to a state waging an unjust war, while it ought to be granted to a state waging a just war.[38]

4. The Law of War and 'Temperamenta Belli'

A major defect of the work is that an important part of it, the exposition of the laws of war in book III, is vitiated by the abandonment of the main purpose with which the author set out, namely, the humanization of the law of war, as recited in his Prolegomena:

Fully convinced, by the considerations which I have advanced, that there is a common law among nations, which is valid alike for war and in war, I have had many and weighty reasons for undertaking to write upon this subject. Throughout the Christian world I observed a lack of restraint in relation to war, such as even barbarous races should be ashamed of; I observed that men rush to arms for slight causes, or no cause at all, and that when arms have once been taken up there is no longer any respect for law, divine or human; it is as if, in accordance with a general decree, frenzy had openly been let loose for the committing of all crimes.[39]

Such was stated to be the primary purpose of his treatise. Some scholars think that the work frustrated its stated purpose. This has nothing to do with the fact that Grotius asserted in book I the lawfulness of the institution of war, basing himself upon the law of nature, the Bible, classical history, and early Christian practice. Rather, it is because Grotius holds that the Law of Nations sanctions the killing of all persons found in enemy territory and of all enemies

---

[37] Ibid., book III, chap. 17, § 3. 1.
[38] Ibid., book II, chap. 2, §§ 13. 1 and 13. 4.
[39] Ibid., Prolegomena 28.

wherever found, as also the killing of captives and those whose surrender is not accepted.[40]

Although in general, as against an enemy, Grotius saw nothing as prohibited by the Law of Nations, he sought to modify the harshness of this conclusion by emphasizing the idea of *temperamenta belli*: this was in essence a plea for moderation, for example in regard to treatment of prisoners and of enemy property. It was more a moral and prudential than a strictly legal idea. Indeed, the very conception of the *temperamenta* makes little sense unless it be assumed that what is to be moderated is necessarily part of the existing Law of Nations.[41]

There are various conjectures as to why Grotius took this approach, which conceded that the Law of Nations permitted many atrocities, and seemed to relegate the *temperamenta* to hortatory status. None of them is very satisfactory. Could he have imagined that the knowledge of the current practices of warfare displayed in his work would induce generals to moderation, or induce statesmen to give him diplomatic employment by reason of his intimate familiarity, as a jurist, with the war practices of states? Neither reason convinces. More probably the effect was the exact opposite. Generals aware of his reputation as a very learned jurist would not readily accept a duty to act otherwise than in the manner that such a jurist asserted to be in accord with the Law of Nations. Certainly, the commanders and generals in the Thirty Years War seem to have been prepared to accept his statements of what accorded with the Law of Nations in the actual conduct of contemporary warfare, as is evidenced by the many sacked cities in Europe at that time. It is a sad reflection upon the influence of Grotius that in the later stages of the war the cruelties committed increased at a time when further editions of his treatise were being published and when his reputation as a jurist stood as high as ever.[12] Grotius' implicit concession that contemporary cruelties were permitted by the Law of Nations inevitably meant that much of the force of his passionate plea for the *temperamenta* was spent and wasted.

---

[40] *JBP*, book III, chap. 4, §§ 6–12.
[41] See ibid., book III, chaps. 11–16.
[42] Lauterpacht, *International Law*, pp. 321–2.

Grotius' purpose was to limit and restrain war in two ways: firstly, by the 'just war' doctrine, with its severe limitations on the causes of resort to it; and second, in seeking some humane limitations upon the means by which wars were waged, that is, his plea for the *temperamenta belli*. In state practice, his 'just war' doctrine certainly was not accepted in his day or for three centuries thereafter, except by way of rhetoric and references in diplomatic exchanges. Yet the Grotian tradition never died. The *temperamenta* were not incorporated into the Law of Nations in his day nor even in the early eighteenth century when some modifications of the harshness of war practices became visible. Such 'moderations' when they came were not attributable to the writings of Grotius, although he had written in their favour with moral force. In the second half of the nineteenth century many of them came to be included in the conventions by which the 'laws and customs of war' were reduced to written agreements. By that time the techniques of war-making had changed almost out of recognition from those in use during the Thirty Years War.

5. *Grotius' Rejection of 'Reason of State'*

It followed from Grotius' conception of the moral, rational, and social nature of man, and the centrality of man as the main object of law, that he rejected any dominant place for 'reason of state' in inter-state relations. Not the least arresting facet of *De Jure Belli ac Pacis* is the absence of any reference throughout the treatise to the views of Machiavelli (1469–1527). Grotius answered him by silence. This is the more surprising having regard to the voluminous works on 'reason of state' that were then in circulation, including that of Father Joseph, Richelieu's adviser.

In the Prolegomena, however, Grotius does address the arguments of proponents of 'reason of state' doctrine. In drawing attention to the value of studying the law governing the relations between states, he tells us that there were in his time those who viewed that law with contempt as lacking reality. Such writers considered that for a state nothing is unjust which is expedient and that the business of a state cannot be performed without injustice.[43] States wielding great power can afford to pursue their policies without regard to law and solely in the light of their own advantage. Grotius contended, in rebuttal of those views, that no state is so powerful that it can afford to dispense with the help of others, such is the impact of economic interdependence and of military security. 'Reason of state' is contrary to Grotius' main theories concerning the 'just war', namely, that there can be no right to resort to war unless there is a just and legal cause for it; that the right of self-defence is under strict limitation debarring a resort to war to ward off an anticipatory attack; and that there is a duty to refrain from 'unjust' wars, or wars the justice of which is doubtful. In truth there is a deep and irreconcilable contradiction between international law and 'reason of state', yet for nearly four centuries 'reason of state' was to be the dominant factor in inter-state relations.

Grotius set out in his Prolegomena his firm rejection of the contention that war and law are irreconcilable, a contention not confined to the ignorant. He then set out what he considered the main arguments in favour of the contention advanced by the supporters of 'reason of state'. Grotius chose Carneades, the Greek philosopher (215–129 BC), as their advocate.[44] He was a leading sceptic who joined issue with the Stoics by rejecting their argument that natural law was discoverable by 'right reason'. He asserted the impossibility of knowledge and the relativity of virtue. He argued that men impose laws upon themselves for expediency and that such laws vary among different peoples and change at different times. The law of nature, he argued, has no basis because all creatures, men and animals, are impelled by nature to ends advantageous to themselves. Therefore, there is no justice, or if there be such, it is supreme folly since a person does violence to his own interests if he is foolish enough to consult the interests of others. This is summed up in one line of Horace's verse: 'And just from unjust Nature cannot know.'

To Grotius, justice is not a folly, as Carneades had argued. Grotius thought that the Law of Nations had as its purpose not the advantage of particular states but rather the advantage

[43] *JBP*, Prolegomena 3.
[44] Ibid., Prolegomena 5, 6, 17, and 18.

of all the members of the great society of states. Just as a subject is not foolish who obeys the laws of his state, so that state is not foolish which does not press its own advantage to the extent of disregard of the Law of Nations. To the extent that a state disregards the law of nature and of nations, it cuts away the safeguards for its own future peace if not its existence.[45]

(g) GROTIUS AND LATER DEVELOPMENTS IN THE LAW CONCERNING WAR

The impact of the distinction made by Grotius between the just and the unjust war, that is, between lawful and unlawful war, was minimal. Generally, later writers used his works largely as rhetorical ornament, and there was little suggestion that they were the basis of the international law and state practice of the ensuing three centuries. During the seventeenth, eighteenth, and most of the nineteenth centuries, 'reason of state' was a more accurate mirror of international law and practice. By the close of the nineteenth century, states had the right in international law to resort to war for the national policy of the moment. Such a right, lodged within the citadel of state sovereignty which itself derived from international law, enabled all state claims to be asserted by resort to war. Might and right were equated. Such a situation seriously weakened the claim of international law to be considered a true system of law, or indeed to be anything more than a system of the utmost weakness. Much of the traditional scepticism of statesmen and jurists towards international law was coloured by this dominant position of war in the international system until the last years of the nineteenth century. In 1880, a leading jurist W. E. Hall wrote:

International law has consequently no alternative but to accept war, independently of the justice of its origin, as a relation which the parties to it may set up if they choose, and to busy itself only in regulating the effects of the relation. Hence both parties to every war

---

[45] Ibid., Prolegomena 18.

are regarded as being in an identical legal position, and consequently as possessed of equal rights.[46]

The first part of his observation overturns the whole of Grotius' distinction between the just and the unjust war; and the second part overtakes it.

At the First and Second Hague Peace Conferences of 1899 and 1907 tentative and modest steps were taken to place the first legal restrictions upon the unqualified right of states to resort to war as an instrument of national policy, an essential part of their inherent sovereignty. However, the Hague Peace Conferences made only minimal impact upon the legality of war as formulated by Hall. By the 1907 Hague Convention II, the use of force to recover public contract debts was prohibited unless arbitration had been refused by either party. The 1907 Hague Convention III required a declaration or ultimatum before armed hostilities began.[47] Such, in the absence of bilateral treaties prohibiting war between the states parties thereto, was the international law position as to resort to war when the First World War began in 1914.

The dramatic changes which came about in international law on resort to war in the period 1920–45 constituted a remarkable legal phenomenon. It is doubtful whether these changes were much influenced by the writings of Grotius, but they do stand in the Grotian tradition. In the Covenant of the League of Nations, which was established by the 1919 Treaty of Versailles and was dissolved in April 1946, lawful resort to war was substantially diminished for the League's member states. It was unlikely that aggressor states would be able to resort to war without breach of one or more of the obligations in the Covenant.[48] Self-defence was not touched in the Covenant.

Such gaps as there were in the Covenant's restrictions upon the right of members to resort to war were reduced by the 1928 Pact of Paris—the Kellogg-Briand Pact. This instrument, whose full title is the General Treaty for the Renunciation of War, is independent of the League Covenant and thus

---

[46] W. E. Hall, *International Law*, 8th edn. (Oxford, 1924), p. 82.

[47] L. Oppenheim, *International Law*, vol. ii, 7th edn., ed. H. Lauterpacht (London, 1952), pp. 179 and 292–9.

[48] Brierly, *Law of Nations*, p. 408.

did not expire with the League in 1946. It reflected the idea, considered at the time of the establishment of the League of Nations a decade earlier, that war should be prohibited except in self-defence. By Article 1, the Parties 'condemn recourse to war for the solution of international controversies, and renounce it as an instrument of national policy in their relations with one another.' By Article 2, the Parties 'agree that the settlement or solution of all disputes or conflicts, of whatever nature or of whatever origin they may be, which may arise among them, shall never be sought except by pacific means.' The sanction for this important instrument, set out in the preamble, was that states which violated the Pact would lose the benefit of it. The weakness of the instrument was that it was confined to 'war', with the result that states resorted to hostilities but declined to consider that there was a 'state of war'. Self-defence receives no express reference in the Pact; a number of states made declarations that their acceptances of the Pact were subject to the right of self-defence.[49] Such prohibitions far exceeded, in their scope and nature, what Grotius had propounded in his treatise when dealing with the 'just war' doctrine.

International law on the right to resort to war was further developed by three important provisions of the UN Charter of 1945. By Article 2(3) 'All Members shall settle their international disputes by peaceful means in such a manner that international peace and security, and justice, are not endangered.' By Article 2(4) 'the threat or use of force against the territorial integrity or political independence of any state' is prohibited. By Article 51 the inherent right of individual or collective self-defence is preserved. Article 2(4) is the greatest inroad upon the sovereignty of states in relation to the use of force yet made by international law.[50]

These provisions go far beyond Grotius' condemnation of resort to war without just cause. However, the idea of 'self-defence' as a justification, which Grotius kept within certain

---

[49] Ibid., pp. 408–12.
[50] Some indication of the categories of aggressive resort to armed force appears in the 1974 General Assembly Resolution 3314 adopted by consensus (i.e. without vote). Although not strictly confined to Article 2(4) of the UN Charter it is essentially an elaboration of that provision. While this resolution does not provide an exhaustive definition of aggression, increasing reference is made to it.

limits, has been widened considerably. In the post-1945 era the idea of collective self-defence, in the form of permanent peacetime alliances, has been central to efforts to preserve international peace. The two main blocs, NATO and the Warsaw Pact, have contrived to bring their respective defence groupings within the ambit of the concept of collective self-defence. It is more than doubtful whether such a system of self-defence in an age of nuclear weapons can be accommodated within the framework of Grotian ideas.

As to internal wars, Grotius' conception does not accord with contemporary developments. Grotius was not prepared to consider internal armed rebellions as 'just wars'.[51] Internal armed conflicts have formed a large proportion of armed conflicts since 1945, together with the 'mixed' armed conflicts in which third states participated on one or other side (or both) in what had originally been essentially an internal conflict. Moreover, armed struggles for 'national liberation' have now gained recognition as lawful resorts to armed force. By virtue of the 1977 Protocol I additional to the 1949 Geneva Conventions, such struggles, essentially internal, have, for the purposes of the application of the modern humanitarian law of armed conflicts been treated as international in character.[52]

Nevertheless, what Grotius had advocated so forcefully in his treatise—the idea that no legal system can afford to disregard the distinction between the lawful and the unlawful resort to war—has now become a fundamental principle (*jus cogens*) of international law. Grotius has to that extent been vindicated. The doctrine of 'reason of state' has been supplanted by international law as regards the resort to war by states. However, Grotius would probably have allowed no place for the use of armed force by internal rebels and 'national liberation movements'. The former is not a violation of, while the latter is now in some circumstances expressly allowed by, international law.

The plea made by earlier writers, including Gentili, but endorsed and fortified by Grotius, namely that limitations on

[51] *JBP*, book i, chap. 4, § 2.
[52] G. I. A. D. Draper, 'Wars of National Liberation and War Criminality', in Michael Howard (ed.), *Restraints on War: Studies in the Limitation of Armed Conflict* (Oxford, 1979), pp. 146–51.

warfare must be observed irrespective of the 'just' or 'unjust' nature of the initial resort to war, has been retained, but not without some hesitation. This was and is a major contribution in legal ideas and forms part of the Grotian tradition.

The Judgment of the International Military Tribunal at Nuremberg of 1945–6, and the experiences in the war to which that Judgment was directed, left misgivings in the minds of some jurists as to whether the contention that the law of war applied equally to the 'just' and 'unjust' belligerents could or should be sustained. In his closing speech the UK Attorney-General said:

The killing of combatants in war is justifiable, both in international and in national law, only where the war itself is legal. But where a war is illegal, as a war started not only in breach of the Pact of Paris but without any sort of declaration clearly is, there is nothing to justify the killing, and these murders are not to be distinguished from those of any other lawless robber bands.[53]

This proposition was rightly rejected by the Tribunal, which followed the Grotian tradition in maintaining that a state acting justly (e.g. in self-defence) is not entitled to disregard the law of war; and that the aggressor is entitled to the benefit and is subject to the burden of it.

Today, the essentially humanitarian quality of the greater part of the modern law of armed conflicts has fortified refusal to allow any weakening of the regime of the law of war in its full and equal application to the 'just' and the 'unjust' belligerent. No less is demanded by morality, the nature of law, humanity, and sheer necessity.[54] There were some attempts in the 1970s to make a breach of this regime of law in favour of 'national liberation movements'. However, the preamble of the 1977 Geneva Protocol I, in which such struggles are included as international armed conflicts, indicates the express rejection of that endeavour. It reaffirms:

that the provisions of the Geneva Conventions of 12 August 1949 and of this Protocol must be fully applied in all circumstances to all

[53] *The Trial of German Major War Criminals: Proceedings of the International Military Tribunal sitting at Nuremberg, Germany* (23 vols., London, 1946–51), part 19, p. 423.
[54] C. W. Jenks, 'Hersch Lauterpacht—The Scholar As Prophet', *British Year Book of International Law 1960*, pp. 82–3.

persons who are protected by those instruments, without any
adverse distinction based on the nature or origin of the armed
conflict or on the causes espoused by or attributed to the Parties to
the conflict.[55]

(h) CONCLUSION: THE GROTIAN LEGACY

Throughout *De Jure Belli ac Pacis* Grotius makes his reader
aware of his hatred of war, although he does accept war as a
legal institution, recognized by Divine Law, natural law, and
the Law of Nations. It was not possible to achieve some legal
regulation of the conduct of warfare if war itself were not
recognized by law.[56] The introduction of his *temperamenta belli*
in book III illuminated the gap between existing practices of
warfare, characterized by great inhumanity, and the 'moderations' which he urged. Indeed his abomination of the cruelties
and destruction during the Thirty Years War was one of the
main inspirations, together with his ideas of religious unity,
for writing the treatise. Grotius advised that if the question of
legal right (the 'just' nature of the 'cause') be doubtful, a state
ought not to resort to war. Even if the cause be 'just', he
cautions against going to war rashly. Wars of aggression, for
example, of conquest, Grotius called 'wars of robbers', as had
St Augustine before him.

  In spite of many defects in his methods, contradictions, and
obscurities, *De Jure Belli ac Pacis* presents a unity and a
cohesion of thought which is impressive and formidable. Thus
Grotius' conception of the 'just war' is derived from his
primary contention that the totality of international relations
are subject to the rule of law, including the resort to war and
the conduct of warfare. His jurisprudential and moral thought
rests in large part upon his idea of the law of nature as an
independent source of international law, independent even
from the law of God and not subject to alteration by the
Divine Will. This fundamental idea played a large part in
severing his doctrine of the 'just war' from the theological

---

[55] A. Roberts and R. Guelff (eds.), *Documents on the Laws of War*, 2nd edn. (Oxford,
1989), pp. 389–90.
[56] Lauterpacht, *International Law*, pp. 358–9.

confines of the medieval schoolmen. In his formulation of the distinction between the 'just' and the 'unjust' war Grotius rejected the doctrine of 'reason of state' although it was dominant for the next three centuries. His idea of qualified neutrality or impartiality of states flowed from his 'just war' doctrine; it was invoked at the time of the US 'lend-lease' assistance before US entry into the Second World War.[57] Finally, there are Grotius' noble pleas for peace, his idealism, and his sense of progress. It has been said that his treatise is really a code of morality.[58]

Modern ideas about 'just' and lawful war are not strictly those advanced by Grotius; but they stand in the Grotian tradition. His great moral principles that resort to war and the conduct of warfare should be subject to law, and that recourse to war should be based upon justice and not upon 'reason of state', form part of a tradition that has now come to be a central part of our contemporary system of international law. That does not indicate that Grotius is the architect of these ideas. What has encouraged posterity is Grotius' impressive expression of his faith in law and progress, something which this age cannot afford to discount.

It is wrong to style Grotius 'the father of international law'. Writers do not make or even beget law, but his writings gave international law a dignity and a moral status at a time when it was vital so to endow it. The Grotian tradition has made international law closer to morality than any other secular branch of law. The modern law of armed conflict has much in common with the spirit of the *temperamenta belli*, although its content may not be the direct heir.[59] Part of the genius of Grotius was to establish international law as a genuine legal science based upon morality and reason. This legacy is enduring.

[57] Ibid., p. 352.
[58] Ibid., p. 363.
[59] *Les Dimensions internationales du droit humanitaire* (Geneva, 1986), Introduction by J. Pictet, pp. 13–15.

6

Grotius and the Law of the Sea

W. E. BUTLER

The legal status of the seas and oceans had engaged the attention of publicists and statesmen for some considerable time before Hugo Grotius appeared on the scene. Venice had since the Crusades pretended to vast maritime dominion in the Adriatic Sea, Denmark sought to control the Baltic Sea until the seventeenth century, China asserted special interests in her coastal waters, and Portugal and Spain in the fifteenth century were prepared to divide the Oceans. Although in the last-mentioned case these claims were intended to lend stability to colonial expansion, for the most part expansive claims at sea frustrated maritime commerce and provoked hostile legal commentary.[1]

(a) DEVELOPMENT OF THE PRINCIPLE OF THE FREEDOM OF THE SEAS

Grotius entered the scene as a young lawyer engaged to elaborate the case on behalf of the principle of the freedom of the seas in a brief on the Law of Prize submitted on behalf of the Dutch East India Company to justify the capture of a Portuguese galleon, the *St Catharine*, in the Straits of Malacca in 1603 by a Company vessel. The full text of Grotius' disquisition remained unknown even in manuscript until discovered in 1864 and published four years later. What turned out to be chapter 12 of *De Jure Praedae Commentarius* had been published separately, following deliberations, in November 1608, under the title *Mare Liberum* (1609), the celebrated

---

[1] See K. R. Simmonds, 'Grotius and the Law of the Sea: A Reassessment', in A. Dufour, P. Haggenmacher, and J. Toman (eds.), *Grotius et l'ordre juridique international* (Lausanne, 1985), p. 43.

exposition substantiating the right of the Dutch to participate in trade with the East Indies. It appears that the subsequent publication of *Mare Liberum* was prompted by negotiations between Spain and Holland culminating in the truce of Antwerp (1609). In these negotiations Spain tried unsuccessfully to persuade the Dutch to renounce their right to trade in the East and West Indies. The Dutch East India Company is believed to have requested Grotius to publish his revised essay in order to strengthen the argumentation on behalf of the Dutch position.[2]

The first two decades of the seventeenth century were replete with conflicting claims to dominion over seas and oceans, not merely by the Spanish and Portuguese, but also by the English and by some of the Mediterranean powers.[3] Whether *Mare Liberum* appeared in time to influence Dutch negotiations with the Spanish is problematic, but in May 1609, shortly after its appearance, King James I proclaimed that foreigners would be allowed to fish in the seas of England, Scotland, and Ireland only when authorized by England; and four years later he granted to the Muscovy Company an exclusive monopoly over whaling in the Arctic seas around Spitzbergen. With regard to claims of this order *Mare Liberum* likewise was apt, and its arguments were quickly taken up by Dutch negotiators in their discussions with the English. A Scottish jurist and Professor of Civil Law at the University of Aberdeen, William Welwood, published a partial response to Grotius in 1613 entitled *An Abridgement of all Sea-lawes* wherein he challenged Grotius' thesis that the sea could not be the subject of ownership by a single sovereign. Grotius' reply, *Defensis Capitis Quinti Maris Liberi*, again remained unfinished, unpublished, and undiscovered until 1864. Welwood returned to the issue in 1615 with yet another publication, but the most celebrated response to *Mare Liberum* came *c.*1617–18 from the

---

[2] See the Introductory Note by James Brown Scott to H. Grotius, *The Freedom of the Seas or the Right which Belongs to the Dutch to Take Part in the East Indian Trade*, trans. R. Magoffin (New York, 1916); J. K. Oudendijk, *The Status and Extent of Adjacent Waters: A Historical Orientation* (London, 1970); C. G. Roelofsen, 'Grotius and International Law', in L. E. van Holk and C. G. Roelofsen (eds.), *Grotius Reader* (The Hague, 1983), pp. 5–15; M. Ahsmann, 'Grotius as a Jurist', in *Hugo Grotius: A Great European* (The Hague, 1983), pp. 38–9.

[3] Simmonds, 'Grotius and the Law of the Sea', pp. 43–5.

pen of John Selden.[1] Although not published until 1635, Selden's *Mare Clausum* defended British claims: the sea, Selden said, under the law of nations is as capable of private dominion as is the land, and the king of Great Britain is lord of all the sea inseparably and perpetually appendant to the British Empire. Others entered the lists on both sides, including the Portuguese Freitas, whose *De Justo Imperio Lusitanorum Asiatico* appeared in 1625, the same year as Grotius' *De Jure Belli ac Pacis* containing his matured views on the freedom of the seas as part of his longer, more systematic exposition of the Law of Nations.

The heart of Grotius' position, espoused in both the *Mare Liberum* and *De Jure Belli ac Pacis*, came eventually to be the foundation of the modern regime of the high seas: namely, that states may not individually or collectively acquire the high seas areas by occupation since they are *res communis omnium* or *res extra commercium*. It took some considerable time for this principle to be accepted in state practice: for the larger part of the seventeenth century claims to closed seas were advanced by Denmark, Spain, Turkey, Portugal, Genoa, Tuscany, the papacy, and Venice. Russia affirmed the principle of freedom of the seas in 1587 in diplomatic correspondence with England: 'The sea is God's road . . .'[5] Elizabeth I in 1602 affirmed the same principle in reply to a Spanish protest against Drake's expedition. But Stuart policies, as we have seen, reversed the trend. Only after the House of Orange succeeded to the English throne in 1689 did England join the Dutch in championing the freedom of the seas. By the late eighteenth century most claims to vast sea areas abated or became special jurisdictional claims—

[1] While the Grotius–Selden controversy is perhaps best known as the 'battle of the books' regarding maritime jurisdiction, a number of individuals from the mid-sixteenth century onward had exercised their minds with the issue. In England these included Edmund Plowden, John Dee, and Sir Thomas Craig, none so prominent in this matter, however, as Welwood, Gentili, Robert Copland, Nicholas Carr, and Thomas Rowghton. On the continent there were many more, including the redoubtable Vitoria and Freitas.

[5] See V. E. Grabar, *Materialy k istorii literatury mezhdunarodnogo prava v Rossii 1647–1917 gg* (Moscow, 1958), p. 16. An English translation, *The History of International Law in Russia 1647–1917*, prepared with the assistance of a translation grant from the National Endowment for the Humanities, is due to be published by Oxford University Press in 1990.

although Russia under Alexander I asserted claim to enormous expanses in 1821.[6] Naval power and commercial shipping interests in the nineteenth century ensured European and American support for, indeed insistence upon, the principle of freedom of the seas. In the twentieth century the freedom of the seas has come to be accepted as a 'general', 'basic', or 'fundamental' principle of international law: some are even prepared to treat it as *jus cogens*.

(b) THE GROTIAN CONCEPT OF FREEDOM OF THE SEAS

The basis of the principle, its spatial reach, and its functional limitations today demonstrate the Grotian tradition in the law of the sea to be obsolete or inappropriate in some respects. However, there are also important elements of continuity. An examination of all aspects is essential if we are to understand the legacy of Grotius and his times.

Grotius' approach to international law reflects the larger literary tradition followed by international legal publicists long before and after him, an 'underlying structure of thought and argument . . . more literary than scientific and more businesslike than concerned.'[7] In *De Jure Belli ac Pacis* he made evident at the outset his intention to avoid intellectual confusion: 'to make the reasons for my conclusions as evident as possible; to set forth in a definite order the matters which needed to be treated; and to distinguish clearly between things which seemed to be the same and were not.'[8] He began this work, as he did the *Mare Liberum*, by explaining the process through which he found rules of the law of nations; amongst all the writers before or since he remains one of the most exemplary for his care in expressly indicating the nature of the authority or source—be it a principle of natural law or philosophy, the Roman *jus gentium* morality, holy scripture, or self-evident truth—on which his argument rested. From

[6] W. E. Butler, *The Soviet Union and the Law of the Sea* (Baltimore, Md., 1971), pp. 27–8.
[7] P. Allott, 'Language, Method and the Nature of International Law', *British Year Book of International Law 1971*, pp. 79–135.
[8] *JBP*, Prolegomena 56.

diverse places and various epochs he amassed 'testimonies' of authorities whose coincident statements can be attributed to some universal cause or element—which in Grotius' view was nothing other than 'a correct conclusion drawn from the principles of nature, or common consent.' The law of nations, he said, rests on the last-mentioned, 'for whatever cannot be deduced from certain principles by a sure process of reasoning, and yet is clearly observed everywhere, must have its origin in the free will of man.' Grotius' method of finding rules of international law, widely followed in doctrinal writings on the subject, requires (and disposes) the reader to perform two mental processes. The first is to make the inductive jump from a cumulation of data of various kinds to a conclusion about the truth or falsity of the proposition being discussed. The second is the leap from a series of 'is' propositions to an 'ought' proposition derived, in the instance of Grotius, from the historical record of state practice, the attitudes of poets, orators, jurists, statesmen, diplomats, princes, and the like, and sometimes his own personal judgements as to where appropriate basic patterns of relationships lie.[9]

How does this style of presentation relate to the principle of the freedom of the seas? Grotius, in *Mare Liberum*, based his argument that by the Law of Nations navigation is free to all persons whatsoever on what he characterized as a

most specific and unimpeachable axiom of the Law of Nations, called a primary rule or first principle, the spirit of which is self-evident and immutable, to wit: every nation is free to travel to every other nation, and to trade with it.[10]

The axiom was laid down by God himself through nature, for since not every place is supplied with the necessaries of life, some excel in some things and others in something else. By 'divine justice' it was brought about that one people should supply certain needs of others. Those who deny this law and remove the opportunities for mutual service do violence to Nature herself.

Grotius then turned to the physical properties of water.

---

[9] Ibid., Prolegomena 40; and Allott, 'Language, Method and the Nature of International Law', pp. 100–2.
[10] Grotius, *The Freedom of the Seas*, p. 7.

Navigable in every direction, constantly in motion, encompassing the entire planet, the seas of the world, just as the air, belonged to the *communia*. In his draft reply to Welwood, Grotius elaborated the reasons why according to the law of nature and nations the seas cannot be divided and owned as other property can. Use of the sea by one country for navigation does not make the sea unnavigable for others, whereas in the case of most movables the contrary is true. Moreover, Grotius added, actual occupation of the seas accompanied by a situation of custody or possession is physically impossible: it is the seas which limit land expanses rather than the contrary. Likewise parts of the oceans or seas cannot be owned: for they are part of a corporeal whole, and lines demarcating them express merely a desire or intention to occupy rather than the capability to do so. Those who build structures at sea occupy merely the sea-bed, and their right of possession exists only so long as the structure itself. Minor coastal appropriations of seas were conceded for purposes of use but these could not be appropriated by prescription, for unlike the civil law, the law of nations gave special protection to the *communia*. Once the use had lapsed, the minor appropriations revert to *communia* again.[11]

The substance and qualities of water being what they are, Grotius elaborated, no part of the seas, irrespective of how large or small, can be in exclusive ownership.[12] If a line is conceded at three, twelve, or one hundred miles, why not beyond? The ruler of a maritime state has the duty to protect the right of all nations to free navigation in adjacent waters, from which it follows that navigation is free not by command of the ruler but by command of the law of nations. In denying the right of any state to assert rights of ownership to the sea, however, which Grotius characterized as *dominium*, he recognized the coastal state's right of *imperium*, or sovereignty, defined by Grotius as rights of protection and jurisdiction. The distinction is not drawn as sharply as it might be in his early works—many writers do not attach the same

---

[11] Oudendijk, *The Status and Extent of Adjacent Waters*, pp. 180–91.

[12] Grotius himself retracted this view in subsequent writings, making an exception for inland seas, bays, and straits in *JBP* (1625) and a territorial sea in 1637. See Ahsmann, 'Grotius as a Jurist'.

consequences to the terms in any event—and it is probable that by maritime jurisdiction Grotius had in view piracy and the law of prize. If so, those were forms of maritime jurisdiction that any power might exercise at sea, although presumably the coastal state would be the one most likely to do so. In so far as the coastal state legislated in furtherance of these jurisdictional rights, it must act so as to protect the basic principles of the law of nations and not to diminish them. To Grotius that position meant the coastal state had no jurisdiction over non-subjects except in so far as an explicit or tacit agreement with other rulers admitted such jurisdiction. The sea-bed in Grotius' view had the same status as the sea waters and was open to common use provided such use did not prejudice others.

That, in brief, was Grotius' view of the freedom of the seas and the basic reasoning underlying it. One does not need to be an international lawyer to realize that the principle no longer has, if indeed it ever did have, the meaning attached to it in Grotius' writings. Natural law in both its divine and secular senses has few adherents; to the extent that international law as a legal system can be said to derive from or conform to some underlying basic pattern or principle, modern theories of international law in the West tend to stress rules whose ultimate *raison d'être* inheres in the international system itself; the principle *pacta sunt servanda*, for example. The freedom of the seas may have been axiomatic to Grotius, but the international system, for all its deference to the principle in theory, has never elevated the freedom of the seas to quite that level.

Grotius' method of finding the law by mixing together a vast assemblage of historical events from remotest antiquity to the seventeenth century, quotations from or reference to poets, orators, politicians, statesmen, lawmakers, and princes from all historical eras, leavened with his own views as appropriate —a dazzling display of learning and erudition in his own day—even by the eighteenth century had been overtaken by a more rigorous level of scientific enquiry and exposition. What persuaded Grotius' contemporaries to make the logical leap from evidence to conclusion was seen by later generations as implausible, unscientific, unresponsive, or irrelevant: the founder of modern international legal doctrine, so forward-looking in his ideas, represented the end of an era in scholastic exposition. The ideas lived on through others, even though much in his exposition declined in importance owing to his antiquated method of presenting argument.

(c) THE GROTIAN CONCEPT ADAPTED AND DEVELOPED

Grotius' arguments rejecting ownership of the seas by reason of the natural properties of water have a compelling logic of their own and considerable physical justification, but the international community has never allowed these to pre-determine the exercise of jurisdiction at sea. As maritime powers seized upon the principle of freedom of the seas in the eighteenth century to secure freedom of commerce and links with overseas possessions or to deploy naval power, coastal states responded by creating coastal zones measured by cannon-range or a specified distance within which certain jurisdictional rights might be exercised. While the terminology for them varied, it very quickly developed that the areas within these belts of up to three nautical miles or so were regarded as coastal state property, precisely the kind of claim Grotius sought to deny in principle.

The international community experienced relatively little difficulty in accommodating such jurisdictional claims by coastal states during the nineteenth and early twentieth centuries, but claims beyond three miles to a territorial sea or to territorial waters did provoke sharp protests, as did claims to ownership of resources, principally fish, in waters beyond that limit. It was a measure of Grotius' durable legacy that even the terminological distinction between the 'territorial sea' and 'territorial waters' concealed a conceptual distinction between a 'high seas' and a 'coastal state' approach to jurisdiction at sea.[13] The state practice and international

[13] 'Territorial sea' historically has tended to connote an expanse of the high seas subject to coastal state jurisdiction for certain purposes. It represented a kind of 'carving out' of an expanse of high seas permitted by international law for the protection of specific coastal interests. 'Territorial waters' tended to convey the opposite presumption: an expanse of coastal waters subject to coastal state sovereignty, the latter, however, being limited by international law to protect certain interests of the international community, e.g. innocent passage. In time the

treaties of the post–1945 era have seriously eroded the original and uncompromising simplicity of Grotius' view of the high seas. Sovereign rights of coastal states over the continental shelf are recognized; and economic zones up to 200 miles in breadth may be established, effectively monopolizing for the coastal state the greater portion of living and non-living resources in and beneath the water column.

(d) THE GROTIAN HERITAGE AND THE 1982 UN CONVENTION ON THE LAW OF THE SEA

The 1982 UN Convention on the Law of the Sea (hereinafter 1982 LOS Convention) constitutes a continuation of the balancing process between coastal and high seas interests to which Grotius had responded so unequivocally. The measure of how far we have departed from Grotius' spatial conception of high seas is expressed in Article 86 of the 1982 LOS Convention: the Convention provisions regarding the high seas apply to all parts of the sea 'that are not included in the exclusive economic zone, in the territorial sea or in the internal waters of a State, or in the archipelagic waters of an archipelagic State.'[14]

Functionally, however, much remains of Grotius' original concept of freedom of the seas.[15] Indeed, in several key

juxtaposed presumptions conveyed by the terminology were lost sight of, and many writers used the expressions interchangeably and synonymously without regard to the original implications. For example, the 1982 Law on the USSR State Boundary uses both terms as express synonyms.

[14] The 1982 UN Convention on the Law of the Sea is reproduced, *inter alia*, in Simmonds, *New Directions in the Law of the Sea* (Dobbs Ferry, NY, 1983–) [looseleaf service]. The Convention will not formally enter into force until 12 months after the 60th ratification or accession is deposited.

[15] Doctrinal writings occasioned by Grotius' quadricentenary exhibited much confusion and inconsistency on this point. One writer claims that two fundamental Grotian premises—that the sea cannot be appropriated and that the freedom of the seas serves the common good—have been 'reaffirmed by the new Convention on the Law of the Sea', citing Arts. 78(1) and 89. See B. Kwiatkowska, 'Hugo Grotius and the Freedom of the Seas', in J. L. M. Elders *et al.*, *Hugo Grotius: 1583–1983 Maastricht Hugo Grotius Colloquium* (Assen, 1984), pp. 29–30. But the sea can in fact be appropriated and its resources exhausted: in this sense the 1982 LOS Convention is a response to the inadequacy in modern times of the Grotian perception. See B. Vermeulen, review of Elders *et al.*, *Hugo Grotius*, in *Grotiana*, 6 (1985), p. 94.

respects it has been clarified and strengthened. Although the high seas are spatially more limited, under the 1982 LOS Convention they are 'open to all States, whether coastal or land-locked' (Article 87). The freedom of the high seas is not an absolute freedom under the Convention, but one which is to be exercised under the conditions laid down by the Convention and by other rules of international law.

In Grotius' day the freedom of the seas meant for all practical purposes the freedom of navigation; it was this that he defended so rigorously in his *Mare Liberum* and distinguished from a related freedom, the freedom of commerce. The 1982 LOS Convention enumerates six freedoms of the high seas without purporting to be exhaustive: freedom of navigation; freedom of overflight; freedom to lay submarine cables and pipelines; freedom to construct artificial islands and other installations permitted under international law; freedom of fishing; and freedom of scientific research. The last four are subject to conditions or circumstances elaborated in other parts of the Convention. All freedoms must be exercised with due regard for the interests of other states in their exercise of the freedom of the high seas and also with due regard for the rights under the Convention with respect to deep sea-bed activities. The Convention imposes another general restriction, namely that the high seas are reserved for peaceful purposes.

The freedom of navigation encompasses rights and duties of navigation for states, whether coastal or land-locked. International law requires, for example: a genuine link between the flag state and the ship; the issuance of ship's documents certifying the right to fly that state's flag; and the duty to exercise effective jurisdiction and control in administrative, technical, and social matters over ships flying its flag and to ensure safety at sea. 'The regime of the high seas' is the expression widely used to express the conditions and rules governing the exercise of the freedom of the seas and to emphasize that the high seas are not a legal vacuum where states may do as they please, but an expanse open to all to engage in lawful activities with due regard to rules developed to protect the interests of other users and the safe exercise of the activities being carried on. The rules comprising this regime comply very much with the spirit of the Grotian tradition, irrespective of how far removed they may be from the technology of navigation in the early seventeenth century.

Expanded uses of the high seas in ways and on a scale unimaginable in Grotius' day necessarily have led to greater regulation of high seas operations, but principally in the spirit of reinforcing the freedom proclaimed by Grotius rather than diminishing it.[16] Directly linked to the Grotian tradition is the 1982 LOS Convention provision that 'No State may validly purport to subject any part of the high seas to its sovereignty.' States on the other hand are obliged, as they were in Grotius' day, to assist in suppressing piracy at sea, and in the course of time the list of responsibilities has been enlarged to encompass the suppression of such activities as the transport of slaves, illicit traffic in narcotic drugs or psychotropic substances, and unauthorized broadcasting from the high seas. The performance of enforcement duties is facilitated by an express but limited right of visit on the high seas.

A thorough examination of the 1982 LOS Convention would disclose dozens of instances of the Grotian tradition of the freedom of the seas exercising some influence upon the draftsmen, not least in the Convention provisions relative to the deep sea-bed, the peaceful settlement of disputes, and the rights of non-coastal powers in the jurisdictional and resources zones or the territorial seas of coastal states.[17]

---

[16] Many would contest this view with regard to the deep sea-bed and subsoil. It is especially in these regions that 'appropriation' is now physically possible and that the Grotian principle of *res communis* has come under severest pressure. Technology is held responsible by some for the triumph of 'individual' over 'common' use. See M. Diesselhorst, 'Hugo Grotius and the Freedom of the Seas', *Grotiana*, 3 (1983), pp. 11–26. For a vigorous argument that 'ocean nationalism' has triumphed in the 1982 LOS Convention and the international community has squandered an opportunity to pursue a more enlightened policy consistent with Grotian principles, see J. J. Logue, 'The Revenge of John Selden: The Draft Convention on the Law of the Sea in the Light of Hugo Grotius' Mare Liberum', *Grotiana*, 3 (1983), pp. 27–56 and sequel: id., 'A Stubborn Dutchman: The Attempt to Revive Grotius' Common Property Doctrine in and after the Third United Nations Conference on the Law of the Sea', in Asser Instituut, *International Law and the Grotian Heritage* (The Hague, 1985), pp. 99–108.
[17] See M. W. C. Pinto, 'The New Law of the Sea and the Grotian Heritage', in Asser Instituut, *International Law and the Grotian Heritage*, pp. 54–93. Also see F. Ito, 'The Thought of Hugo Grotius on the Mare Liberum', *Japanese Annual of International Law*, 18 (1974), pp. 1–15, and a subsequent article, ibid., 20 (1976), pp. 1–16.

(e) CONTINUING VALIDITY OF THE GROTIAN HERITAGE

Merely to compare the origins and spatial reach of Grotius' notion of the freedom of the seas to that of today, instructive as the comparison is, would gravely understate the continuing vitality of the Grotian heritage in the law of the sea. The principle of freedom of the seas expounded by Grotius has served and continues to serve as rhetorical reinforcement for the point of departure when deliberating about matters of maritime jurisdiction. Rather like the presumption of innocence in criminal proceedings, we invoke it constantly to remind ourselves that whatever developments in the law of the sea are to be contemplated, we should measure their validity and impact with reference to the freedom of the seas. Grotius left embedded in our consciousness a phrase and a standard of community awareness on the international level: anyone doubting the magnificence of that legacy need merely contemplate what might have been if adherents of *Mare Clausum* had triumphed in their seventeenth-century conception. On the whole we have been well served by a doctrine that has required us to evaluate the propriety and legitimacy of individual claims against the international community interest, rather than the opposite process of carving an area of community concern from a myriad of conflicting claims to ownership of the seas.

7

Grotius and International Equality

HIDEMI SUGANAMI

The doctrine of the equality of sovereign states is one of the central postulates in the theory and practice of international law and international relations in the contemporary world. The idea that sovereign states are equal had already been given considerable prominence by the natural law theorists of the Law of Nations especially in the eighteenth century. It was strongly defended by smaller states at the Hague Peace Conferences of 1899 and 1907, and is now enshrined in Article 2 of the UN Charter, which provides that the Organization is based on the principle of the sovereign equality of all its Members. The Charter of Economic Rights and Duties of States, adopted by the UN General Assembly in 1974, repeatedly refers to the sovereign equality of each state as a basis of a New International Economic Order.

Concomitantly with the (not-unchallenged) view that Hugo Grotius is the father of international law, it is sometimes held that he was also an advocate of the doctrine of the equality of sovereign states. However, some writers, most notably E. D. Dickinson, dispute the idea that Grotius was a champion of international equality. The aim of this chapter is to examine how Grotius treated this subject in his most important work, *De Jure Belli ac Pacis*, with a view to assessing the continuing relevance of his ideas in the context of contemporary international relations.

The doctrine of the equality of sovereign states, clearly, is incomplete unless what is to count as a sovereign state is also spelt out. Once this is done, a question arises as to how those associations or entities which are not sovereign states are to be treated. The doctrine, moreover, must square with the undeniable fact that sovereign states are vastly unequal not only in terms of their power, influence, and prestige, but also with regard to legal rights and freedoms which they enjoy. In addition, the expansion of the international society since the time of Grotius has meant that its institutions have come to encompass non-European nations. In this process a question arose as to how Western sovereign states should treat those nations which did not satisfy the Western standard of civilization. It is not surprising therefore that the doctrine of the equality of sovereign states has encountered numerous problems both in the theory of international law and in the practice of diplomacy from the formative period of the states-system to the present. Grotius' positions on these related issues will be explained in the course of this chapter in order to give a full account of his ideas on the subject of international equality.

(a) THE DIFFERENT MEANINGS OF 'EQUALITY'

References to the doctrine of the equality of sovereign states seldom make clear in what ways they are equal. To understand what is meant by state equality, and to assess Grotius' position on this subject, it is necessary to begin by distinguishing two different senses in which sovereign states may be said to be equal.

1. Equality before the Law

Most fundamentally the notion of sovereign equality means that sovereign states are equal *before* the Law of Nations. When they are so characterized, however, nothing more is meant than that they are all equally bound by international law, that they all have an equal obligation to obey the Law of Nations.[1] This is a fundamental postulate on the basis of which international relations have come to be conducted in peace and war.

　　Writing in the midst of the Thirty Years War, characterized by 'a lack of restraint in relation to war, such as even barbarous races should be ashamed of',[2] Grotius saw an

---

[1] See Hans Kelsen, *General Theory of Law and State*, trans. Anders Wedberg (New York, 1945), pp. 252–3.

[2] *JBP*, Prolegomena 28.

urgent need to establish in the minds of sovereigns that international relations were regulated by law, and that international law bound all states. How far Grotius' writings themselves contributed to this end in the subsequent practice of international relations cannot easily be assessed, but his argument, outlined below, has had continuing influence, and merits the attention of contemporary readers.

According to Grotius, men are not purely self-interested creatures. Justice is possible in human relationships because

among the traits characteristic of man is an impelling desire for society, that is, for the social life—not of any and every sort, but peaceful, and organized according to the measure of his intelligence, with those who are of his own kind.[3]

Man's innate sociability is, therefore, the source of the 'law of nature'. The law emanating from human nature, however, is not alone in regulating human relationships since expediency too produces legal principles. Internationally, the consideration of expediency has established a body of law based on consent. This body of law, which Grotius distinguishes from the 'law of nature' and calls the 'law of nations', had in view 'the advantage, not of particular states, but of the great society of states.'[4]

Obeying the laws of nature and nations, moreover, is not a folly even when it is against a state's immediate interest to do so. Comparing the case to that of the domestic law, Grotius argues as follows:

For just as the national, who violates the law of his country in order to obtain an immediate advantage, breaks down that by which the advantages of himself and his posterity are for all future time assured, so the state which transgresses the laws of nature and of nations cuts away also the bulwarks which safeguard its own future peace. Even if no advantage were to be contemplated from the keeping of the law, it would be a mark of wisdom, not of folly, to allow ourselves to be drawn towards that to which we feel that our nature leads.[5]

[3] Ibid., Prolegomena 6.
[4] Ibid., Prolegomena 17.
[5] Ibid., Prolegomena 18. By 'our nature', of course, Grotius meant our sociable nature.

'Most true is the saying,' Grotius continues, 'that all things are uncertain the moment men depart from law.'[6] 'If no association of men can be maintained without law . . . surely also that association which binds together the human race, or binds many nations together, has need of law.'[7] This need should be felt, according to Grotius, even by powerful states since 'there is no state so powerful that it may not some time need the help of others outside itself, either for purposes of trade, or even to ward off the forces of many foreign nations united against it.'[8]

The laws of nature and nations, moreover, are applicable not only in peace but also in war. To show their applicability to the latter, Grotius resorts to the analogy of war with a judicial process. He writes:

Demosthenes well said that war is directed against those who cannot be held in check by judicial processes. For judgements are efficacious against those who feel that they are too weak to resist; against those who are equally strong, or think that they are, wars are undertaken. But in order that wars may be justified, they must be carried on with not less scrupulousness than judicial processes are wont to be.[9]

In the absence of organized sanctions the effectiveness of the laws of nature and nations may be limited, particularly in war. Yet, Grotius maintains, in war the consciousness that one has justice on one's side greatly contributes to victory.[10] Furthermore, a 'reputation for having undertaken war not rashly nor unjustly, and of having waged it in a manner above reproach'[11] is exceedingly efficacious in winning friends and allies. These factors do not guarantee, but contribute towards, the effectiveness of the laws of nature and nations in time of war.

These are, then, the grounds upon which Grotius tried to defend the thesis that international relations were properly legal relations. Laws are binding on sovereigns in their mutual

---

[6] *JBP*, Prolegomena 22. [7] Ibid., Prolegomena 23.
[8] Ibid., Prolegomena 22. [9] Ibid., Prolegomena 25.
[10] Ibid., Prolegomena 27. A similar line of argument is advanced with reference to the Congolese and Nigerian civil wars by F. S. Northedge and M. D. Donelan, *International Disputes: The Political Aspects* (London, 1971), pp. 57 and 132.
[11] *JBP*, Prolegomena 27.

relationships in peace and in war; they emanate from human sociability and are supported by common interests; and they can operate tolerably well without centralized sanctions.

In his defence of the idea that the relations of sovereigns or sovereign states are properly legal relations, Grotius does not say that this is true only with respect to a certain class of sovereign states, such as Christian, European, or 'civilized'. In his view all sovereign states are bound by international law. And since if all sovereign states are bound by international law, they cannot but all be equally so bound, Grotius must be said to have committed himself to the idea of the equality of all sovereign states *before* international law. This is so because the equality of sovereign states before the law simply means that they are all equally bound by international law.

When it is said that all sovereign states are equally bound by international law, it is not meant that all sovereign states have equal international legal rights or duties. This is clearly untrue. Sovereign states do not possess identical rights or duties in international law. If all the rights or duties of one state were to be listed, they would inevitably be different, in extent and content, from the rights or duties of another sovereign state.[12] The idea that states *ought to* possess identical rights or duties in international law is also untenable. Even in the most egalitarian of all societies, there would be a division of labour and role-differentiation, resulting in the inequality, or in the absence of identity, of legal rights (and duties) on the part of its constituent members. Nevertheless sovereign states are equal *before* the law in that they are equally subjected to, bound by, or obligated to act in accordance with, international law. Nothing in *De Jure Belli ac Pacis* contradicts these elementary observations regarding the meaning of 'equality'.

2. Equal Capacity for Rights

It is very often said that states have equal rights in international law when what is meant is merely that they have

---

[12] Kelsen, *General Theory of Law and State*, p. 252. Even according to general international law, Kelsen remarks, 'all the States have not the same duties and rights. A littoral State, for example, has other duties and rights than an inland State.'

an equal capacity for rights in international law. When states are said to have an equal capacity for rights what is meant is that there is nothing in the institutional arrangements of international society precluding any class of sovereign states from acquiring legal rights, or from maintaining legal freedoms, which another class of sovereign states are permitted. An institutional arrangement providing different degrees of capacity for rights for different classes of states would constitute an international caste system, so to speak. Such a hierarchically stratified system would divide sovereign states into various classes, and treat a state's class identity as the ground for discrimination in the law.

Despite a great deal of inequality in the law, it is one of the fundamental postulates of contemporary international relations that all sovereign states have an equal capacity for rights in general international law. Needless to say, there is a vast difference in the degree of external activism from one country to another, and also a good deal of difference in the prestige of various sovereign states. Given the unequal distribution of capability, wealth, and resources, it is unavoidable that a certain class of states, notably great powers, will play a predominant role in the running of international relations. Some writers take note of this and interpret it as an institutional feature of international relations.[13] There is little doubt that the great powers of various historical periods acted at times as though they had formed a directorate. None the less, there is no general international law principle which confers special privileges on great powers as such. In the words of Oppenheim,

Politically, States are in no manner equals, as there is a difference between the Great Powers and others . . . But, however important the position and the influence of the Great Powers may be, they are by no means derived from a legal basis or rule.[14]

---

[13] See Hedley Bull, *The Anarchical Society* (London, 1977), chap. 9.

[14] Lassa Oppenheim, *International Law: A Treatise*, i, *Peace*, 1st edn. (London, 1905), p. 163. To be more precise, the phrase, 'from a principle of general international law' should replace 'from a legal basis or rule' in the final part of the quoted passage since, as in the League of Nations or the United Nations, the position and influence of the great powers can be defined and protected by rules of particular international law. At the other end of the spectrum from the great powers are 'mini' and 'micro' states.

Grotius shares this fundamental approach. In *De Jure Belli ac Pacis* he does not attempt to introduce general legal distinctions between classes of sovereign states.

Even though there is no general international legal rule which confers special privileges upon the great powers, the principle of the equal capacity for rights cannot be said to prevail in international society if there is a class of states which is legally discriminated against on account of their class identity. For example, in the nineteenth century, it was held by writers on international law that a certain class of states, because they did not live up to the Western standard of civilization, were in effect second-class citizens of international society.[15] This was a doctrinal sanctification of the practice of Western states at that time which imposed a series of 'unequal' treaties on countries such as China and Japan.

However, the idea that a class of states has a limited capacity for rights in international law because of their uncivilized character was largely a nineteenth-century phenomenon. Grotius, in the early seventeenth century, did not discuss it. In recent decades this idea has lost legitimacy. In contemporary international relations there are certain states, such as South Africa and Israel, which, because of their deviance from internationally acknowledged norms, have sometimes been described as 'pariah states'. But such a description is not normally meant to suggest that these states are deprived of full capacity for rights in international law. Grotius' treatment of 'unequal' treaties and his positions on deviant entities will be discussed later in this chapter.

(b) GROTIUS' IMAGE OF SOCIETY AND OF INTERNATIONAL RELATIONS

E. D. Dickinson, in his study of the doctrine of state equality in international law, contends that while Grotius advanced

---

Their legal status as sovereign entities subject to international law, however, is substantially identical to that of ordinary states. See Alan James, *Sovereign Statehood: The Basis of International Society* (London, 1986), pp. 111–15.

[15] See Gerrit W. Gong, *The Standard of 'Civilization' in International Society* (Oxford, 1984).

the idea that sovereign states were equal *before* international law, he did not adhere to the doctrine of equal capacity for rights.[16]

The doctrine of equal capacity for rights in international law was historically a consequence of a number of assumptions which authoritative writers on the Law of Nations upheld in the formative period of international law. The most crucial among these assumptions was the idea that sovereign states in international relations were analogous to individual free persons in the state of nature. Since in the state of nature men were equal as individual free persons, so by analogy it was held that in the international state of nature states were also equal.[17] Such a conception of international relations, as is well known, originated in the writings of Hobbes, and was handed down among subsequent writers on the Law of Nations, most notably, Pufendorf, Wolff, and Vattel.[18]

In the writings of these authors, the idea that sovereign states are as equal as individual free persons in the state of nature is given considerable prominence. It was partly because sovereign states were considered as being in the 'state of nature' that the 'law of nature' was thought by these writers to apply to international relations.[19]

The analogy between sovereign states in international relations and men in the state of nature is indeed, as Hans Morgenthau puts it, the 'main stock-in-trade' of modern international thought.[20] However, Grotius' *De Jure Belli ac Pacis* appeared about a quarter of a century before Hobbes' *Leviathan*, and the state-of-nature analogy was of marginal significance in Grotius' depiction of international relations. For Grotius, the 'law of nature' applied to international relations not because sovereigns or sovereign states were in the 'state of nature' but because the rational nature of man

[16] See Dickinson, *The Equality of States in International Law* (Cambridge, Mass., 1920), chap 2.

[17] See ibid., chap. 1.   [18] See ibid., chap. 3.

[19] See Pufendorf, *De Jure Naturae et Gentium*, book II, chap. 2, § 4; book II, chap. 3, § 23; book VII, chap. 1, § 8; book VIII, chap. 4, § 18; Wolff, *Jus Gentium Methodo Scientifica Pertractatum*, Preface and Prolegomena, § 2; Vattel, *Le Droit des gens*, Preface and Introduction. See also Walter Schiffer, *The Legal Community of Mankind: A Critical Analysis of the Modern Concept of World Organization* (New York, 1954), chap. 3.

[20] H. J. Morgenthau, *Scientific Man versus Power Politics* (Chicago, Ill., 1946), p. 113.

demanded it. According to Dickinson, the difference of attitude between Grotius on the one hand and certain post-Hobbesian writers on the other towards the state-of-nature analogy is a crucial factor which divided them on the question of equal capacity for rights in international law.[21]

It must at any rate be accepted that Grotius did not give much prominence to the idea of equal capacity for rights in international law, and a further reason for this may be sought in the fact that his image of society was itself predominantly a hierarchical, as opposed to an egalitarian, one. The types of social relationship which he took to be primordial were father and son, husband and wife, master and slave, king and subjects, patron and clients, older and younger brothers, and male and female children.[22] These were considered as hierarchical by Grotius, and the laws pertaining to such relationships he called 'rectorial' as opposed to 'equatorial'.[23] Grotius also talked of friends and citizens, implying the possibility of equal relationships.[24] But, characteristically, he considered the state as an association, not of atomized individuals, but of households headed by fathers.[25]

Starting from a virtually identical notion of society to that of Grotius, some Confucian cultures, such as those of China and Japan, had produced hierarchical conceptions of international relations.[26] We might expect Grotius to have held a similar conception. We might expect him to have entertained an

---

[21] Dickinson, *Equality of States*, chap. 2, esp. pp. 37–8 and 47–9.

[22] See *JBP*, book I, chap. I, § 3. 2; book I, chap. I, § 14. 1; book I, chap. 3, § 7. 2; book I, chap. 3, § 16. 1; book I, chap. 3, § 21. 3; book I, chap. 5, § 3; book II, chap. 26, § 1.

[23] Ibid., book I, chap. I, § 3. 2.   [24] Ibid.

[25] Ibid., book II, chap. 5, § 23.

[26] See Gong, 'China's Entry into International Society', in H. Bull and A. Watson (eds.), *The Expansion of International Society* (Oxford, 1984), pp. 171–83, esp. pp. 173–5; Hidemi Suganami, 'Japan's Entry into International Society', ibid., pp. 185–99, esp. pp. 185–90. It was partly through experiencing the disadvantages of being at the receiving end of unequal treatment that these countries began to accept the Western concept of state equality. For a 20th-century Chinese view of 'unequal' treaties, see Gary L. Scott, *Chinese Treaties: The Post-Revolutionary Restoration of International Law and Order* (Dobbs Ferry, NY, 1975), pp. 85–99. It is interesting to observe that in the case of Japan the idea of equality was introduced to her primarily through certain Western textbooks of international law, and that the idea of state equality preceded that of individual equality. This was the opposite of the Western experience. On this point, I am indebted to Michiari Uete, 'Taigaikan no Tenkai', in B. Hashikawa and S. Matsumoto, *Kindai Nihon Seiji Shisoshi* (2 vols., Tokyo, 1971), i, 33–74, esp. pp. 59 ff.

image of international society which was essentially hierarchical, with different classes of states enjoying different
degrees of capacity for rights in international law. Such a
conception of international relations would be entirely consistent with his hierarchical notion of domestic society, and would
not be contrary to his assumption of the equality of sovereign
states *before* the law.

This is in fact what Dickinson suggests the Grotian
conception of the social world amounted to. He concludes:

> Instead of conceiving of a society of states having equal capacity for
> rights, Grotius deferred so far to contemporary practice as to
> recognize the existence of a society among whose members there
> were many differences of status, with corresponding differences of
> capacity.[27]

Indeed, the Grotian world was inhabited not by atomized
sovereign states, as in the case of some later writers, but by
kings (sometimes states headed by kings) of varying strengths
and prestige, as well as by pirates, brigands, tyrants, and
infidels. He also spoke of feudal and tributary relationships as
modes of international intercourse.[28] All this would seem to
reinforce our theoretical expectation that the Grotian view of
the world was one of hierarchical stratification. To examine
this point conclusively, we need to study his treatment of two
key concepts, 'sovereignty' and the 'unequal treaty'.

(c) GROTIUS ON 'SOVEREIGNTY' AND 'UNEQUAL TREATIES'

In book I, chapter 3, section 7 of *De Jure Belli ac Pacis*, Grotius
spells out what 'sovereignty' is:

> That power is called sovereign whose actions are not subject to the
> legal control of another, so that they cannot be rendered void by the
> operation of another human will . . . The subject of a power is either
> common or special. Just as the body is a common, the eye a special

---

[27] Dickinson, *Equality of States*, p. 60.

[28] *JBP* abounds in references to kings, but Grotius, as in Prolegomena 17,
occasionally refers to the 'society of *states*'. References to pirates, brigands, tyrants,
and infidels occur in various places in *JBP*. Some of these references will be examined
below, together with Grotius' treatment of feudal and tributary relationships.

subject of the power of sight, so the state, which we have defined above as a perfect association, is the common subject of sovereignty.

We exclude from consideration, therefore, the peoples who have passed under the sway of another people, such as the peoples of the Roman provinces. For such peoples are not in themselves a state, in the sense in which we are now using the term, but the inferior members of a great state, just as slaves are members of a household.

Again, it happens that several peoples may have the same head, while nevertheless each of them in itself forms a perfect association. While in the case of the natural body there cannot be one head belonging to several bodies, this does not hold also in the case of a moral body. In the case of a moral body the same person, viewed in different relations, may be the head of several distinct bodies . . . It may also happen that several states are bound together by a confederation, and form a kind of 'system', as Strabo in more than one passage calls it, while nevertheless the different members do not cease in each case to retain the status of a perfect state . . . It may be granted, then, that the common subject of sovereignty is the state, understood as we have already indicated. The special subject is one or more persons, according to the laws and customs of each nation; 'the first power', according to Galen, in the sixth book of his treatise *On the Teachings of Hippocrates and Plato.*

In this passage, although the language now seems somewhat archaic, Grotius clearly exhibits his awareness of an important distinction between two questions regarding 'sovereignty': one is about whether a given human association can be said to be a sovereign entity, and the other is about who in that association can be said to be sovereign. The failure to distinguish between these questions has led to much seemingly intractable confusion in the discussion of sovereignty, but, as Georg Jellinek was later also to note, 'the sovereign organ within the state and the sovereign state are . . . two entirely different things.'[29]

Having understood 'sovereignty' in the context of the first question noted above as signifying 'legal independence', Grotius explores the conditions under which the sovereignty of a state may be said to be lost. As indicated in the above passage, becoming part of another sovereign state, clearly, is one such condition: becoming a member of a 'personal union'

---

[29] Georg Jellinek, *Allgemeine Staatslehre*, 3rd edn., ed. W. Jellinek (Berlin, 1922), pp. 457–8. Translation mine.

or a 'confederation' is not. This is in line with the modern, orthodox doctrine on the loss of sovereignty.

But what of unequal treaties? Are they not in some cases signs of the loss of sovereignty on the part of the inferior states? Grotius deals with this question in some detail.

By an unequal alliance or treaty Grotius does not mean a compact between sovereign states of an unequal strength, but an alliance or treaty which by *its* very character can be said to give one of the contracting parties 'a permanent advantage over the other'.[30] According to him: 'Such terms are unequal on the part of the superior if he promises aid, but does not require it, or promises greater aid. Unequal terms on the part of the inferior . . . are those . . . "arrangements imposed by command".'[31]

Thus there are two types of unequal compact. In the one, the superior power extends protection to the inferior in exchange for honour. This is analogous, in Grotius' view, to the patron–client relationship. Grotius' example is found in the following passage:

Of the ancient treaty between the Romans, who had obtained a complete mastery over Alba, and the Latins, who were natives of Alba, Livy says: 'In that treaty the Roman state had greatly the advantage.' Rightly did Andronicus of Rhodes, following Aristotle, say, that this is characteristic of a relation of friendship between those who are unequal, that more honour is granted to the stronger, more help to the one that is weaker.[32]

In the other type of unequal treaty, 'arrangements imposed by command', the superior party oppresses the inferior 'more than is just'.[33]

It is interesting to note that not all unequal treaties are thought by Grotius to fall into the second category, and that he appears to have thought it possible for an inferior party to be the real beneficiary in an unequal compact. Whichever the party that gains most from an unequal treaty, a question arises as to whether the terms of the treaty are such that the inferior party can no longer be regarded as a sovereign entity. Grotius' answer to this is straightforward. The inferior party

[30] *JBP*, book I, chap. 3, § 21. 1.
[31] Ibid., book II, chap. 15, § 7. 1.
[32] Ibid., book I, chap. 3, § 21. 2.
[33] Ibid, book II, chap. 15, § 7. 1.

remains sovereign so long as its legal independence is not lost, provided (and here Grotius is somewhat imprecise) the party is 'under protection, not under domination', 'under patronage, not under subjection'.[34] He remarks:

Just as private patronage in the case of individuals does not take away individual liberty, so patronage in the case of a state does not take away independence; and independence without sovereignty is inconceivable.[35]

Accordingly, in Grotius' judgement, neither tributary nor even feudal relationship removes the sovereignty of the inferior party.[36]

Grotius acknowledges that in many cases the dominant party in an unequal relationship might act as though it ruled the weaker. He writes:

It is, nevertheless, true that in the majority of cases he who has the position of vantage in a treaty, if he is greatly superior in respect to power, gradually usurps the sovereignty properly so called. This is particularly liable to happen if the treaty is perpetual, and if it contains the right to introduce garrisons into towns, as the Athenians did, when they allowed appeals to be made to them by their allies—something that the Spartans had never done. The rule of the Athenians over the allies in those times Isocrates compares to the rule of a king.[37]

Grotius also says that an unequal treaty may impair the sovereignty of the inferior party if, 'as the second treaty of the Carthaginians with the Romans', it contains the provision that the inferior party should not make war on any one without the sanction of the superior.[38] It should be noted in interpreting this statement, however, that Grotius distinguishes between an 'impairment' of sovereignty and its 'transfer': the former is a matter of degree, the latter absolute.[39] This suggests that in the above passage Grotius was not arguing that the inferior party, such as the Carthaginians in the second treaty with the Romans, was no longer a sovereign (legally independent) entity, but rather that it suffered a major curtailment of its legal freedom.

---

[34] Ibid., book I, chap. 3, § 21. 3.
[35] Ibid.
[36] Ibid., book I, chap. 3, §§ 22 and 23.
[37] Ibid., book I, chap. 3, § 21. 10.
[38] Ibid., book II, chap. 15, § 7. 2.
[39] Ibid.

What Grotius' treatment of unequal relationships in international society reveals is his awareness of the extent to which the sovereign states system can tolerate inequality in terms of power, prestige, and legal rights and freedoms. These are distributed in a vastly unequal fashion among sovereign states, but sovereign they remain so long as their legal independence has not been transferred to another authority.

Moreover, despite what Dickinson attributes to Grotius, there is nothing in what Grotius says about inequality in international relations which shows him actually to believe in an international caste system which would divide sovereign states into separate classes with varying degrees of capacity for rights. Those states which are in an inferior position in an unequal treaty can be known to be in that position only through the analysis of the terms of the treaty,[40] and they are placed in that position not because they belong to an inferior class beforehand, but because they happen to be weaker than the superior states. Under Roman domination, the Carthaginians suffered an impairment of sovereignty (until it was completely lost following their defeat in the Third Punic War in 146 BC) not because they did not have the same degree of capacity for rights as the Romans, but because they turned out to be weaker. Had the Romans been defeated the position would have been reversed.

But what of pirates, brigands, tyrants, and infidels? Are they not of an unequal status in relation to Christian sovereign states because of what they are? Do they not, in the Grotian system, genuinely belong to a different class with restrictions on their legal capacity?

As for pirates and brigands, Grotius deals with these separately partly because of their special status in Roman law. He maintains that since they are associations banded together for wrongdoing they do not qualify as states, but that it is possible for them to transform into states upon embracing another mode of life.[41] In his support he quotes St Augustine, who says: 'If by accessions of desperate men this evil grows to such proportions that it holds lands, establishes fixed settlements, seizes upon states and subjugates peoples, it assumes

---

[40] *JBP*, book I, chap. 3, § 21. 1.
[41] Ibid., book III, chap. 3, §§ 2 and 3.

the name of a kingdom.'[42] And as for states run by tyrants, Grotius accuses Cicero of speaking 'too sweepingly' in remarking that 'where an unjust man is king . . . there is not a wicked state, but none at all.'[43] In Grotius' opinion, 'a state, although seriously diseased, is a state so long as there remain tribunals and the other agencies that are necessary in order that foreigners, no less than private citizens, in their relations one with the other may there obtain their rights.'[44]

Therefore Grotius does not accord sovereign statehood to associations of pirates and brigands, or to those entities run by tyrants without a legal system. Agreements made between such entities on the one hand, and sovereign states on the other, Grotius argues, are not valid according to the Law of Nations. None the less, he insists that faith ought to be kept with these associations. Since pirates, brigands, and tyrants are human beings, and since obligations to abide by agreements are universal under the law of nature which binds all human beings, it follows that agreements with them are as obligatory as those between sovereign states.[45]

As regards the 'strangers to the true religion', Grotius maintains that all Christians are under obligation to enter a league against the enemies of Christianity, but that wars cannot justly be waged against those who are unwilling to accept Christianity.[46] It is right to wage wars, however, against those who treat Christians with cruelty for the sake of their religion alone.[47] Thus it appears that in Grotius' view peaceful coexistence is possible between Christians and non-Christians so long as both sides refrain from resorting to hostile actions against each other on account of religious differences.[48]

[42] Ibid., book III, chap. 3, § 3.
[43] Ibid., book III, chap. 3, § 2. 2.
[44] Ibid.
[45] Ibid., book III, chap. 19, § 2.
[46] Ibid., book II, chap. 15, § 12; and chap. 20, § 48. Grotius adds that wars may not justly be waged against those who unknowingly err in the interpretation of Divine Law, a heretic being one who either creates or follows new and false opinions for the sake of some temporal advantage and especially for his own glory and pre-eminence. Ibid., book II, chap. 20, § 50.
[47] Ibid., book II, chap. 20, § 49.
[48] One qualification which should be added here is that Grotius considers that it is just to wage war against those who show impiety towards the (non-Christian) gods

Such coexistence may involve the establishment of legal relationships between them, and Grotius says that by the law of nature treaties with those who are strangers to the true religion are permissible. This is because the right to enter into treaties is so common to all men that it does not admit of a distinction arising from religion.[49]

Grotius' position on the treatment of pirates, brigands, tyrants, and infidels is therefore that while they are either not states or are not in the same class as Christian states, relationships with them should still be regulated by the law of nature which binds all mankind.

Grotius considers the argument that pirates, brigands, and tyrants, since they are atrocious criminals who do not belong to any state, can be punished by any person whatsoever. Since this punishment may involve the death penalty, they can also rightfully be subjected to lesser forms of deprivation, such as loss of property or rights. It follows that they can be deprived of the right arising from a promise made to them.

Grotius accepts the force of this argument in principle, but remains sceptical of the extent to which ordinary sovereign states can in practice *consistently* deal with these entities as criminals. If consistency is lacking, he argues, we must abandon the claim that they are outlaws. Thus, for example, a sovereign state which at one time made an alliance with a tyrant must, out of regard for consistency, abandon the claim that the latter is deprived of protection under the law of nature.[50]

(d) GROTIUS' CONTEMPORARY RELEVANCE

The analysis in the previous section casts doubt on Dickinson's claim that Grotius advanced a hierarchically stratified vision

they believe in. *JBP*, book II, chap. 20, § 51. Therefore, Christian nations may choose not to coexist peacefully with those non-Christians who are, as it were, beyond the pale.

[49] Ibid., book II, chap. 15, § 8.

[50] Ibid., book III, chap. 19, § 3. Grotius appears to hold that, like criminal associations, miscreant states too can be punished by any state. See book II, chap. 25. It may be noted here that the 1982 UN Convention on the Law of the Sea stipulates in its Art. 100 the duty of all states to cooperate in the repression of piracy on the high seas or in any other place outside the jurisdiction of any state.

of international relations according to which the actors on the international stage would be divided into separate classes with varying degrees of capacity for rights. There are two main reasons for arguing that Grotius did not go so far. First, Grotius believed in sovereign equality, implicitly holding that despite an unequal distribution of power and prestige, and despite the existence of unequal, and sometimes unjust, treaties, sovereign states were equal in their capacity for rights in international law. Second, where pirates, brigands, tyrants, and infidels were concerned, while Grotius did not place them in the same class as Christian sovereign states, he insisted that the law of nature would apply to them since, however wicked, they were human beings. Grotius, as we saw, recognized the force of the argument that pirates, brigands, and tyrants were outlaws, but doubted if they could in practice consistently be treated as such. In practice, therefore, they would be brought back to inhabit the legal world governed by the law of nature, the common law of mankind.

It was therefore the combination of three factors—the adherence to the idea of sovereign equality (in the sense of equal capacity for rights), belief in the law of nature binding on all mankind, and the appreciation of the practical need of international intercourse regulated by law—that caused Grotius to refrain in the end from advancing a hierarchically stratified vision of international relations.

From the viewpoint of contemporary international relations, it is of great interest to find that Grotius, writing in 1625, was already upholding ideas and principles which are not only comprehensible and familiar to us, but are felt to be of increasing importance in the closing decades of the twentieth century. The principle of sovereign equality, as we noted, is enshrined in the UN Charter, is reiterated more recently in the Charter of Economic Rights and Duties of States, and forms one of the fundamental postulates upon which contemporary international relations are conducted. The idea of natural law which embraces all mankind and protects a minimum standard in the treatment of human beings *qua* human beings regained support in the aftermath of the atrocities experienced in the Second World War; and the closely related issue of international human rights has

attracted increasing attention in the post-1945 period.[51] It is
now virtually unchallenged that international intercourse
must be regulated by law. However, the idea that certain
miscreant states should be treated as outlaws has not entirely
disappeared.[52] Grotius' writings offer one counter-argument
which those urging such outlaw treatment should take into
consideration.

In sharp contrast to Grotius' time, the topic of sovereign
equality cannot be discussed today without reference to the
claim that the substantive inequality among nations in wealth
and resources must be reduced, and a more equitable
international system be created. Such a claim is advanced by
those theorists, imbued with a global outlook, who see no
reason why the concern for distributive justice should not be
extended beyond national boundaries to embrace the world
economic system.[53] However, the proposals for a 'New
International Economic Order' have not escaped criticism.
For example, it has been argued that the demands of the
poorer states for the redistribution of wealth are not solely
motivated by a genuine regard for equality, but are propelled
also by a desire to increase the power of their governments.[54]
Whatever the merits of these redistributive demands, it is of
great historical significance that the language of justice is
available at the international level with respect to the
distribution of global wealth and resources. This, however, is
a very recent development in the history of international
thought, and it would be utterly unrealistic to expect a writer
in the early seventeenth century to have considered substantive
international inequality as in need of rectification. The
Grotian epoch was much closer in time and in spirit to the

[51] See R. J. Vincent, *Human Rights and International Relations* (Cambridge, 1986);
R. J. Vincent (ed.), *Foreign Policy and Human Rights: Issues and Responses* (Cambridge,
1986). Note, however, the chapter by Hedley Bull in the present volume.
[52] See Georg Schwarzenberger, *International Law and Totalitarian Lawlessness*
(London, 1943).
[53] See e.g. Christopher Brewin, 'Justice in International Relations', in Michael
Donelan (ed.), *The Reason of States: A Study in International Political Theory* (London,
1978), pp. 142–52; Charles R. Beitz, *Political Theory and International Relations*
(Princeton, NJ, 1979). Beitz, unlike Brewin, goes beyond international distributive
justice, and argues for a cosmopolitan justice in the distribution of global wealth and
resources.
[54] See Robert W. Tucker, *The Inequality of Nations* (London, 1977).

Treaty of Tordesillas (1494), by which Spain and Portugal divided the world with respect to the newly discovered and yet to be discovered territories,[55] than to the philosophy of the Charter of Economic Rights and Duties of States (1974).

There is, however, one interesting passage in *De Jure Belli ac Pacis* which indicated Grotius' awareness of the necessity to modify the strict conception of private ownership in case of overriding needs. He wrote:

Now let us see whether men in general possess any right over things which have already become the property of another.

Some perchance may think it strange that this question should be raised, since the right of private ownership seems completely to have absorbed the right which had its origin in a state of community of property. Such, however, is not the case. We must, in fact, consider what the intention was of those who first introduced individual ownership; and we are forced to believe that it was their intention to depart as little as possible from natural equity . . .

Hence it follows, first, that in direst need the primitive right of user revives, as if community of ownership had remained, since in respect to all human laws—the law of ownership included—supreme necessity seems to have been excepted.

Hence it follows, again, that on a voyage, if provisions fail, whatever each person has ought to be contributed to the common stock. Thus, again, if fire has broken out, in order to protect a building belonging to me I can destroy a building of my neighbour. I can, furthermore, cut the ropes or nets in which my ship has been caught, if it cannot otherwise be freed . . .

Even among the theologians the principle has been accepted that, if a man under stress of such necessity takes from the property of another what is necessary to preserve his own life, he does not commit a theft.

The reason which lies at the back of this principle is not, as some allege, that the owner of a thing is bound by the rule of love to give to him who lacks; it is, rather, that all things seem to have been distributed to individual owners with a benign reservation in favour of the primitive right. For if those who made the original distribution had been asked what they thought about this matter they would have given the same answer that we do.[56]

---

[55] Arthur Nussbaum, *A Concise History of the Law of Nations*, rev. edn. (New York, 1954), p. 63.

[56] *JBP*, book II, chap. 2, § 6.

Grotius' ideas of 'primitive right to satisfy one's needs', 'the natural state of community of property', and 'the presumed intention of those who introduced the institution of private ownership' find their contemporary counterparts in the idea of basic human rights and John Rawls's theoretical device of the 'original position' and the 'veil of ignorance'.[57] By extrapolating those ideas from Grotius' writings, a present-day follower of his teachings might argue that sovereign states were entitled to the ownership of wealth and resources located within their boundaries, but that exceptions be made where basic human needs could not be met within particular states, and that these states be entitled to emergency measures to alleviate their shortfalls.

However, Grotius himself did not apply these ideas to international relations, and the passage quoted above indicates that he would not have argued for a general obligation on the part of the richer states to aid those citizens of the poorer countries who were in direst need. In any event, to confront a writer from the early seventeenth century with a problem which began to be formulated in the second half of the twentieth century would be to commit an unfair anachronism.

The continuing relevance of Grotius on the question of international equality is therefore to be appreciated primarily in terms of his defence of the idea that sovereign states are equal before the law; his acceptance of the view that sovereign states possess an equal capacity for rights in international law; and his argument that even those entities which do not belong to the same class as sovereign states are none the less under the protection of the law of nature.

[57] See John Rawls, *A Theory of Justice* (Oxford, 1971).

8

Grotius, Human Rights, and Intervention

R. J. VINCENT

'The freedom and equality which the makers of the coming peace must seek to establish is not a freedom and equality of nations, but a freedom and equality which will express themselves in the daily lives of men and women.'[1] It is a measure of the impact of Grotianism on the theory and practice of international politics in the twentieth century that these words were written towards the end of the Second World War not by a reformist allowing his vision to distort his interpretation of reality, but by E. H. Carr, the realist destroyer of an earlier reformism.[2] They assert the importance of a great society of humankind, of which the society of states however prominent is only one strand, and in doing this they may be said to go to the heart of the Grotian or Rationalist conception of international relations.[3] This is the conception of international relations which regards them as taking place within a real society where rules and institutions confine the behaviour of individuals and states alike. The purpose of this chapter is to examine the vitality of this conception of international relations, focusing particularly on the great contemporary questions of human rights and intervention in world politics.

The contemporary investigation of these questions does not conventionally begin with Grotius. For while he gives one of the earliest statements of our modern idea of rights as moral possessions, and goes so far, it has been said, as to turn the law

---

[1] E. H. Carr, *Nationalism and After* (London, 1965 edn.), p. 43.

[2] See id., *The Twenty Years' Crisis* (London, 1939).

[3] For Grotians or Rationalists as one of the three great schools of thought about International Relations see Hedley Bull, 'Martin Wight and the Theory of International Relations', *British Journal of International Studies*, 2 (1978).

of nature into an injunction to 'respect one another's rights',[4] he does not explicitly distinguish a category of *human* rights from those of states or citizens or princes. And while it is possible to read into his work the basis of a fully fledged principle of non-intervention, and also a doctrine of humanitarian intervention as an exception to it, it is anachronistic to take Grotius' writings as indicating the arrival of these ideas in international society. The explicit statement of the principle of non-intervention awaited the work of the eighteenth-century writers Wolff and Vattel, and became the positivist orthodoxy only in the nineteenth century. And as for the doctrine of humanitarian intervention, we may even now doubt whether it has arrived at all, as will be discussed below.

There are, however, themes which arise from Grotius' work which give shape to the contemporary discussion of human rights and intervention. The first is the similarity of the scenery passed: Grotius' time marked the transition from a great society of humankind to a society of states, whereas now some see a movement in the opposite direction, from international society to a more inclusive world society. The second is the legal reflection of the first: it is the way in which Grotius' own transition from the old task of describing the law common to most nations to the new one of charting the law between nations is mirrored in the work of his present-day counterparts by a move back from the 'new' to the 'old': so that, in the discussion of the international law of human rights, we are observing a return to the medieval concern with the *jus gentium intra se* (the law of nations within the state) to run alongside the *jus gentium inter se* (the law between states). And the third Grotian theme which assists our contemporary understanding is the contest between liberty and peace, between the prerogatives of princes and the rights of subjects—especially when the prince is of one state and the subjects of another; that is to say when what is at issue is the justification of intervention. In all these matters Grotius' work is a text for our own times, and is dated not in substance but merely in style.

[4] Richard Tuck, *Natural Rights Theories: Their Origin and Development* (Cambridge, 1979), p. 67. See also Hugo Grotius, *The Jurisprudence of Holland*, trans. and ed. R. W. Lee (Oxford, 1926), pp. 315, 293.

(a) GROTIUS ON HUMAN RIGHTS AND STATE SOVEREIGNTY

Human rights, the rights that everyone is said to have by virtue of his or her very humanity, have become so much the language of our time as to be taken for granted as the starting-place for political argument. And in western politics, in any event, this is a starting-place which assumes the importance of the interests of individual human beings in justifying this or that political programme. While the expression 'human rights' is not associated with Grotius (or indeed with any publicist before the twentieth century), nevertheless it has been impressively argued that the reading of the Law of Nations according to Grotius should begin with the individual.[5] There are two aspects to this. The first has to do with the status of law as a body of rules. The second is concerned with the place occupied by individuals in the rules making up international law.

Law as a body of rules, Peter Paul Remec suggests, is unthinkable unless it applies to rational beings capable of obeying it.[6] Such are individual human beings, and law is a body of rules to discipline their conduct. And it is through their individuality, their reason, and their will, that the law can be understood and obeyed. International law is not different, in this regard, from any other law, and Grotius thought of it as directly binding on princes.[7] After Grotius, the idea emerged, reaching the full light of day in the nineteenth century, that it was the states themselves, and not the princes personally that were the subjects of international law. But the idea, also reaching its apogee in the nineteenth century, that states were *exclusively* the subjects of international law, and individuals merely its objects, Grotius would have found a peculiar one.

This leads to the second aspect. For Grotius the *jus gentium* consisted in the rules covering all relations taking place

---

[5] See Peter Paul Remec, *The Position of the Individual in International Law according to Grotius and Vattel* (The Hague, 1968); Hersch Lauterpacht, 'The Grotian Tradition in International Law', *British Year Book of International Law 1946*.

[6] Remec, *The Position of the Individual*, p. 23.   [7] Ibid., p. 23.

outside the bonds of municipal law[8]—the relations of princes between themselves, certainly, but also any other relations that went beyond the boundary of the state. The society formed between societies was, as we have seen, a great society of humankind and not a society of states alone. In this society the individual had a dignified place and was not merely an object. Indeed, Sir Hersch Lauterpacht took it to be one of the major features of Grotius' scheme that it endorsed the fundamental rights and freedoms of the individual.[9]

Grotius' *De Jure Belli ac Pacis* is often combined with the Peace of Westphalia to locate in the second quarter of the seventeenth century the origins of the modern states-system. In this regard, it is Grotius' recognition of the importance of sovereignty that is celebrated rather than his attachment to the individual. What is not contested is the idea that in Grotius' scheme rights had a central place. Humans had a sociable instinct. They sought moreover to live tranquilly and reasonably with each other. Personal security, property, contracts, and the like were necessary to the achievement of this tranquillity. Human nature mothered natural law. Natural law dealt with what was just and due. Rights derived from this calculation.[10] And no society whatever could be preserved without the recognition of rights.[11] International society was no exception to this, and the warfare that was a feature of this society was never to be undertaken except to assert rights, and never to be carried on except within the limits of rights.[12]

Grotius' discussion of the *idea* of a right (or *jus*) dealt with it in two aspects. One meaning of the word, he said, was to convey what is just, as when what is being discussed is whether any war is just, or what is just in war.[13] But right had another meaning when what was being discussed was *my*

---

[8] Remec, *The Position of the Individual*, p. 60.

[9] Lauterpacht, 'The Grotian Tradition', pp. 43–5.

[10] *JBP* (Whewell's trans., Cambridge, 1853), Prolegomena 16; book I, chap. I, §§ 3 and 4. The treatment in the text follows Whewell's tendency to use 'right' as a synonym for law as well as for our modern notion of a right as a moral possession. This tendency is illustrated by Whewell's translation of Grotius' title as *The Rights of War and Peace*. All references in this chapter are to Whewell's translation, rather than to the later one by Kelsey in the Classics of International Law series (1925).

[11] *JBP*, Prolegomena 23.

[12] Ibid., Prolegomena 25.

[13] Ibid., book I, chap. I, § 3.

right.[14] Here it was a moral quality by which 'a person is competent to have or to do a certain thing justly'.[15] When perfect this moral quality was called a *facultas*, a jural claim; when imperfect, an *aptitudo*, a moral claim.[16] A fully fledged right, a jural claim, involved a compact or pledge with a corresponding debt on the other side.[17] In this notion of a correlative obligation Grotius' conception of rights is both modern and strong.[18]

But while the concept of rights was strong, the political theory associated with it was not. Grotius seemed to deny individuals the right of resistance against the unjust acts of their own rulers. Because civil society was established to maintain public tranquillity, the state acquired a right—to the extent necessary to achieve this goal—to limit the right of resistance.[19] He was also sceptical of the doctrine of the sovereignty of the people. Kings who were subject to the people, he thought, were only improperly called kings.[20] The good of the governed might be the object of government, but it did not follow that people were superior to kings, 'for guardianship is for the sake of the ward, and yet the guardian has authority over the ward'.[21] And the guardian might decide under pressure that in order to preserve the tranquillity of his people he should enslave them to a foreign power. For life was of more value than liberty, and God himself spoke of it as a benefit that he does not destroy men but delivers them into slavery.[22] Quoting Aristides, Grotius says that 'men are accustomed to save the ship by throwing overboard, not the passengers, but the cargo.'[23]

This right to life, a more basic right than any right to liberty, is not absolute. There is a simple right 'to those acts without which life cannot conveniently be sustained', and to the 'necessaries of life, food, clothing, medicaments'.[24] All men

[14] Ibid., book I, chap. I, § 4.
[15] Ibid. [16] Ibid. [17] Ibid., book I, chap. I, § 5.
[18] For a discussion of the correlativity question see David Lyons, 'The Correlativity of Rights and Duties', *Noûs*, 4 (1970).
[19] *JBP*, book I, chap. 4, § 2. I. [20] Ibid., book I, chap. 3, § 8. II.
[21] Ibid., book I, chap. 3, § 8. 14.
[22] Ibid., book II, chap. 24, § 6. 2. The biblical reference is to 2 Chr. 12: 7 and 8.
[23] *JBP*, book II, chap. 24, § 6. 5. [24] Ibid., book II, chap 2, § 18.

had a right to purchase these things at a fair price, but not when their possessors needed them.[25] The right was in that sense conditional. Indeed all human rights were so conditioned that they did not bind in cases of extreme necessity.[26] As the common rights of mankind, they obliged others as 'external rights'—rights which existed between persons of different nations—and not as the bond of municipal law. The thinking here seems, by comparing mere external rights to municipal solidarity, to put domestic law before universal law and to acknowledge that the fact of state sovereignty weakened the theory of human rights. So it is with the rule of non-resistance to sovereign authority. Grotius appeals to the practice of civilized nations to establish it, and not to the principles of natural law.[27]

There are then difficulties for those who wish to uphold Grotius as a father of human rights as well as of international law, especially because of his attitude to the right of resistance. Acknowledging this, Hersch Lauterpacht fell back not on the hackneyed explanation based on Grotius' being a pensioner of the King of France (which he became after his exile from Holland), nor on the number of exceptions he entertained to the rule of non-resistance, but on the centrality of the individual human being in Grotius' system. Lauterpacht thus connected Grotius through Locke to the liberal revolutions of the eighteenth century.[28] But this nevertheless begs the question of the weight which we are to give to the individual as against the state, and it is the ambiguity on this issue in Grotius' work which allows him to be called up in support of both the positivist doctrine of state sovereignty and the naturalist notion of the rights of individuals.

(b) GROTIUS ON INTERVENTION

Grotius may be counted as a non-interventionist in international relations because of the deference he shows to sovereign

[25] *JBP*, book II, chap. 2, § 19.   [26] Ibid., book II, chap. 18, § 4. 6.
[27] Remec, *The Position of the Individual*, pp. 214–15.
[28] Lauterpacht, 'The Law of Nations, the Law of Nature and the Rights of Man', *Transactions of the Grotius Society*, 29 (1944), pp. 24–5.

authority and the doubts he entertained about any right of resistance. The defence of his position is the prudential one having to do with the maintenance of international order. He says, quoting Ambrose, that peoples should not run into wars by usurping the care for those who do not belong to them.[29]

But the rights of individuals are not completely eclipsed by this arrangement among sovereigns. For the sovereigns themselves retain a residual responsibility for humankind at large. They ought to care not only for the single nation which is committed to them, said Grotius, but for the whole human race. They should be (and he is quoting here Themistius in an oration to Valens) not philo-Macedonian only, or philo-Roman but philanthropic.[30] So if a tyrant practises atrocities towards his subjects, even though those subjects cannot take up arms against him, it does not follow that others in a position of responsibility regarding humankind as a whole could not take up arms on their behalf.[31] So to a general principle of non-intervention (the actual language here came after Grotius) is added an exception, especially when subjects are persecuted for their religious beliefs.[32]

Lauterpacht has suggested that this is 'the first authoritative statement' of the principle of humanitarian intervention,[33] which he defines as the 'principle that the exclusiveness of domestic jurisdiction stops where outrage upon humanity begins.' The difficulty with this resounding interpretation is twofold. In the first place, it seems too zealous to call Grotius' tentative admission of the possibility in some circumstances of rights being vindicated by outsiders, a doctrine of intervention. Second, it runs two separate questions together. One is about the boundaries of domestic jurisdiction—how far is it legitimate for foreign states ever to pay attention to some matter which another state claims to be an internal affair? The second is about the definition of intervention. Taking up arms on behalf of oppressed subjects is plainly to make war on another sovereign, whereas the use of the term intervention in modern international law has often been to depict an activity that is less than war but more than mere diplomatic persuasion.

---

[29] *JBP*, book II, chap. 25, § 8. 1.
[30] Ibid., Prolegomena 24.
[31] Ibid., book II, chap. 25, § 8. 3.
[32] Ibid., book II, chap. 25, § 8. 2.
[33] Lauterpacht, 'The Grotian Tradition', p. 46.

Because the development of the doctrine of humanitarian intervention has been closely linked to this modern definition of intervention—a term which Grotius himself did not use— there is an element of licence in calling Grotius its first authoritative exponent.

Moreover, we now read Grotius in an intellectual climate influenced by the nineteenth-century liberal doctrine that a people that is not prepared to brave labour and danger for its liberation is not worth intervening for.[34] So we find it curious that outside authorities should somehow be licensed to produce a result that cannot be pursued domestically. We shall return to this question in the conclusion, dealing before that with the question of humanitarian intervention in the context of contemporary international politics.

(c) IS HUMANITARIAN INTERVENTION NOW LEGITIMATE?

In order to establish the legitimacy in international society of a doctrine of humanitarian intervention, it may be said that three things are required. First, it has to be shown that individual human beings have some independent standing in international society in order that their rights can constitute a reason for intervention. Second, it has to be shown that this status is something established in general international law which cannot simply be trumped by an appeal by this or that state to a doctrine of domestic jurisdiction which retains its vitality. Third, in the correct positivist manner, we would need to show that the doctrine of humanitarian intervention is supported by state practice. Let us take these three require- ments in turn.

1. The Standing of Individuals in International Society

The idea that individuals have standing in international society was given its classic statement in the twentieth century by Hersch Lauterpacht even before the international covenants

---

[34] See J. S. Mill, 'A Few Words on Non-Intervention', in *Dissertations and Discussions: Political, Philosophical and Historical*, 4 vols. (London, 1875), iii. 175.

on human rights became law for the international community. He argued that in so far as the international law embodied in the UN Charter and elsewhere recognized 'fundamental rights of the individual independent of the law of the State, to that extent it constitutes the individual a subject of the law of nations.'[35] Developments since these words were written—the international covenants, the provision under the 1950 European Convention on Human Rights for individuals to appeal to central institutions over the heads of their governments, the procedure under ECOSOC Resolution 1503 allowing individuals to communicate directly with the UN Sub-Commission when consistent patterns of gross violations of human rights take place[36]—might be said to have given them greater force. The evidence that Lauterpacht sought for asserting that individuals are subjects of international law is now much more abundant. The difficulty with the idea is not the lack of evidence for its existence, but the lack of substance in the status. Individuals may now, for some purposes, be called subjects of international law, but they are hardly equal members with states in international society, and they cannot hope to *enforce* their rights in that society. Developments such as that under the European Convention on Human Rights are real steps in this direction, but they are the exception rather than the rule, and are local rather than global.

2. *Human Rights* v. *Domestic Jurisdiction*

Our second requirement for the establishment of a doctrine of humanitarian intervention concerns the tension between the international law of human rights and the state's right to exclusive domestic jurisdiction. In terms of the UN Charter this tension is found between Articles 55 and 56 on human rights and Article 2, especially Article 2(7) reserving domestic jurisdiction. Lauterpacht's own mode of resolving this tension relied on the definition of intervention as 'dictatorial interference'.[37] What Article 2(7) excluded was 'direct legislative

---

[35] Lauterpacht, *International Law and Human Rights* (London, 1950), p. 4.

[36] These developments are described and assessed in R. J. Vincent, *Human Rights and International Relations* (Cambridge, 1986), chap. 6.

[37] Lauterpacht, *International Law and Human Rights*, p. 167.

interference by the United Nations—that is, an attempt to
impose upon States rules of conduct as a matter of legal
right.'[38] Discussion, study, and recommendation on the
matter of human rights in any state, however, did not breach
the principle of domestic jurisdiction.

The practice of the United Nations since 1950 has been to
shrink the area reserved to domestic jurisdiction, especially
in regard to issues like that of apartheid.[39] But the debate
continues in the international community about where the
boundary lies between international concern and national
sovereignty, and about what the implications of the distinction are.

One notable arena in which this issue has been discussed is
that of the Helsinki Conference on Security and Cooperation
in Europe (1975) and the subsequent review conferences. In
the Final Act of the Helsinki Conference (which, while not a
treaty binding in law, was a solemn agreement) a strong and
detailed statement of the doctrine of non-intervention appeared
as Principle VI, and an equally forthright statement of
universal human rights as Principle VII.[40] In general the
Western powers lined up behind Principle VII, arguing that
human rights were now a matter of international concern, that
an appeal to the principle of non-interference in relation to
them was no longer acceptable, and that 'intervention' was to
be defined (much as Lauterpacht had suggested) as dictatorial
interference—the implication being that lesser forms of
'interference' were not illegal. The Soviet Union's first
response to this was not to deny that human rights were a
matter of international concern, but to insist that their
implementation was a matter of domestic jurisdiction which
ruled out the monitoring activity which the West took to be
not merely legitimate but necessary if the Helsinki process was
to continue. This attitude of the Soviet Union has changed as
the Helsinki process has developed. At the 1988–9 Vienna
follow-up meeting, for example, the Concluding Document
not only set out a very extensive listing of human rights, but
also contained a provision that any participating state could

---

[38] Lauterpacht, *International Law and Human Rights*, p. 171.
[39] See Vincent, *Nonintervention and International Order* (Princeton, NJ, 1974), chap. 6.
[40] For a fuller discussion see id., *Human Rights and International Relations*, chap. 4.

at any time bring cases in the human dimension of the CSCE to the attention of other states through diplomatic channels. This seems to involve outsiders in implementation as well as proclamation. But the reflex of an appeal to non-intervention remains an instinctive one when states are under attack for their record on human rights. To the extent that this is a general tendency in inter-state relations, it produces a second reason for caution in response to claims made about the legitimacy of humanitarian intervention in contemporary international society.

3. *Humanitarian Intervention in State Practice*

The most important criterion by which the legitimacy of humanitarian intervention may be judged is the third one, state practice. Does the actual conduct of states suggest any acceptance of the enforcement of human rights by one state or states within another sovereign jurisdiction? There is a dispute about this among international lawyers. One the one hand there are those who point to the strength of the prohibition of the unilateral use of force in the UN Charter, and who observe in addition the lack of support for a policy of humanitarian intervention in past and contemporary state practice.[41] On the other hand there are those who regard the achievement of human rights as a purpose of the UN Charter that ranks with the pursuit of peace and security, and who are prepared to sanction unilateral action if the collective action envisaged in the Charter comes, as it characteristically has, to nought.[42]

This is not merely a legal dispute, but also one of policy. Those who argue against the legitimacy of humanitarian intervention are inclined to observe that it is a doctrine used by the great against the small, that it smacks of imperialism, that it disguises ignoble motives (or, conversely, that it expects too high a standard of behaviour), that it might

[41] See esp. Ian Brownlie, 'Humanitarian Intervention', in J. N. Moore (ed.), *Law and Civil War in the Modern World* (Baltimore, Md., 1974); and M. Akehurst, 'Humanitarian Intervention', in Hedley Bull (ed.), *Intervention in World Politics* (Oxford, 1984).

[42] See esp. Richard B. Lillich, 'Humanitarian Intervention: A Reply to Dr Brownlie and a Plea for Constructive Alternatives', in Moore (ed.), *Law and Civil War*.

provoke counter-intervention, and that it is in general heedless of consequences. On the other side the argument is that the costs of non-intervention have to be counted alongside those of intervention, and that the policy of the doubters amounts to doing nothing, leaving the international community impotent however shocked its conscience. Good policy, in the view of this side of the argument, should shape the interpretation of the law, and indeed good policy is part of the definition of what the law is.[43]

It is hard to find in the contemporary practice of states a robust doctrine of humanitarian intervention. Moreover, in a contemporary international society which is strikingly pluralist (in contrast to the solidarism of Grotian doctrine),[44] where new states having just gained their sovereignty are quick to protect it, and where old states are no less concerned to safeguard their ancient freedoms, the prospects for entrenching a doctrine of humanitarian intervention seem remote. This does not necessarily mean, however, that we can dismiss the concern with human rights in contemporary international society as merely a superficial phenomenon having to do with the words states speak in the international community rather than with the action they undertake in their foreign policy. A return to the Grotian themes with which this chapter began may show why such a dismissal is not possible.

(d) GROTIAN THEMES IN CONTEMPORARY DEBATES ON HUMAN RIGHTS AND INTERVENTION

The first theme identified earlier in this chapter was about the transition from medieval to modern society, from the great society of humankind to the society of states. We suggested that it may be helpful to compare Grotius' treatment of the emergence of the states-system with our contemporary preoccupation with its actual or potential decline. In regard to human rights and intervention this comparison concerns the marking out of the sovereign state as a special actor in world

[43] See Myres S. McDougal, Harold D. Lasswell, and Lung-chu Chen, *Human Rights and World Public Order* (New Haven, Conn., and London, 1980).
[44] For this distinction see Bull, 'The Grotian Conception of International Society', in H. Butterfield and M. Wight (eds.), *Diplomatic Investigations* (London, 1966).

society leading in the nineteenth century to the submergence of the individual and his or her rights, and then the twentieth century's rediscovery of individual rights in the passage back from international to world society (and the search for a doctrine of humanitarian intervention). This comparison may have nothing more useful to offer than that entrances are instructive for the contemplation of exits. And it is a static comparison which assumes that nothing much of interest happened between the entrance and the exit (that is, during the heyday of the nation-state). Accordingly, it might be argued that such a static comparison should be abandoned in favour of a more dynamic model of human evolution which sees the nation-state as a stage in the development of human beings away from their womb-like attachment to the local tribe and towards the situation in which individual human beings encounter each other not as members of this or that department of humanity but as fully human beings.[15] But even if we were to accept such a historicist account, as Lauterpacht does to the extent that he sees Grotius as passing on the baton of individual emancipation to Locke, it would still be useful to consult Grotius not merely as a defunct publicist, someone who ran his lap some time ago, but as a scholar who has thought deeply about the tension between the attachment to a local community and the more abstract obligation to world society as a whole.

Our second Grotian theme concerned the transition from the *jus gentium intra se* to the *jus gentium inter se*, and the traffic now in the opposite direction in virtue of the establishment of a body of doctrine called the international law of human rights. This is sometimes referred to dismissively, by lawyers themselves, as 'soft law', recommendations as to standards of behaviour which may or may not harden into proper international law, but it also contains some principles such as that of non-discrimination on racial grounds which apply to everyone in the international community, and are counted as *jus cogens*—'having the status of peremptory norms'.[46] If there

---

[15] See Andrew Linklater, *Men and Citizens in the Theory of International Relations* (London, 1982).

[46] Brownlie, *Principles of Public International Law*, 3rd edn. (Oxford, 1979), pp. 596 and 512–15.

is a body of law of this kind which is accepted to varying degrees by the international community as a whole, and is not simply the political preferences of the strong imposed on the weak, we may see in it a set of principles, akin to the *jus gentium intra se*, by which states undertake internationally to abide domestically.

This leads to our third introductory theme, which, put at its strongest, was about what is to be done when rules agreed are not only disobeyed but massively violated within one of the constituents of the global society. Grotius, we have seen, was very cautious about this, seeing at every turn the virtue of international tranquillity and of allowing the guardians to get on with their domestic tasks as best they could. And it was the same concern for (this time domestic) order that led him to sanction the use of force by princes against threats to public order in a way that might now be regarded as over-reaction. In turn, because princes carried the responsibility, not merely for those who were their own nationals, but also for humankind as a whole, then it was they who, on the rare occasion when intervention was justified, should be entrusted with it rather than allowing the wards of other guardians to take the law into their own hands. Whether or not it is true to claim with Lauterpacht that Grotius made a first authoritative statement of the doctrine of humanitarian intervention (and reasons were earlier given for scepticism about this), his perception of the difficulty that interference produced for international order is still instructive.

In our democratic age, there is less of a disposition either to trust the guardians, or to expect that foreigners can perform better what is now taken to be the proper work of nationals. Both these things reinforce the principle of non-intervention. But the same democratic age has produced declarations about the rights of all men and women, which, if they are to mean anything at all, must reduce the domain defended by non-intervention. We illustrated this ambiguity above by reference to the tension between Principle VI and Principle VII of the Helsinki Final Act, but it is an ambiguity that is general in the international community. International legitimacy, that which is sanctioned by law or right, includes both non-intervention and universal human rights. The former principle obstructs the doctrine of humanitarian intervention, while the latter rejects the idea that behind the walls of non-intervention anything goes. Offences against human rights are a matter of international concern, but they do not trigger intervention except perhaps when outrageous conduct shocks the conscience of mankind.[47]

But the absence of a well-established doctrine of humanitarian intervention does not evaporate international concern, and now each state is quite legitimately exposed to the scrutiny and criticism of the international community on the relationship beween government and governed within it.

This may not have produced a *significant* improvement in the way that states conduct themselves, but in so far as reputation counts in international society the inability to hide the disreputable behind any doctrinal bulwark may be a factor in favour of the expectation that improvement might take place. Against this it might be argued that making human rights a matter of international concern gives states, and especially the superpowers, merely another matter about which, in Burke's phrase, to equivocate, scuffle, and fight. Moreover, it may be argued that it is not through expressions of international concern, but through domestic change within a political tradition that improvement in rights records might take place. So that by virtue of both these points, the activities of outside powers may sometimes be counterproductive rather than a constructive contribution to change.

It is difficult, however, to be dogmatic about the superiority of domestic change over international pressure, because of the blurring of the boundaries between domestic and international society which become fuzzier with the accumulation of more conventions in the international law of human rights. These conventions bear witness to the spread of a global cosmopolitan culture, the human rights elements of which are penetrating 'domestic jurisdiction' to the extent that they establish standards which any government is supposed to meet. But this penetration has not necessarily spelled the

---

[47] For a discussion of this question see Vincent, *Human Rights and International Relations*, chaps. 7 and 8; and Michael Walzer, *Just and Unjust Wars* (New York, 1977), chap. 6.

demise of the state, which may even be strengthened by the successful cosmopolitanization of its élites, rather than weakened.[48] In any event, the division remains between the human being and the citizen. So long as it does, and world politics continue to be organized as the relations of states, the question of the relationship between human rights and intervention will be asked, and the work of Grotius on the rights of mankind and the rights of states will continue to be helpful to the questioner.

[48] See Ronald Dore, 'Unity and Diversity in Contemporary World Culture', in H. Bull and A. Watson (eds.), *The Expansion of International Society* (Oxford, 1984); and Vincent, *Human Rights and International Relations*, chap. 8.

9
Grotius' Influence in Russia
W. E. BUTLER

At about the time of Hugo Grotius' birth, European merchants
and adventurers were just beginning to discover Muscovy,
then at the earliest stage of re-establishing links destroyed by
the Tartars when they razed Kievan Rus. It was in the 1580s
that the Muscovite Tsar reminded Queen Elizabeth of
England that the sea was 'God's road' and not subject to
appropriation by any state. The constant religious strife
underlying the Thirty Years War (1618–48) that strangled
Europe and partly inspired Grotius to write his epic treatise
affected Russia but little, the more so since Russia had been
cut off from the intellectual and other currents of the age that
shaped Grotius' life. But as Russia opened her frontiers to
Westernization from the mid-seventeenth century, Grotian
views entered to compete with other philosophies and take
their place in the education of the enlightened Russian
diplomat or statesman. From the eighteenth century Russian
students of the Law of Nations were expected to know
something of his basic ideas, albeit usually filtered through the
utterances of his critics. Russia has remained one of the
important—although lesser-known—areas of his influence.

Grotius died in what is now the German Democratic
Republic only two years before the publication in Russian
translation (1647) of a substantial German work on the art
and laws of war (1615–17) by J. J. von Wallhausen.[1] The
translation is regarded as the first printed work treating the
Law of Nations in the Russian language, but of course it
reflected the state of the law of war on the eve of Grotius'

---

[1] Von Wallhausen, *Kriegskunst zu Fusz, darinnen gelehrt und gewiesen werden*
(Oppenheim, 1615–17); trans. into Russian as *Uchenie i khitrost' ratnogo stroeniia
pekhotnykh liudei* (Moscow, 1647). A facsimile of the 1647 edition was printed in 200
copies at St Petersburg (1904). Copies of both are extremely rare.

celebrated treatise rather than in the light of Grotius' teachings. Nevertheless, it is evident from the inventories of seventeenth- and eighteenth-century personal and institutional libraries in Russia that editions of *De Jure Belli ac Pacis* had been acquired, including by the Ambassadorial Department, later the College of Foreign Affairs. Among the important Petrine libraries containing copies of Grotius were those of the Russian ambassador A. A. Matveev, who had copies of Grotius' books on the freedom of the seas and on the law of war and peace, and the Vice-Chancellor of the Russian Empire, P. P. Shafirov, who possessed copies of Grotius on the law of peace and war in the original Latin and in French translation.[2]

In the reign of Peter the Great (1682–1725), the Tsarevich Aleksei was schooled in the views of Grotius and Pufendorf through translations into Russian of the 1712 edition of Grotius' *De Jure Belli ac Pacis* and the 1672 edition of Pufendorf's *De Juris Naturae et Gentium Libri Octo*. Both translations remained in manuscript, although some of Pufendorf's other works translated at Peter's behest were published. The Russian translators of the day experienced tremendous difficulties with Grotius' style and terminology and reported to the Ambassadorial Department: 'It is impossible to translate some words of these books without studying jurisprudence because the terms and rhetoric of jurisprudence are special.'[3] When books of this nature fell into the hands of inexperienced translators, the original became unrecognizable. Grotius' book was entrusted to the Kiev Theological Academy for translation, and the rendering was a combination of old Church Slavonic and the Russian of the day. The manuscript translation survives still in the Leningrad Public Library.

Baron Huyssen's Instruction regarding the Tsarevich's training in the Law of Nations, it should be noted, was

[2] See the Introduction by the present author: 'P. P. Shafirov and the Law of Nations', in Shafirov, *A Discourse Concerning the Just Causes of the War Between Sweden and Russia: 1700–1721* (Dobbs Ferry, NY, 1973), pp. 25–7.

[3] Quoted in V. E. Grabar, *Materialy k istorii literatury mezhdunarodnogo prava v Rossii 1647–1917 gg.* (Moscow, 1958). An English translation, *The History of International Law in Russia 1647–1917*, is due to be published by Oxford University Press in 1990.

preceded on 22 April 1703 by a similar recommendation from
P. P. Shafirov, who in 1717 was himself to publish the first
unofficial Russian work on international law:

It is possible . . . to use as an introduction to the law of nations either
Grotius or Pufendorf on natural law and the law of nations, in which
one can study the basis of all law, and especially the law of war and
peace between potentates . . .[4]

Russian readers learned something of Grotius through
translations by other jurists who cited or quoted from him,
among them J. F. von Bielfeld (1717–70).[5] A brief conspectus
of Grotius' teaching was given in 1839 by K. A. Nevolin.[6]
Students at Kharkov University in the 1851–2 academic year
were required to write an essay on the topic: 'A Critical
Evaluation of Hugo Grotius' *De Jure Belli ac Pacis* Showing the
Influence of this Publicist's Works on the Development of the
Science of the Law of Nations.'[7] Several nineteenth-century
Russian jurists drew substantially upon Grotius in specialized
works on international law: N. A. Bezobrazov,[8] V. N.
Leshkov,[9] M. N. Kapustin,[10] among others. By the turn of the
twentieth century brief biographical sketches of Grotius were
being included in the standard encyclopaedias; V. N.
Aleksandrenko in 1905 published an article contrasting
Gentili and Grotius.[11] But still the only version of Grotius in
Russian remained the unpublished manuscript of 1712.

In 1902 a heavily censored summary of Grotius' treatise on
the law of war and peace appeared, his theological views
rather than his legal doctrines evidently giving offence.[12] A
lengthy summary of *De Jure Belli ac Pacis* based on the French

---

[4] Ibid., p. 44.

[5] J. F. von Bielfeld, *Nastavleniia politicheskiia barona Bilfelda* (Moscow, 1768–75).

[6] K. A. Nevolin, *Entsiklopediia zakonovedeniia* (Kiev, 1839); repr. in id., *Polnoe sobranie sochinenii* (St Petersburg, 1857–9).

[7] Grabar, *Materialy k istorii*.

[8] N. A. Bezobrazov, *Issledovanie nachal vneshniago gosudarstvennogo prava, ili ob"iasnenie svoistv vzaimnykh otnoshenii gosudarstv* (St Petersburg, 1838).

[9] V. N. Leshkov, 'Ob osnovnom istochnike i obshchem stroe prava', *Iuridicheskii vestnik*, no. 1, pt. 1 (1873), pp. 44–55.

[10] M. N. Kapustin, *Obozrenie predmetov mezhdunarodnogo prava* (Moscow, 1856–9).

[11] V. N. Aleksandrenko, 'Ocherki po istorii nauki mezhdunarodnogo prava. A. Dzhentili i G. Grotsii', *Zhurnal ministerstva narodnogo prosveshcheniia*, no. 5, part III, NS (1905), otdel nauk, pp. 109–24.

[12] Grotius, *O prave voiny i mira* (St Petersburg, [1902]).

translation published in 1867 by P. L. E. Pradier-Fodéré was included in Gorovtsev's Encyclopaedia of International Law (1909),[13] and by then the place of Grotius in developing international legal doctrine, if not his actual writings, was standard fare in all the Russian textbooks on the subject. In 1915 V. A. Ovchinnikov succeeded in having Grotius' chapter on the law of embassies reprinted as an Annex to his monograph on the doctrine of ambassadorial inviolability.[14]

When Russian international lawyers came to give serious consideration in the late nineteenth century to Grotius' role in the development. of international legal doctrine, they were disposed on the whole to rest upon the findings of their European predecessors and contemporaries. The Russian jurist who by linguistic accomplishment and intellectual inclination was best qualified to assess Grotius, V. E. Grabar, believed that Grotius was essentially a popularizer of doctrines and principles developed in the works of dozens of earlier medieval scholars, most long since forgotten, whose perception of the existence of an international system was far more sophisticated and informed than we tend to suppose.[15]

Others were more generous in their assessment. The leading Russian publicist of the day, F. F. Martens, accepted that the appearance of Grotius' *De Jure Belli ac Pacis* in 1625 marked the emergence of international law as an 'autonomous legal science'.[16] Theoretically, however, Martens found Grotius to be 'casuistic'. With regard to Grotius' view that international legal rules are drawn from international custom and treaties, Martens observed that in Grotius' time there were no treaties which could be regarded as generally binding; Grotius failed to draw, in other words, upon empirical observations of international politics in his day and should have confined himself, said Martens, to expressing the wish that international law were based on treaty and custom. The evidence adduced by Grotius in support of his propositions bore little relationship to the 'positive elements of international law' in

[13] A. M. Gorovtsev, *Mezhdunarodnoe pravo. Izbrannaia literatura. Kratkaia entsiklopediia* (St Petersburg, 1909).

[14] V. A. Ovchinnikov, *K ucheniiu o posol'skoi neprikosnovennosti* (Warsaw, 1915).

[15] Grabar, *Materialy k istorii.*

[16] F. F. Martens, *Sovremennoe mezhdunarodnoe pravo tsivilizovannykh narodov*, 5th edn. (St Petersburg, 1905), i. 158.

the seventeenth century. Moreover, added Martens, it was doubtful that Grotius' work contained a concept of a 'system of international law', for most of the questions treated exclusively with the law of war, and naturally so since the book was inspired by the excesses of the Thirty Years War.

On the impact of Grotius' work, Martens quoted Sir Henry Maine[17] with regard to the success of *De Jure Belli ac Pacis*, and noted that Gustav Adolf always took a copy with him on his campaigns, together with his Bible, and used it as a manual. And the German universities, Martens believed, had founded chairs of international law under the impact of Grotius' teachings. Finally, in Martens' view Grotius' book was the forefather of the philosophical and positivist orientations that dominated in the post-Grotian era of international law.

Grotius ultimately found his Russian translator in the person of A. L. Sakketti, whose attempt in 1902 to publish Grotius was frustrated by the censor. Sakketti persisted, and in 1948 book I of *De Jure Belli ac Pacis* was issued with a preface by A. I. Denisov,[18] and in 1956 the entire work, translated from the Latin text published at Amsterdam in 1646 containing Grotius' last corrections.[19] The 1956 edition appeared under the general editorship of the former Soviet judge on the International Court of Justice, S. B. Krylov.

Soviet legal scholarship has had a high opinion of Grotius and his writings on international law. The 'vitality' and 'genius' of Grotius' works, Krylov wrote, outlived their author; his writings are part of the treasure-house of world legal literature. In a sense *De Jure Belli ac Pacis* was an encyclopaedia of the humanities as then understood and even in the realm of law it reached beyond the Law of Nations to civil, criminal, and public law.[20]

Sakketti saw Holland, in Grotius' lifetime, as emancipating herself from Spanish feudal domination and being transformed into a modern bourgeois society. Grotius well expressed the 'interests of the bourgeois development of society' in his work

---

[17] H. Maine, *Ancient Law* (London, 1861), p. 111: 'The great marvel of the Treatise . . . was its rapid, complete, and universal success.'

[18] Grotius, *O prave voiny i mira* (Moscow, 1948), pp. i–xv.

[19] Id., *O prave voiny i mira* (Moscow, 1956).

[20] S. B. Krylov, ibid., pp. 4–5.

and was a founder of the new progressive bourgeois legal science. The esteem for Grotius and his works expressed in the Programme of the Dutch Communist Party, said Sakketti, where reference was made to spiritual freedom, freedom of conscience, and freedom of thought, was further evidence of Grotius' contribution to the Dutch cultural heritage.[21]

In a more detailed critique offered in prefatory remarks by A. Zheludkov, Grotius is seen as one of the first to use natural law concepts in order to substantiate the transition of society from a feudal to a higher level of development.[22] For despite its shortcomings, the 'rule of reason' postulated by Grotius played a 'positive role' and inflicted a blow against teleological theories of state and law, although remnants of feudal jurisprudence were still to be found within. Especially 'positive' was Grotius' secularization of natural law theory— as compared, for example, with Thomas Aquinas—and his view (in *De Jure Belli ac Pacis*) that natural law extends exclusively to humankind, the last position all the more noteworthy in the light of Grotius' inability to understand that it is 'labour' which separates man from beast.

Since Grotius did not appreciate the class essence of law, a number of issues could not be satisfactorily treated in his writings. His efforts to trace the roots of 'human reason' as the source of natural law accordingly were defective. Amongst several examples given by Zheludkov, we dwell on private property. Grotius' approach was said to bear the clear imprint of bourgeois ideology. To Zheludkov it was evident that Grotius linked to the right of private ownership the possibility for individuals to own and use their property, to derive income, to satisfy their personal needs, and to alienate their property to others. The duties to refrain from violating another's property rights, to restore property unlawfully taken, and to compensate for property damage caused, all arose directly from the community nature of man and were protected by natural law. However, the state's right to assert an interest in private property and seize it for compensation, also upheld by Grotius, was viewed by Zheludkov as a survival of feudal views in the former. Other aspects of

[21] *O prave voiny i mira* (Moscow, 1956), pp. 8–9.
[22] A. Zheludkov, ibid., pp. 10–38.

Grotius' treatise, for example, the treatment of punishment, the relationship between the Law of Nations and municipal law, the concept of the just war, and the rules of warfare, Zheludkov summarized in a positive way. By way of conclusion he offered the following:

the general progressive orientation of Grotius' international legal views is evident. These views reflected the requirements of the bourgeoisie in the historical period when it, as the leading class, united opposed elements of society for the struggle against feudalism. The class interests of the bourgeoisie at that time found support in the objective laws of historical development and to some extent coincided with the interests of the toiling masses. In endeavouring to create the conditions for consolidating the capitalist order, it did not raise the issue of territorial conquests for itself and opposed, as a rule, feudal wars which were alien to its interests and onerous in their consequences. This also predetermined the progressive character of this situation in the domain of international law set out by ideologies of the bourgeoisie, including Grotius.[23]

Sakketti's introductory essay to the Russian edition of *De Jure Belli ac Pacis* was remarkably brief in comparison with what might have been expected from the pre-eminent Soviet student of Grotius. That expectation was more than satisfied by a lengthy study of Grotius as a scholar, humanist, jurist, and historian published two years later.[24] There Sakketti set out the most thorough account in Russian of the range of Grotius' accomplishments and, just as importantly, the modern perception of Grotius' role in developing the science of international law.

Here the influence of V. E. Grabar's work is paramount. Sakketti would not go so far as Grabar in characterizing Grotius as a 'popularizer' of earlier doctrines, but he does observe impartially that the oft-claimed distinction for Grotius of being the 'founder' of the science of international law can be legitimately contested by both Vitoria and Gentili. Grotius is part of a lengthy continuum of writers on the Law of Nations, Sakketti suggests, dating back to Roman law. The originality of Grotius' contribution lay in his utterances on the law

---

[23] Ibid., p. 37.

[24] Sakketti, 'Gugo Grotsii kak uchenyi-gumanist, iurist i istorik', *Sovetskii ezhegodnik mezhdunarodnogo prava 1959* (1960), pp. 261–71.

concerning war, a theme to which Sakketti returned several years later in a two-page essay on Grotius:

it is necessary once and for all to renounce war as a means for settling disputes between States and through a universal agreement of nations and governments to resolve such disputes only by peaceful means.[25]

The quatercentenary of Grotius' birth (1983) was commemorated in the Soviet Union by a lengthy assessment of Grotius' place in the development of international legal doctrine.[26] Baskin and Fel'dman, in the Grabar tradition, saw Grotius as *one* of the founders of modern international legal doctrine. In their perception Grotius was a fundamental figure of transition: on one hand he was a source for the classical bourgeois 'legal world view' that law must be transformed into a fundamental principle of social life, yet he retained in his doctrine 'elements of old views' and even remained 'the prisoner of certain early teleological feudal dogmas'. In his recourse to two sources of law—'nature (and God) as well as will (agreement) between people'—Grotius continued to synthesize 'the natural law and positivist approaches'. It is therefore not surprising that 'the proponents of both doctrines thereafter had recourse to the authority of Grotius'.[27]

Among the several merits of Grotius in comparison with his predecessors, Baskin and Fel'dman claim, is that his definition of the Law of Nations discloses more profoundly the essence of the 'specific nature of international legal relations' as compared with other branches of law. Baskin and Fel'dman have in mind Grotius' emphasis upon the treaty character of the Law of Nations based on the will of those nations. In elevating this facet of international law to the 'first plane', Grotius is credited with creating the prerequisite for acknowledging the sovereign equality of subjects of international law. Further, and here they differ from F. F. Martens, Baskin and Fel'dman

[25] Sakketti, 'Gugo Grotsii o voine i mire', *Sovetskii ezhegodnik mezhdunarodnogo prava 1964–1965* (1966), pp. 202–3.
[26] I. I. Baskin, and D. I. Fel'dman, 'Rol' Gugo Grotsiia v stanovlenii i razvitii nauki mezhdunarodnogo prava', *Sovetskii ezhegodnik mezhdunarodnogo prava 1982* (1983), pp. 252–75.
[27] Ibid., p. 261

believe Grotius to have been the 'first who created a true system for the science of international law'.[28]

That 'system' was primarily concerned with the law of war, because Grotius was writing during the Thirty Years War, but the 1648 Treaty of Westphalia rested 'on the principles and institutes advanced or defended by Grotius':

At the same time he formulated a number of new principles of international relations and institutes of international law which exerted enormous influence on the entire system of law prevailing in Europe until the French Revolution of the eighteenth century. It must also be noted that the majority of bourgeois international lawyers until the beginning of the twentieth century had recourse to Grotius when considering the system of international law. Probably for the simple reason that he was its progenitor.[29]

While Baskin and Fel'dman consider Grotius' views on individual principles and rules of international law (treaties, succession, nationality, territory, ambassadors, war, reprisals, and settlement of disputes) and note their constructive contribution to the development of international law, in certain areas they suggest Grotius' positions continue to be of modern significance. Examples are chosen from the law of treaties and the law of the sea. Grotius' recognition of the importance of the 'will' of peoples in forming rules of international law has achieved culmination, Baskin and Fel'dman point out, in what they perceive as a transition from custom to treaties as the principal source of international law. Innocent passage is regarded as originating in the Grotian era, and Grotius' utterances on the freedom of the seas are seen as influencing the formulation of the 1958 and 1982 UN Conventions on the Law of the Sea.

That Grotius should finally have been translated in full into the Russian language and published in the 1950s, as well as into certain Eastern European languages,[30] is testimony to his continuing importance in a living, developing, international legal system. Historical figure though he be, his doctrinal writings comprise part of the continuum in the development of

[28] Ibid., p. 262.
[29] Ibid., p. 263.
[30] See A. M. Stuyt, 'Grotius et la pensée Marxiste–Leniniste', *Grotiana*, 6 (1985), pp. 25–37.

international law and a subsidiary source to which international tribunals may and do refer when applying rules of international law to cases before them. Students of international law and relations require an understanding of Grotius and his teachings not merely better to comprehend the present in the light of the past, but because there is a direct normative link between the rules for state conduct in Grotius' time and our own. Baskin and Fel'dman put the issue for Soviet international legal doctrine as follows:

[According to Marx and Engels] 'history is nothing other than the successive change of individual generations, each of which uses the materials, capital, and productive forces transmitted to it by preceding generations. By virtue thereof a given generation, on one hand, continues the activities inherited under completely changed conditions and, on the other, alters the old conditions by means of completely changed activities.' The socialist science of international law has taken the best traditions of the past, and armed itself with everything valuable and progressive contained in the doctrines of international lawyers who endeavoured to serve the cause of peace between peoples, the cause of humanism. Hugo Grotius has occupied an eminent place among those whom Karl Marx named as being in the ranks of outstanding thinkers of the past, such as Hobbes, Spinoza, Rousseau, Fichte, and Hegel. They all have left an indelible trace in the history of international legal doctrine.[31]

Recalling something of Grotius' presence in the history of Russian international legal doctrine likewise is more than a token genuflexion towards acknowledging the breadth of his influence over the centuries. The development of Soviet attitudes toward the law of the sea from the 1960s to the 1980s reflected the Soviet Union's almost unprecedentedly rapid transition from a land power defending vast vulnerable sea frontiers to the second largest maritime power on the planet. The accompanying reassessment of attitudes towards the freedom of the seas has been comparable in fascinating respects to the 'battle of the books' between Hugo Grotius and John Selden in the early seventeenth century.

[31] Baskin and Fel'dman, 'Rol' Gugo Grotsiia v stanovlenii i razvitii nauki mezhdunarodnogo prava', p. 274.

10

Grotius and the Development of International Law in the United Nations Period[1]

ROSALYN HIGGINS

For any international lawyer, an understanding of what has gone before includes a broad familiarity with the thoughts and writings of Hugo Grotius. We witnessed around the time of the quatercentenary of Grotius' birth (1983) a great contribution to the understanding of Grotiana.[2] That year provided the impetus for many who specialize in particular areas of international law to go back to his writings—whether *Mare Liberum*, *De Jure Belli ac Pacis*, or *De Jure Praedae*—to discover how the developments of today accord with the thoughts expressed therein.[3]

Those who specialize in the law of the sea, the international law of trade, or matters relating to the use of force have found much to comment on. Obviously, no references to the United Nations are to be found in his work, but to link Grotius with the United Nations seems apposite, for three reasons. First, the UN Charter deals with certain aspects of international law central to the writings of Grotius: questions of sovereignty, the use of force between nations, and what we today term self-determination, are examples.[4] Second, the United Nations,

---

[1] This article is based in part on a lecture given to the Westminster UN Association in Dec. 1983. An earlier version was published in *International Social Science Journal*, 37 (1985), pp. 119–27.

[2] See e.g. C. F. Murphy, 'The Grotian Vision of World Order', *AJIL* 76 (1982), p. 477; Charles Edwards, *Hugo Grotius: The Miracle of Holland* (Chicago, Ill., 1981); M. Lachs, *The Teacher in International Law* (The Hague, 1982); L. E. van Holk and C. G. Roelofsen (eds.), *Grotius Reader* (The Hague, 1983).

[3] The splendid commemorative booklet, *The Grotius Collection at the Peace Palace: A Concise Catalogue* (Peace Palace Library, The Hague, 1983), reveals the astounding number of editions and translations of all of Grotius' works.

[4] See Arts. 1(2) and 2(1) of the UN Charter.

through its remit in Article 13 of the Charter[5] to assist in the codification and progressive development of international law, has over the years provided the framework for important lawmaking endeavours, particularly in the form of multilateral treaties. The Third UN Conference on the Law of the Sea, culminating in the opening of the 1982 Convention for signature and ratification, is an example. It is natural, therefore, to see whether in so doing the United Nations has adhered to the Grotian principles spelt out in *Mare Liberum*. Third, if we step back from the specific rules of international law, the UN Charter is permeated with a certain spirit and ethos (no matter how far contemporary practice may seem to stray from it). And it may be pertinent to ask how closely that ethos reflects the spirit of Grotius, and whether it remains viable in our present difficult times.[6]

What relevance does the Grotian spirit have for us today, and especially for the United Nations, which has undergone a period of considerable crisis? What does it mean when we speak of Grotius as the founding father of international law, when we recall his insistence upon the freedom of the seas, and upon limits to the authority of states to act as they wish? Have not times changed so as to make the legal sentiments with which he is particularly associated simply obsolete?

The UN Charter contains important clauses on the curtailment and limitation of the use of force by states which reflect the idea that states may use unilateral force only for the purpose of self-defence and not in the pursuit of foreign-policy objectives.[7] The road back from this precept to the ideas of Grotius is a long one indeed, with many intervening landmarks on the way, but its starting-point is *De Jure Belli ac Pacis*.

---

[5] Art. 13(1) provides: 'The General Assembly shall initiate studies and make recommendations for the purpose of: (a) promoting international co-operation in the political field and encouraging the progressive development of international law and its codification . . .'.

[6] On the UN generally, and its work in lawmaking, see D. Bardonnet (ed.), *The Adaptation of Structures and Methods at the United Nations*, Académie de Droit International de La Haye Colloque 1985 (Dordrecht, 1986); E. McWhinney, *United Nations Law-Making* (New York, 1984); T. Meron, *Human Rights Law-Making in the United Nations* (Oxford, 1986); A. Roberts and B. Kingsbury (eds.), *United Nations, Divided World* (Oxford, 1988).

[7] See esp. Arts. 2(4) and 51.

(a) THE LAWFULNESS OF RESORT TO WAR

On the lawfulness of resort to war—*jus ad bellum*—the forthright views of Hugo Grotius marked a break with the past, and the beginning of the contemporary formulation of international law. He wrote in book II of *De Jure Belli ac Pacis*: 'No other just cause for undertaking war can there be excepting injury received.' He further elaborated three justifiable causes: 'defence, recovery of property, and punishment'. It is evident that although this placed constraints upon states, it did not limit the use of force to self-defence as we understand it today. Grotius' formulation included 'the obtaining of that which belongs to us or is our due'—a general expression of the entitlement to use force in self-help. 'That which is our due' specifically included the right to free navigation and trade.[8]

This is not, of course, what the UN Charter provides. The prohibition on the unilateral use of force laid down in Articles 2(4) and 51 makes clear that self-defence is the only exception. The International Court of Justice confirmed in the *Corfu Channel* case in 1949[9] that it was not right to use force to ensure freedom of passage through the Corfu Channel—even though that freedom was certainly 'our due' and acknowledged as such. The Court expounded further on the limits of any right to use force unilaterally in its decision in 1986 on the merits in the case of *Nicaragua v. United States of America*.

For Grotius, his formulated doctrine of the 'just war' was a method of controlling the unbridled power of states to act as they chose. The Kellogg–Briand Pact of 1928[10] outlawing war as an instrument of national policy echoed the Grotian view, and indeed represented further progress. The Pact declared that international controversies were not to be resolved by resort to force, and the contracting parties undertook that, no matter what the nature or origin of a conflict, they would

---

[8] *JBP*, book II, chap. 1, § 1.4 and § 2; chap. 2, § 13; *JP*, chap. 12; and the comments of B. V. A. Röling, 'Jus ad Bellum and the Grotian Heritage', in Asser Instituut, *International Law and the Grotian Heritage* (The Hague, 1985), p. 117.
[9] *Corfu Channel* case, Merits, Judgment, *ICJ Reports*, 1949, p. 4.
[10] 1928 General Treaty for the Renunciation of War, *LNTS* 94, p. 57.

resolve it only by peaceful means. This instrument went beyond the position of Grotius in decoupling the 'justness' of the cause from the necessary entitlement to use force. Some sixty-three states became party to the Pact. Yet to those drafting the UN Charter in 1945, this was not a satisfactory point at which to rest: it had to be made more explicit that force could only be used in self-defence, and not to pursue legal rights or genuinely held notions of justice. It has been put this way by a fellow contributor and leading jurist in the Netherlands, the late Professor Röling, who wrote:

A less restrictive just war doctrine which emphasizes war as a means of maintaining law and order is a dangerous doctrine, as it demands the right to initiate a war. By accentuating the purported aim— preservation of law and order—the tendency develops to pay less attention to the nature of the means, namely war. Thus to plead for the maintenance of such a doctrine implies a plea for violence, which in our time has become totally unacceptable.[11]

Of course, the UN system was meant to resolve this fearful dilemma in a way totally beyond the vision of Grotius. The Charter was meant to provide for collective security. At the heart of the Charter was the idea that it would be realistic to enjoin states to use force only in self-defence, because collective security would be provided to ensure that rights would not be denied in a manner which might threaten international peace. The reality is that the UN collective security system has totally failed. It is of critical importance frankly to acknowledge this and to focus our minds on the consequences that flow from this reality. From the outset the United Nations has been unable to set up the forces whereby it was envisaged that the Security Council would provide collective security. The umbrella which was to encourage members to limit their use of force to self-defence has never really been unfurled. The determination of the Charter that the end should no longer justify the means, taken together with an apparent inability of the United Nations itself to guarantee the end, has exacted a fearful price. As Röling himself acknowledges:

[11] Röling, 'Jus ad Bellum and the Grotian Heritage', pp. 125–6. Röling also discusses this question in his chapter in this volume, below, pp. 284–5.

The taking of hostages, as in Iran, would have been unthinkable if the Iranian Government could have expected war with the United States. The misconduct of the many present dictatorships is outrageous, and would probably be less gruesome if external intervention were still to be feared. The elimination of war gives weak States greater freedom for internal misbehaviour. Genocide in all its various forms is an everyday reality.[12]

We see this dilemma all around us. The 1979 Soviet intervention in Afghanistan, clearly condemned by the United Nations, lasted for ten years in part because the United Nations could not risk doing more than organizing the long-drawn-out 'proximity talks' to promote a Soviet withdrawal. Conversely, those who supported the US action in Grenada in 1983 emphasized that the military intervention was in a 'just cause'—namely, the removal of 'repression' and the restoration of 'democracy'. Many who supported the action simply dismissed international law: what was important to them was the chance of achieving legitimate ends. Yet others, such as Ambassador Kirkpatrick, actually sought to invoke international law in support of their position.[13] But the truth is that this cannot be done without returning to a Grotian concept of the lawfulness of the use of force: it does not fit with today's Charter.

The contemporary problem of humanitarian intervention is another difficult aspect of the same matter. In the Grotian view, humanitarian intervention could be a just war. Under the UN Charter, this is harder to maintain. Whether the Charter forbids all such intervention has indeed been the subject of scholarly debate among international lawyers.[14] Grotius had some pertinent remarks to make on the matter. In

[12] Röling, 'Jus ad Bellum and the Grotian Heritage', p. 126.

[13] Address to the American Society of International Law, Apr. 1984. *Proceedings of the American Society of International Law 1984*, pp. 59–68. See, however, Detlev F. Vagts, 'Grenada and the International Double Standard', *AJIL* 78 (1984), p. 145; Christopher C. Joyner, 'The United States Action in Grenada', ibid., p. 131; and the impressive Report of the Committee on Grenada by the American Bar Association Section on International Law and Practice, 10 Feb. 1984.

[14] See Lillich (ed.), *Humanitarian Intervention and the United Nations* (Charlottesville, Va., 1973); Akehurst, 'Humanitarian Intervention', in Bull (ed.), *Intervention in World Politics* (Oxford, 1984), pp. 95–118; and Doswald-Beck, 'The Legal Validity of Military Intervention by Invitation of the Government', *British Year Book of International Law 1985*, pp. 198–252.

book II of *De Jure Belli ac Pacis* he declared that 'wars are justly waged against those who treat Christians with cruelty for the sake of their religion alone.'[15] Yet we know today that religious persecution abounds, and that states, for good or ill, will not normally intervene except perhaps where the lives of co-religionists are immediately in danger.

What was especially important about Grotius' contribution in this context was that while he upheld as a just war a humanitarian intervention to protect oppressed Christians, his was an extraordinarily early voice in rejecting the proselytizing underpinnings to this view: 'Wars cannot justly be waged against those who are unwilling to accept the Christian religion'[16] he wrote at the beginning of the seventeenth century. Cortez had completed his defeat of the Aztecs in 1581, some two years before Grotius' birth; Pissaro had landed in Peru in 1532 and began his cruel suppression of the Incas immediately thereafter. Notwithstanding these terrible events, Grotius nurtured a seed that was eventually to thrive—namely, the restriction of the use of force to just causes, and the refusal to allow the imposition of one's religion on others to be deemed a just cause.

The failure of the UN collective security system has meant that some interventions for utterly unacceptable purposes have occurred, as well as some unlawful interventions for more acceptable purposes. The picture is alarmingly random and unpredictable. Of course, the gap between what was intended and what was attainable was plugged in part by the evolution of the concept of UN peacekeeping.[17] Even if the United Nations could not enforce the peace, and thereby discourage the unilateral use of force, they could encourage the protagonists to disengage by moving into a vacuum, supervising military withdrawals, and overseeing cease-fires. All these peacekeeping functions had to be based on consent. From 1956 onwards it seemed that peacekeeping was a major contribution of the United Nations. However, by the 1970s, UN peacekeeping was becoming unacceptable to certain states, which looked to alternative solutions. While the

---

[15] *JBP*, book II, chap. 20, § 49.   [16] Ibid., book II, chap. 20, § 48.

[17] See Higgins, *UN Peacekeeping* (Oxford, 1969–81), i–iv; Wiseman, *Peacekeeping: Appraisals and Proposals* (New York, 1983).

detailed reasons are beyond scope of this chapter, they seemed to fall broadly into two categories.

First, some states—perhaps not entirely without reason—felt that the United Nations had not always dealt fairly with the problems of their region. Unlawful military action in which they engage is always (quite properly) condemned; but action taken against them, equally unlawful under the Charter, does not always receive comparable condemnation in the General Assembly and the Security Council. This, certainly, is Israel's perspective: and when it is combined with the establishment of a UN force with an inadequate mandate to tackle the real problems,[18] it is not surprising that UN peacekeeping has been unable to secure the confidence of all the states in the area. Again, the growth of the concept of regionalism has meant that the United Nations has been unable to offer peacekeeping in conflict situations exactly of the type that it is best suited to deal with. The attempts of the Organization of African Unity to deal with the paramilitary aspects of the dispute between Chad and the Libyan Arab Jamahiriya are a case in point.[19] And whereas in the late 1950s UN peacekeeping had significantly contributed to the stabilization of the Lebanon, in October 1976 it was the League of Arab States that sanctioned the presence of an overwhelmingly Syrian force. Later, the Syrian force was matched by a further non-UN force—the Multinational Force (MNF), with its American, British, French, and Italian contingents. The problems faced by such a force are prodigious, as events illustrated all too graphically.

The MNF was in August 1982 requested by the Government of the Lebanon to assist the Lebanese Armed Forces in facilitating the withdrawal from Lebanon of Palestinian leaders and combatants in a manner to 'further the restoration of the sovereignty and authority of the Government of Lebanon over the Beirut area'.[20] The MNF was then reconstituted in September 1982 to provide an interposition

[18] For the mandate given to the United Nations Interim Force in Lebanon (UNIFIL) see Security Council Resolutions 425–7 and 434 of 1978.

[19] See UN Security Council Documents S/15011–S/15013 (1982); and Security Council Resolution 504 of 30 Apr. 1982.

[20] Exchange of letters between Lebanon and US, 18 and 20 Aug. 1982. Similar agreements were concluded with France and Italy.

force between the various factions in and around Beirut. It
consisted of American, French, and Italian contingents, to
which was added a fourth contingent when British soldiers
arrived in Beirut in early February 1983. From early 1983
onwards the MNF found itself drawn into combat, and the
French and US contingents were subjected to sniping,
bombardment, and acts of terrorism. By the spring of 1984 all
the contingents had withdrawn.[21] In February 1987 it was
again Syrian armed forces which entered strife-torn Beirut.

It is not appropriate for UN forces to be established to meet
every conflict or problem. However, the evidence overwhelmingly points to the fact that where an outside force is needed,
the United Nations can do the job in a way that national
forces cannot. Even if a country uses force only in self-defence,
any military action is inevitably perceived in the context of the
power position and diplomatic posture of that country. The
United Nations has no foreign policy of its own. By contrast,
every action of the United States in the Lebanon was seen,
inevitably, as furthering American foreign policy in that
country. Retaliation, reprisal, maintenance of the credibility
of Western world leadership, are all perfectly understandable
elements of American foreign policy, but they are not part of
the vocabulary of UN peacekeeping. It was inevitable that the
MNF should be withdrawn, but lessons could be learned for
the future. A serious effort needed to be made to ensure that
the United Nations was able to regain the confidence of states
and resume its peacekeeping role, in respect of which it had
so painstakingly built up experience over a long period. In
1988–9 the deployment of the UN observer force to monitor
the Iran–Iraq ceasefire, and the UN force deployed under the
1988 Namibia accord, were evidence of a significant return to
peacekeeping under UN auspices.

In addition, efforts must be made to see if any progress can
be achieved on the provision of collective security. The call of
Secretary-General Pérez de Cuéllar in 1982 to turn our

---

[21] For a clear exposition of the role and functions of the MNF, see R. Nelson,
'Multinational Peacekeeping in the Middle East and the United Nations Model',
International Affairs, Winter 1984/5, pp. 67–89; and Marianne Heiberg and Johan
Holst, 'Peacekeeping in Lebanon: Comparing UNIFIL and the MNF', *Survival*,
Sept.–Oct. 1986, pp. 399–422.

attention once again to this unfashionable topic remains salutary.[22]

(b) THE MEANS OF PURSUING WAR

Hugo Grotius contributed not only to the idea that international law places limits upon the circumstances in which a state is able to resort to war, but also to our perception that the means of pursuing war—even war lawfully entered into— may not be unlimited. *Jus in bello*, as this branch of international law is called, is not explicitly mentioned in the UN Charter. But the United Nations, especially since the early 1970s, has shown a keen interest in promoting *jus in bello* and in developing international humanitarian law, alongside the International Committee of the Red Cross. Grotius, long before the 1899 and 1907 Hague Conventions, argued that the prohibition of unnecessary suffering was the leading precept of *jus in bello*. He urged that unnecessary fighting be avoided, and he advanced early and constraining ideas on the doctrine of military necessity. As Geoffrey Best put it in a paper on Grotius and humanitarian law:

It was above all Grotius who brought the non-combatant firmly onto the stage of warfare and set the pattern for that categorization of 'protected persons' which provides the *dramatis personae* of international humanitarian law. It must be doubtful whether any greater single stroke has ever been struck on the non-combatant's behalf.[23]

This Grotian principle has, of course, been under enormous pressure in recent years, not only because military convenience has often urged that it should be ignored (this is nothing new) but because the methods of contemporary warfare, with their reliance on guerrillas and irregulars, make it increasingly hard to distinguish combatant from non-combatant. However, in all the horrors we have witnessed, and in the important

[22] Report of the Secretary-General, GAOR, 37th session, Supplement No. 1, A/37/1.

[23] Geoffrey Best, 'The Place of Grotius in the Development of International Humanitarian Law', in A. Dufour *et al.* (eds.), *Grotius et l'ordre juridique international* (Lausanne, 1985), p. 105.

diplomatic negotiations that led in 1977–81 to the conclusion of various legal instruments on humanitarian law,[24] the Grotian distinction between combatant and non-combatant has never been lost from sight.

(c) THE STATE'S MONOPOLY ON THE USE OF FORCE

Central to Grotius' enunciation of the law is the insistence that *bellum privatum* is largely forbidden.[25] War is essentially limited to the state. It was, in Grotius' view, critical to move away from what was commonplace at the time he was writing—namely, violence between families, groups, cities. The individual had an alternative remedy, that of litigation: and only if war was limited to states could it possibly be controlled. The limitations on the use of force imposed by Grotius' notions of *bellum justum* could only work if states asserted a monopoly over the use of force.

The law's increasing emphasis over the last 400 years on the state as the major actor on the international scene has, of course, reflected the reality. Until very recently this emphasis has been at the expense of the capacity of the individual to invoke international law. Indeed, the positivists of the nineteenth and early twentieth centuries denied a place to the individual as a subject of international law: any rights which the individual had in international law were made to depend solely upon the beneficence of the state. This was not Grotius' view. The invocation of human rights—rights inherent in the individual *vis-à-vis* the state—has only comparatively recently begun to present a release from the grip of the inter-state system.[26]

[24] Notably the 1977 Geneva Protocols I and II additional to the Geneva Conventions of 1949, the 1978 Red Cross Fundamental Rules of International Humanitarian Law Applicable in Armed Conflicts, and the 1981 UN Convention on Prohibitions or Restrictions on the Use of Certain Conventional Weapons which may be Deemed to be Excessively Injurious or to have Indiscriminate Effects; all conveniently reprinted in A. Roberts and R. Guelff (eds.), *Documents on the Laws of War*, 2nd edn. (Oxford, 1989).

[25] On this point see esp. Röling, 'Jus ad Bellum and the Grotian Heritage', p. 115 n. 5.

[26] See Higgins, 'Conceptual Thinking about the Individual in International Law', *New York Law School Law Review*, 24 (1978), pp. 11–29; and id., 'Human Rights: Some Questions of Integrity', *Modern Law Review*, 52 (1989), pp. 1–21.

The view that the state should have the monopoly of the use of force seems also to have had its heyday. So long as individuals did not resort to international force, they could be treated as non-combatants, states would know that they were limited in their responses, and violence could be controlled. Yet in recent years the United Nations has passed many resolutions which offer material and moral support to those fighting in 'wars of national liberation', though no clear basis for this is to be found in the text of the Charter.[27] Lest it be thought that this is simply a matter of the Third World and Eastern Europe imposing their numerical weight upon a reluctant West, it is appropriate to recall the UK and US support for the Mujaheddin of Afghanistan from 1979 onwards, and the US assistance to the 'contras' of Nicaragua in the 1980s. Support of non-state violence is all around us, and we should heed Grotius' warning that it is incompatible with the control of force, not least because, as he pointed out, only states have the authority to achieve their objectives without committing all the fire-power at their disposal. Self-restraint is a more plausible policy option for the nation-state than for non-state groups.

The main reason for the post-Second World War revival of the legitimation of non-state violence has been the emergence of the concept of self-determination.[28] So-called wars of national liberation occur when people entitled to self-determination take up arms against the government ruling the territory where they seek to exercise that right. It is thus impossible to speak of wars of national liberation without first having some idea of the right to self-determination. Broadly speaking, it is a right of peoples to decide upon their own economic and political destiny, and over the years the Western countries (which obviously include among their number many

[27] See Richard Falk, 'Intervention and National Liberation', in Bull, *Intervention in World Politics*, pp. 119–33; Ronzitti, 'Resort to Wars of National Liberation', in A. Cassese (ed.), *Current Problems of International Law* (Milan, 1975), pp. 319–50; and Heather Wilson, *International Law and the Use of Force by National Liberation Movements* (Oxford, 1988).

[28] Rigo Sureda, *The Evolution of the Right of Self-Determination: A Study of UN Practice* (Leiden, 1973); James Crawford, *The Creation of States in International Law* (Oxford, 1979), pp. 84–103; and Michla Pomerance, *Self-Determination in Law and Practice* (The Hague, 1982).

colonial and ex-colonial powers) have moved from the belief that this is a mere political aspiration to the acknowledgement that it is a legal right.

Grotius had some things to say about this topic, even though it did not go by this name. On the one hand: 'An unjust cause of war is the desire for freedom among a subject people.' On the other hand, with extraordinary liberalism he declared: 'An unjust cause of war also is the desire to rule others against their will on the pretext that it is for their good'.[29] He viewed the native Americans as having rights under international law, and rejected many of the legal pretexts for taking their tribal lands from them by force. The respect that he accords to indigenous peoples, and his refusal to use international law to justify, whether on grounds of religion or cultural superiority, their domination, shines out like a beacon among his contemporaries and successors.

Today the great debate is as to whether self-determination is a right applicable only to persons under alien or colonial rule (as some of the UN membership would hold) or whether it applies to all those who do not have the opportunity to participate in the public life of their own country and choose their own political system. Although Grotius did not, of course, address this point, the generosity and spirit of his remarks leave one in no doubt as to the answer that must be embraced by the international lawyers of today.

(d) THE SIGNIFICANCE OF GROTIUS TODAY

There are so many aspects of international life about which Grotius wrote that investigating whether contemporary developments properly reflect the ideals to which he pointed would be a huge task. In the contributions that were made to the various quatercentenary commemorative colloquia, for example, much attention was paid to whether his notions of distributive justice may be seen as supporting the so-called 'New International Economic Order'. There has also been study of whether the principles emerging from the 1982 Law

[29] *JBP*, book II, chap. 22, §§ 11 and 12.

of the Sea Convention represent a shift from traditional notions of freedom of the seas, notwithstanding the cooperative endeavour which has been the vehicle of such changes.

Grotius did not elaborate his great ideas in a vacuum. He wrote against the background of the struggle between the Dutch Republic and its component provinces. The Netherlands were at war with the King of Spain, who in 1580 also succeeded to the Portuguese crown. There was a struggle with the Portuguese for the control of overseas trade routes. Grotius' advocacy of the freedom of the seas and of the liberty of the Dutch to trade with the East Indies fitted entirely with the political objectives of his country.[30] By 1625 Grotius' views on this had been somewhat qualified; the Dutch East India Company had in its turn concluded exclusive trade treaties with local princes. Grotius defended this, not wholly convincingly, by contending that treaties were an exception to the general requirements of the Law of Nations, and that, in any event, the arrangement was less than monopolistic. Such points should not be ignored: we should not look at Grotius naïvely, blocking out that which we do not wish to see. But it is exactly because Grotius was a realist, and not what some today would pejoratively call a 'do-gooder', that his views command our respect. And even without donning rose-coloured retrospective spectacles, there has to be something extraordinary about a man who wrote in Latin in the early seventeenth century and whose words we study and invoke today in a vastly changed world.

Scholars have spoken of the articulation of great ideas (such as freedom of the seas, and restraint in war) as 'Grotian moments'. Richard Falk has suggested that the continuing relevance of such ideas is assured by focusing, not on the minutiae of international law rules, but on the spirit that underlies them. This has been termed the 'Grotian quest'—'a special sort of creativity that blends thought and imagination without neglecting obstacles to change.'[31]

---

[30] See the hard-headed appraisal by Roelofsen, 'Grotius and International Law', *Grotius Reader*, pp. 12–13. See also the chapters by Roelofsen and Röling in the present volume.

[31] Falk, 'Introduction' in Charles S. Edwards, *Hugo Grotius: The Miracle of Holland* (Chicago, Ill., 1981), p. xiii.

The United Nations is often regarded as an exasperating body. But it simply reflects the world we live in—and we no longer live in a world where the West can command automatic majorities or where indeed Western views necessarily prevail on a range of issues. Nor are our own actions and positions always as free from blemish as we would like to think. To seek to turn our back on the United Nations is as wholly unrealistic as to seek to opt out of the real world in which we live. While we may disagree with particular conduct, it is in fact extraordinary that the international community continues to have no quarrel with the text of the Charter which, many years after it was written, still effectively captures a Grotian moment. It is really up to all of us— whether diplomats, lawyers, politicians—not to turn aside now from the enormous difficulties that lie in the way of an effective United Nations, but to listen to the message of Hugo de Groot to this generation, and to renew our commitment to the Grotian quest.

Are Grotius' Ideas Obsolete in an Expanded World?

B. V. A. RÖLING

What is the significance of Grotius for our time and our world? Our interest specifically concerns work in the field of international law, the law of the sea, *jus ad bellum* (the law on resort to war), *jus in bello* (the law on the actual conduct of war), and his attitude with respect to the non-European world.

Do his teachings and opinions still have any significance for us? It is my thesis that in general they do not. I suggest that they have lost much of their import due to radical changes over the last four centuries. Three areas in which important changes have occurred are:

1. The development of technology.
2. The process of democratization within the nation-state.
3. The process of democratization in the world at large, that is, in the expansion of the number of states forming the legal community in which international law plays its role.

Largely as a result of these changes, many of Grotius' teachings are obsolete or even dangerous. However, he does provide us with an inspiring example of how law can and must be reshaped to meet vastly changed circumstances.

(a) THE IMPACT OF TECHNOLOGICAL CHANGE

It is quite clear that the development of technology has an impact on the social effects of prevailing principles and rules. This is clearly illustrated by the law of the sea. Grotius advocated the freedom of the seas, including the freedom of traffic and trade thereon as a God-given order through which the fruits of the earth might be shared by all people.[1] Freedom of action is the ageless wish of the powerful who are able to look after their own interests. The freedom of the seas concerned not only traffic and trade, but also exploitation and fishing. With the growth of technology came the possibility of exploitation of the sea-bed and subsoil (oil, minerals). Freedom of exploitation would lead to exploitation by the rich and technologically highly developed states. They would be the only states able to use this freedom. They would dominate the sea and sea-bed economically, as in former centuries they had dominated foreign lands politically.[2] Freedom, one might think, is a device of universal justice since, legally, it means equality for everyone. In practice, however, it opens possibilities only for those who have the means of making use of the opportunity. It serves in fact the interests of the rich and powerful.

Hence, with respect to the sea-bed, Malta proposed at the 1967 UN General Assembly to replace the regime of freedom by a regime of order, serving the whole of mankind, an order in which the poor and less developed nations might share in the benefits of exploitation. According to Ambassador Pardo's

---

[1] That at least was his original viewpoint. About the special situation which influenced this standpoint in 1604, see C. G. Roelofsen, 'Grotius and International Law: An Introduction to Some Themes in the Field of Grotian Studies', in L. E. van Holk and Roelofsen (eds.), *Grotius Reader* (The Hague, 1983), pp. 12 ff. Later, at a time when the United East India Company had concluded treaties with some native rulers, Grotius taught that the principle of freedom recognized exceptions concerning exclusive trade. In *JBP*, book II, chap. 2, § 24, Grotius answers in the affirmative to the question: 'Whether a contract is permissible with a people that it should sell its crops to those with whom it has made the contract, and not to others.' Such an arrangement is allowable 'if the people which buys is prepared to sell to others at a fair price. It makes no difference, in fact, to other nations, from whom they buy what satisfies the demands of nature.' This is especially lawful 'if the people which has obtained the concession has taken the other under its protection and on that account is incurring expense'. On this fundamental change in Grotius' teachings see Frans de Pauw, *Grotius and the Law of the Sea* (Brussels, 1965).

[2] US President Lyndon Johnson declared in 1966: 'Under no circumstances, we believe, must we ever allow the prospects of rich harvest and mineral wealth to create a new form of colonial competition among the maritime nations. We must be careful to avoid a race to grab and hold the lands under the high seas. We must ensure that the deep seas and the ocean bottoms are, and remain, the legacy of all human beings.' Quoted N. S. Rembe, *Africa and the International Law of the Sea* (Alphen aan den Rijn, 1980), p. 38.

initiative the riches of the sea-bed should be considered as the 'common heritage of mankind'.

The Maltese proposal led to a thorough review of the law of the sea by the Third UN Conference on the Law of the Sea (1973–82). The developing countries generally supported restriction of the 'freedom of the seas', which they considered to be a reprehensible product of the mighty maritime nations. In its report on the twenty-sixth session of the UN General Assembly, the Dutch Foreign Ministry wrote: 'The Western and East European nations were united in the defence of the universal value of the principles of law developed during the ages.'[3] It might as well have written: 'The highly developed capitalist and communist states were united in the defence of their economic interests in exploiting the sea-bed.'

After long diplomatic negotiations the UN Convention on the Law of the Sea was adopted in 1982. This treaty seeks to restrict the freedom of the seas, especially with respect to the exploitation of the sea-bed. It aims to replace the traditional freedom by a new international order, a segment, as it were, of a New International Economic Order.

The Reagan Administration, however, more or less killed the whole enterprise by withdrawing all former US support and by refusing to sign the treaty. The national economic interest in exploitation apparently prevailed over the world interest in the sharing of benefits. Regrettable as it is, this US attitude is more in conformity with Grotius' teachings than are the principles underlying the 1982 treaty.

Technological development has also, especially in recent decades, brought about fundamental changes in the field of weaponry: for example, nuclear weapons, missiles, and precision-guided munitions. If nuclear weapons—of which there are at present about 50,000—are ever used, the contesting parties will be totally destroyed; and there may be a risk, according to some experts, that human life on earth no longer will be possible. It is now possible that any limited war, started with conventional weapons, may escalate into a nuclear war between the great military alliances, even into a total nuclear war. This is much too great a risk!

[3] *Report on the 26th Session of the UN General Assembly, 21 Sept.–23 Dec. 1971* (State Printing Office, The Hague, 1972, Publ. no. 100), p. 71 (in Dutch).

Hence the conclusion: technology has made our weapons
unusable. Their use has become too risky. Should we,
therefore, abolish them? General disarmament—in the sense
of common reduction of armaments to an acceptable level—
has proven to be an impossibility up to now. Negotiations
since the Second World War have led to practically nothing:
instead an arms race has developed, resulting in an unprecedented capacity for overkill.

Would one-sided, unilateral disarmament be the solution?
If NATO were to disarm the Soviet Union could use its armed
power again. It could threaten with its nuclear power, and use
it without fear of retaliation. Consequently, the possession of
weaponry is needed to assure that the arms of the opponent
will remain unusable.

That is the present weapon dilemma: modern weapons are
unusable but for the time being indispensable. In such a
situation the only reasonable function of national armed
power is to provide for 'military security', and to try to ensure
that weapons will not be used; in short, to assure the
maintenance of peace. That is not only its sole reasonable
function, it is also its only legitimate function under present
international law. The UN Charter, in Article 2(4), forbids
the initiation of war. The state may use its armed power in
self-defence against an armed attack (Article 51), but only if
the opponent has initiated the use of force. This fundamental
prohibition of the use of force is reaffirmed and clarified by the
'definition of aggression' formulated in General Assembly
Resolution 3314 (XXIX) of 14 December 1974. According to
Article 5(1): 'No consideration of whatever nature, whether
political, economic, military or otherwise, may serve as a
justification for aggression.'[4]

[4] For elaboration of the present *jus ad bellum*, see my 'On the Prohibition of the Use of Force', in A. R. Blackshield (ed.), *Legal Change: Essays in Honour of Julius Stone* (Sydney, 1983), pp. 274–98. Many scholars accept a wider concept of the right of self-defence: they take the view that a state may defend with military means its vital interests against non-military violation. This opinion, however, runs counter to the wording and the system of the UN Charter. Art. 51 recognizes the right to use force in case of armed attack only. However, even this right is not unrestricted. It exists only 'until the Security Council has taken measures necessary to maintain international peace and security'. It is inconceivable that the Charter would recognize, next to this restricted right of self-defence against an armed attack, the unrestricted right of self-defence against a non-military violation of interests.

Great powers, however, are inclined to extend the function of their national armed power, so as to include also military defence against non-military violation of their interests. It is undeniable that national interests can be threatened or violated by non-military events, including developments in the political-ideological or economic spheres. Great powers are prone to adhere to a wider concept of security, including not only 'military security' but also 'ideological security' and 'economic security'. This means that they are prepared to react with military power in cases where their interests are affected by ideological developments or economic events. The Soviet Union reacted with armed power against ideological developments in Hungary (1956), Czechoslovakia (1968), and Afghanistan (1979). The United States interfered militarily in Guatemala (1954), Cuba (1961), the Dominican Republic (1965), and Grenada (1983). The United States seems to view revolts against military dictatorships, and indeed many other forms of social emancipation, as a first step to communism. The dependence on raw materials in foreign countries is considered by the United States as incompatible with national security. Hence the establishment of rapid deployment forces, now not used as a reaction against 'creeping communism' (as in Kennedy's time), but designed to assure a regular inflow of oil and scarce minerals for 'the satisfaction of our growing industrial needs'.[5]

Such policies are incompatible with the situation of unusable weaponry. They are, however, bolstered by Grotius' teachings about the 'just war'. From its inception the just war doctrine has been a doctrine concerning the right to start war. That doctrine not only has become obsolete, but outright dangerous. It is the hard-liners and the militarists in our society who appeal to that Grotian doctrine.[6]

[5] Further details in my paper, *The Impact of Nuclear Weapons on International Relations and International Law* (Polemological Institute of the University of Groningen, 1982), pp. 9 ff.

[6] Strong advocacy of the just war doctrine can be found in James Turner Johnson, *Just War Tradition and the Restraint of War: A Moral and Historical Inquiry* (Princeton, NJ, 1981). Johnson speaks of 'the contemporary rediscovery of just war thought as a source of moral wisdom' (p. 366). He holds the view that 'the *jus ad bellum* of contemporary international law does not measure up to the moral standard of justice; rather, its coalescence around the "aggressor-defender" dichotomy has led to an erroneous stress on the first resort to military force' (p. 328).

The third field in which the teachings of Grotius have been rendered obsolete by technology concerns the laws of war. Grotius' basic principle is that anything is allowable in war that is *ad finem belli*: 'In war things which are necessary to attain the end in view are permissible.'[7] Unnecessary suffering should be avoided. This principle is still a ground-rule of the laws of war, the only undisputed rule as a matter of fact. It is moreover a rule acceptable to the military. Unnecessary killing and devastation should be prohibited if only on military grounds. It merely increases hostility and hampers the willingness to surrender. But this rule is no longer deemed sufficient. Especially in this era of atomic weapons, nerve gases, biological weapons, and environmental modification techniques, more specific prohibitions are needed. The laws of humanity play a role.

In respect of new weapons, the parties to the 1868 St Petersburg Declaration reserved to themselves the right to come to an understanding 'to conciliate the necessities of war with the laws of humanity'. Weapons useful from the military point of view can still be forbidden as too cruel or too inhumane, as for example, the chemical and bacteriological weapons the use of which is outlawed in the 1925 Geneva Protocol.

The time of Grotius was an era of national arms build-up, not of arms restrictions. National armed power served the aim of state-building. The era of colonial conquests by European states had begun. The unrestrained freedom of the state to arm was an undisputed principle.

Because of the technological development of weaponry, the present world needs 'a new international military order' in which the right of a state to possess arms is not unlimited, and in which the right of the state to *possess* arms is linked with its right to *use* armed power.[8]

---

[7] *JBP*, book III, chap. 1, § 2.

[8] Treaties exist which restrict freedom of the state to arm, such as the 1968 Non-Proliferation Treaty and the 1972 Biological Weapons Treaty. The 'freezing' treaties (1959 Antarctica Treaty, 1967 Outer Space Treaty, 1971 Sea-bed Treaty), and the 'ceiling treaties' (as 1972 SALT 1) have the same effect. But most treaties contain a special *clausula rebus sic stantibus*, which entitles the state to withdraw from the treaty if new developments have jeopardized its supreme interests, that is its security. The world needs law of arms control and disarmament that is binding, and not dependent

The only legitimate function of national armed power is deterrence and defence—the provision of 'military security'. 'Military security' has two aspects. First of all it means that national armed power is sufficient to ensure that the opponent will not dare to attack. This is the aspect of 'enemy security'. The second aspect arises because weapon postures can form a danger of their own by putting a premium on haste: haste to start hostilities (for example, if both parties assume that they each possess the capability of a disarming first strike), or haste to escalate the fighting (for example, vulnerable weapons of mass destruction will be attacked immediately in case of hostilities; the expectation of this attack may lead to their immediate use before destruction). A military posture should aim at eliminating such destabilizing features. If the weapons are such that they do not contribute to the danger of war, one may speak of 'weapon security'. The distinction is useful. Measures to enhance 'enemy security' may diminish 'weapon security'—as in the case of the building up of 'superiority' in armed power. All this points to the need for a prohibition of an offensive military posture, of destabilizing armed power, and of excessive weaponry.

In such a 'military order' deterrence would have the features of defensive, inoffensive, unprovocative deterrence. If both parties in the Cold War relationship would agree to restrict their armed power to such a military posture, their security would be enhanced. Carter and Brezhnev agreed on 18 June 1979 to continue

for the purposes of reducing and averting the risk of outbreak of nuclear war, to seek measures to strengthen strategic stability by, among other things, limitations on strategic offensive arms most destablizing to the strategic balance and by measures to reduce and to avert the risk of surprise attack.

on the moods of a government. For further elaboration of the concept and indication of the steps that could lead to this progressive development of international law see my contributions 'Arms Control, Disarmament and Small Countries', in *Impact of Science on Society*, 31 (1981), pp. 97–112; and 'The International Law of Arms Control and Disarmament', in Marek Thee (ed.), *Armaments, Arms Control and Disarmament* (UNESCO, 1981), pp. 272–80.

These negotiations might have led to the first step in the direction of a strategy of inoffensive deterrence.[9]

(b) DEMOCRATIZATION IN THE NATION-STATE

The second factor of change since Grotius' time is the development of democracy within the nation-state, meaning the development from government by a small élite to participation by the whole adult population. As a consequence the character of the national state changed from the 'night watchman state', which is responsible only for law and order, and internal and external security, to the Welfare State, which is responsible for the well-being of all its subjects, including the poor. This implies intervention where needed in the economic market-mechanism, adoption of a full-employment policy, and the assumption of some responsibility with respect to medical care, housing, and education.

This democratic development also caused a change in domestic law: from 'liberal law' to 'social law', from law having as its main function the adjustment of the freedom of the one to the freedom of the other, to a law aiming at the protection of the weak against the might of the powerful, and aiming to assist the helpless where needed. Principles of law concerning the duties of the community to those of its subjects not able to take care of themselves were recognized, as well as principles of law expressing solidarity and awareness of the fact that the well-being of the one was related to the well-being of the other.

All this contributed to such an enormous extension of the function of the nation-state, that in many fields state functions could not be fulfilled without international co-operation. Thus it contributed to the growing international interdependence, needing new international structures and new principles and rules of international law.

[9] US–USSR Joint Statement of Principles and Basic Guidelines for Subsequent Negotiations on the Limitation of Strategic Arms, Vienna, 18 June 1979. Further elaboration of the concept of 'defensive deterrence' is contained in my contribution, 'The Feasibility of Inoffensive Deterrence', in *Bulletin of Peace Proposals*, 1978, pp. 339–47.

(c) THE DEVELOPMENT OF DEMOCRACY IN THE WORLD
COMMUNITY

The third reason why Grotius' teachings have become
obsolete is the change in the composition of the international
legal community, and the gradual development of democracy
in the world community.

Grotius lived in a transition period. Behind him lay the
medieval period, in which Europe was more or less vertically
organized under Emperor and Pope. Before him lay the
modern world of national sovereign states, horizontally
organized in a more or less anarchical order, a world which
found its formal establishment in the 1648 Peace of Westphalia.

It was also a transition period in respect of the *kind* of law
that played a role. A gradual change has taken place from
'natural law' to the 'positive law' expressed in treaties or
customs. Grotius' *De Jure Praedae* (1604) was still based on
natural law, and partly on 'God-ordained' law. In his *De Jure
Belli ac Pacis* (1625) we find a mixture: natural law still plays a
considerable role, but he recognizes the impact of treaties,
which can even make exceptions to some rules of natural law.
This change in type of law implied a change in the
applicability of the law: a change from universal law (the law
of nature applied in principle to everyone) to law that
pertained in Europe, between European states based on
European treaties and customs.

1. Amity Lines and Spheres of Influence

The remnants of medieval institutions were still in evidence in
Grotius' time. One example was the concept of the 'amity
lines', the *'lignes d'amitiés et d'alliances'*, separating Europe
from the non-European world.

The background to this concept lay in the Pope's commission
to Portugal in the fifteenth century to bring the Christian
message to the non-European world. It was the beginning of
colonization, justified by the blessings of Christianity, but at
the same time leading to the dominating position of him who
brought the happy message. It was the first clear case of what

we nowadays call 'ideological aggression'. Spain then demanded its share, and the Pope, in the Bull *'Inter Caetera'*, divided the world between Portugal and Spain.[10] This first division of the non-European world was demarcated in degrees of longitude and latitude.

The northern European countries refused to recognize the authority of the Pope to grant the non-European world (in a typical feudal medieval setting) to Spain and Portugal. Negotiations between France and Spain followed, leading to the second division of the non-European world in the form of the 1559 Treaty of Cateau-Cambrésis. Reibstein describes this treaty as the first 'agreement to disagree'.[11] The treaty provided for the drawing of 'amity lines' along the first meridian and the Tropic of Cancer. Beyond those lines Spain claimed the monopoly of relations with what we now call the 'Third World', but France rejected this claim. It was agreed that 'beyond the line' power would decide. In practice it amounted to this: beyond the line colonization would proceed in military competition, but such fighting need not necessarily mean war in Europe.

Grotius did know about these 'amity lines', but he does not mention the concept in his writings. At the Colonial Conference between England and Holland, in 1615, he proposed to King James I that Spain be ejected from its possessions by a joint military action. James refused, declaring that he did not wish to start a war against Spain. Grotius explained, according to the official record, that he had not asked for offensive war or for a general rupture of the English peace with Spain, and that it was well known how little peace the English and the French already had with the Spaniards 'beyond the line'. Grotius maintained that hostilities 'beyond the line' need not involve war in Europe.[12]

---

[10] On the history of the division between Spain and Portugal and the 'amity lines' see Adolf Rein, *Der Kampf Westeuropas um Nordamerika im 15. und 16. Jahrhundert* (Stuttgart, 1925). Ernst Reibstein gives in his *Völkerrecht I Von der Antike bis zur Aufklärung* (Freiburg, 1958) the text (in German) of the pertinent parts of the Bull *'Inter Caetera'* (pp. 268–72) and of the Treaty of Tordesillas (pp. 272–6).

[11] Ernst Reibstein, *Völkerrecht I Von der Antike bis zur Aufklärung*, pp. 417–18.

[12] See G. N. Clark and W. J. M. van Eysinga, 'The Colonial Conferences between England and The Netherlands in 1613 and 1615', *Bibliotheca Visseriana*, 17 (1951), p. 114.

Another form of division, and one proclaimed unilaterally from outside Europe, was the Monroe Doctrine (1823). This division, however, still had a European origin: Canning proposed the doctrine to the American president as a riposte to the Holy Alliance's effort to expand its power in South America. Later Canning stated, not without some pride: 'I called the New World into existence to redress the balance of the Old.' The Monroe doctrine still plays a role. It was cited in the American gunboat diplomacy against Grenada in 1983.

The concept of the amity lines seems to have some validity even in our time, not in a competition about colonial possessions but in the struggle for 'spheres of influence', the modern form of political domination. In Vietnam half a million American soldiers fought against Soviet weapons. But in the mean time there was peace in Europe, and arms control agreements were even concluded between the United States and the Soviet Union.

2. *The Expansion of the International Community*

From the sixteenth century onwards, notions of universal natural law represented by such writers as Francisco de Vitoria (1480–1546) were replaced by the positive international law of the small group of European states. Gradually this élite group grew to include non-European states. This gradual extension is clearly shown in the growing number of states participating in what were considered to be 'world conferences'. Five states participated in the 1648 Peace of Westphalia, eight in the 1814–15 Congress of Vienna, sixteen in the 1863 Red Cross Conference, 14 in the 1885 Berlin Africa Congress, 26 in the 1899 First Hague Peace Conference, and 44 in the 1907 Second Hague Peace Conference. The membership of the League of Nations grew from 42 to 63. The 1928 Pact of Paris (the Kellogg–Briand Pact) was binding for 63 states. The United Nations started with 51 members and by 1985 had 159 members.

In that gradual extension and in this process of gradual democratization of the world community we can distinguish three periods. The members of the first small élite group called themselves 'Christian Nations', the central common value being Christianity. This phase lasted from about 1648 to 1856. By the 1856 Peace Treaty of Paris, Turkey was admitted 'to participate in the public law and concert of Europe'. Henceforth the members of the group referred to themselves as the group of 'civilized nations'. The central common value was considered to be 'civilization', a vague concept which primarily connoted the capacity and willingness to give legal protection to foreign trade and merchant traffic. But military power and military conduct could also play a role. At the beginning of the twentieth century Japan was admitted after its victorious wars against China and Russia. At a celebration of this happy admittance a Japanese diplomat is reported to have said: 'As soon as we showed ourselves your equals in scientific butchery we were at once admitted at your council tables as civilized men.' The period of the 'civilized nations' lasted until 1945. According to the UN Charter membership of the organization is open to 'peace-loving states' (Article 4). Christianity, civilization, peace. The central value gets diluted and loses some of its content, and the numbers of adhering nations become bigger, now even tending towards universality.

Officially all nations are now peace-loving. In the first years—after the outbreak of the Cold War—the non-communist majority of the UN members refused to admit several 'socialist countries' with the argument that such states were not peace-loving. But in the package deal of 1955 these states were admitted, and at present every independent state able and willing to accept the obligations of the Charter can become a UN member.

The legal world has expanded and now comprises almost all nations.[13] Positive international law, originally European law, has now become world law.

In each of the different periods the significance of the central value—Christianity, civilization, peace—was three-fold. First, it determined the group of states to which international law pertained. Second, arguments in favour of progressive development of international law referred to the requirements of the central value: Christianity, civilization, or

---

[13] Further elaboration of this process in my *International Law in an Expanded World* (Amsterdam, 1960).

peace. Third, the common value formed the reason and justification of dominant positions. At the 1885 Berlin Africa Congress, a part of Central Africa was given to the Belgian king as a colony 'to bring the blessings of civilization to the natives'. In our time appeals are made to the demands of peace to justify the discrimination in the 1968 Nuclear Non-Proliferation Treaty which intends to ensure that the 'nuclear have-nots' are 'nuclear have-nevers'.

The broadening of the international legal community from a small group to practically the whole world signified not only a change in quantity but also in quality. The original small group was formed by rather well-to-do, self-supporting states. They were in favour of the freedom to pursue their own interests. They created liberal law to regulate their mutual relations and considered the law's most important function to be the adjustment and harmonization of their respective freedoms. The states which were admitted in the period of the 'civilized nations' belonged to approximately the same category. At least they accepted the prevailing international law as a condition of admittance to the 'charmed circle'. With the entry of Latin American states came a demand for some alterations, and the development of the concept of regional American international law.

After the decolonization of Asia and Africa the new independent states demanded entry into the world legal community but without accepting all the provisions of prevailing international law. As a matter of course they claimed equality and the right to participate in decision-making in the various international organizations. But their main point of difference concerned the great underlying principles of law. It was not primarily freedom they expected from international law, because they knew from experience that liberty favours the strong and the wealthy. As relatively poor and powerless states they wanted not 'liberal law' but 'social law'. They wanted legal protection against the power-ful, assistance from the international community in their state of disadvantage, changes in the structure of international society, and interference where necessary with the economic market-mechanism through a New International Economic Order. These claims were analogous to the earlier claims of the working classes in the North concerning the domestic legal systems.[14]

(d) GROTIUS' IRRELEVANCE TO PRESENT NEEDS

Positive law as considered from the viewpoint of sociology is the product of three factors: interests, power positions, and prevailing values. All three factors changed when poor and underdeveloped states came to form a majority in the world legal community. Consequently international law should be adapted to the new factual situation if it is to be recognized and respected by all participants. A plea for such a change is not an expression of idealism and is not asking for Utopia. It is realism in the sense of taking reality into account. What we were willing to do and achieved in domestic law, *mutatis mutandis*, must be applied to international law. That is not a question of good will, but a question of good sense. It means progressive development of international law; it is an attempt to change the primitive anarchy of the world state system into a mature anarchy.[15] That implies an international order in which the state system is maintained. States and peoples differ too much in interests and in values for 'one world' to be feasible. The slogan 'One world or none' may contain more than a grain of truth, but 'one world' is impossible without an unacceptable dictatorial setting. A mature anarchy means an international order in which states are willing to respect each other's sovereignty, but in which this sovereignty is restricted by legal rules. It is an order in which 'the benefits of fragmentation could be enjoyed without the costs of continuous

[14] The analogy between the national and international process of democratization is striking in many respects. In both communities the newcomers' behaviour differed from that of the former élite. This is unsurprising, for they had been excluded from that company and had lived in different circumstances. The newcomers were resented and were often not taken seriously because they spoke 'slang' and did not behave in the usual manner. But their proposals were rational and valuable, because—living at the shadowy side of society—they had 'the relevant experience'. One might say that in a democratizing society good legislators may have bad manners.

[15] Suggestions of required changes are discussed by Hedley Bull, *The Anarchical Society* (London, 1977), pp. 315 ff.

struggle and instability'.[16] It would imply the acceptance of a New International Economic Order, needed for the short term to promote and stimulate economic development in the Third World, and for the long term to establish the framework for the management of economic interdependence.

In all this Grotius cannot be our guide. He formulated a law that served the needs of the existing legal community—a law that made it possible for the European states to conquer and dominate the greater part of the non-European world, and to do so in good conscience, firm in the conviction that, as Grotius affirmed, God was the source of this right.

Grotius' achievement was the introduction of the principle that sovereign states, too, are bound by rules of law. But he formulated a system of legal rules which implied that it was the sovereign state itself which was to decide when its rightful interests were threatened or had been violated, or when injustices demanding punishment had been committed. If rights were threatened or harmed and injustices were in evidence, the state had the right to go to war, for this was a means whereby justice might be maintained.

In the Middle Ages the just war doctrine had served to buttress the claims and practices first of the papacy and then of the national monarchies and city-states.[17] The just war doctrine as elaborated by Grotius served the European states' desire for expansion and conquest very well. On balance, it recognized that states could legally resort to war for many reasons. In book II of *De Jure Belli ac Pacis* Grotius starts with the question: 'What causes of war may be called justifiable?' The answer is clear: 'No other just cause for undertaking war can there be excepting injury received.'[18] The list of just causes amounts to defence, recovery of property, and punishment.[19] The state does not, in strict law, need to wait until interests are violated, as the threat of such violation already justifies military action if the danger is immediate and certain.[20] Punishment is allowed not only for injury received

---

[16] Barry Buzan, *People, States and Fear: The National Security Problem in International Relations* (Brighton, 1983), p. 96.

[17] Frederick H. Russell, *The Just War in the Middle Ages* (Cambridge, 1975), p. 297.

[18] *JBP*, book II, chap. 1, § 1.4.   [19] Ibid., book II, chap. 1, § 2. 2.

[20] Ibid., book II, chap. 1, § 2. 1 and § 5. 1.

by the states that inflict the punishment but also 'on account of things done contrary to the law of nature, although not against them or their subjects.'[21] 'Wars are justly waged against those who treat Christians with cruelty for the sake of their religion alone'; 'war may justly be waged against those who show impiety toward the gods they believe in'; 'wars may rightfully be undertaken . . . on behalf of allies of equal or unequal standing'; 'wars may rightfully be undertaken on behalf of friends'; 'wars, finally, may rightfully be undertaken on behalf of any persons whatsoever'.[22]

In *De Jure Praedae* Grotius wrote: 'A just cause of war exists when the freedom of trade is being defended against those who would obstruct it.'[23] In *De Jure Belli ac Pacis* he made an exception to this in case of treaties with the native government concerning exclusive trade.[24]

Grotius spoke of 'the great society of states', but it was rather Europe he had in mind. He was a typical representative of a powerful state, convinced of the righteousness of his government. (This is especially evident in *De Jure Praedae*.) He was silent about the horrors committed in the Indies and elsewhere; he was also silent about the contents of the iniquitous peace treaties concluded with subjected peoples.

Grotius was praised all over the world, by hawks and doves. What he wrote sounded lofty and could be considered to be on a high moral level. It is therefore understandable that jurists, moralists, and theologians praised Grotius highly as a man of peace who had demonstrated that the behaviour of states was governed by rules of law.

---

[21] *JBP*, book II, chap. 20, § 40. Emer de Vattel criticized this opinion: 'It is surprising to hear the learned and judicious Grotius tell us that a sovereign can justly take up arms to punish Nations which are guilty of grievous crimes against the natural law, which treat their parents in an inhuman manner . . .'. In this respect Vattel wonders: 'Did not Grotius perceive that in spite of all the precautions added in the following paragraphs, his view opens the door to all the passions of zealots and fanatics, and gives to ambitious men pretexts without number?' *The Law of Nations*, 1758 (Classics of International Law, Washington, DC, 1916), book II, chap. I, par. 7, p. 116.

[22] *JBP*, book II, chap. 20, § 49; chap. 20, § 51; chap. 25, § 4; chap. 25, § 5; chap. 25, § 6.

[23] *Commentary on the Law of Prize and Booty* (Classics of International Law, Oxford, 1950), chap. 12, p. 262.

[24] *JBP*, book II, chap. 2, § 24.

But kings and governments too could accept Grotius' teachings with eagerness. For they alone were called upon to interpret these rules. And this at a time when the European powers—in the usual manner of mighty states—judged their actions to be always right and benevolent.

In short, the enormous popularity of Grotius' doctrine becomes comprehensible when we recognize that in theory it could gratify the high-minded because it pointed to the way which could reasonably lead to a better world—while in practice it did not restrict in any way the endeavour to subjugate the non-European peoples to European authority. It justified with moral prescripts even the most selfish political acts. Thus was inaugurated an epoch in which aggressive state behaviour, aimed at the expansion of power and wealth, could perpetually be disguised in terms of the preservation of rights and of the costly duty of upholding justice.

(e) THE RESPONSIBILITIES OF LAWYERS AT A 'GROTIAN MOMENT'

No other conclusion is possible: in view of the changed circumstances Grotius' teachings are for a considerable part obsolete. In many respects they are even dangerous, when advocating the right to start war.

Why then the many commemorations of his quadricentenary? Why still pay attention to his work?

Grotius is still an inspiring figure. He lived in a period of fundamental transition: transition from the Middle Ages to modern times. He did much to develop a modern international law suitable to meet the needs of the new nation-states which had arisen on the ruins of the medieval world.[25]

He lived in what Richard Falk called 'a Grotian moment':[26] a time in which a fundamental change of circumstances

---

[25] E. H. Carr, *The Twenty Years' Crisis 1919–1939: An Introduction to the Study of International Relations* (London, 1939), p. 223.

[26] Richard A. Falk, 'On the Recent Further Decline of International Law', in A. R. Blackshield (ed.), *Legal Change: Essays in Honour of Julius Stone* (Sydney, 1983), p. 272.

created the needs for a different world structure and a different international law. At the present we are living in a similar situation, again in a Grotian moment. Our needs are clear. They are the needs of an interdependent world, threatened by weapons of mass destruction, a world that knows of mass poverty and hunger. Present international law and the contemporary world structure are no match for these challenges. Our legal needs are determined by the hard facts of atomic weapons, of 800 million starving people, of interdependence. But we are not only concerned with those hard facts: the soft facts—tradition, our fears and mistrust, our nationalism, our short-sightedness—determine what is attainable. A wide gap exists between our needs and our capacities.

Lawyers have a special responsibility in such circumstances. They are the experts who should recognize that present international law—measured according to its own values and goals—is bad law. They are also the ones who can formulate the 'natural law of the atomic age': the law capable of serving the goals and values of our present time. They can use this natural law as an inspiration and as a guiding principle to achieve a change in positive international law—a gradual change, a peaceful change—with the aim, not to create paradise on earth, but to make our world more livable, with a diminished fear of mankind's destruction and with the prospect of an end to mass starvation. Modest aims! But aims of vital importance.

It is the task of governments to reach for these aims. But the lawyers are indispensable for the opening of feasible roads, and for the introduction of methods and steps that may lead to a law suited to serve the needs of the time.

We live in a Grotian moment and apparently are unable to fulfil the Grotian task. Here I see the significance of honouring Grotius: not in an adherence to his teachings which are hardly applicable in our time, but to be reminded of his achievement in formulating a new law for a new time that could serve the interests of the legal community for which he wrote: the élite circle of European states.

At present international lawyers serve a greater community, an expanded world, the whole of mankind. This demands another kind of law, a law that has still not been adequately formulated, let alone realized.

It is my deep conviction that lawyers fail in their historic mission if they hesitate to tackle the political and sensitive issues connected with the progressive development of international law. In honouring Grotius, we lawyers are reminded of a gigantic task before us, and of a heavy responsibility.

The Grotius Factor in International Law and Relations: A Functional Approach

GEORG SCHWARZENBERGER

With commendable decisiveness, two crowned heads expressed themselves on Huig de Groot or, in his Latinized version, Hugo Grotius (1583–1645).[1] While Henry IV of France exalted him as 'le miracle de Hollande',[2] James I of England considered him a 'pedant, full of words'.[3] More ambiguously, Gustavus Adolphus of Sweden is supposed to have rested his royal head during his campaigns on Grotius' *De Jure Belli ac Pacis Libri Tres*.[4]

Assessments of Grotius by other, and less exalted, figures across three centuries range from various shades of grey to whiter than white.[5] More than one distinguished critic has described Grotius' *chef-d'œuvre* as unreadable, and Grotius has

[1] On the history of Grotius' family name, see 'Grotius on Good Neighbours', *Times Literary Supplement*, 1 Sept. 1945, p. 409.

[2] Actually, Henry IV was merely replying in kind to the fifteen-year-old Grotius' flattering ode in his honour—partly perhaps because, as fate would have it, Grotius was also a protégé of the leader of a politically important Dutch mission to France. On this meeting see Jean de Burigny, *Life of Grotius* (orig. pub. in French, Paris, 1752; ref. is to the English trans., London, 1754), pp. 9–11; W. S. M. Knight, *The Life and Works of Hugo Grotius* (London, 1925), pp. 34–5; and F. E. Wolf, *Grotius, Pufendorf, Thomasius* (Tübingen, 1927), p. 9.

[3] If Archbishop Abbot's report is accurate, it reflects the irritation of James I on at least three grounds: undue length of Grotius' addresses in the royal presence during his 1613 London visit, inopportune and highly pragmatic proposals of his to the English merchants, and unwelcome solicitations of support for the Arminian section of Dutch Calvinism. Knight, *Life and Works of Hugo Grotius*, pp. 143–5.

[4] De Burigny, *Life of Grotius*, pp. 135–6, maintains that a copy of *JBP* was found in Gustavus' tent after his death.

[5] For early illustrations see ibid., pp. 314–17; and for a balanced assessment, see J. L. Brierly's observation that Grotius 'is great enough to dispense with the undiscriminating adulation which is often showered upon him. This adulation has done disservice to international law by encouraging a servile imitation of his methods.' *The Law of Nations*, 2nd edn. (Oxford, 1936), p. 27.

gradually faded into a Grotian tradition or has come to be claimed as part and parcel of a Grotian heritage.

The problematical character of Grotius' 'afterlife' suggests that a different approach should be adopted: isolation, as far as possible, of the Grotius factor in international law and relations, and functional analysis of the liability of his name and fame to be used for extraneous purposes.

This chapter is divided into three sections. Section (a) is concerned with Grotius' *persona*—a term intended to draw attention to the conditioning elements in Grotius' family background, upbringing at home, and further education at Leiden University. In Grotius' *fama*, discussed in section (b), his *persona* with all its masks tends to become over-shadowed by contemporary and posthumous awareness on the part of others of—at least to them—attractive and useful features of his work. It forms the basis of Grotian traditions, and of claims to participation in a Grotian heritage. The compound of Grotius' *persona et fama* may be termed the Grotius *factor*, which is the subject of section (c). Both constituent elements of the Grotius factor vary according to the changing selections made by 'Grotians' and others at different times.

(a) PERSONA

Grotius was born into a Delft patrician family, closely linked with Holland's other burgher oligarchies. The financial security of this background, and the assurances which Calvinist determinism held out to the elect, provided a measure of stability during the struggle of the Low Countries for independence from Spain.

Hugo's brightness, and his father's own intellectual interests and ambitions for the most promising of his sons, led almost automatically to the next phase in the growing-up process of a gifted youngster: a classical education in a humanist atmo-sphere at a hothouse pace.

His professional career also promised to develop according to a stereotype—based on a combination of merit and the hardly veiled preference of his senior peers for a deserving scion of the ruling caste. Yet the liberal Calvinists and opponents of centralized political power in Holland, a group to which Grotius and his family belonged, underestimated both the possibility of Prince Maurice, the Stadtholder, making common cause with the forces of orthodox Calvinism, and his ruthlessness in pursuing his political objectives. The anti-centralist and moderate Calvinist opposition suffered defeat, and Grotius was imprisoned for life. By his wife's ingenuity, he made his legendary escape to Antwerp and Paris. Yet Richelieu's earlier interest in Grotius did not prevent the exile from being treated whenever possible as a purely nominal ambassador of the Swedish Crown to the French Court. In the circumstances, Grotius had ample leisure to excel as a man of letters, pursue his diverse interests, and publish several of the major works on which his fame came to rest.

(b) FAMA

As might be expected from a seventeenth-century polymath, Grotius' fame extends to a number of fields. They include theology, history, social philosophy, jurisprudence, and law.

1. Persona et Fama

Grotius' *persona*—his family background, readiness to accept established authority, successful passage through a demanding education, and his own perceptiveness—provided a tempting object for self-identification for contemporary and subsequent generations of academics and practitioners. What proved especially attractive to Grotius' personality were his erudition and touches of Erasmian liberalism, self-doubt, and a tendency towards middle positions between contending camps. What was even more reassuring was his almost automatic, and positive, response to the needs of congenial establishments and the rewards they could be expected to bestow on him.[6]

---

[6] See e.g. Grotius' treatment of the form of Dutch government at the time in his *De Antiquitate Reipublicae Batavicae* (1610), and D. P. O'Connell, *Richelieu* (London, 1968), p. 304.

2. From Advocacy to System

A long-hidden continuity in effort and reasoning links Grotius' probable advocacy on behalf of the Dutch East India Company in a famous prize case in 1604 before the Admiralty Court of Amsterdam with *De Jure Belli ac Pacis* (1625).[7]

It took over three hundred years to uncover the gradual process of abstraction and generalization that led Grotius from a brilliant *ad hoc* effort in about 1604 to his *magnum opus* of 1625. In between, Grotius elaborated his original argument more fully in his *De Jure Praedae Commentarius* (written *c.*1604–6 and eventually published 1868), *Mare Liberum* (published anonymously in 1609—actually a chapter from *De Jure Praedae*), and his response (eventually published in 1872) to Welwood's attacks in 1613 and 1615 on *Mare Liberum*.[8]

As a prominent member of a Dutch diplomatic mission to London in 1613, Grotius responded to the needs of his employers and artfully defended a position more akin to that of *mare clausum* than *mare liberum*.[9] Similarly, during his Paris exile, he found it prudent to express complete concurrence with Welwood's attempted refutation of *Mare Liberum* and

---

[7] See, further, Robert Fruin, *An Unpublished Work of Grotius* (1868), English translation in *Bibliotheca Visseriana*, 5 (1925). Subsequent references to *JBP* are to the *last* edition revised by Grotius (1646), repr. in facsimile (Classics of International Law, Washington, DC, 1925).

[8] With a not uncommon identification of the interests of his employer—then the Dutch East India Company—with those of his country, Grotius admitted: *'opus de Mari libero optimo scriptum in patriam animo'*. Letter to Camerarius, 20 May 1637, in B. L. Meulenbroek (ed.), *Briefwisseling van Hugo Grotius*, viii (The Hague, 1971), p. 303.

It is also rewarding to consider Lauterpacht's hypothesis *ad hominem* on Grotius' motivations for writing *JBP* in 1623–4: 'Neither can the possibility be dismissed that the treatise which he was writing—an exile without private means to support himself and his large family—was being prepared with an eye to diplomatic employment and that, for that purpose, it would have been of advantage to gain the reputation of a lawyer who takes fully into account the practice of states.' 'The Grotian Tradition in International Law', *British Year Book of International Law 1946*, p. 13.

[9] On Grotius' 'volte-face', see J. H. W. Verzijl, *International Law in Historical Perspective*, iv (Leiden, 1971), p. 35; and T. W. Fulton, *The Sovereignty of the Sea* (Edinburgh, 1911). Actually, the thesis advanced by Grotius in London could be squared with the view that, like other principles of secondary natural law, the principle of the freedom of the seas could be overriden by positive law, municipal law, and international law alike. See e.g. *JBP*, book II, chap. 3, §§ 8, 10, and 12–14.

remain silent on the claims of Gustavus Adolphus to *dominium maris Baltici.*[10]

Any novel emphasis on the international law of peace as the counterpart to the law of war is less than apparent from the main divisions of Grotius' *De Jure Belli ac Pacis Libri Tres*, or from the arrangement of the individual chapters in each of its three books. Similarly, in the subject-matter covered under the heading 'The Law of Peace', *De Jure Belli ac Pacis* exceeds less than may be thought the topics treated in Alberico Gentili's *De Jure Belli Libri Tres* (London, 1598–9, and Hanover, 1612). Thus, Grotius' decision to amplify the title of Gentili's work may well have been due to awareness of the unwisdom of appropriating to himself a title that was not his, and doubts on the adequacy of his acknowledgements to an earlier fellow-author in their common field.[11]

The claim to the presentation of a comprehensive system of international law, implicit in the title, gave Grotius' treatise a special appeal. It also strengthened the case for presenting the 1648 Peace of Westphalia as the beginning of a new era, founded on the preponderance, on the Continent, of France and aligned anti-Habsburg powers, as well as on claims in favour of Grotius as *the* father of international law.

3. The Grotian Approach

The Grotian treatment of natural and international law can be condensed into three propositions: First, primary natural law is immutable and would exist even if God did not.[12] Second, secondary natural law, which is based on primary

[10] On Grotius' silence after the publication of Selden's *Mare Clausum*, see Willem de Groot's letter of 14 Jan. 1636 to his brother Hugo, in B. L. Meulenbroek (ed.), *Briefwisseling van Hugo Grotius*, vi (The Hague, 1967), p. 474. On the claims of Gustavus Adolphus and his successors to sovereignty of the Baltic Sea, which were well served by Selden's argument, see Fulton, *The Sovereignty of the Sea*, p. 375.

[11] *JBP* contains six citations from Gentili's *JB*. In general terms, Grotius acknowledged (with qualifications) his indebtedness to Gentili in Prolegomena 38. What is more problematic is whether Grotius acknowledged his debt to Gentili in the places in which he 'borrowed' most. See, further, T. E. Holland's Oxford Inaugural Lecture (1894), repr. in *Studies in International Law* (Oxford, 1898), p. 2; and Peter Haggenmacher's chapter in the present volume.

[12] In the 1631 edition of *JBP*, Grotius strongly qualified the passage (Prolegomena 11) on God's inability to change primary natural law which had appeared in the 1625 edition. See also Prolegomena 12, and book I, chap. 1, § 10. 5.

natural law, coexists with positive law but may be modified by the latter.[13] Third, the principles of natural law and rules deduced from these principles may manifest themselves at any time and in any walk of life. Thus, they can be demonstrated by evidence of any kind and from any quarter—holy or otherwise.[14]

4. Grotius' Uses

In his declining years, Grotius—unwanted in his homeland, without offers of condign posts from other princes, and precariously poised in his Swedish employment—considered himself as having failed in his life's ambitions.[15]

Actually, Grotius remained highly esteemed by other literati. Yet there was little that guardians of *raison d'état* of his time in the class of Richelieu and Father Joseph could learn from Grotius. Their secret archives, diplomatic correspondence, sophisticated treaties, and the pamphlets of their scribes for public consumption, all attest to the competence, the training in casuistry, and the growing richness, of the practice of European international law.[16]

Even so, these masters of statecraft would concede the marginal usefulness of works such as *De Jure Belli ac Pacis*. Their clerks and pamphleteers might beneficially adumbrate some of their *ad hoc* arguments with selective references to, and quotations from, suitable sections in Grotius' treatise.

Among topics in Grotius' discourses that come to mind are

[13] On permissible modifications of natural law by positive national or international law, see e.g. Grotius' doctrines on the freedom of the seas and *bellum justum*.

[14] In some cases as, for instance, on the prohibition of retaliation against an ambassador for offences of the sending state (*JBP*, book II, chap. 18, § 7), Grotius evaluates the evidence offered. In others, he draws from conflicting evidence merely the conclusion that, as on the choice of government, everybody may please himself (ibid., book I, chap. 3, § 8). This approach provides splendid opportunities for arguments either way.

[15] The writer respectfully dissents from Grotius' last words: 'By undertaking many things I have accomplished nothing.' Knight, *The Life and Work of Hugo Grotius*, p. 289. On the tercentenary of Grotius' death, Cecil Hurst, President of the Grotius Society, described Grotius as 'a great man, and yet a lonely and pathetic figure'. Letter to *The Times*, 29 Aug. 1945.

[16] See e.g. Thomas Rymer's *Foedera* (20 vols., London, 1704–35); C. J. Burckhardt, *Richelieu* (4 vols., Munich, 1935–67); E. A. Beller, *Propaganda in Germany during the Thirty Years War* (Princeton, NJ, 1940), p. 13.

sovereignty and the legitimacy of all civil authority,[17] the
scope for subversion and intervention in the dominions of
other sovereigns,[18] hegemonial preponderance,[19] relativity of
the pledged word,[20] the right to take reprisals and the
elasticity of just causes of resort to war (*jus ad bellum*),[21]
freedom of action in warfare (*jus in bello*) and neutrality,[22] the
right of unilateral annexation of occupied enemy territory,[23]
overseas expansion,[24] and the legality of slavery.[25]

Growing forces of public opinion with tendencies towards
rationalism, liberalism, and pacifism could only increase the
attractiveness of an approach, such as that of Grotius, that
was safe on the essentials of establishment policies but could
be used selectively whenever convenient in diplomatic exchanges,[26] adversary proceedings,[27] and, on suitable occasions,

[17] Grotius defines sovereignty as that power 'whose actions are not subject to the
legal control of another, so that they cannot be rendered void by the operation of
another human will' (*JBP*, book I, chap. 3, § 7). For all practical purposes, the
internal monopoly of legitimate force held by governments is complete. See ibid.,
book I, chap. 4, §§ 1, 2, 7, 8, and 20; book III, chap. 19, § 6.

[18] In *JBP*, Grotius provides most of the ideological justifications required for
purposes of subversion *or* intervention. See book II, chap. 20, § 40; and chap. 25,
§§ 2–3. See also the chapter by R. J. Vincent in the present volume.
On the competition between Spain and France for control of the border of
Switzerland and Italy, see Duke of Sully (Maximilien de Béthune), *Memoirs* (English
trans., Edinburgh, 1770), iii. 365–70; iv. 213–4. For the continuation of this rivalry in
the Thirty Years War see C. V. Wedgwood, *The Thirty Years War* (London, 1938),
p. 31.

[19] Relying on Thucydides, Grotius in *JBP* upheld both the compatibility of
hegemony with the sovereignty of the unequal party, and the legality of such
hegemonic arrangements. See *JBP*, Prolegomena 22; book I, chap. 3, § 21; book III,
chap. 3, § 4.

[20] See ibid., book III, chaps. 19–25. There always remains *clausula rebus sic stantibus*.
See ibid., book III, chap. 19, § 14.

[21] On reprisals, see ibid., book III, chap. 2, § 2; and chap. 19, § 15. On *jus ad bellum*,
see ibid., book II, chap. 1, § 2; chap. 17, § 19; and chap. 23, § 5.

[22] On killing and inflicting injury, see ibid., book III, chap. 4, §§ 2, 6, 8, 9, 15, and
17. On acquisition of enemy property, see ibid., book III, chap. 4, § 1; chap 5, §§ 1 and
4; and chap. 6, § 18. On neutrality, see ibid., book III, chap. 17, § 3.

[23] See ibid., book III, chap. 6, § 4; chap. 8, § 4.

[24] See ibid., book II, chap. 5, § 31; chap. 9, § 5; chap. 15, § 8; chap. 20, § 49.

[25] *JBP*, book III, chap. 7, §§ 1 and 2; and chap. 14, § 9.

[26] See e.g. the US argument of 24 June 1824, and the British reply of 19 July 1824,
in the St Lawrence controversy. H. A. Smith, *Great Britain and the Law of Nations*, ii
(London, 1935), pp. 329 and 332–6; or Clive Parry (ed.), *A British Digest of
International Law*, iib, Part III (London, 1967), p. 132.

[27] See e.g. the *Lusitania Cases* (German–US Mixed Claims Commission, 1923):
referring to *JBP* (book II, chap. 17, § 22) on money as the common measure of

even in faint support of public yearnings for better things to come.[28]

5. The Mantle of Grotius

Were Grotius to review his afterlife, he might find that what he regarded as failure in his lifetime was not the worst fate that could have befallen him. What fame brought to him, as to others before and after, was reduction to a mere object at anyone's mercy.

Successive political systems in countries existing in Grotius' time and in others then unborn have differed but little in their own hierarchical structures and oligarchic 'élites' from those of their predecessors. Similarly, international systems of open power politics and power politics in disguise have come and gone over the generations since Grotius. They all required establishment-orientated professionals and intellectuals at large. If these were to perform their appointed tasks well, they could hardly avoid using eclectic techniques in their masters' service, and never was this type of pragmatism more in vogue than in the institutional superstructure of our latter-day world systems of power politics in disguise. Yet who would want to be called an eclecticist or pragmatist if, in full concord with other augurs in similar predicaments, he was welcome to common cover under the ample mantle of Grotius, a Grotian tradition or a Grotian heritage?

(c) THE 'GROTIUS FACTOR': PRESENT-DAY RELEVANCE

In the present phase of an increasingly irrational confrontation between the superpowers, the over-mighty and their advisers might do worse than recall at least one of Grotius'

---

valuable things (*Reports of International Arbitral Awards*, vii. 35); and *The Trial of German Major War Criminals: Proceedings of the International Military Tribunal sitting at Nuremburg, Germany* (23 vols., London, 1946–51): de Menthon, Counsel for France, part 4, p. 369; Stahmer, Counsel for the Defendant Göring, part 18, p. 120; and Krantzbühler, Counsel for the Defendant Dönitz, part 19, pp. 9 and 23.

[28] On arbitration as a consensual alternative to war, see *JBP*, book II, chap. 23, § 8; book III, chap. 20, § 46.

counsels: *temperamentum* (moderation).[29] Yet while there is life there is hope. While both last, it may be permissible (if primarily for purposes of *l'art pour l'art*) also to reflect on narrower and more technical facets of Grotius' continuing relevance.

1. Methods

Empirically verifiable evidence of international law and relations was harder to come by in the early years of the seventeenth century than in the following century with its steadily growing volume of published state papers and treaty collections. Moreover, with Article 38 of the 1920 Statute of the Permanent Court of International Justice—re-enacted with minor modifications in Article 38 of the 1945 Statute of the International Court of Justice—organized international society took a major step forward in the codification and development of international law. These two Statutes provide, in legally binding form for the Court and parties before it, a readily verifiable basis for ascertaining the actual rules of international law, the range of principles abstracted from these rules, and the transformation of natural law—that is, international morality—into international law.

Naturalist philosophers, including Grotius, made a major contribution of their own to the study of international relations: their reflections and speculations on the nature of international society provided the beginnings of a framework for understanding international relations, including international law.

That these synopses should have been coloured by the optimistic or pessimistic predispositions of their authors is understandable. What is less easy to accept is the failure of subsequent generations of 'Grotians' to refine the analyses of pioneer-thinkers by using the aids offered by such scholars as Henry Sumner Maine, Karl Mannheim, and R. G. Collingwood.

To Maine, and to subsequent continental sociologists, we owe the distinction between models of *society* and *community*. A

[29] Ibid., book III, chaps. 11–16.

society requires but a low level of social integration and consists principally of members with, in the typical case, diverging or conflicting interests. A community tends to attain a higher degree of integration, and primarily relies on the service principle and the overriding character of common interests.

To Mannheim we owe the distinction between *ideologies* and *Utopias*. While the typical object of ideologies is the defence of sectional interests in a particular group, that of Utopias is to suggest improvements which, without fundamental changes in the character and structure of the group concerned, are likely to remain unattainable.

Finally, to Collingwood we owe a refinement of a distinction familiar to the naturalists, including Grotius. While they treated states of *savagery* and *barbarism* as synonymous, Collingwood limited savagery to a state preceding civilization, and barbarism to a state following more civilized behaviour in and by the group concerned.

Each of these six categories can assist in assessing more accurately the specific character of past and present international societies. Conversely, the non-use of these categories provides its own clues. For example, to call societies 'communities', or to say of contemporary world society that it is an 'international community', serves an ideological or Utopian purpose rather than a descriptive one.

2. *International Law*

Six fundamental principles can be abstracted from the practice of international law in different international societies across nearly three millennia: sovereignty, recognition, consent, good faith, international responsibility, and self-defence. Yet it was not until the writings of Grotius that European international law came to include what might be regarded as the seventh fundamental principle: the freedom of the seas.

Notwithstanding an impressive extension of the functional scope of contemporary international law and the addition of a hypertrophy of institutional superstructures, the Law of Nations, especially at the level of the superpowers, still appears to be as liable to self-interpretation and abuse as at

the time of Grotius. It must suffice to illustrate this sceptical
diagnosis by reference to five of the areas mentioned in section
(b) above on *fama*.

(i) Heterogeneity of World Society Similar to the Grotian
legitimation of almost any civil authority, contemporary
international customary law and the law of the United
Nations treat alike democratic, authoritarian, and totalitarian
states (or, with stronger emphasis on their socio-economic
structure, mixed, near-monopolistic, and state-capitalist entities) as well as groups in various stages of the civilizing process
or decline into barbarism at home and abroad.

(ii) Destabilization Since the days of Richelieu and Gustavus
Adolphus, subversion and intervention in other sovereign
states have changed in form rather than substance. Recognition and support of rival regimes in one and the same state
have become widely practised routines of 'destabilization'.

(iii) Hegemony In Thucydides' apt terminology, dominant
partners of alliances and members of global and sectional
confederations exercise their pre-eminence as of old.

(iv) Relativity of the Pledged Word Unless strong reciprocal
interests or an occasional acknowledgement of overriding
common interests generate the requisite good faith,[30] the
techniques of unilateral interpretation, suspension or termination of consensual obligations, especially on sensitive political
or military issues, have remained remarkably constant.
Especially in the relations between the superpowers, general
unwillingness to agree to third-party examination of contested
facts, let alone the arbitral or judicial settlement of any issue
in dispute—and their pronounced distrust of the good faith of
the other side on matters of political significance—appear to
have been as prevalent as they were in the seventeenth
century.

(v) Jus in Bello In the scale of destruction of life, property,
and environment, the Second World War and the *de facto* wars
fought since by the superpowers or their proxies appear to

[30] On this point, Grotius remains as relevant as ever. See *JBP*, book III, chap. 25,
§ 1.

compare unfavourably even with the horrors of the Thirty Years War. Yet who would deny the present-day relevance of Grotius' verdict, above all if applied to the potential and actual use of biological, chemical, and nuclear doomsday-weaponry: 'a lack of restraint in relation to war, such as even barbarous races should be ashamed of'?[31]

3. International Relations

In any assessment of the present-day relevance of the Grotius factor in international relations, a question that deserves reconsideration is the optimal scope of the interdisciplinary exploration of contemporary world affairs.

There will always be the need for specialization. Yet if this takes place otherwise than within the framework of a general theory of international relations, specialization is likely to produce technicians and robots for ideological or Utopian uses, rather than teachers and scholars worthy of the name. In the present-day condition of the world as a single activity area, the notion of a world society appears to offer the most promising framework for the study of international relations.

Similarly, while in its global character present-day international society differs from its predecessors, it shares with them reliance on power as the overriding motivation in matters considered vital, especially in the higher echelons of a highly stratified world oligarchy.

---

[31] *JBP*, Prolegomena 28.

Select Bibliography

This is an introductory guide to further reading on the themes explored in this book. It includes some, but by no means all, of the works referred to in the chapters in this book. It is concerned only with works bearing on the subject of Grotius and International Relations, and the emphasis is on those written in English. Standard general works on international law, the history of international law, political philosophy, and the history of ideas have in most cases been omitted. A useful bibliography of major pre- and post-Grotian works in international law is included in Haggenmacher, *Grotius et la doctrine de la guerre juste* (Paris, 1983).

For further references the reader can consult works listed in the bibliographical section below. These works have been very helpful in the preparation of this select bibliography; we gratefully acknowledge also the kind assistance provided by the staff of the Grotius Institute in The Hague.

Relatively few articles are listed here. Several important articles and essays are included in the collections of essays listed in sections 3 and 4 below. Periodicals containing germane articles have included:

Bibliotheca Visseriana (Leiden, 1923–64).
Grotiana (1928–47).
Grotiana, NS (Assen, 1980–) (cited in this bibliography simply as *Grotiana*).
Grotian Society Papers (Madras, 1964; The Hague, 1968 and 1972).
Grotius annuaire international (The Hague, 1913–48).
Transactions of the Grotius Society (London, 1916–59).

This select bibliography is divided into the following sections: 1. Grotius' Works (main editions of relevant works by Grotius, and English translations of these works); 2. Bibliographical Works; 3. Biographical works (accounts of Grotius' life and works in the context of the seventeenth century); and 4. Secondary Literature (works dealing with Grotius' ideas and bearing on international relations issues: (a) books and (b) articles).

1. GROTIUS' WORKS

Mare liberum sive de iure quod Batavis competit ad Indicana commercia dissertatio. Leiden: Elzevier, 1609.

—— trans. Ralph van Deman Magoffin. New York: OUP, 1916; repr. New York: Arno, 1972.

De Jure Belli ac Pacis Libri Tres. In quibus ius naturae & Gentium, item iuris publici praecipua explicantur. Paris: Buon, 1625; Amsterdam: I. Blaeu, 1646; Leiden: Brill, 1939 (ed. B. J. A. de Kanter-van Hettinga Tromp).

—— abridged translation by William Whewell. Cambridge and London: John W. Parker, 1853.

—— trans. Francis W. Kelsey, with the collaboration of Arthur E. R. Boak, Henry A. Sanders, Jesse S. Reeves, and Herbert F. Wright. Oxford: OUP, 1925 (Classics of International Law); repr. New York: Oceana; London: Wildy & Sons, 1964.

Inleidinge tot de Hollandsche Rechts-Geleerdheid. The Hague: Van Wouw, 1631; Leiden: Universitaire Pers Leiden, 1952.

—— trans. R. W. Lee. Oxford: OUP, 1926.

Annales et Historiae de Rebus Belgicis. Amsterdam: Blaeu, 1657.

—— trans. T. Manley. London: Twyford and Paulet, 1665.

De Jure Praedae Commentarius. Ed. G. Hamaker. The Hague: Nijhoff, 1868.

—— trans. Gwladys L. Williams with the collaboration of Walter H. Zeydel. Oxford: OUP, 1950 (Classics of International Law); repr. New York: Oceana; London: Wildy & Sons, 1964.

Defensio Capitis Quinti Maris Liberi, in S. Muller, *Mare Clausum.* Amsterdam: Frederik Muller, 1872, pp. 331–61.

—— trans. Herbert F. Wright. *Bibliotheca Visseriana,* 7 (1928), pp. 154–205.

The Opinions of Grotius as Contained in the Hollandsche Consultatien en Advijsen, collated, trans., and annot. D. P. de Bruyn. London: Stevens and Haynes, 1894.

Briefwisseling van Hugo Grotius. 12 vols. to 1988, ed. P. C. Molhuysen, B. L. Meulenbroek, *et al.* The Hague: Nijhoff, 1928– (continuing).

2. BIBLIOGRAPHICAL WORKS

EYFFINGER, A. C., *et al. The Grotius Collection at the Peace Palace: A Concise Catalogue.* The Hague: Peace Palace Library, 1983.

—— 'Grotius Commemoration 1983: Inventory of Major Events and Issues'. *Grotiana,* 6 (1985), pp. 71–83.

GELLINEK, CHRISTIAN. *Hugo Grotius*. Boston, Mass.: Twayne, 1983, pp. 147–57.

HAGGENMACHER, PETER. *Grotius et la doctrine de la guerre juste*. Paris: Presses Universitaires de France, 1983, pp. 645–72.

HOLK, L. E. VAN. 'Selective Bibliography of Books on the Life and Legal Writings of Grotius', in *Grotius Reader: A Reader for Students of International Law and Legal History*, ed. L. E. van Holk and C. G. Roelofsen. The Hague: T. M. C. Asser Instituut, 1983, pp. 45–54.

MEULEN, JACOB TER, and DIERMANSE, P. J. J. *Bibliographie des écrits imprimés de Hugo Grotius*. The Hague: Martinus Nijhoff, 1950.

—— *Bibliographie des écrits sur Hugo Grotius imprimés au XVIIe siècle*. The Hague: Nijhoff, 1961.

NELLEN, HENK J. M. 'Grotius, l'homme et l'œuvre: aperçu bibliographique'. *XVIIe Siècle*, 35 (1983), pp. 499–502.

SCHOEPKE, KARL. 'Hugo Grotius (10 Apr. 1583–28 Aug. 1645): Eine teilweise annotierte Auswahlbibliographie', in *Beiträge zum nationalen und internationalen Seerecht*, vii, *Hugo Grotius: 1583–1645*, ed. Friedrich Elchlepp, *et al.* Rostock: Gesellschaft für Seerecht der Deutschen Demokratischen Republik, 1983, pp. 39–132.

WILLEMS, J. C. M. 'Bibliography'. *Grotiana*, 1 (1980), pp. 141–54; ibid., 2 (1981), pp. 123–33; ibid., 6 (1985), pp. 115–23; ibid., 8 (1987), pp. 120–31 (continuing).

3. BIOGRAPHICAL WORKS

BRANDT, CASPAR, and CATTENBURGH, ADRIAAN VAN. *Historie van het leven des heeren Huig de Groot*. Dordrecht and Amsterdam: Van Braam en Onder de Linden, 1727; 2nd edn., 1732.

BURIGNY, JEAN-LEVESQUE DE. *Vie de Grotius, Avec l'Histoire de ses Ouvrages, Et des Négociations auxquelles il fut employé*. Amsterdam: M. M. Rey, 1754. (First publ. in 2 vols., Paris, 1752.)

DUFOUR, ALFRED. 'Grotius—homme de loi, homme de foi, homme de lettres', in *Grotius et l'ordre juridique international*, ed. A. Dufour *et al.* Lausanne: Payot, 1985, pp. 9–32.

DUMBAULD, EDWARD. *The Life and Legal Writings of Hugo Grotius*. Norman, Okla.: University of Oklahoma Press, 1969.

EYSINGA, W. J. M. VAN. *Hugo Grotius: Eine biographische Skizze*, trans. Plemp van Duiveland. Basle: Benno Schwabe, 1952.

FRUIN, R. 'Hugo de Groot en Maria van Reigersbergh'. *De Gids*, 22 (1858), pp. 289–323 and 417–74.

HOLK, L. E. VAN. 'Hugo Grotius, 1583–1645, A Biographical Sketch', in *Grotius Reader: A Reader for Students of International Law and Legal History*, ed. L. E. van Holk and C. G. Roelofsen. The Hague: T. M. C. Asser Instituut, 1983, pp. 23–44.

Hugo Grotius: A Great European 1583–1645. Delft: Meinema, 1983.

KNIGHT, W. S. M. *The Life and Works of Hugo Grotius*. London: Sweet & Maxwell, 1925.

LEE, ROBERT W. *Hugo Grotius*. London: H. Milford, 1930.

—— 'Grotius: The Last Phase, 1635–45', *Transactions of the Grotius Society*, 31 (1945), pp. 193–215.

NELLEN, HENK J. M. *Hugo de Groot (1583–1645): De loopbaan van een geleerd staatsman*. Weesp: Uitgeverij Heureka, 1985.

PATTISON, MARK. 'Grotius', in *Encyclopaedia Britannica*, 11th edn. Cambridge: 1910, xii. 621–4.

VREELAND, HAMILTON. *Hugo Grotius, the Father of the Modern Science of International Law*. New York: OUP, 1917.

4. SECONDARY SOURCES

(a) Books

ALTING VON GEUSAU, F. A. M., *et al. Ex Iure: Veertien Opstellen bij het Veertiende Lustrum van Societas Iuridica Grotius en de Vierhonderdenvijfde Geboortedag van Grotius*. Arnhem: Gouda Quint, 1987.

ASSER INSTITUUT. *International Law and the Grotian Heritage*. The Hague: T. M. C. Asser Instituut, 1985.

BLACK, VIRGINIA (ed.) *Vera Lex*, 4 (1983–4), nos. 1–2.

BOXER, C. R. *The Dutch Seaborne Empire, 1600–1800*. London: Hutchinson, 1965.

DICKINSON, EDWIN DE WITT. *The Equality of States in International Law*. Cambridge, Mass.: Harvard University Press, 1920.

DUFOUR, ALFRED, HAGGENMACHER, PETER, and TOMAN, JIRI (eds.) *Grotius et l'ordre juridique international: travaux du colloque Hugo Grotius, Genève, 10–11 novembre 1983*. Lausanne: Payot, 1985.

EDWARDS, CHARLES S. *Hugo Grotius The Miracle of Holland: A Study in Political and Legal Thought*, with an Introduction by Richard A. Falk. Chicago, Ill.: Nelson-Hall, 1981.

ELCHLEPP, FRIEDRICH, *et al.* (eds.) *Hugo Grotius: 1583–1645*. Rostock: Gesellschaft für Seerecht der Deutschen Demokratischen Republik, 1983.

ELDERS, J. M., *et al.* (eds.) *Hugo Grotius: 1583–1643* (Maastricht Colloquium). Assen: Van Gorcum, 1984.

EYSINGA, W. J. M. VAN. *Sparsa Collecta: een aantal der verspreide geschriften*. Leiden: Sijthoff, 1958.

FIGGIS, JOHN. *Studies of Political Thought from Gerson to Grotius, 1414–1625*. Cambridge: CUP, 1907.

FIKENTSCHER, WOLFGANG. *De fide et perfidia: Der Treuegedanke in den "Staatsparallelen" des Hugo Grotius aus heutiger Sicht*. Munich: Bayerischen Akademie der Wissenschaften, 1979.

FORTUIN, HUGO. *De natuurrechtelijke grondslagen van de Groot's volkenrecht*. The Hague: Nijhoff, 1946.

FULTON, THOMAS W. *The Sovereignty of the Sea*. Edinburgh and London: Blackwood, 1911.

HAGGENMACHER, PETER. *Grotius et la doctrine de la guerre juste*. Paris: Presses Universitaires de France, 1983.

HOFFMAN, G. (ed.) *Rostocker philosophische Manuskripte* 23 (1982).

HOLK, L. E. VAN, and ROELOFSEN, C. G. (eds.) *Grotius Reader: A Reader for Students of International Law and Legal History*. The Hague: T. M. C. Asser Instituut, 1983.

HUIZINGA, J. H. *Dutch Civilization in the Seventeenth Century and Other Essays*, trans. Arnold J. Pomerans. London: Collins, 1968.

KALTENBORN VON STACHAU, CARL, BARON. *Die Vorläufer des Hugo Grotius auf dem Gebiete des Ius naturae et gentium sowie der Politik im Reformationszeitalter*. Leipzig: Gustav Mayer, 1848.

KEEN, MAURICE H. *The Laws of War in the Late Middle Ages*. London: Routledge & Kegan Paul, 1965.

LANGE, CHRISTIAN L. *Histoire de l'internationalisme*, i. *Jusqu'à la paix de Westphalie (1648)*. Kristiania: Norwegian Nobel Institute, 1919.

MEULEN, JACOB TER. *Der Gedanke der Internationalen Organisation in seiner Entwicklung*, i. *1300–1800*. The Hague: Nijhoff, 1917.

MICHELIS, FIORELLA DE. *Le origini storiche e culturali del pensiero di Ugo Grozio*. Florence: La Nuova Italia Editrice, 1967.

MOLEN, GESINA H. J. VAN DER. *Alberico Gentili and the Development of International Law: His Life, Work and Times*. 2nd edn., Leiden: Sijthoff, 1968.

MURPHY, C. F. *The Search for World Order*. Dordrecht: Nijhoff, 1985.

Na Oorlog en Vrede: Twaalf opstellen bij het dertiende lustrum van Societas Iuridica Grotius en de vierhonderdste geboortedag van Grotius. Arnhem: Gouda Quint, 1984.

OMPTEDA, DIETRICH H. L. VON. *Litteratur des gesammten sowohl natürlichen als positiven Völkerrechts*. Regensburg: J. L. Montag, 1785.

OTTENWÄLDER, PAUL. *Zur Naturrechtslehre des Hugo Grotius*. Tübingen: Mohr, 1950.

OUDENDIJK, JOHANNA K. *Status and Extent of Adjacent Waters: A Historical Orientation*. Leiden: A. W. Sijthoff, 1970.

Panebianco, Massimo. *Ugo Grozio e la Tradizione Storica del Diritto Internazionale.* Naples: Editoriale Scientifica, 1974.

Pauw, Frans de. *Grotius and the Law of the Sea,* trans. P. J. Arthern. Brussels: Éd. de l'Institut de Sociologie, 1965.

Phillipson, Coleman. *The International Law and Custom of Ancient Greece and Rome,* 2 vols. London: Macmillan, 1911.

Remec, Peter Pavel. *The Position of the Individual in International Law according to Grotius and Vattel.* The Hague: Nijhoff, 1960.

Riphagen, W., *et al. Hugo de Groot 1583–1645* (Amsterdam Symposium). Zwolle: Tjeenk Willink, 1983.

Royal Netherlands Academy of Arts and Sciences. *The World of Hugo Grotius (1583–1645).* Amsterdam and Maarssen: APA–Holland University Press, 1984.

Russell, Frederick H. *The Just War in the Middle Ages.* Cambridge: CUP, 1975.

Schama, Simon. *The Embarrassment of Riches: An Interpretation of Dutch Culture in the Golden Age.* London: Collins, 1987.

Tex, Jan den. *Oldenbarnevelt,* 2 vols. Cambridge: CUP, 1973.

Todescan, Franco. *Le radici teologiche del giusnaturalismo laico,* i. *Il problema della secolarizzazione nel pensiero giuridico di Ugo Grozio.* Milan: Giuffrè, 1983.

Tooke, Joan. *The Just War in Aquinas and Grotius.* London: SPCK, 1965.

Tuck, Richard. *Natural Rights Theories: Their Origin and Development.* Cambridge: CUP, 1979.

Vollenhoven, Cornelis van. *The Three Stages in the Evolution of the Law of Nations.* The Hague: Nijhoff, 1919.

—— *Verspreide Geschriften,* i. Haarlem: Tjeenk Willink, and The Hague: Nijhoff, 1934.

Wolf, Dieter. *Die Irenik des Hugo Grotius nach ihren Prinzipien und biographisch-geistesgeschichtlichen Perspektiven.* Marburg: N. G. Elwert, 1969.

Wolf, Erik. *Grosse Rechtsdenker der deutschen Rechtsgeschichte.* 4th edn., Tübingen: Mohr, 1963, pp. 253–310.

(b) Articles

Ago, R. 'Le Droit international dans la conception de Grotius'. *Recueil des Cours de l'Académie de Droit International,* 182 (1983), pp. 375–98.

Basdevant, Jules. 'Hugo Grotius', in *Les Fondateurs du droit international. Leurs œuvres—leurs doctrines.* Éd. A. Pillet, Paris: V. Giard & E. Brière, 1904, pp. 125–267.

BOURQUIN, MAURICE. 'Grotius est-il le père du droit des gens?', in *Grandes figures et grandes œuvres juridiques*. Geneva: Georg, 1948.

—— 'Grotius et les tendances actuelles du droit international'. *Revue de Droit International et Législation Comparée*, 7 (1926), pp. 86–125.

BOZEMAN, ADDA B. 'On the Relevance of Hugo Grotius and De Jure Belli ac Pacis for Our Times'. *Grotiana*, 1 (1980), pp. 65–124.

BULL, HEDLEY. 'The Grotian Conception of International Society', in *Diplomatic Investigations*. *Essays in the Theory of International Politics*, ed. Herbert Butterfield and Martin Wight. London: Allen & Unwin, 1966, pp. 51–73.

CHIU, H. 'Hugo Grotius in Chinese International Law Literature', in Asser Instituut, *International Law and the Grotian Heritage*. The Hague: T. M. C. Asser Instituut, 1985, pp. 310–13.

CLARK, G. N., and EYSINGA, W. J. M. VAN. 'The Colonial Conferences between England and The Netherlands in 1613 and 1615'. *Bibliotheca Visseriana*, 15 (1940); ibid., 17 (1951).

DONELAN, MICHAEL. 'Grotius and the Image of War'. *Millennium*, 12 (1983), pp. 233–43.

DRESDEN, SAMUEL. *Beeld van een verbannen intellectueel: Hugo de Groot*. Amsterdam: Noord-Hollandsche Uitgevers Maatschappij, 1983.

DUFOUR, A. 'Grotius et le droit naturel du dix-septième siècle', in *The World of Hugo Grotius (1583–1645)*. Amsterdam and Maarssen: Royal Netherlands Academy of Arts and Sciences, 1984, pp. 15–41.

EIKEMA HOMMES, HENDRIK VAN. 'Grotius on Natural and International Law'. *Netherlands International Law Review*, 30 (1983), pp. 61–71.

FEENSTRA, R. 'Quelques remarques sur les sources utilisées par Grotius dans ses travaux de droit naturel', in *The World of Hugo Grotius (1583–1645)*. Amsterdam and Maarssen: Royal Netherlands Academy of Arts and Sciences, 1984, pp. 65–81.

FORIERS, PAUL. 'L'Organisation de la paix chez Grotius et l'école du droit naturel'. *Recueils de la Société Jean Bodin pour l'Histoire Comparative des Institutions*, 15 (1961), pp. 275–376.

FORTUIN, HUGO. 'Grotius en de neutraliteit'. *Tijdschrift voor International Recht*, 1 (1953–4), pp. 121–39.

FRUIN, ROBERT. 'An Unpublished Work of Hugo Grotius's'. *Bibliotheca Visseriana*, 5 (1925), pp. 1–74.

GREWE, W. G. 'Grotius—Vater des Völkerrechts?' *Der Staat*, 23 (1984), pp. 161–78.

GROS ESPIELL, HECTOR. 'En el IV centenario de Hugo Grocio. El nacimiento del Derecho de Gentes y la idea de la comunidad internacional', in *Pensamiento jurídico y sociedad internacional. Estudios en honor del profesor D. Antonio Truyol y Serra*, i. Madrid: Centro de Estudios Constitucionales, 1986.

GUGGENHEIM, PAUL. 'Les Origines de la notion autonome du droit des gens', in *Symbolae Verzijl*. The Hague: M. Nijhoff, 1958, pp. 177–89.

HAAKONSSEN, KNUD. 'Hugo Grotius and the History of Political Thought'. *Political Theory*, 13 (1985), pp. 239–65.

HAGGENMACHER, PETER. 'Genèse et signification du concept de "ius gentium" chez Grotius'. *Grotiana*, 2 (1981), pp. 44–102.

—— 'Mutations du concept de *guerre juste* de Grotius à Kant'. *La Guerre: Actes du Colloque de Mai 1986*. Cahiers de philosophie politique et juridique, No. 10. Caen: Université de Caen, 1986, pp. 107–25.

—— 'On Assessing the Grotian Heritage', in Asser Instituut, *International Law and the Grotian Heritage*. The Hague: T. M. C. Asser Instituut, 1985, pp. 150–60.

—— 'Sur un passage obscur de Grotius: Essai de réponse à Cornelis van Vollenhoven'. *Tijdschrift voor Rechtsgeschiedenis (The Legal History Review)*, 51 (1983), pp. 295–315.

HART, A. C.'t. 'Hugo Grotius and Giambattista Vico'. *Netherlands International Law Review*, 30 (1983), pp. 5–41.

HAUSMANINGER, HERBERT. '"Bellum iustum" und "iusta causa belli" im älteren römischen Recht'. *Österreichische Zeitschrift für öffentliches Recht*, 11 (1961), pp. 335–45.

HOLLAND, THOMAS E. 'Alberico Gentili'. In Thomas E. Holland, *Studies in International Law*. Oxford: OUP, 1898, pp. 1–39.

JIMÉNEZ DE ARÉCHAGA, E. 'The Grotian Heritage and the Concept of a Just World Order', in Asser Instituut, *International Law and the Grotian Heritage*. The Hague: T. M. C. Asser Instituut, 1985, pp. 5–24.

JOHNSON, JAMES TURNER. 'Grotius' Use of History and Charity in the Modern Transformation of the Just War Idea'. *Grotiana*, 4 (1983), pp. 21–34.

KENNEDY, DAVID. 'Primitive Legal Scholarship'. *Harvard International Law Journal*, 27 (1986), pp. 1–98.

KILNER, JOHN F. 'Hurdles for Natural Law Ethics: Lessons from Grotius'. *American Journal of Jurisprudence*, 28 (1983), pp. 149–68.

KOOIJMANS, P. H. 'How to Handle the Grotian Heritage: Grotius and Van Vollenhoven.' *Netherlands International Law Review*, 30 (1983), pp. 81–92.

KOSTERS, J. 'Les Fondements du droit des gens. Contribution à la théorie générale du droit des gens'. *Bibliotheca Visseriana*, 4 (1925), pp. 1–273.

LACHARRIÈRE, GUY LADREIT DE. 'The Controversy Surrounding the Consistency of the Position Adopted by Grotius', in Asser

Instituut, *International Law and the Grotian Heritage*. The Hague: T. M. C. Asser Instituut, 1985, pp. 207–13.

LACHS, M. 'The Grotian Heritage, the International Community and Changing Dimensions of International Law', in Asser Instituut, *International Law and the Grotian Heritage*. The Hague: T. M. C. Asser Instituut, 1985, pp. 198–206.

LANDHEER, BART. 'The Grotian Model of a World System'. *Grotiana*, 1 (1980), pp. 17–32.

LAUTERPACHT, HERSCH. 'The Grotian Tradition in International Law'. *British Year Book of International Law 1946*, pp. 1–53.

LE FUR, LOUIS. 'La Théorie du droit international depuis le XVIIᵉ siècle et la doctrine moderne'. *Recueil des Cours de l'Académie de Droit International*, 18 (1927), pp. 263–442.

MEYLAN, PHILIPPE. 'Grotius et l'école du droit naturel', in *Hommage à Grotius*. Lausanne: F. Rouge, Librairie de l'Université, 1946.

MÜNCH, FRITZ. 'Gedenken an Grotius'. *Die Friedenswarte*, 66 (1986), pp. 5–22 and 125–204.

MURPHY, CORNELIUS J. 'Grotius and the Peaceful Settlement of Disputes'. *Grotiana*, 4 (1983), pp. 35–42.

OUDENDIJK, JOHANNA K. 'Van Vollenhoven's "The Three Stages in the Evolution of the Law of Nations"'. *Tijdschrift voor Rechtsgeschiedenis*, 48 (1980), pp. 3–27.

PINTO, M. C. W. 'The New Law of the Sea and the Grotian Heritage', in Asser Instituut, *International Law and the Grotian Heritage*. The Hague: T. M. C. Asser Instituut, 1985, pp. 54–93.

POUND, ROSCOE. 'Grotius and the Science of Law'. *American Journal of International Law*, 19 (1925), pp. 685–8.

REIBSTEIN, ERNST. 'Von Grotius zu Bynkershoek'. *Archiv des Völkerrechts*, 4 (1953–4), pp. 1–29.

ROELOFSEN, C. G. 'Some Remarks on the "Sources" of the Grotian System of International Law'. *Netherlands International Law Review*, 30 (1983), pp. 73–9.

—— 'The Sources of Mare Liberum: The Contested Origins of the Doctrine of the Freedom of the Seas', in *International Law and its Sources: Liber Amicorum Maarten Bos*, ed. Wybo P. Heere. London: Kluwer, 1989.

RÖLING, B. V. A. 'Jus ad Bellum and the Grotian Heritage', in Asser Instituut, *International Law and the Grotian Heritage*. The Hague: T. M. C. Asser Instituut, 1985, pp. 111–35.

SIMMONDS, KENNETH R. 'Hugo Grotius and Alberico Gentili'. *Jahrbuch für Internationales Recht*, 8 (1959), pp. 85–100.

—— 'Some English Precursors of Hugo Grotius'. *Transactions of the Grotius Society*, 43 (1957), pp. 143–57.

STARKE, J. G. 'The Influence of Grotius upon the Development of International Law in the Eighteenth Century', in *Grotian Society Papers 1972*. ed. C. H. Alexandrowicz. The Hague: Nijhoff, 1972, pp. 162–76.

TUCK, RICHARD. 'Grotius, Carneades and Hobbes'. *Grotiana*, 4 (1983), pp. 43–62.

VITANYI, B. 'Treaty Interpretation in the Legal Theory of Grotius and its Influence on Modern Doctrine'. *Netherlands Yearbook of International Law*, 14 (1983), pp. 41–67.

VOLLENHOVEN, CORNELIS VAN. 'The Framework of Grotius' Book De Iure Belli ac Pacis (1625)'. *Verhandelingen der Koninklijke Akademie van Wetenschappen*, Afd. Letterkunde, 30 (1931).

—— 'Grotius and the Study of Law'. *American Journal of International Law*, 19 (1925), pp. 1–11.

—— 'Grotius and Geneva'. *Bibliotheca Visseriana*, 6 (1926), pp. 1–81.

—— 'The Growth of Grotius' De Iure Belli ac Pacis as it Appears from Contemporary Correspondence'. *Bibliotheca Visseriana*, 6 (1926), pp. 131–77; and ibid., 8 (1929), pp. 103–70.

—— 'Het Theorema van Grotius'. *Verspreide Geschriften*, i. Haarlem: Tjeenk Willink, and The Hague: M. Nijhoff, 1934, pp. 461–68.

—— 'Un passage obscur dans le livre de Grotius'. *Grotiana*, 5 (1932), pp. 23–5.

WRIGHT, HERBERT F. 'Some Less Known Works of Hugo Grotius'. *Bibliotheca Visseriana*, 7 (1928), pp. 131–238.

Index

The index does not refer to the bibliography nor to authors when merely cited. Dates are given for writers born before 1600.

nation-states 72, 75, 86–7, 281, 288–9, 297
national liberation, wars of 277–8
NATO 204
natural law
  as basis of international law 4, 12, 30–8, 73, 78, 166, 170–1, 200, 215, 228, 289, 309
  contemporary views of 79–80, 237
  eighteenth-century natural law theorists 11, 220, 228
  and equality of states 221
  Grotius on 30–6, 78–80, 170–1, 192–4, 228–9, 244, 305
  sixteenth-century Hispanic jurists on 159, 170, 186–9
  universality of 47–8, 80–2, 200–1, 236–7
neutrality, qualified 88–9, 196–7, 207
Nevolin, K. A. 259
New International Economic Order 238, 278, 283, 293, 295
Nicaragua 277
Non-Aligned Movement 35
non-European world 281
  European intervention in 42–7, 80, 290, 296–7
  rights of 82–3, 222, 225, 227, 291, 293
non-intervention, principle of 242, 247, 250–1, 254–5
non-state groups 84–5, 277
Nuclear Non-Proliferation Treaty (1968) 293
nuclear weapons 18, 66, 283–4
Nuremberg war crimes tribunal 89, 205

Oldenbarnevelt, Johan van 68, 99, 103–20 *passim*, 122, 144
Olivecrona, Karl 31
Ompteda, Dietrich von 135
Oppenheim, Lassa 226
Organization of African Unity 273
Ostiensis (Henry of Susa) (c.1210–71) 81
Ovchinnikov, V. A. 260
Oxenstierna, Axel (Regent of Sweden) 69, 127–30

Panormitanus, Niccolo Tedeschi (1386–1445) 146
Papacy
  opposition to Grotius 77
  powers of 44, 71–2, 77, 295

Pardo, Arvid 282
Paris, Pact of (Kellogg–Briand Pact) (1928) 202, 269, 291
Paris, Treaty of (1856) 292
Pauw, Reynier 106, 116n.
Pérez de Cuéllar, Javier 274
Peter the Great of Russia 258
Philip II of Spain 188, 189
Philip III of Spain 105
Phillipson, Coleman 156n., 168n., 169n.
Piccolomini, Francesco (1520–1604) 149–50
pirates, brigands, etc. 41, 150, 182–3, 185, 190, 236–7
Portugal
  conflict with Dutch 70, 71, 104–7, 112, 142
  overseas claims 106, 210, 211, 239, 289–90
positivism, legal 31–4, 73, 78–80, 82, 84, 86, 223, 242, 264, 289, 292, 294, 307
positivist legal theorists 24, 37, 49, 79
Pradier-Fodéré, P. L. E. 260
Prague, Peace of (1635) 69
Prierias, Sylvester Mazzolini (1460–1523) 146, 154
prize, law of 70, 104, 143, 215
Protestant states in Europe 69, 105, 117, 128
Pufendorf, Samuel
  influence in Russia 258
  on international society 11, 17, 61, 174, 228
  on natural law 78, 166

Rawls, John 61, 240
Raymond of Penafort, St (c.1185–1275) 182
reason of state doctrines 25, 72, 199–201, 204, 207, 306
Red Cross
  Conference (1863) 291
  International Committee of 275
Reigersberch, Nicolaas van 114, 121–2
religious conflict in Europe 67, 69, 76–7, 112–13, 128
Remec, Peter Paul 243
Remonstrants 112–13
  see also Arminian faction
resistance, right of
  in Grotius 62, 66, 85–6, 102n., 204, 245